AQA (A)

Advanced
General Studies

Trevor Green

Editor: Eric Magee

Philip Allan Updates, an imprint of Hodder Education, part of Hachette Livre UK company, Market Place, Deddington, Oxfordshire OX15 0SE

Orders

Bookpoint Ltd, 130 Milton Park, Abingdon, Oxfordshire OX14 4SB

tel: 01235 827720

fax: 01235 400454

e-mail: uk.orders@bookpoint.co.uk

Lines are open 9.00 a.m.–5.00 p.m., Monday to Saturday, with a 24-hour message answering service. You can also order through the Philip Allan Updates website: www.philipallan.co.uk

© Philip Allan Updates 2008

ISBN 978-1-84489-603-5

First printed 2008
Impression number 5 4 3 2 1
Year 2012 2011 2010 2009 2008

AQA material is reproduced by permission of the Assessment and Qualifications Alliance.

All photographs are reproduced by permission of TopFoto, except where otherwise specified.

In all cases we have attempted to trace and credit copyright owners of material used.

Crown copyright material is reproduced under the terms of the PSI licence number C2007001851.

Some of the websites referenced in this textbook may no longer be available.

Printed in Italy

Hachette Livre UK's policy is to use papers that are natural, renewable and recyclable products and made from wood grown in sustainable forests. The logging and manufacturing processes are expected to conform to the environmental regulations of the country of origin.

P01185

Contents

A2

UNIT 3 CULTURE AND SOCIETY

UNIT 4 SCIENCE AND SOCIETY

Introduction

This textbook has been written specifically to meet the needs of AS and A2 students of General Studies who are following the AQA Specification A in General Studies. It is based on the subject content that has been approved by QCA for teaching from September 2008, with the first, two-unit, AS examinations in 2009 and the first, two-unit, A2 examinations in 2010.

Course coverage and how to use this book

The book is divided into two main sections: AS and A2. There are many ways of approaching General Studies, but each chapter aims to provide wide coverage of the topic under consideration, enabling you to start reading wherever you or your teacher decide to begin the course. There are cross-references within the chapters to other chapters where an issue is discussed. This is important because the subject content for AS and A2 is sometimes quite similar, although A2 study requires greater depth and more analysis. In addition, you can use the contents page and the index to lead you to the section containing the information you require.

As far as possible, this book seeks to contain everything you need to achieve a high grade; but you should recognise that General Studies covers a wide area of knowledge under the two main groupings of Culture and Society and Science and Society. Topical issues arise that might form the basis of some examination questions. Consequently, you may choose to read newspapers and magazines to supplement the material provided in each chapter.

This book contains examples of examination questions that might be set in all four units at AS or A2. Answers to these questions, together with other information covering successful preparation and examination technique, can be found in a separately published **Teacher Guide**.

Special features

There are several special features in this book that are designed to help your understanding of the AQA Specification A course in General Studies, including the following.

Bullet pointing

Most questions used in AS and A2 examinations require you to write in continuous prose. However, particularly in a subject like General Studies, which covers different disciplines and a wide range of knowledge, it is often easier for a student to present some information in bullet-point form. This helps to identify the main points, aids understanding and is a useful revision technique.

Key terms

Wherever possible, clear and concise definitions of important terms that are commonly used on the course are given. These appear in the relevant chapters rather than in a glossary at the end of the book.

Examples

Examples are used to support and develop particular points. These are important because a common criticism made by examiners — especially in the essay writing that forms an important part of A2 assessment — is that potentially good answers don't always reach the highest levels because they lack examples to support the points being made.

Viewpoints

In General Studies, it is important to develop personal viewpoints and also to recognise that other views might be equally legitimate. While views based on prejudice or unsupported opinion do not count for much, examiners do expect you to be able to offer your own logically argued viewpoint based on evidence. An entirely neutral response based on 'playing safe' is not always the most appropriate.

Using evidence

Evidence can come in many forms, and in General Studies you will be asked to look at it critically so that you can assess its strengths and weaknesses. Many kinds of extract and stimulus material can be used as evidence and this book includes written and visual sources where appropriate — photographs, diagrams and statistical tables. References are made to additional evidence that you can seek out, for example from websites.

Ask the examiner

The author has over 30 years of examination experience, much of it at a senior level. Most chapters offer examiner tips. Although only you can do the work that will increase your knowledge and develop your skills, the examiner tips advise you on how to show these off to best advantage and how to avoid common pitfalls.

Practice exercises and sample questions

The examiner knows nothing about you. Your school is not identified and the assessment of your work is based solely on the quality of your answers, judged against the exam's assessment objectives and mark scheme. Practising typical examination questions improves technique and boosts confidence, and each of the four units of the book includes examples of these.

Assessment objectives

There are four separate, nationally agreed, assessment objectives on which your marks for the examination will be based. These assessment objectives are:

AO1: demonstrate relevant knowledge and understanding applied to a range of issues, using skills from different disciplines

AO2: marshal evidence and draw conclusions; select, interpret, evaluate and integrate information, data, concepts and opinions

AO3: demonstrate understanding of different types of knowledge, appreciating their limitations

AO4: communicate clearly and accurately in a concise, logical and relevant way

Particularly at AS, most of your marks are awarded for AO1 (your knowledge and understanding of the key topics of the specification) and for AO2 (your ability to select, interpret and evaluate relevant information and opinions). Good communication skills (AO4) are important for all examinations at this level and, for A2 in particular, AO3 is designed to test a deeper understanding and greater awareness of how complex issues can be examined from different perspectives.

Scheme of assessment

The scheme of assessment is modular. AS and A2 each consist of two units and each makes up 50% of the total award. In both AS and A2, one unit covers Culture and Society and the other covers Science and Society. There is no coursework and the structure of the examination and assessment of the four units is described below.

AS

Unit 1: Culture and Society (1½ hours)

Section A: 30 marks

30 multiple-choice questions based on a cultural/sociopolitical passage for comprehension.

Section B: 35 marks

Three compulsory documentary source analysis questions based on three short extracts on a single cultural/sociopolitical theme.

Unit 2: Science and Society (1½ hours)

Section A: 30 marks

30 multiple-choice questions based on a predominantly scientific passage for comprehension and mathematical reasoning (arising naturally from the passage).

Section B: 35 marks

Choose one from three questions linking science and society. Each question will begin with its own brief source designed to serve as stimulus material and each question will be divided into two parts.

A2

Unit 3: Culture and Society (2 hours)

Section A: 20 marks

One compulsory source evaluation exercise based on a cultural/sociopolitical source.

Section B: 25 marks

Choose one from four culture essays.

Section C: 25 marks

Choose one from four sociopolitical essays.

Unit 4: Science and Society (2 hours)

Section A: 45 marks

Short-answer questions assessing pre-released case-study material (approximately four extracts) plus unseen extracts (approximately two) contained in the examination paper. Material will be released approximately 2 months before the examination. Teachers will be allowed to discuss the pre-release materials with you.

Section B: 25 marks

Choose one from four science and society essays.

Command words used in the examinations

A common error — and one that results in lower marks than might have been anticipated — is the failure of candidates to answer the question set. Perhaps out of a sense of relief, candidates write a lot about the theme of a question without really answering the question itself. The 'command word' in the question is crucial and so is the selection of relevant information.

Command words vary. Among the most straightforward are words like 'describe', 'identify' or 'outline' — write a straightforward account. Such words are sometimes used in AS General Studies but are unlikely to appear in A2. In A2 there are more demanding command words such as 'analyse', 'explain' and 'discuss'. These words require wider and deeper skills. It is always a good idea to identify, perhaps by underlining, the command word(s) in a question before you begin your answer.

Below is a glossary of command words that may be used in the AS and A2 examinations.

analyse: analysis requires a number of skills which entail probing a particular issue, using some detailed knowledge, to find underlying key factors which help to explain why it is complex or controversial. Material used needs to be relevant and communicated in a clear and logical manner.

compare: a more demanding task which often focuses on two different viewpoints relating to the same issue. Making a comparison involves identifying both differences and similarities and then reaching a conclusion.

define: more likely to be found in scientific sections and in areas where there is little scope for argument. It can require quite specific knowledge but is often used for short-answer questions.

describe: a factual description does not look for explanation or analysis.

discuss: a commonly used higher-level command word which involves constructing detailed and analytical arguments based on evidence rather than opinion, perhaps reflecting different points of view and recognising that there is often legitimate disagreement about complex problems which do not have simple solutions.

evaluate: possibly the most demanding of all the command words, although sometimes the word '**assess**' is used to make it a little less intimidating. It involves both discussion and an attempt to judge the worth of different viewpoints or evidence. It requires a certain detachment — a sense of standing back in an effort to make an objective appraisal.

explain: whereas 'describe' looks for what happened, 'explain' requires you to probe more deeply so that you say why events might have happened in a particular way.

identify: pick out or select the most important features or issues.

outline: another way of seeking a description or narrative and another way of seeking to show that you can identify a range of mostly factual points.

select: both Unit 1 and Unit 2 contain multiple-choice questions based mostly on comprehension of a passage. In each case, the question will be followed by four options and you are asked to select the one that is correct. Never leave a multiple-choice question unanswered.

using only...using both...: sometimes used in source/extract-based questions. You will be asked to use information either only from the source or from both the source and your own knowledge.

20 top exam tips

1 Prepare thoroughly and in a way that suits you. Different revision methods suit different people.

2 Check exam dates carefully, identifying which exams take place in the morning and which in the afternoon.

3 Draw up a revision timetable and stick to it.

4 Bear in mind that the General Studies paper that you are sitting will have been set at least 18 months earlier.

5 Although some past papers might be of help, papers set before 2009 should be used with caution. Initially, specimen papers issued by AQA for each of the four units in the new specification will be the only reliable guide.

6 Practise examination questions, including writing against the clock.

7 If you are sitting exams in the summer don't let hay fever ruin your chances. Consult your doctor at an early stage.

8 Don't stereotype the examiner by trying to write what you think will please him or her. Examiners look for responses that are different, stimulating and challenging.

9 In Unit 4, the questions in Section A (where 45 marks are on offer) are based wholly on case-study materials, most of which are released 2 months before the exam. It is vital that you familiarise yourself fully with these materials in advance. Your teacher can help and advise.

10 Read the questions carefully and answer the questions set, not the ones you might have liked. Don't write all you know about the subject but select from your knowledge what is relevant to answer the question.

11 Do what the command words ask of you.

12 Each question shows the total number of marks awarded. The length of your answer should reflect this.

13 If you use a plan as the basis for your answer keep it brief, make it clear that it is a plan and don't cross it out. The examiner may allow some credit for points not in the main body of your answer.

14 Remember that the best marks usually reflect a combination of knowledge and skills.

15 Use a clear structure for extended writing: an introduction, followed by the main body of your essay, ending with a logically argued conclusion. This should follow from the arguments used and should not lead to a lot of repetition.

16 Always use up-to-date examples to support and illustrate your arguments.

17 Bear in mind, particularly for essay answers, that there are marks for clear and accurate communication.

18 Don't be unnerved in the exam room by somebody who constantly raises his or her hand to request extra sheets. The longest answers are not always the best.

19 Allow sufficient time to answer all the questions required. If you are short of time, use notes and bullet points. These may gain you some credit.

20 Try to leave time at the end to read through your answers.

AS

UNIT 1

CULTURE
AND SOCIETY

An understanding and appreciation of the changing nature and importance of culture

There is a danger that our views of **culture** might become stereotyped. One way of illustrating this is the distinction that is sometimes made between '**high**' (appreciated and understood by an intellectual elite) and '**low**' culture (easier to understand and approved by the masses). Such distinctions, largely based on stereotypes, are out-of-date and insulting.

They are based on a class system that, in the twenty-first century, is far less easy to recognise and define. There is also an underlying assumption that certain types of culture are intrinsically worth more than others. Typical of the sort of shorthand used is the distinction made between classical music and popular music.

'Culture' is a word that is used widely in conversation and it appears many times on the printed page and in arts blogs. Language is a very important part of culture because we use it to describe our ideas, feelings, values and preferences. It helps to shape our identity and it is not difficult to summon up an image of a 'cultured' person. Yet to do so would be to submit too readily to stereotypes because culture, like society, is always changing — sometimes slightly, sometimes significantly.

Key terms

culture: a total way of life that is central to our identity as individuals, and helps to give us our place in society and to understand our society in relation to others. Culture is constantly evolving, and central to it is language, which we use to communicate ideas, share experiences and express feelings.

high culture: traditionally associated with the tastes of the upper classes (an elitist minority), who are sufficiently educated to appreciate the finer points of performing arts such as opera and ballet and great works of classical music and art. High culture is likely to be long established, is probably expensive (especially if without subsidy) and perhaps involves specialist knowledge and vocabulary.

low culture: usually known as **popular** or **mass culture**, it appeals to a majority; this is often taken to imply that it might contain little of quality and be short-lived, relatively undemanding, cheap and easily accessible to audiences and consumers. Tabloid newspapers, many magazines and popular music often come into this category.

Culture also takes on a geographical dimension. Most people in the United Kingdom are likely to be more familiar with Western culture (which might include the USA), if only because they experience it more often. Alternatively, some refer to a European culture that would exclude examples from the United States.

Equally valid would be references to Eastern culture, but this is a broad term and might incorporate many examples from different art forms. The boom in Indian art has created one of the fastest-growing markets among exiled Indian, and Western, buyers in the West. Prices of Indian art were more than 20 times higher in 2007 than they were in 2001. In the Arab world, the ruling family of Qatar are financing a Museum of Islamic Arts to hold their collection of manuscripts, books, coins, paintings, glassware and weaponry. In marked contrast, the National Museum of Iraq was looted after the US-led invasion.

Another important distinction that is sometimes made is between mainstream or dominant culture (an example of this is the way that the importance of Shakespeare's writings is widely recognised) and **subculture**. A subculture might represent a minority view, possibly signifying a protest against mainstream views. Graffiti tags for some people are the signatures of urban artists. For others they simply represent another form of vandalism.

Key term

subculture: reflects the practices of a minority group with its own behaviour and preference codes. It signifies rejection (sometimes referred to as **counterculture**) or avoidance of mainstream cultures.

In recent years, a graffiti street artist called Banksy has achieved both fame and notoriety. His identity remains a secret but it is believed that his name is Robin or Robert Banks and that he is a Bristolian in his early 30s. Banksy is best known for his stencil works but he also does parodies of major works such as Monet's *Water Lillies* and the American artist Edward Hopper's *Nighthawks*.

Banksy's work often has a political message and is admired by many young people, but the artist also has many admirers in the art world and auctions have led to fierce bidding. His *Avon and Somerset Constabulary*, featuring two policemen looking through binoculars, sold for £96,000. His 'self-portrait', featuring a stencil of a chimp's head, fetched £198,000 and his most expensive work, *Space Girl and Bird*, sold for £288,000 — a remarkable sum for a street artist who once painted 'Mind the crap' on the steps of Tate Britain. Meanwhile, both Tower Hamlets and Hackney councils have pledged to remove what they consider to be no more than graffiti.

Subcultures and countercultures can have many different origins and may, like Banksy, use a distinctive style or language (such as rap music with its often-criticised lyrics). Age may also be an important factor, with subcultures perhaps reflecting the rebelliousness of youth. Since the 1960s, and perhaps even earlier, we have often referred to 'youth culture' — almost as if 'youth' can be accepted as a homogenised grouping. Yet there might be much that is distinctive and much that challenges conventional thinking about some of the subcultures (and their attitudes, clothing and language) often associated with young people. As Tony Blair said in 2007, 'culture spans so many disciplines'. Perhaps that is why it is so difficult to define.

Banksy's *Avon and Somerset Constabulary*

Ask the examiner

Q **Aren't all examiners going to support high culture? Do they know anything about subcultures and countercultures?**

A Examiners have to be anonymous, so assumptions are sometimes made that they belong to a different, more conservative generation that is fundamentally out-of-date and that places considerable value on 'highbrow' activities like classical music, ballet and opera. The dangers of stereotyping have already been mentioned.

Examiners come from all walks of life but their common feature is that they must be objective, following an agreed mark scheme (which covers all parts of the question) and giving credit for knowledge, the quality of arguments and the extent of analysis. They may or may not agree with the views you express. Unsupported opinions and generalisations get few marks whatever the views expressed. Well-crafted and well-supported arguments will always be fully rewarded, so don't try to write with your own image of an examiner in mind.

What do we mean by 'the arts'?

The phrase 'the arts' can cover a number of activities and sometimes a distinction is made between 'creative' (e.g. painting, sculpture) and 'performing' (theatre, dance) arts. In broad terms, 'the arts' may cover:

- ballet
- cinema
- comedy
- dance
- fiction
- music
- opera
- poetry
- sculpture
- television
- theatre
- visual art (perhaps in the form of exhibitions of paintings or photography)

Alternatively, the Arts Council — a significant provider of funding for the arts in England and Wales — groups the arts as follows:

- combined arts
- dance
- interdisciplinary arts (recognising that artists sometimes work across boundaries)
- literature
- music
- theatre
- visual arts

The lists are not exhaustive and 'sport' remains a controversial area, as many continue to see it as a recreational, rather than an art, form.

Ask the examiner

Q Are we expected to know about all the arts?

A No, that would be impossible. An awareness of what the arts encompass is expected and many students will have some specialist knowledge of one or more of the arts, gained from their other A-level subjects, personal involvement as performers or their own particular interests. Obviously, if you have this, use it to your advantage when answering a question.

At AS, questions are based either on the comprehension of a passage or the use of three fairly brief sources. Some additional knowledge to supplement that contained in the sources is always helpful, but detailed, specialist knowledge is not required for AS General Studies.

The Department for Culture, Media and Sport

The arts, however they might be defined, are largely dependent on the government for funding. The government department responsible for the arts is the Department for Culture, Media and Sport and its title is informative. 'Culture' cannot be rigidly or securely defined. 'Media' is a more modern term, but it applies to a rapidly changing area as global communications and new technology play their part. 'Sport' is a newer and more contentious addition, yet sport is massively important both as a spectator pursuit, a media focus and a participant activity.

The Secretary of State (senior minister) concerned enjoys cabinet rank and he/she is assisted by three other MPs — a Minister of State for Sport, and Parliamentary Under-Secretaries responsible for culture (arts, museums, libraries and heritage), creative industries (broadcasting, film and music) and tourism. The 15 members of the governing body of the Arts Council are appointed by the Secretary of State.

A key figure in the often political world of the arts is the Permanent Secretary — the most senior (and often highly influential) civil servant responsible for the smooth running of the department. In 2006 the post was advertised, and the advertisement gave an indication of how much things are changing. Three of the key areas of importance were:

- Financing the Olympic Games due to take place in London in 2012.
- The switch from analogue to digital television, which is taking place over a 5-year period, having begun in Whitehaven, Cumbria, in 2007 and ending in 2012.
- Proposed changes in the gaming laws that (if Parliament votes in favour) will see the opening of more casinos, including one 'super-casino'. Soon after Gordon Brown became prime minister, he gave a clear indication that his government no longer favoured such large-scale developments that might be seen to encourage gambling. Subsequently, plans for the super-casino in Manchester were shelved.

This is an indication of how widely we need to think about what is meant by 'culture and the arts' and what a wide area they embrace.

Vibrant communities and celebrating diversity

The Arts Council has an important role in planning for the future in the arts, not least for new, or expanded, communities that are likely to emerge as the UK's population continues to grow. It states that 'the arts have a major part to play in helping to galvanise community engagement and participation...and in creating a common sense of identity and pride'.

'Vibrant communities' are envisaged in which:

> ...artists and arts organisations might extend their work beyond designing and constructing housing to partnership work in non-established arts settings such as health, community regeneration and criminal justice; cultural opportunities can be promoted, meeting the creative needs of people by providing them with facilities that they can use and activities that they value.

'Celebrating diversity' reflects a recognition that race, ethnicity and faith are important elements of an increasingly diverse society in which many different cultures play their part. Increasingly the arts are seen as a way of helping to develop our sense of identity within our communities. In particular, the Arts Council recognises a need to tackle 'any social or institutional barriers that prevent people from participating in and enjoying the arts'. In 2004/05, nearly 25% of those receiving Arts Council grants defined themselves as black and minority-ethnic artists.

Key term

the Arts Council: strictly speaking, 'the Arts Council' usually means 'the Arts Council of England', although there are equivalent bodies for Northern Ireland, Scotland and Wales so that arts right across the UK are covered. The Arts Council was set up in 1947 to support arts of the highest quality and to increase public access to them. It is the national development agency for the arts, distributing money from government and the National Lottery. It funds 1,100 arts organisations in England.

Ethnic music — a vibrant contribution to an increasingly diverse society

Political spin: buzzwords, the arts and culture

In comparison with issues like global warming, education, crime, taxation and terrorism, culture and the arts rarely rank high on any government's list of political priorities. In party manifestos, published when a general election is about to take place, the arts usually warrant no more than a brief mention, with most parties indicating their general support while fighting shy of making promises about specific areas such as the all-important funding.

As we saw at the beginning of the chapter, high culture is traditionally often associated with what are sometimes deemed to be elite art forms that may (often quite wrongly) be linked to small, privileged groups of society. They may be art forms that are more demanding for audiences, including areas such as ballet, opera, classical music and 'great' works of literature. Popular culture, in contrast, appeals to a great many people and may range from television soaps to concerts given by popular entertainers. In reality the distinction is more complex.

Key terms

political spin: a way of communicating information in politics that presents an individual or policy in the best possible light. It does not mean lying, but it may contain a little distortion because only the most favourable information has been selected or emphasised.

elites: relatively small and often powerful groups, usually selected rather than elected, on the basis of expertise, wealth, specialist skills, access to positions of power etc.

political lobbying: the attempt by specialist firms or individuals to influence the opinions of those (such as politicians and senior civil servants) who may be responsible for policy formulation and decision making in politics.

For politicians this presents a dilemma. Their aim is to secure enough votes to win the election. Theoretically their appeal should be to the masses and ministers are not slow to take up photo opportunities alongside popular entertainers, some of whom may endorse their policies.

There will be buzzwords, such as 'greater relevance' to ordinary people, or 'broadening participation', as populism comes to the arts, but the brutal political reality is that there are not significant votes in the arts. 'Cool Britannia' was a populist theme used soon after Labour returned to power in 1997, but it quickly disappeared. Perhaps we need to see what results from Liverpool's stint as European capital of culture in 2008.

Elites, although not numerically large, are powerful. They can secure access to politicians and civil servants easily. State patronage of the arts goes back many centuries and most people believe that the state, and thus the taxpayer, should continue to subsidise the arts to prevent admission prices from becoming prohibitive.

Ultimately, though, funds are limited; there are lots of competing priorities and there is much **political lobbying** by individuals and their organisations. Increasingly, artists working in all art forms are expected to become more aware of the commercial potential of their work.

Early in March 2007, Tony Blair looked back on his 10 years as prime minister and on Labour's contribution to the arts in a speech delivered at one of the country's most prestigious arts venues, the Tate Modern. Inevitably, he claimed that the arts and culture were central to the new modern Britain, referring to 'the whole process of stimulation through books, plays, films and works of art'. If there is dynamism in the arts, that dynamism might be reflected in the achievements of the country. Funding for the arts doubled between 1997 and 2007 and that, in itself, was no small achievement.

Funding the arts

Central to any debate about the arts and culture should be diversity, artistic talent and achievement. We have already established that there are many artistic forms, and we may also need to be reminded that the arts are not only features of major cities but also of much smaller venues such as village halls. Though a few, often nationally known, individuals may become rich because of their talents, many more do not and lots of people participate in the arts as amateurs or members of the audience.

Nevertheless, the arts are expensive to develop, produce and sustain, especially if they have what is known as 'minority appeal'. The arts are also competitive, and a feature of life that has become more distinctive since the Thatcherite years of the 1980s and 1990s is what many see as the more competitive, acquisitive and consumer-driven nature of society. State subsidies, though common in many areas of life, such as farming and public transport, are looked down upon by those who favour a greater sense of individual achievement.

A number of organisations are involved in the funding of the arts (and national museums and galleries are funded directly by the Department for Culture, Media and Sport) including the Arts Council, the biggest single funding body, and the National Lottery.

For politicians, whatever they may say about the importance of the arts in national life, there are always conflicting spending priorities. Voters may express many preferences for what they would like to see but tax rises are rarely one of them.

Viewpoints

The case for subsidised funding

Subsidies:

- enable the arts to be extended so that minorities are not excluded
- help to keep ticket prices at affordable levels
- allow the arts to be available to a relatively wide audience, making certain art forms less elitist than they would otherwise be
- offer some financial guarantees and security to arts organisations, enabling them to plan and develop
- help to protect vulnerable areas of the arts, such as regional theatre, orchestras, art education, and the British film industry, instead of leaving them to 'market forces'; many would otherwise be unable to survive and cultural life would become impoverished
- help people to establish a right of access to culture in the same way that they have a right of access to other services such as health and education
- can be seen as a form of investment — the arts generate funds, often attracting tourists and bringing in foreign currency

> **Key term**
>
> **subsidised funding:** financial support, often directly or indirectly from central government and local councils, to supplement the income of organisations like arts bodies, which might not be able to generate sufficient income from other sources to finance their activities.

Free museums and galleries

Although there is no longer a charge to enter our national museums and galleries, their running costs — staffing, energy, maintenance — may be quite high. The costs, in the case of 22 national museums and galleries, are met directly by the Department for Culture, Media and Sport rather than by grants from organisations such as the Arts Council. In 2006, the cost of this subsidy was £320 million, including £40 million to cover the cost of free admission.

In effect, they are subsidised and paid for by the taxpayer. A political decision has been taken to facilitate free entry to encourage more people to visit museums and to make their attractions available to all groups in society. After charges were scrapped in 2001, an extra 30 million visits had taken place by 2006 (see Table 1.1).

Free admissions — widely seen as a major success — come at a price and Britain's leading museums lack the money available in many of their American and European counterparts to spend on their collections. Consequently, when important works of art come up for auction, British museums and galleries are often outbid and the National Art Collections Fund has warned of the difficulties faced if funding becomes insufficient, especially as the income of museums has not been rising as quickly as staff costs and inflation.

There is a lot of debate about whether the public really cares that much about art but the success of this appeal seems to answer the question in the affirmative. Critics of subsidised art suggest that we value more the things that we pay for directly.

Table 1.1 Percentage increase in museum visits since the scrapping of admission charges

Museum	Increase in numbers since scrapping of admission charges (%)
National Museums, Liverpool	138
Victoria and Albert Museum, London	122
Natural History Museum, London	112
Natural History Museum, Tring	81
Science Museum, London	81
National Railway Museum, York	55

In 2007 the Conservative shadow Culture Secretary, Hugo Swire (a former head of development at the National Gallery and a director of the art auctioneers Sotheby's), caused a storm when he suggested in the *Mail on Sunday* that the right of museums and galleries to make charges might be restored, with the proceeds used to finance new activities.

His remarks drew sharp criticism from the General Secretary of the National Union of Teachers, who pointed out the benefits of free admission to children, and from senior Labour and Liberal Democrat politicians. Soon afterwards, Swire was forced to make a speedy U-turn, with Conservative Party officials suggesting that he was referring only to proposals in the party's manifesto for the 2005 general election. As against the new emphasis on 'social inclusion', Swire's proposals might have led to a return of greater 'exclusivity' in the arts.

The case against subsidised funding

- Subsidised funding comes with 'strings' attached: targets, bureaucracy and links with policy areas such as 'social inclusion', with the arts having to relate to prisons, hospitals, ethnic minorities, the disabled and areas of economic deprivation.
- Too much attention is paid to political correctness, stifling creativity and innovation.
- Creative people and visionaries have become less important than those who place emphasis on policies, reports, targets and risk assessments for health and safety. Efficiency appears to be more important than artistic flair.
- Reliance on subsidies can foster a dependency culture because the subsidies provide certain financial guarantees perhaps irrespective of artistic quality.
- Political priorities change and there are conflicting pressures on public spending so the level of subsidy fluctuates, making planning in the arts difficult and bringing to the arts the 'boom and bust' cycle that sometimes affects the economy.
- Subsidies may seem like 'handouts' or charity, perhaps leading artists to respectability rather than innovation.

Q **What conclusion should I reach on funding for the arts?**

A There are not always clear-cut and predictable answers to questions in General Studies, and funding the arts is one of the most contentious areas. The conclusion is the one that you believe and the examiner will not have a 'correct answer' in mind. Marks are awarded for the quality of your arguments, and you may be asked to put the case both for and against subsidising the arts.

This does not mean that you should always 'sit on the fence' — on the contrary, a clear and well-argued case with plenty of supporting examples will be generously rewarded. Without subsidies, the arts would undoubtedly become less accessible, their availability would be reduced and the lives of many people would be less enriched.

Subsidies, however, are paid for by the taxpayer, and there are those who argue that the arts should be left to market forces. 'Popular' arts would survive, as would those that people could afford to meet the full cost of. Subsidies offer a form of protection that might be seen as 'cosseting' and guaranteed income from subsidies may encourage complacency and mediocrity.

Ultimately, very few people beyond free market purists would support a system in which there were no subsidies so the argument may, principally, be about the level of subsidies, how they should be distributed and to whom. Much may depend on individual beliefs, values and even political preferences — but they will be yours rather than the examiner's.

Key term

democracy: the term originated in ancient Greece and describes a form of government, the exercise of power and the way choices are made. It means the rule of the many or even by the people as a whole. In modern times we have 'representative democracy' in which adults represent people by taking decisions on their behalf. In other respects, 'democracy' suggests the ability to 'have a say' through different forms of consultation. It does not mean that the majority is always right.

'Democracy' and the cost of staging the Olympic Games

The 2005 decision that the 2012 Olympic and Paralympic Games should take place in London (rather than Paris, which was widely regarded as the favourite) was not met with universal approval by UK citizens. Whereas many saw it as a great opportunity to achieve success on the world sporting stage, and as an opportunity for urban and environmental regeneration of local communities, concern was expressed about the likely cost of staging the games. (An important political consideration is the claim that the Olympics will bring 40,000 new homes and 50,000 new jobs to one of the poorest parts of London.)

In particular, many organisations were concerned that lottery funding for the Olympics might mean cuts for other groups, reducing future provision for grass-roots participation in arts, culture and sport (see Table 1.2).

Table 1.2 Escalating cost projections for staging the Olympic Games

July 2005	Estimated cost of staging the games was £2.4 billion.
Nov 2006	Tessa Jowell (Secretary of State for Culture, Media and Sport) informed the Culture, Media and Sport Select Committee that costs had risen to £3.3 billion.
Feb 2007	*The Sunday Times* reported that the cost of staging the games would be more than double the cost originally quoted.
Mar 2007	Tessa Jowell announced to Parliament that costs had escalated to over £9 billion.

The trebling of the estimated cost of staging the games perhaps established a new and unwelcome Olympic record and generated fierce political debate. There was even fierce criticism of the design of brand consultants Wolff Olins for the Olympic logo, which took a year to produce, cost £400,000 and was dismissed by critics as a graffiti tag or a mosaic of beer mats, although its creators defend it as 'dynamic, modern and flexible'.

Where the money is coming from:

£6 billion government

£2.2 billion National Lottery

£1.2 billion former Mayor of London (Ken Livingstone declaring: 'I have no interest in sport. I did the Olympics for the regeneration of East London.'

Where the money is going to:

£3.1 billion Olympic park and venues

£2.7 billion contingency fund

£1.7 billion regeneration and infrastructure

£840 million value added tax (VAT)

£600 million security

£390 million community sport/Paralympic funds

Viewpoints

Are the Olympic Games really worth it?

Politically, concern has been expressed about the planning process and the lack of consultation among people already living in the area. Planning permission for the Olympic Park was given in 2004, a year before London's bid for the games succeeded. It was subsequently modified and the plans of the Olympic Delivery Authority (ODA) eventually amounted to more than 10,000 pages with supporting documents. Ultimately, there were 6 weeks for consultation — if all the documents could be obtained. Applications for an extension were turned down by the ODA. In such circumstances, opportunities for genuine participation in decision making seem limited.

Many in the arts see the 2012 Olympic Games as a huge distraction, siphoning vital National Lottery funds essential to a range of artistic organisations into a short-lived sports programme and large-scale, but non-artistic, geographical regeneration in London. Perhaps this is simply another form of culture, although successful regeneration often makes the area concerned more attractive so that the original residents are pushed out by wealthier incomers as both rents and house prices rise. Similarly, debts associated with staging the games may take years to pay off.

Alternatively, there is massive prestige involved in staging the Olympic Games and the world's attention will be centred on the UK and will bring in large sums from spectators and television rights (although this, in itself, makes London more vulnerable to terrorist attacks and security costs will be considerable). The new facilities will be available for national use at the end of the games and the area of London concerned is in need of regeneration.

Practice question

Below is a typical source and question that might be used in Section B of the Unit 1 examination.

Many connected with the arts have ambiguous feelings about politicians and tend to treat them with suspicion. Hitler liked to see himself as an artist but fascism was not known for its tolerance, and a number of art forms were outlawed as subversive or degenerate. Similarly, key figures among the communist leaders of the former Soviet Union had fixed ideas about what was acceptable as art.

Ideally, many might wish art to be free from political influence altogether but the arts are rarely self-funding and, without what amounts to a measure of political patronage and funding, old accusations of elitism would quickly emerge. Contemporary British politicians rarely seem at ease with the arts, although Tony Blair was known to court celebrities from the pop world on occasion. This may smack of opportunism, but if they distance themselves from the arts, politicians are quickly criticised for their lack of aesthetic taste and understanding.

Yet if they are too involved, especially when they stray into the world of modern art, awkward questions are asked and they stand accused of frittering away the taxpayers' money on what critics would see as adolescent drooling or pseudy nonsense that bears a remarkable resemblance to the emperor's new clothes. Far from being the Capital of European Culture, such critics see Liverpool as the capital of binge drinking. If there is money to spare it should go on tackling alcoholism and not subsidising mediocrity. It is difficult to see how politicians can win.

Art is never going to be in the top ten political priorities and often it rates no more than a passing reference in the party manifesto. The arts simply are not a vote winner, but if both artists and politicians do agree it is likely to be on the value of publicity. Artists need the money to sustain their careers and, irrespective of how creative they might be, there is a growing appreciation of the arts as an economic as well as a creative force.

Using the source and your own knowledge, explain why the arts are both beneficial and problematic to politicians. *(12 marks)*

Creativity and innovation

The role of art and artists

London houses one of the most famous art galleries in the world, Tate Modern, which opened in 2001. The job of the curators of Tate Modern is to present art from the last 100 years. It is no easy task to span Picasso and the pop art of Andy Warhol and Roy Lichtenstein, and initially much of the UK's national collection of twentieth-century modern art was kept in storage as Tate Modern went for a 'thematic' rather than chronological approach — sometimes criticised by art purists but seemingly popular with a range of visitors.

Speaking at Tate Modern (a speech said by the Tate's director, Nicholas Serota, to be the longest ever made by any prime minister on the arts) in 2007 about the role of the arts in society, Tony Blair claimed that London had become 'the creative capital of the world', although it is unlikely that patrons of the arts in Paris or New York would agree. The French capital has much larger exhibition spaces, such as the Grand Palais, and more objective observers than Blair might claim that New York's Museum of Modern Art has the capacity to outdo Tate Modern — although not in terms of the sort of access that free entry brings.

Nevertheless, the arts scene in London is vibrant and exciting — a fitting rival to the best. Listeners to Blair were no doubt reassured to hear that the arts and culture are at the heart of what is sometimes packaged as new, modern Britain. For him, 'stimulation through books, plays, films, works of art; the delight in design, in architecture, in crafts all enlarges a country's capacity to be reflective, interested and bold'. The vision of British arts as the envy of the world is not entirely a figment of a politician's imagination.

Arts prizes

The Turner

- Few awards create more controversy than the annual Turner Prize, which is worth £25,000 to the winner and open to all British visual artists under 50.
- The prize has existed since 1984 and is named after J. M. W. Turner, the famous nineteenth-century English Romantic painter whose most famous work is shown in Tate Britain.

- It was originally intended to promote British art but quickly became not only prestigious but highly controversial for its shortlist exhibits.
- All forms of art can be entered but it is frequently associated with conceptual art and media.
- Judging is based on a wide body of each artist's work rather than just that shown in the exhibition.
- Initially funded by an investment bank, sponsorship then passed to Channel 4 but the prize's current sponsor is Gordon's Gin.
- The four artists on the 2007 shortlist provided examples of just part of the breadth of the arts encompassed, with the prize being judged on the artists' contribution to art over the previous year.
- The annual show can attract up to 100,000 visitors and generates much public debate and controversy about what constitutes 'art'.
- In many respects, a significant purpose of the Turner Prize is to generate publicity for its sponsor, the Tate, for younger British visual artists and for contemporary art.
- Without such media exposure it might not amount to very much. That was certainly the view in 2002 of one culture minister, Kim Howells, who thought that contemporary British art was lost if the Turner represented the best of its output — he dismissed it as 'conceptual bullshit'.

In 2006 the Turner Prize was won by **Tomma Abts** a painter with an essentially abstract approach who exhibited 11 paintings, all identically sized.

The 2007 Turner exhibition was held at Tate Liverpool prior to Liverpool becoming European Capital of Culture in 2008. The shortlist was:

- **Zarina Bhimji:** a photographer and film-maker forced to leave Uganda with her family in 1974. At Liverpool she uses photographs drawn from Africa and India and is also showing a new film of an African sisal rope factory, an old and atmospheric building empty of people and containing by-products of rope making.
- **Nathan Coley:** a maker of architectural installations whose three cardboard sculptures of a church, a mosque and a synagogue were disguised using a candy-stripe camouflage pattern. Coley's Liverpool exhibition includes *Untitled*, a threshold using a hefty block of oak and a scaffold where lightbulbs have been installed to spell out the message *There Will Be No Miracles Here*.
- **Mike Nelson:** his medium is interiors into which the viewer enters. At Liverpool, his main piece in the show is *Amnesiac Shrine* (based on Nelson's mythical band of bikers called the Amnesiacs). He uses piles of driftwood and bits of red plastic that may appear like flames and which may be viewed through a hole in the wall of four inner rooms, crisscrossed by narrow corridors.

- **Mark Wallinger** (the winner): short-listed originally for his *State Britain* — a 40 m re-creation of Brian Haw's anti-Iraq-war display of banners, placards and flags originally set up as a protest action in Parliament Square. It labels Tony Blair and George Bush as 'baby killers' and was forcibly removed by police acting under new powers in 2006. In Liverpool he exhibited only a 2 ½ hour video titled *Sleeper*, featuring Wallinger dressed in a bear suit and moving around an empty gallery in Berlin, where the bear is the city's symbol.

Mark Wallinger with his installation *State Britain*

Not all were impressed. One blogger called for 'an end to this kind of boring rubbish that passes itself off as an art form' and another denounced the Turner Prize as 'an annual festival of anti-Western, anti-capitalist junk'.

Viewpoints

Artists or imposters?

The artists concerned work in innovative media but many people have asked if their creations are really art.

Supporters say:

- New names in visual arts are introduced to the public.
- There is scope for a genuinely creative and unencumbered approach to the visual arts.
- Much of the work is genuinely innovative.
- Art is not necessarily easy to understand and may be open to different interpretations.
- The award helps to encourage younger artists and viewers.

Opponents say:

- Too often the aim is to shock rather than to provide anything of artistic merit.
- Many of the works demonstrate little in the way of skill and technique.
- Too many of those shortlisted are represented by a small number of London dealers.
- There are no clear and agreed criteria to judge the merits of the work.
- The exhibition discredits British art in the eyes of many members of the general public, who see the exhibits as incomprehensible.

The Man Booker

- The Booker prize for fiction was founded in 1968. More recently it has become the Man Booker prize (the Man Group plc is involved in international finance and investment).
- Sponsorship enables a prize of £50,000 to be made available for what is judged to be the best novel of the year.
- Entrants must be citizens of either the Commonwealth or the Irish Republic.

The 2006 winner was *The Inheritance of Loss* by Kiran Desai and in 2007 Dubliner Anne Enright surprised many by winning with *The Gathering*, her bleak and uncompromising tale of an Irish family. Like all others shortlisted except Ian McEwan's huge commercial success, *On Chesil Beach*, it had sold few copies prior to the award.

The Orange Broadband

- This is the top literary prize for women novelists and is worth £30,000 and has been sponsored by Orange since 1996.
- It took the name 'Orange Broadband' in 2007, when it began to feature readers voting for their favourite three books from the shortlist.

The 2007 winner was the Nigerian-born Chimamanda Ngozi Adichie for her book *Half of a Yellow Sun*, based on the Nigerian civil war of 1967–70.

Important contemporary artists

Damien Hirst

Damien Hirst rose to fame in 1988 by curating the exhibition *Freeze* in a London Docklands warehouse. In 1995 he won the Turner Prize. During the 1990s and until 2003, he benefited from the support of the art patron Charles Saatchi.

Death is a central theme in Hirst's work and his first major animal installation, *A Thousand Years*, featured a large glass case containing maggots and flies feeding off a rotting cow's head. He is most famous for preserving animal corpses in formaldehyde (his bisected tiger shark displayed in two tanks of formaldehyde was titled *Death Explained*), reflecting his exploration of the relationship between science and art. Perhaps the most notorious, but certainly the richest, of the group originally called Young British Artists (or Britart), Hirst was awarded a grade E in A-level art.

By 2007 Hirst was exhibiting a £50 million work of art, *For the Love of God*, at London's White Cube gallery. *For the Love of God* is a platinum cast of a human skull set with 8,601 flawless diamonds. The raw materials alone cost over £14 million. The skull was made by the Bond Street jewellers Bentley & Skinner and is a replica of a skull purchased from a London taxidermy shop, *Get Stuffed*, which is estimated to be nearly 300 years old. According to the artist, his creation was produced as a celebration against death because its beauty offers hope.

Tracey Emin

Tracey Emin had her first solo show, *My Major Retrospective*, at the White Cube gallery in London. Much of the exhibition was based on personal photographs and other details of her private life shown in public. She is best known for her installation works, especially *My Bed* — the artist's unmade bed complete with stained sheets, rumpled quilt, soiled underwear and used condoms — which was part of her Turner Prize exhibition in 1999. In 2007 Tracey Emin became a Royal Academician when she was elected to the elite group of artists who are members of the Royal Academy of Arts.

Her 2007 redesign of the London Oyster travel-card wallet to mark the sixtieth anniversary of the Arts Council of England featured a drawing of her cat, Docket, with the caption 'We've got fur and lots of ears. Love Tracey Emin.' Ironically, when *My Bed* is showcased in an exhibition ('Aftershock: Contemporary British Art 1990–2006') in the Chinese capital, Beijing, it is being re-titled *The Simple Truth*. In recognition of Chinese sensibilities, the bed is neatly made and covered by an embroidered quilt showing an American flag containing the words 'Tracey Emin — Here to stay'.

Antony Gormley

A sculptor, Gormley is a legend in the northeast of England, where his *Angel of the North* at Gateshead, with its 54 m wing span, kick-started a process of regeneration. Gormley won the Turner Prize in 1994 with *Fields for the British Isles*.

Gormley uses materials to interpret the human body and he is particularly well known for *Another Place*, his 2005 installation of 100 cast iron men, made from a mould of his own body, on the tidal beach at Crosby on Merseyside. (They have previously featured in Germany, Norway and Belgium.) A characteristic of Gormley's work is its installation in public places. Despite some continuing local protests and safety concerns, Sefton council reversed an earlier decision that would have sent the statues packing. It is estimated that more than 700,000 visitors have been attracted to his *Another Place* installation.

Another Place by Antony Gormley on Crosby Beach, Merseyside

Best-sellers and booksellers

At the weekend, broadsheet newspapers (*The Times, Telegraph, Guardian, Observer* and *Independent*) publish lists of fiction and non-fiction best-sellers. Rarely do the names there correspond to those of 'literary giants' or contemporary writers whose merit is such as to guarantee them inclusion on the set book list.

Nevertheless, there are writers such as Dan Brown (of *Da Vinci Code* fame), Ruth Rendell, Danielle Steel, Josephine Cox, Patricia Cornwell, Ian Rankin, Lee Child and John Grisham whose paperback fiction is so popular that each of their novels will sell many thousands.

Non-fiction is less predictable, but the Galaxy British Book Awards are often barometers of popular taste. In 2007, comedian Peter Kay's *The Sound of Laughter* (the best-selling hardback autobiography ever, selling over 800,000 copies) won Biography of the Year. Another comedian, Ricky Gervais, won Children's Book of the Year with *Flanimals of the Deep*. Author of the Year was Richard Dawkins with *The God Delusion*, his best-selling demolition of religion. Book of the Year was the remarkable *The Dangerous Book for Boys* by Conn and Hal Iggulden.

All these books sold in huge numbers and say something not only about the potential of the contemporary book market but also about the changing ways in which demand is met. It is increasingly difficult for small, independent booksellers to survive because they cannot match the significant price discounts given by online giants such as Amazon or by Waterstones (itself part of the HMV chain) with its national network of bookshops. Major supermarkets sell books (often popular fiction) at reduced prices and charities such as Oxfam and Barnardo's operate specialist bookshops stocked by donations from the public.

Viewpoints

Are best-sellers the best books?

Yes

- They appeal to, and are bought by, a lot of people.
- People get pleasure from reading the books.
- They are financially successful for publishers, booksellers and authors.
- They help people to get away from the idea that books are for a highly educated minority.
- Recognition and acknowledgement of diversity in reading habits are important.

No

- They have little intrinsic literary merit.
- They have no lasting appeal.
- They often use familiar and unadventurous formulas.
- There are other ways of judging a book as well as total sales and financial success.
- High sales are based more on selection for promotional campaigns by booksellers.

Conclusion

Ideally there should be an objective (value-free) way of judging the merits of a book using commonly agreed criteria. In reality, most people make a more subjective judgement based primarily on their own values, opinions and tastes. The ability to recognise this is very important.

Ask the examiner

Q **How far should I use books in General Studies that are set for other subjects?**

A One of the problems of General Studies is its breadth. The most successful students are those who can use knowledge from their other subjects, or wider study, to help with their answers to questions in General Studies. 'Set books' are just one opportunity to do this when the opportunity arises.

What you should try to avoid is 'name dropping' — quoting for the sake of quoting. Any quotes or other references must be relevant to answering the question asked and they certainly need not be confined to 'set books'. Once again, it is worth emphasising that relevant supporting examples or quotes are always likely to gain additional marks. It demonstrates that you can 'think outside the box' — that you are able to transfer knowledge across subjects and disciplines.

Celebrity culture

Celebrity culture is often derided and dismissed as vulgar or trashy. Yet it fills our television screens and substantial parts of tabloid newspapers. It is a manifestation of popular culture — something that lots of people are interested in. Magazines such as *Heat* and *Closer* focus almost entirely on celebrities, often in a state of semi-undress or apparent drunkenness. Television programmes such as *Celebrity Big Brother* have proved popular and, in the case of the fall-out between Jade Goody and Shilpa Shetty in the show's fifth series, with its attendant allegations of bullying, class conflict and racial abuse, highly controversial.

Whether they are A-, B- or C-list celebrities, almost anyone can be caught almost anywhere on a mobile or by the paparazzi. Identifying the qualities that determine celebrity status is sometimes a frustrating process; but, whatever their appeal, celebrities — particularly those on the A-list — are used because they sell — warts and all. Perhaps celebrity nurtures our voyeurism in an age of multimedia, representing a seemingly insatiable demand to observe the not-always-private lives of famous people.

Dumbing down

Ratings can be as important in the arts as in other areas, not least because popularity, and large numbers of viewers or readers, may attract advertisers or simply be good box office business. Arguments about 'high' and 'low' culture re-open and there are increasing allegations of dumbing down — making content more bland and 'accessible'.

> **Key term**
>
> **dumbing down:** making things easier and simpler to understand. Sometimes quite complex books, television programmes and pieces of music are oversimplified to have wider popular appeal.

Going downmarket?

- Compared to BBC1, BBC2 is generally seen as a minority channel. In 2004 it launched a weekly arts programme, *The Culture Show*. There are increasing accusations that in order to boost audience figures the programme has been seeking to move 'downmarket' — in effect putting more emphasis on popular culture with a wider appeal. Yet does this represent a rather British obsession with whether culture is 'high' or 'low'? Does it really matter if *The Culture Show* lacks the popular appeal of its Saturday night competition — celebrities dancing, dancing on ice, or the draw for the National Lottery?
- Television is full of 'reality' shows, the content of which is often criticised as voyeuristic, artificial and degrading. Such criticisms may be valid but these are shows that bring in many younger viewers. They create a 'buzz' that helps to dispel the view of art and culture as belonging to dusty backwaters where silence is necessarily the order of the day.

- Kylie Minogue is not a name associated with high culture so it was a surprise to some when, early in 2007, the famous Victoria and Albert Museum mounted an exhibition of Kylie as an icon, featuring the pop singer's costumes, photographs and music. A seemingly incompatible pairing and clear evidence of dumbing down, it might be said, yet it attracted many new and young visitors to see the work of a highly regarded performer.

- The appreciation of classical music requires time, thought, knowledge and patience — rare commodities in the days of more accessible forms of culture characterised by the short attention span of the audience. There is a musical language based on harmonic tonality and concentration — something that very few people experience. Today's audience may become familiar with orchestral music through films or even computer games. Perhaps, as in fiction, where works for teenagers meet those intended more for adults, there is a 'crossover'.

- The once elitist BBC Radio 3 still offers more for classical music 'purists', but the commercial station Classic FM (which is among the five most listened-to radio stations nationally), specialising mainly in brief excerpts from mostly well-known pieces, has widened the audience for classical music massively. Critics claim that it has done this by selecting brief and 'easier' excerpts that are not necessarily representative of works as a whole, thus distorting their effect.

Viewpoints

Dumbing down: a genuine concern or clinging on to elitism?

Genuine
- Not everything can be simplified.
- Audiences and consumers need to be able to respond to a challenge.
- Some areas of the arts are genuinely more demanding than others.
- Egalitarianism is false and life is much more likely to be based on hierarchies and competition.
- Elitism is inevitable given differences which exist between people.

Elitist
- The use of a phrase like 'dumbing down' is insulting to a great many people.
- Accusations of 'dumbing down' are typical of those who would like to preserve the arts for elite groups.
- Widening access to the arts does not necessarily mean dumbing down.
- Modern media and new forms of technology have enabled new art forms to emerge and have increased the numbers who have access to and can appreciate many art forms.
- A hierarchy of arts has more to do with class and status than the arts themselves.

Practice questions

The following five paragraphs are part of a longer passage typical of one that might be used for Section A of Unit 1. Seven objective-type (multiple-choice) questions are asked on these five paragraphs. In a normal exam there will be 30 multiple-choice questions based on the whole passage and, in all cases, there is only one correct answer.

Don't write off television just yet

(1) It is easy to dismiss today's television as something that proves its popularity by appealing to the lowest common denominator. It is just as easy to be cynical and to say that we can't trust the BBC any more and that all the old certainties have gone. Families are dysfunctional and gran watches soaps in a soporific haze while dad is upstairs watching the latest sports channel and paying heavily for the privilege. Mum is at the gym and the kids are in that part of their PC world that adults avoid through either fear or ignorance.

(2) Television becomes a backwater — or so we are led to believe. It is just another gadget, as we boast at the dinner table of being part of the digital revolution. It becomes another part of the acquisitive society. A bigger and better screen, or something truly sensational in high definition. There it sits in the corner, supposedly unloved save for a few devotees lost in an age when Morecambe and Wise sent 28 million people into fits of laughter. Those days — with comedians who were truly funny and audiences nearly half the size of the population — will never return.

(3) Yet there are still nuggets of delight, not least from Andrew Davies, who brings history back to life. He shocked the nation with *Tipping the Velvet*, with its raunchy journey back to the era of the Victorian music hall — for once not sanitised lest we take offence at being challenged and invited to consider reality. A more recent offering takes us back to the eighteenth century with his two-part adaptation of John Cleland's novel *Fanny Hill*.

(4) *Fanny Hill* is a world of brothels and brothel keepers, of country girls both naïve and, perhaps, deceived. Costume drama perhaps, but we are invited to draw modern parallels. Expansion of the European Union has helped to expand an unwelcome trade — sex trafficking, as girls are lured from eastern Europe by extravagant promises of a new and better life. We are invited to make moral judgements about now and then. Perhaps Cleland intended it to be a morality tale, though he wrote his book in a debtor's prison so perhaps his intentions were more mundane. As for Fanny herself, we were left to wonder about her exploitation, for Davies's message was not one-dimensional and we did not rush to condemn.

(5) Then there's *Spooks*, back for another series. This often shows a bleak and murky world, but one full of intrigue and excitement, as we enter the world of counter-espionage and open a peephole into the lives of those who are said to keep us safe in our beds at night.

They should, of course, be the 'goodies', but to make them so would take away their credibility. These are mavericks — mostly men who are never far away from amorality with a touch of misogyny. It is a world away from *Fanny Hill* yet there is a common thread of moral ambiguity. We thought we knew the baddies, but could they really be British agents planting an explosive device among civilians in a country regularly portrayed in real life as one of the most hostile to the Western world? They couldn't be... could they?

---

1 **The phrase 'appealing to the lowest common denominator' (paragraph 1) refers to programmes that**

A   are popular but have little artistic merit.

B   appeal only to the lower classes.

C   make no demands on the audience.

D   rely on phone-ins and audience participation.

2 **The 'acquisitive society' referred to in paragraph 2 is most likely to emphasise**

A   expertise in the use of IT.

B   material success.

C   rapid change.

D   high crime rates.

3 **In paragraph 2 which of the following is implied about comedians?**

1   No modern comedians are funny.

2   Morecambe and Wise are legends of comedy.

3   Nostalgia still influences some current viewers.

4   There is no real interest in contemporary comedians.

Answer:

A   if 1 and 2 only are correct.

B   if 2 and 3 only are correct.

C   if 3 and 4 only are correct.

D   if all are correct.

4 **The reference to 'sanitised' in paragraph 3 suggests that *Tipping the Velvet***

A   had to be censored for television audiences.

B   was suitable for showing before the 9 p.m. watershed.

C   may have reflected what went on in Victorian music halls.

D   failed to ask the viewers the right questions.

5 According to paragraph 4 the most likely reason why John Cleland wrote *Fanny Hill* was

A to satisfy a creative instinct.

B as a source of income.

C to start a moral debate.

D as a way of passing the time.

6 The reference to 'a touch of misogyny' in paragraph 5 suggests that

A maverick characters are usually lonely and miserable.

B morality is not a quality shown by most males.

C viewers forgive the flaws of maverick characters.

D some characters show a dismissive attitude towards women.

7 'Moral ambiguity' as referred to in paragraph 5 suggests that

A it is easy to identify good and bad actions.

B characters in modern dramas are immoral.

C audiences should not need to judge morality.

D clear judgements about morality are difficult to make.

Ask the examiner

Q **How many units in General Studies use multiple-choice question?**

A Both AS Units 1 and 2 contain 30 compulsory multiple-choice questions based on passages contained in the examination paper.

Q **Aren't these really easy because they will always contain the answer?**

A They are not as easy as you might think. Great care is taken in selecting the passage for the examination paper. A small team of writers will draft about 80 questions. After much discussion, a smaller number will be selected for pre-testing. After pre-testing and further discussion, the final 30 questions will be selected for the examination.

Comprehension (in this case of the passage) is an important skill. The correct answer keys are varied so that simple sequences of Question 1 is A, Question 2 is B, Question 3 is C etc., are avoided. Writing the questions is a skilful task — and so is answering them correctly.

CULTURE AND SOCIETY
Chapter 3

Aesthetic evaluation

Evaluating the arts

Appreciation of the arts is based on building arguments for and against the appeal or qualities of an art object or performance and making various aesthetic judgements. Often there are no absolutes but there is a lot of ambiguity. The arts are emotive. Works and performances are evaluated and re-evaluated, often in a changing climate of artistic opinion, judgement and argument.

There are differing opinions about the 'quality' of art and how to evaluate the extent to which a work of art possesses, or lacks, qualities such as 'beauty'. Beauty, it is often said, is in the eye of the beholder. It is a personal judgement and, if pressed for reasons why something is deemed to be beautiful, we may become vague and evasive. It is beautiful because, intuitively, we feel that it is — or perhaps because we have been conditioned by our upbringing or environment to think in a particular way. It might be equally difficult to decide why we consider something to be funny — or tragic.

Aesthetic judgements in art are often about the 'beauty' or 'appeal' of an object. An aesthetic object might be a piece of music, a painting or a sculpture. It might involve the appreciation of a piece of the landscape such as a water feature or a mountain range. This will involve the impact an object might have on the emotions, our capacity to experience pleasure and enjoyment, and how we might discriminate at a sensory level.

These are all feelings, and feelings cannot be proved right or wrong. Sometimes we are moved when we listen to a piece of music or watch a play because they arouse feelings in us. Yet someone else may be unmoved by the same experience. Consequently, there may be many differing opinions regarding the qualities of the arts and how they can best be evaluated.

In a broader sense, the issue of cultural conditioning might be raised. We are all brought up in a particular environment and we experience different forms of socialisation, all of which influence the values that we develop and the judgements that we make. A wider area of social, political and moral life is opened up by the arts. We have to think about what we are interpreting, perhaps within a particular context, and what something means to us.

This raises the central issue of whether aesthetic judgements are subjective or objective. Writing in the 1740s, the eminent philosopher David Hume identified some of the difficulties in formulating aesthetic judgements because they might be both partly **subjective** and partly **objective**. Many writers and critics tend towards the view that such judgements are far more likely to be subjective.

Contemporary art, in particular, is problematic because it tends to emphasise process and concept over the final product. Often it is dismissed as transient or ephemeral — like much pop music. Perhaps much of it is, but the quality of the work of some artists now regarded as great (such as Vincent van Gogh) was not always recognised in their lifetimes.

> ### Key terms
>
> **subjective judgement:** a judgement that is made on the basis of personal feeling, values and preferences. Such a judgement might be primarily intuitive.
>
> **objective judgement:** an unbiased judgement that might be based on external proof. It is impartial and without prejudice, the result of an attitude of mind proper to a scientific investigator.

Similarly, broadsheet newspapers and some entertainment magazines give marks out of ten, or stars, as an accompaniment to reviews of the performing arts. The *Guardian* does this in tabular form, comparing the judgements of different critics. That they vary is not surprising. That they sometimes vary by wide margins is more puzzling. 'How did you judge that film or concert?' we want to ask, but there need be no common criteria, no common boxes in which every critic must enter a tick or a cross.

Ask the examiner

Q How can I learn to make more informed judgements about the quality of the arts?

A
- Select an area of the arts which you are particularly interested in and curious about.
- Visit museums and galleries or watch films and plays. Try to determine what makes art worthy of display or why audiences react in a certain way.
- Identify and analyse the qualities of actors or consider factors that might be relevant in judging a painting, e.g. look at composition, colour, content, line, shape etc.
- Do some background reading around the subject and read critical reviews if appropriate.

- Discuss the arts with as many people as you can so that you are familiar with different viewpoints.
- Given that many judgements in the arts are likely to be subjective, try not to be too judgemental about the tastes, views and preferences of others.
- Remember that being critical does not just entail being negative. Try to add constructive comments to your criticism.

In addition, you could try to answer a list of questions:
- What is the artist or performer seeking to express?
- Does he or she succeed? If so why (or why not)?
- Are there recognisable qualities or technical skills?
- How far does the art object fit into the stated theme of the exhibition and why is it displayed prominently (or not)?
- What is its contemporary or historical context, and how far does it fit in?
- What does the work or performance say to me, personally?

Assessing artistic quality: the Arts Council view

Just like critics and audiences, there are many others in the world of the arts who need some sort of evaluative criteria:

- Museum directors and curators need to determine what to exhibit and what to place in store.
- Jurors have to judge those appearing on the popular television programme *The X Factor* or decide which book should win a prestigious literary award.
- Patrons must form a judgement on artists they wish to support.
- Funding agencies like Arts Council England are accountable for how they spend public money.

A common, though not necessarily informed, criticism of the Arts Council is that it gives money away for 'anything', or for work of seemingly dubious artistic merit. Perhaps to counter these accusations — and to satisfy politicians sensitive to this sort of public criticism — the Arts Council seeks to demonstrate how it assesses artistic quality. It sets out the following points:

- Everyone experiences artistic work in their own way.
- People respond to artistic experiences in different ways.
- As a result of the experience, people may be thrilled, inspired or challenged.
- Responses can be emotional, intellectual, physical or spiritual.

X-Factor judges at the National Television Awards, 2007

- A strength of the arts is that they have the capacity to engage us directly and in different ways — perhaps producing a life-changing experience.

The Arts Council's approach to the assessment of artistic quality is based on three dimensions of artistic work:

- **idea:** the concept or artistic impetus behind the work
- **practice:** the effectiveness of how the work is put into practice and the impact it has on those experiencing it
- **development:** the contribution the work makes to the development of the artist, the art form and the arts more widely

Central to the process is the Arts Council's belief that artists and organisations are usually best placed to evaluate the quality of the work they produce and that the starting point for assessment is self-assessment.

In addition, artists and organisations are encouraged to involve their peers in the self-assessment process. As part of this process, independent arts reporters are being used on the basis of their experience and engagement with the arts. Arts Council staff also write reports which are shared with artists and organisations.

Ask the examiner

Q **Is the search for objective criteria as the basis for judging the quality or value of the arts a waste of time?**

A Experts continue to disagree but many in the arts world believe that the arts need things like freedom and imagination and that, because of the sensory reactions involved, our feelings are likely to be personal and subjective. Feelings cannot be right or wrong. They are simply feelings. Tick-the-box judgements become as absurd as painting by numbers.

Yet, in accepting what seems to be the inevitable, we are left with a situation in which subjective judgements may be hopelessly inconsistent. We are back to beauty being in the eye of the beholder. In itself, this is not a satisfactory position because judgements are based on like and dislike.

Ultimately, what we should seek to do is to follow the line of so many examination questions and 'give reasons for'. An answer which says, basically, that an art object is 'good because I think it is' will not score well. An answer which says it is 'good because I think it is and my reasons for responding in this way are as follows' will do much better. Most of us can offer our opinions but they might not be very informed. If we can offer reasons, it is likely that our judgement will be much more informed.

Beliefs, values and moral reasoning

Beliefs and their origins

Beliefs are based on personal thoughts and opinions, perhaps with reference to some form of external authority or teaching. People have individual beliefs — which might differ from those held by others — and they may belong to groups and organisations where beliefs are shared.

In some respects, beliefs may be theories, because beliefs cannot be proved. For example, a religious person may believe in God and may do so with a fervent conviction and a deep and unshakeable faith. However, that person is unable to offer factual proof that God exists, so cannot claim to be telling the truth because what is true is capable of being verified.

Initially we learn from those immediately around us — in most cases our parents. They are the prime socialisers because, as babies or very young children, we are almost wholly dependent on them. Depending on the size and structure of the family, others contribute to our beliefs, in that young children copy what older children and adults say or do.

Many children now start some form of education from the age of 3, so we also learn from other children and from teachers. As we get older, school plays a more important role, as do our peers. Individuality is sometimes prized, but people aim for conformity so as to be 'in with the crowd', to behave in a way based on shared beliefs. The influence of others may be extended at secondary school, where there are more pupils and more teachers, and then further with entry to some form of further or higher education or to work.

Work is just one example of the widening of the environment. Where we grow up can have an important influence on our beliefs. Rural environments are prized by some people for their beauty, peace and quiet. Yet young people growing up in a rural environment often complain that they lack facilities, are isolated and do not offer stimulation. Inner-city environments may be characterised by more crime, vandalism and drug taking but cities can be more vibrant as far as many young people are concerned.

As we grow up the media become more important. At first we are likely to be passive learners lapping up programmes for young children. As we get older, we learn to read and gradually become more independent learners. There is often a 'generation' gap between young people and their parents, with the former rebelling against the beliefs of the latter. Television, radio, DVDs, newspapers, magazines and the internet all help to form just part of the world of global communications.

Moral values and their origins

Commonly linked to beliefs are values, although in the latter we move towards morality and making judgements about what we regard as being right and wrong. As we grow up, we develop value systems that influence the way we behave. Moral values become rules — perhaps loosely written and understood — that determine how we interact with others. From our beliefs and values we learn responsibility, both as individuals and towards others.

Often moral values are simply accepted as a matter of custom. Yet they, and the **moral codes** based on values and principles, may vary from individual to individual. There may be no direct sanction against people whose value system is different from that of others, say in their peer group, but behaviour arising from that difference may lead to some form of social isolation. By contrast, those who break the law of the land, as set down by Parliament, face more clearly determined sanctions if detected.

> **Key term**
>
> **moral code:** a set of informal and unwritten rules based on commonly accepted values that helps to regulate the behaviour of individuals towards other individuals or members of a group.

Ideally, it should be possible to establish a commonly accepted set of moral values to form a moral code that can govern our behaviour. In reality, this happens only in part. For example, most people wish to be treated with 'respect' — but what do we mean by this?

Old people may feel that they should command respect because of their age and their earlier contribution to their families and society. Young people may wish to gain respect from adults, yet this respect may depend on responsible behaviour. Some young people see respect — respect from their peers rather than adults — as gained by what others might regard as deviant behaviour. In some communities, those with Anti-Social Behaviour Orders and with access to guns may command more respect than those who, say, are successful at school.

Moral issues: euthanasia

Some issues can be very contentious. One is euthanasia. The term itself is derived from the Greek for 'good death' and has come to mean the premature ending of the life of a terminally ill or severely disabled person either at their request or by taking the decision to end artificial life support. Although suicide is legal in Great Britain under the 1961 Suicide Act, helping a person to commit suicide is a criminal offence and carries a long prison sentence.

Euthanasia is illegal in the UK and many people feel that 'assisted death' is also morally wrong. Conversely, some argue that terminal illnesses can be extremely painful and sometimes very protracted if sufferers go into a slow but irreversible decline, and that to allow this to continue is also morally wrong. Such people would consider an 'assisted death' to be a 'mercy killing'.

The law did move a little in the case of Anthony Bland, a 17-year-old left severely brain damaged in the 1989 Hillsborough Football Stadium disaster (which involved a fatal crush of supporters). In 1993 the High Court and the House of Lords agreed to a request from Anthony's parents and the NHS trust that, because Tony was in a persistent vegetative state, his life support should be turned off.

In 2001 Diane Pretty, who suffered from the degenerative and incurable motor neurone disease, asked the Director of Public Prosecutions that her husband should not be prosecuted if he helped her to carry out her wish to end her life. The DPP refused and his decision was upheld by the High Court and the House of Lords. In 2002, the European Court of Human Rights upheld the decisions. Three days later, 43-year-old Mrs Pretty died.

Diane Pretty with her husband

The pressure group Dignity in Dying continues to campaign for terminally ill people to be allowed to ask for medical help to end their lives at a time of their choosing, subject to strict legal safeguards. Surveys frequently show a large majority of respondents in favour of allowing those with painful terminal illnesses to seek further intervention from doctors with a view to ending their suffering.

In 2006 Lord Joffe introduced a bill on assisted suicide into the House of Lords, restricting the doctor's role to supplying the medicine and with 20 built-in safeguards. The bill was rejected, with strong opposition from religious groups, an umbrella group of charities and healthcare organisations called Care Not Killing, the disability group RADAR and a cross-party group of MPs seeking better end-of-life care called Dying Well.

Doctors' organisations such as the British Medical Association and the Royal College of Physicians are broadly opposed to euthanasia, although it is estimated by the journal *Palliative Medicine* that individual doctors in the UK were responsible for 3,000 euthanasia deaths in 2005, and that about a third of all deaths came more speedily because treatment was withheld. It is a dilemma for doctors, who risk prosecution or being struck off by the General Medical Council.

There are a few countries that allow some form of euthanasia:
- The practice of voluntary euthanasia was ruled acceptable by the Dutch Supreme Court in 1984, although it was not until 2002 that the Netherlands legalised adult euthanasia. 'Physician-assisted' euthanasia is now practised and about 5,000 deaths a year fall into this category even though most requests are turned down. Non-adult euthanasia is also permitted in the Netherlands.
- 'Assisted suicide' exists in Switzerland, where it can be practised by non-physicians. Some Britons, aided by the charity Dignitas, have travelled there to end their lives, although they must first be seen by doctors and lawyers, and family members returning to Britain risk prosecution. Euthanasia remains illegal in Switzerland.
- After initial legislation in 2002, Belgian pharmacists have been permitted since 2005 to supply doctors with fatal doses of medicine to facilitate assisted suicide. Patients who seek euthanasia must have 'constant and unbearable physical or psychological pain'.
- One American state, Oregon, allows doctors to give lethal prescriptions, although they are not allowed to administer the drugs. Oregon publishes few details, but it is estimated that only about 200 people have been able to take advantage of the state's 1998 Death with Dignity Act, mostly because of the Act's many safeguards.

Viewpoints

For euthanasia

- It allows terminally ill people to control timing and place of death.
- It can bring an end to the suffering of terminally ill people in severe pain.
- It allows terminally ill people to die with dignity.
- Choosing when to die is part of personal freedom.
- Palliative care is of uneven quality.
- An unsustainable burden can be placed on relatives.
- From an economic point of view, as people live longer more will become terminally ill and care costs will rise dramatically.
- Legalising euthanasia would regularise the present situation, which leaves some doctors vulnerable to prosecution, and would eliminate grey areas.
- Suicide is no longer a criminal act, so why should assisting suicide remain so?

Against euthanasia

- It is the deliberate killing of human beings.
- Death should not be controlled by a doctor, especially as hastening death is against medical ethics.
- Life is sacrosanct and euthanasia is against all religious teaching.
- It is open to abuse, particularly by unscrupulous relatives.
- A cure may be found for a particular illness.
- Good-quality palliative care is now available.
- The elderly may worry that someone wants them dead.
- It compromises the relationship between patients, carers and doctors.
- Relatives may suffer from guilt if they consent.
- As in Nazi Germany, euthanasia could lead to racial cleansing.
- It assumes that the lives of the terminally ill or severely disabled are less valuable than others.

CULTURE AND SOCIETY
Chapter 5

Religious beliefs: the major world religions

Christianity

Christianity originated 2,000 years ago as a development of the much older religion of Judaism. Today it is the largest religion in the world, although there are many different denominations, the largest of which are the Roman Catholic and Protestant Churches.

It was founded by followers of Jesus of Nazareth, who at the beginning of his ministry taught in Jewish synagogues. He was a travelling preacher who was eventually crucified on the orders of the Roman governor, Pontius Pilate. His followers proclaimed that he was the **Messiah** (Special Messenger of God). For centuries the Jews had waited for a Messiah; at the time when Jesus lived they were waiting for someone who would free them from Roman rule. The Jews, however, rejected the claim that Jesus was the Messiah, which led to Christians and Jews splitting. Opposition to Jesus, sometimes based on jealousy and rivalry, grew quickly. Religious leaders claimed he was breaking Jewish law and the Romans feared that he was trying to incite popular uprisings against them.

In 1054 (long after the fall of the Roman Empire) there was a split between eastern Christianity (the Orthodox Church) and western Christianity (Roman Catholicism — a church headed by the Pope, with a strong belief in the Virgin Mary as the mother of Jesus, who conceived him supernaturally). In the early sixteenth century, a German monk, Martin Luther, led a protest movement against his own Catholic church. This led to the start of the Reformation and the emergence of the Protestant Church. Shortly afterwards, Henry VIII split from the Roman Catholic Church over the issue of divorce, and the Church of England was born. Further splits in the Church of England occurred with the start of the Baptist Church (early seventeenth century), the Quakers (mid-seventeenth century) and John Wesley's Methodist Church (eighteenth century).

The teachings

Christianity's teachings are contained in the holy book (or collection of books), the Bible: 39 books in the Old Testament, which is largely shared with Judaism, and 27 in the New, the specifically Christian part. Four Gospels in the New Testament of the Bible provide information about the teaching of Jesus. The first might have been Mark's Gospel, probably written about 35 years after Jesus had died. In these Gospels we are told about the miracles that Jesus performed.

On the night before his death, Jesus celebrated the Jewish Passover with his disciples in Jerusalem. He used bread and wine to teach the disciples, and this 'Last Supper' has been commemorated ever since through the regular celebration of **Communion** (called Mass by Roman Catholics and the Eucharist by Anglicans).

Christians remember the crucifixion of Jesus on Good Friday. They teach that his body was placed in a tomb by a follower, Joseph of Arimathea. When three women visited it to embalm the body 3 days later they found that the tomb was empty. An angel told the women that Jesus had been brought back to life, and Jesus also appeared again among the disciples. News spread quickly that he had been resurrected. Peter was an early spokesman for the disciples, and Paul travelled extensively to spread the gospel (the 'good news') about the death and resurrection of Jesus, writing many letters to support the churches he founded.

A vicar conducting a Communion service in an Anglican church

Other beliefs and practices

- Some Christians believe that the Bible is the literal truth. Others see it more as a guide to the principles of everyday life.
- Christians believe that Jesus is the 'Son of God'.
- The 'Trinity' is God as three persons in one — God the Father, God the Son and God the Holy Spirit. Christians believe that obedience to God will bring them everlasting life in heaven (God's Kingdom).
- The main festivals of the Christian year are Christmas (birth of Jesus), Easter (his death and resurrection) and Pentecost (or Whitsun: the giving of the Holy Spirit to the first Christians in Jerusalem on the Day of Pentecost).

- People may join the Christian community through baptism, which is the initiation ceremony into church membership and a symbol of cleansing from sin.
- The Lord's Prayer is the only prayer common to Christians of all denominations.
- Although different Christian churches worship God in their own ways, most have an altar, representing the table at the Last Supper; a raised platform for preaching from, known as the pulpit; and fonts which hold the water used for baptism. Many church buildings have decoration such as stained glass windows.

Hinduism

Hinduism originated in India over 3,500 years ago but its foundations are uncertain. It is the oldest world religion still practised today.

Estimates suggest that there are over 900 million Hindus scattered in over 100 countries, although the great majority continue to live in India. One of the largest Hindu communities outside India is probably Great Britain, as a result of immigration from Asia and the West Indies.

There are millions of Hindu gods and goddesses and all are reflections of **Brahman** — the one universal and supreme spirit. Brahman is the origin of all creation and can take male, female or animal form. It represents both the entire world and the inner world of the individual. Brahman is often mentioned alongside Saraswati, the goddess of learning. The inner world in Hinduism is called **atman**, the soul. Hindu understanding of human life centres on the relationship between the imperfect body and perfect soul.

The main beliefs are reincarnation and **karma** (the law of cause and effect). There is an endless cycle of birth, life on earth, death and rebirth. Each believer is reincarnated and this is determined by how he or she spent his or her previous existence. So each Hindu tries to remove bad effects of karma on their next rebirth by living a virtuous life.

There are many sacred writings of Hinduism. They are divided into two broad groups: the Shrutis and the Smritis. The Shrutis are seen as divine in origin and include the ancient hymns of the Vedas. The Smritis are holy books of human origin; and the Ramayana is a 48,000-line poem.

The **caste system** came to be closely associated with Hinduism. People were placed in different castes based on their occupation. This system determined social contacts and marriage prospects. 'Untouchables' do not belong to any caste and carry out the most menial tasks. The caste system has dominated social life in India for centuries but it has been modified, particularly after the campaign led by the famous reformer Mahatma Gandhi.

Hindu practice

- Hinduism is a way of life covering all forms of behaviour. There are four recognised religious paths to personal salvation. These are:
  - **Bhakti:** loving devotion to one of the gods.
  - **Karma:** the chain of cause and effect, with good deeds leading to more good deeds.
  - **Jnana:** a formidable path requiring an understanding of the scriptures and constant guidance from a spiritual guru.
  - **Yoga:** a special discipline of physical and mental exercises practised in India for centuries.
- Worship is mainly in home-based shrines (where women take a major spiritual responsibility) and is practised on a daily basis; but some is communal and many Hindus visit the temple regularly. Each Hindu temple is dedicated to a particular god. Worship takes place through the acknowledgement of the sacred syllable, the singing of mantras and the use of geometric patterns called **mandalas**.
- There are many festivals, most notably Divali (the autumn Festival of Lights), and sixteen ceremonies (**samskaras**) marking the most important stages of life, from birth and name-giving to death and the funeral ceremony. Festivals help to ensure the continuation of human traditions and help to educate children.
- Many parts of India are regarded as sacred by Hindus and seven rivers are regarded as holy. Washing in rivers such as the Ganges is believed to have religious significance because they help to convey life and energy.
- The cow is often seen as the universal symbol of Hinduism. Anything produced by the cow is seen as purifying.

Islam

Islam originated 1,400 years ago in Mecca through Muhammad (the greatest prophet of God and his last messenger). Muhammad was a deeply religious, politically influential Arab, who was concerned about social injustice and excesses such as drunkenness. Muslims believe that Muhammad was human. They do not see him as the founder of a new religion. They recognise the work of Abraham, Moses and Jesus but believe that their messages became distorted over time. Jews and Christians are recognised as early monotheists (believers in one God) even though the Torah and the Gospels became distorted.

Muhammad was particularly concerned about polytheism (worshipping several gods) and preached against this in Mecca. Following persecution, Muhammad and his Muslim followers undertook the **Hijra** (emigration) to Medina but soon afterwards returned to take control of Mecca.

Muslims believe in one God, Allah ('Muslim' means one who submits to one God). The Arabic word 'Islam' means the complete surrender of the individual to God (Allah).

Today, Islam is the second biggest and the fastest growing religion. There are believed to be over 1,000 million followers of the faith. There are two groups of Muslim believers, **Sunnis** (the great majority) and **Shi'ites**, who disagree about the successors of Muhammad.

The teachings

The holy book, the Qur'an (sometimes referred to as the Koran in English), was revealed to Muhammad by Allah. Muhammad had a vision, revealed by the Angel Gabriel, in which he saw a superhuman figure who called him the 'messenger of Allah'. The text recited by Muhammad later became part of the Qur'an.

The Qur'an is central to Muslim belief and is treated with the utmost respect as it represents the literal word of God. Though translations are allowed, it is often read aloud in the original Arabic as this represents the perfect form of the Qur'an. The Qur'an rules that women should cover their bodies and that Muslims cannot be moneylenders. In the holy month of Ramadan, time is often set aside by Muslim males to read the whole book.

Muslims believe in the resurrection and life after death. Belief in angels is also an important part of Islamic faith. Angels worship God, bring down revelations and record every person's actions prior to the Day of Judgement. (Islamic belief involves belief in God, his revelations, his angels, his messengers and the Day of Judgement.)

Muslim practice

- Prayer is central to Islam and prayers are said five times a day. Muslims can pray anywhere, but all males endeavour to be in the mosque for noon prayers on a

Friday. The Qur'an teaches Muslims how to live their lives and how to prepare for the Day of Judgement, when they will stand before Allah and account for their lives. The mosque is both a place of prayer and a gathering place for the Muslim community. Muslims must wash thoroughly and remove their shoes before praying in the mosque.

Muslims praying outside Finsbury Mosque in London

- The Muslim way of life is based on the Five Pillars of Islam. These are:
  - **Shahadah:** belief that there is one God, Allah, and that Muhammad is his messenger
  - **Salah:** ritual prayer performed five times a day at set times
  - **Zakat:** giving support to the poor — Muslims are supposed to give 2.5% of their wealth to charity annually
  - **Sawm:** fasting during Ramadan by healthy adult Muslims
  - the **Hajj:** pilgrimage to Mecca
- The **Jihad** is sometimes seen as the sixth pillar of Islam. It symbolises a struggle on God's behalf and is often seen as an armed struggle in defence of the Muslim faith. It can also mean battling against injustice and different forms of helping to promote and defend Islam.
- Islamic laws (the **Shariah**) influence all aspects of daily life. Marriage and family life are considered central. Muslims must only eat **halal** food prepared under strict conditions. Eating pig products and drinking alcohol is forbidden.
- Every healthy Muslim who can afford to do so should make a pilgrimage to Mecca once in their lifetime.

Ask the examiner

Q Will I need to know about every religion in detail?

A No. An AS comprehension passage or source used in Unit 1 might contain references to specific religions but detailed knowledge will not be required. Essay questions set in A2 Unit 3 may ask for knowledge of one or more specific religions and more detailed knowledge and analysis is required.

Practice questions

The following six paragraphs are part of a longer passage typical of one that might be used for Section A of Unit 1. Nine objective-type (multiple-choice) questions are asked on these six paragraphs. In a normal exam there will be 30 multiple-choice questions based on the whole passage and, in all cases, there is only one correct answer.

Are we still tolerant?

(1) Britain has always prided itself as being characterised by religious toleration and is a country of many different faiths in a world society increasingly described as 'secular'. In many ways, however, things have changed since the 9/11 attack on New York and the London transport bombings of 2005 in which many people lost their lives or were maimed. The perpetrators of the violence were religiously inspired terrorists, and it is difficult to believe that such acts of savagery can be undertaken in the name of God when we are taught to believe that religion is a force for peace and understanding, not a vehicle for malevolence.

(2) We have become suspicious, and if suspicion extends to Muslims more widely then that suspicion can become prejudice — something usually born of ignorance. We are not seeking evidence of a Jihad lurking somewhere in the recesses of the mosque around the corner, but people interpret religious teaching — whether it be the teaching of Judaism, Christianity or Islam — in different ways, and one lesson of history is that these are not always peaceful.

(3) While terrorist activity fills the news screens, another area of controversy has focused on the wearing of the niqab and the jilbab. The niqab is a face veil and, in November 2006, Aishah Azmi, a bilingual teaching assistant, lost her job because she refused to remove it when helping children. Similarly, Shabina Begum, who had been banned from her school for wearing a head-to-toe Islamic dress, lost her case that her human rights had been violated after a decision in the House of Lords. The situation is similar in other European countries. France does not allow the wearing of 'conspicuous' religious symbols in schools and some German states do not allow the wearing of hijab.

(4) Is this simply prejudice? Alan Johnson, the Education Secretary, has given his support to headteachers who ban their pupils from wearing the full Muslim veil on 'safety, security and teaching' grounds, although this does not appear to extend to the wearing of a headscarf. It appears to be a pragmatic decision in an age of insecurity, in which tolerance of diverse religious beliefs assumes lesser importance.

(5) It is all, seemingly, a long way from the world of al-Qaeda and its figurehead Osama bin Laden, who declared war on the West in 1998, and from the mountains in or near the lawless, tribal areas of Pakistan where he is said to hide — from the training camps, fundraisers and ideologues. Britain is said to be in the firing line because of its strong support for American foreign policies, its greater ease of accessibility compared with the USA and its historic links with Pakistan, which allow British subjects to travel with relatively limited monitoring.

(6) The fundamentalists have an unwavering faith in their cause and are masters of ideology. Thousands of young Muslims have been mobilised across the world in the last 5 years. Their radicalisation, and the spread of slick, effective and pernicious propaganda, has been helped by the internet. Many are young and impressionable teenagers operating and learning from their own bedrooms. Others are in their mid-20s, often graduates whose parents have emigrated from parts of Asia or Africa to Western countries. Religious dress may be little more than symbolic but the threat from al-Qaeda-related terrorism is deadly and enduring.

1 **A 'secular society' (paragraph 1) is best described as one**
   A   in which the importance of religion is declining.
   B   where different faiths are flourishing.
   C   in which attendances at places of worship are rising.
   D   which has a single, dominant religion.

2 **The 9/11 attack focusing on New York**
   A   had been widely predicted.
   B   was a shock because it was unexpected.
   C   confirmed the existence of weapons of mass destruction.
   D   was an act of retaliation by Iraqi forces.

3 **A 'Jihad' (paragraph 2) is**
   A   a radical preacher.
   B   a religious symbol.
   C   a holy book.
   D   a holy war.

4 **According to paragraph 2 a problem with religion is that it**
A   inevitably leads to prejudice and bigotry.
B   appeals only to the less well educated.
C   does not always offer clear teaching.
D   always leads to conflict and war.

5 **In paragraph 3 the author's attitude to Aishah Azmi and Shabina Begum is**
A   hostile.
B   sympathetic.
C   neutral.
D   indignant.

6 **A 'pragmatic decision' (paragraph 4) is best described as one that**
A   reflects a clear political ideology.
B   is shaped to meet particular circumstances.
C   is based on the culture and beliefs of others.
D   is based entirely on health and safety considerations.

7 **Osama bin Laden (paragraph 5) is**
A   a symbolic figure for al-Qaeda supporters.
B   an important Muslim prophet.
C   one of the tribal leaders in Pakistan.
D   a mythical figure revered by al-Qaeda supporters.

8 **According to paragraph 5 Britain is a terrorist target because**
1   of its special relationship with the USA.
2   it is more geographically vulnerable than the USA.
3   of serious flaws in British immigration policy.
4   of its hostility to the Pakistan government.

Answer:
A   if 1 only is correct.
B   if 1 and 2 only are correct.
C   if 2, 3 and 4 only are correct.
D   if all are correct.

9 **The author's attitude to the propaganda used by Muslim fundamentalists mentioned in paragraph 6 is**
A   wholly condemnatory of the techniques used.
B   typical of those who do not understand Muslim teaching.
C   anger that the internet does not censor the messages.
D   a mixture of disgust and recognition of skills.

Examination and appreciation of ideologies and values

We all have our own personal beliefs and values. As individuals we value our freedom but we also have to accept that if everyone were completely free to do as they chose we might soon find ourselves in a state of **anarchy** in which there was no established order or framework for behaviour. Consequently, we accept that there have to be certain restrictions that help to maintain a balance between our own freedom to do things and freedom from actions and forms of behaviour that might prove harmful.

We also enjoy a series of rights as individuals and these rights allow us considerable freedom of expression, to associate with other people and to take a whole range of other actions. With these rights come responsibilities in terms of how we behave. In addition, there are some things that nearly everybody accepts as desirable social goals, such as equality of opportunity. This does not mean that we can, or should, all be equal. Instead it represents the ideal that all members of society should have an equal ability to succeed if they have the capacity to do so.

Ideologies

Ideologies are connected with our core beliefs and the way we look at things, usually in a wider social, political and economic context. Followers of the teaching of Karl Marx believed in the significance of economic status and the power of the working class to become a revolutionary force to overcome the ruling class. In the twentieth century there was a sharp ideological division between Western countries such as the USA and UK, with their emphasis on democracy and competing political parties, and countries such as Russia and China, where a communist ideology was based on a single party exercising power.

Key terms

anarchy: the breakdown of established systems of government.

ideology: a perspective that represents a particular view; a distinctive and identifiable way of representing or examining issues.

In the 1950s and 1960s there was talk of an imaginary 'Iron Curtain' between East and West and there were often acute tensions between the major powers. In the last 20 years, differences have been less pronounced and ideologies have become more blurred. Many eastern European countries, once part of a vast communist bloc, have become more democratic and market-oriented in recent years. A number have now gained membership of the European Union (EU).

The rise of Hitler was accompanied by Nazism and the belief in a super-race, embodied in handsome Germanic types with blue eyes and fair hair. In the Nazi state there was certainly no thought of equality of opportunity, and some groups were discriminated against in the extreme manner commonly referred to today as 'ethnic cleansing'. Jews, in particular, and also many non-whites and Romany travellers, were identified and dealt with ruthlessly.

Even in Great Britain the sort of ideology that characterised the two main political parties when the Second World War ended in 1945 is far less evident today. When the Labour Party swept to power in 1945 it had what many considered to be an avowedly

Margaret Thatcher, 1985

socialist agenda. Key industries such as power, coal, steel and the railways were nationalised (brought under state control) and the welfare state was widened, most notably by the creation of a National Health Service that was free for all at the point of delivery. Labour was identifiably 'left-wing'.

The Conservative Party put more emphasis on the freedom of the individual and private businesses, and favoured lower taxes and a less pronounced role for the state. In some respects the party distrusted ideologies, and in the 1950s and 1960s there was a broad measure of consensus between the two major parties.

This changed in the 1980s when Margaret Thatcher became party leader, prime minister and champion of the 'New Right'. With its desire to 'roll back the frontiers of the state', the party became more noticeably 'right-wing' and pursued a vigorous programme of encouraging competition and privatisation, selling industries to private companies and council houses to their tenants, and creating a 'share-owning democracy' for millions of people.

'Thatcherism' almost became a new ideology in itself. Supporters regarded Margaret Thatcher as an overwhelming success, but she was a controversial figure with many critics of the undesirable effects of her policies, particularly in the old industrial regions.

In 1997, Labour swept to power after an absence from government of 18 years. The new prime minister, Tony Blair, completed the transformation from 'Old Labour' to 'New Labour', the latter being based on thinking that had moved from left to centre and, for some, was indistinguishable from the 'one nation' Conservatism of the 1950s and 1960s.

General election victories were repeated in 2001 and 2005. After David Cameron was elected its leader the Conservative Party also moved to more central ground, prompting some commentators to ask if there was any ideology left and cynics to claim that the two parties had become almost indistinguishable.

Perhaps Gordon Brown, who became prime minister when Tony Blair stepped down in 2007, has different ideas; but ideologies are sometimes said to represent extremes and British voters have rarely shown a taste for these. Politics almost inevitably involves a measure of compromise. Increasingly, the most successful politicians are often the most **pragmatic**.

> **Key term**
>
> **pragmatism:** a willingness to avoid extremes and to accept that, to achieve success, actions might require some degree of compromise and partial dilution of principles.

Unquestionably, in recent years the ideological differences between the two main parties have narrowed — so much so that an increasing number of voters find it difficult to distinguish between the policies of the two main parties and to identify any distinctive form of ideology. The danger is that disillusionment will turn to apathy. If it still exists, ideology might be more readily associated with the nationalist parties of Northern Ireland, Scotland and Wales, or with parties that have a more distinctive agenda (such as the Green Party or the United Kingdom Independence Party) or are seen as more 'extreme', such as the British National Party.

Q I have strong political views. Should I keep them to myself? If I do express them, will examiners who don't agree with me mark me down?

A Many people have strong views about politics, but you need to avoid giving answers that are strongly opinionated and very biased towards the view of a particular political party. All parties have strong points and weak points — though dedicated supporters are often blind to the latter.

In general, you should always try to take into account both sides of an argument. However, this often results in a neutral view and a danger is that it will become too bland and that you will try to produce an answer that you think the examiner wishes to read. A well-reasoned argument will avoid becoming too emotionally involved or excessively biased, but you need to avoid sidestepping some of the controversy that might be built into a question.

Much depends on the extent to which you are able to provide a critical response, and how far you can express your views in the form of balanced arguments, with a logically argued conclusion rather than one that is full of assertions and sweeping statements.

Examiners as individuals may or may not have strong views about politics and the merits of a particular political party and it would be dishonest to pretend otherwise. However, when acting as examiners they will set these aside and mark strictly according to the mark scheme, which will reward knowledge and reasoned arguments supported by examples irrespective of the perspective taken.

Law and morality

To operate in an orderly way society requires rules, and these rules reflect a mixture of values, beliefs and moral concerns. Often we look to moral codes and the formulation of laws by those elected to represent us. Consequently, we can live our daily lives and conduct our affairs with a reasonable amount of freedom. Those who disregard and flout the law will, if detected, face sanctions and may lose their freedom.

Moral codes do not have the force of law but they are said to represent a shared value system. Often these operate in fairly simple ways, summed up by the phrases 'doing good' or behaving as a 'good citizen'. Other moral codes, which may also reflect religious beliefs and values, may be more elaborate. Some people see moral codes in a strict way — they see moral absolutes which must always be followed. Others talk in more relative terms, suggesting that judgements may differ according to changing circumstances.

One way of illustrating the differences is by looking at attitudes to the age of consent for sexual activity. The law fixes the age at 16. Anyone who indulges in certain forms of non-consensual, or even consensual, sexual activity below the age of 16 has broken the law and could be prosecuted. For those over 16 the position changes. The activity becomes legal but it may not be moral in the eyes of those who argue that sex before marriage is wrong. Others may feel that, under certain circumstances, it is both legally and morally acceptable.

Similarly, murder is always seen to be wrong both morally and legally. In the UK, euthanasia is illegal yet not everyone agrees about the moral position. There are those who feel that, given the sort of strict safeguards that are applied in countries like the Netherlands and Switzerland, there is a case for changing the law to help end the suffering and pain of terminally ill people.

Abortion in the UK is legal within specified time limits, yet people are divided over its morality. Supporters believe in the right of women to choose whether to continue or terminate a pregnancy. Opponents represented by the pressure group SPUC (Society for the Protection of the Unborn Child) campaign for the right of the foetus.

Though we have said that murder is always regarded as wrong, controversial issues like abortion and euthanasia are much more difficult. Assisting somebody to end his or her own life is regarded as a serious offence and may be punished by a long period of imprisonment. For many religious people the thought of someone 'playing God' is abhorrent.

Yet we cannot readily say that those who sincerely believe in euthanasia have beliefs that are necessarily right or wrong. They are wrong only if they break the law. Feelings over abortion run even higher and, in the USA, anti-abortionists have sometimes resorted to violence against medical professionals. The anti-abortionists feel that their beliefs are right; yet many would judge their actions to be wrong, especially as, in extreme cases, their actions have resulted in murder.

Ask the examiner

Q **For religious reasons, I believe that abortion is wrong. Can I express this viewpoint?**

A Firmly held and sincere religious beliefs will always be respected, but questions about abortion are rarely clear-cut and you might be expected to consider arguments used by both supporters and opponents of abortion. In your conclusion you will be able to make your own position clear, perhaps saying whether you would or would not approve of the use of violence to support a particular belief.

Rights and responsibilities

It is often said that nobody in the world should live without basic human rights (such as the rights to education, to follow one's own religion and to meet freely with friends), but many do. Guidelines have been established by the following milestones in the history of human rights:

- **1948 — The Universal Declaration of Human Rights (UDHR).** Coming 3 years after the end of the Second World War, the UDHR was drawn up by the United Nations (UN), which wanted to establish and protect freedoms such as speech, movement and the right to a fair trial.
- **1950 — The European Convention on Human Rights (ECHR).** The ECHR set out a framework of human rights for European countries, with ultimate access for aggrieved citizens to the European Court of Human Rights.
- **1989 — The Convention on the Rights of the Child (CRC).** The CRC requires governments around the world to consider the rights of children. This may be especially important in countries where there are many orphans as a result of civil war or the ravages of AIDS.
- **1998 — The UK Human Rights Act.** This Act was passed by Parliament to make the ECHR part of UK law, thus helping to avoid the costly and time-consuming process of taking a case to the European Court in Strasbourg. Coming into operation in 2000, it gave the UK its own laws on human rights as set out originally in the ECHR. With its identification of basic human rights, the Act was designed to protect the rights of everyone in the UK. The key human rights under the Act are:
  - the right to life
  - freedom from torture and degrading treatment
  - freedom from slavery and forced labour
  - the right to liberty
  - the right to a fair trial
  - the right not to be punished for something that wasn't a crime at the time of the action
  - the right to respect for private and family life
  - freedom of thought, conscience and religion
  - freedom of expression
  - freedom of assembly and association
  - the right to marry or form a civil partnership and start a family
  - the right not to be discriminated against in respect of these rights and freedoms
  - the right to own property

- the right to an education
- the right to participate in free elections
- **2000 — The Freedom of Information Act.** This Act gives individuals a general right of access to personal information held on them by various public bodies. It also requires these bodies to publish a range of information but, in both cases, a number of exceptions exist and critics argue that individuals cannot always gain full access to information in the ways initially envisaged.

When a law protects a human right, it becomes a legal right in the country concerned. For example, the Universal Declaration of Human Rights provides for a right to work; and in the UK there are a variety of additional legal protections that limit the working age and hours of young people, seek to guarantee a minimum wage for adults, and outlaw discrimination at work on the grounds of race, gender, disability or sexual orientation.

There is a useful website at **www.direct.gov.uk**.

Equality of opportunity

Theoretically, every UK citizen has the same rights and nobody is above the law. In practice, however, some people are more likely than others to be able to put their rights under the Human Rights Act into practice, for a variety of reasons:

- Success, however it might be defined, depends partly on individual skills, talents and application. These qualities are not equally distributed in society.
- There are marked variations in incomes. The best-paying jobs tend to be those that need the most qualifications or, perhaps in the case of sportspeople, depend on particular gifts that very few possess.
- Wealth is also unequally distributed and people may inherit large sums.
- In some postcode areas there is considerable poverty. People who live in those areas may find it difficult to get credit, be more exposed to crime and antisocial behaviour and attend schools with poorer facilities.
- Certain groups suffer from discrimination even though such actions are illegal. Women may not receive the same pay as men for equal work; members of ethnic minority groups may be discriminated against because of the colour of their skin; homosexuals of either sex may be discriminated against because of their sexual orientation; and disabled people may find that their access is limited in many areas. Such discrimination is often very difficult to prove.

However, values are never static and part of the responsibility of politicians is to recognise when they are changing — and possibly to give a lead to public opinion.

In the 1960s significant changes took place, which perhaps reflected the changes in education after free secondary education became available to all in 1944.

By the 1960s, the universities — previously limited in number and accommodating only a tiny proportion of 18–21-year-olds — were beginning to expand, as did courses in the social sciences such as social policy, sociology, politics, economics and psychology. Old values were repeatedly questioned and the Labour government of 1964–70 recognised the need for change. Parliament enacted new laws that saw the suspension and subsequent cessation of capital punishment, the legalisation of homosexuality between consenting adults in private and the legalisation of abortion.

These were momentous changes and met with great resistance from those who saw capital punishment as a deterrent to murder, who deemed homosexuality to be deviant behaviour or an illness that could be 'cured' and who saw abortion as a signal that casual sexual relationships would threaten the institution of marriage. The dangers of 'back street abortionists' who operated when abortion was illegal were rarely referred to.

From 1970, governments increasingly took action to limit discrimination and to make opportunities more equal:

- **Equal Pay Act.** First passed in 1970, this Act sought to give an individual a right to the same contractual pay and benefits as a person of the opposite sex in the same employment, where a man and a woman are doing 'like work' or work that can be rated as equal. This led to a significant erosion of the differences in pay for men and women doing equal work, but it has not yet eliminated unequal pay.
- **Sex Discrimination Act.** First passed in 1975, this Act established guidelines for fair employment practices so that there was less likelihood that women would be denied access to certain jobs or senior posts on grounds of gender or marital status. Although primarily intended to protect the interests of females, the Act offers the same protection against discrimination to males. Exemptions may be claimed if an employer can prove that the determining requirement of a job is one associated with a particular gender.
- **Race Relations Act.** First operative from 1976, this Act set up the Commission for Racial Equality to support those who had legitimate claims that they had been discriminated against, perhaps in employment, because of the colour of their skin. Under the Act, it is an offence to treat a person differently on the grounds of race, colour, nationality or ethnic or national origin.
- **Disability Discrimination Act.** First passed in 1995, this Act set up the Disability Rights Commission to support people discriminated against on the grounds of

mental or physical disability. It applies to both employment and the provision of services, not least in terms of access to shops and public buildings.

- **Minimum Wage Act.** First passed in 1998, this Act set out a national minimum wage for adult workers. It applies to nearly all workers and sets hourly rates below which pay must not be allowed to fall. The January 2008 minimum hourly rate for those aged 22 and over was £5.52, with lower 'development rates' for those aged between 16 and 21.
- **Employment Equality (Religion or Belief) Regulations.** Since 2003, these regulations have sought to outlaw discrimination in employment and vocational training on the grounds of religious belief or similar philosophical belief.
- **Employment Equality (Sexual Orientation) Regulations.** Since 2003, these regulations have meant that employers cannot refuse to employ people just because they are gay, lesbian or bisexual.
- **Civil Partnership Act.** First passed in 2004 and operative from 5 December 2005, this Act established civil partnership as a completely new legal relationship which can be formed by two people of the same sex and is distinct from marriage. It gives same-sex couples the ability to obtain legal recognition for their relationship.
- **Employment Equality (Age) Regulations.** Age discrimination in employment and training has been unlawful since 2006.

In 2007, a single commission called the Commission for Equality and Human Rights replaced the Equal Opportunities Commission, the Commission for Racial Equality and the Disability Rights Commission.

In some respects, laws passed by Parliament help to reflect changing public opinion. It is important that the rights of people are protected by a legal framework and that they can seek redress for their grievances, if necessary in the courts. However, even though there are now many laws to protect against discrimination and to promote equality this does not necessarily mean that discrimination does not exist.

Viewpoints

There have been a number of Acts to prevent discrimination and promote equality of opportunity. Have they worked?

Yes
- There is a comprehensive system of legislation.
- People who have been discriminated against have plenty of opportunities to seek redress and secure compensation.
- Companies and individuals guilty of discrimination may get bad publicity and may have to pay large fines.

- People are much more aware of their rights and can get advice from trade unions, the Citizen's Advice Bureau or anti-discriminatory bodies.
- The move to a single commission will help to streamline the system and give it a sharper focus.

No

- Not all discrimination is direct, and it may be difficult to prove.
- Discrimination can take more subtle forms of harassment or bullying at work.
- Many people are not aware of their rights.
- People either don't know how to complain or are reluctant to do so.
- Enforcement of the law is often difficult.
- Sanctions are not sufficiently strong to act as a deterrent.

Practice questions

The following three sources are typical of those that will be used in the Unit 1 Section B AS examination paper. In each case, a question is based on the source and the candidate's own knowledge of the theme is used.

Source 1

I am 18 and have the right to vote in UK elections but what use is that? When you really think about it, the vote's a waste of time, especially for young people. Voting takes place once every few years and changes nothing. How can MPs know what young people are thinking? I don't think that's proper democracy. I'd like a say in some of the decisions being taken in Parliament. We don't make enough use of referendums in this country, especially when there are big decisions to be made about issues such as the European Union and immigration.

Question
Develop two arguments against and two arguments in favour of the viewpoint of the 18-year-old expressed above.
(9 marks)

Source 2

I believe in socialism and that's what we've not had in this country for a long time. It was different between 1945 and 1951. Those were the golden years of socialism. Industries were nationalised and controlled by the state for the people. A welfare state was set up with a new National Health Service. People pulled together. It was clear what the Labour Party stood for.

Now it's different. All the old certainties have gone. What we've got now is 'New Labour', with competition, privatisation, no power for the trade unions. There's no difference between New Labour and the Conservatives. They all want to support big business and fat cats. The gaps between rich and poor are greater than ever.

We need a new socialist party that stands for more equality, for taxing the rich to help the poor and for stopping the privatisation of our education and health service.

We need to scrap private schools so everybody has a fair chance to get a decent standard of education.

We need proper human rights for people, not racist immigration laws which give all the powers to the police and the government.

We need decent benefits for people to live on. It's a disgrace that old people, the disabled and the unemployed have to live on a pittance. We're the fourth richest country in the world.

Question

Using your own knowledge and information from the source, consider why it might be difficult for anyone to form a new political party based on the aims stated in Source 2.

(11 marks)

Source 3

First letter to a newspaper, supporting experiments using animals

I wonder what the animal rights supporters would feel if they had someone close to them who was ill and research hadn't been done on the drugs that a loved one might need. Don't get me wrong. I don't want to see animals suffering, but research on animals is done in a very humane way and it's the only way that proper testing can be done to see if drugs work without serious side effects. We don't live in an ideal world and we have to put our trust in the companies and their employees who work in research.

We simply have to establish priorities and the reality is that humans are much more developed than animals so that's where our priorities must lie. Animal rights supporters make lots of claims about cruelty, but have you ever seen any proof? Not likely. Their claims are false and misleading and if they terrorise research staff in their own homes they should be treated for what they are — terrorists.

Second letter to a newspaper, opposing experiments using animals

I sympathise with the staff who have been threatened, but this is part of the risk that they take when they work for a firm connected with doing research on animals. Perhaps they will experience some of the pain and fear that animals have to go through. A lot of experiments mean that animals feel pain, and that's cruel. They are defenceless so that's what animal rights supporters try to do — offer them a bit of protection.

We only get to learn what they tell us in these research labs and we don't know if it's the truth. My feelings are much more for the innocent animal kingdom and for the suffering that animals go through. Vivisection favours multinational companies and their real interests are in maximising profits. Other methods of testing are available and these should be properly researched and funded. They don't want to do this because it's cheaper to exploit animals.

Question

Discuss the views expressed by the writers of the two letters shown above. Which of the two viewpoints do you support? Give reasons for your answer. *(15 marks)*

Media and communication

Communication is central to the lives of almost everyone. Much of it takes place on a day-to-day basis through conversation. Often we use an intermediary form of communication through a medium (perhaps television) or, more commonly, several different intermediaries, which help to form what is sometimes referred to as the mass media.

The major forms of mass media include:

- newspapers
- books
- magazines
- film
- television
- videos
- CDs/DVDs
- internet/e-mail
- mobile phones

The press

Newspapers and magazines play an important part in our lives. A visit to a major newsagent will reveal a dazzling array of magazine titles, often produced for target groups with specific interests. Newspapers can be local or national; both daily and Sunday papers remain important to many adults, but their circulation is declining by about 4% a year and 'circulation wars', using incentives such as free gifts and temporarily reduced prices, are common. There is a lot at stake for national newspapers, fighting for around £2 billion of advertising revenue, which provides about 50% of their income.

A distinction is often made between 'popular' and 'quality' newspapers — between those with daily sales figures of over a million copies and those with lower circulation figures. Another way of making the distinction is to refer to popular newspapers as 'tabloids' and quality newspapers as 'broadsheets'. Traditionally, tabloids were smaller in size and broadsheets were much larger. However, over the last 10 years, most broadsheets (with the exception of the *Telegraph*) have become smaller and a new name has emerged — 'compacts'. Tabloids have also developed an alternative description — 'redtops'.

The tabloids/redtops are said to aim at what they deem to be 'popular' taste. The best-selling example, the *Sun*, with daily sales hovering around 3 million copies, contains brief news stories with an emphasis on bold and inventive headlines, photographs, celebrity culture, gossip, entertainment, scandal and advertisements for mobile phones and financial loans. That may, indeed, reflect popular taste, or it may just be the way in which the *Sun* seeks to interpret what it believes to be popular taste. Ultimately, newspapers are commercial concerns and higher sales bring in more revenue and attract more advertisers. 'Taste' may be important but profit is the key goal.

Broadsheets/compacts are ostensibly more 'upmarket' — perhaps aimed at people who have remained for longer in the education system. Pictures and banner headlines are less common and the focus is on longer, more serious, and more balanced news reporting. The danger is that readers and markets become stereotyped. Broadsheets become the preserve of the upper classes (a common misconception) and tabloids are for those who occupy lower places in the class structure (an equally common misconception). 'High' and 'low' culture take on another dimension and it is unwise to oversimplify categories of newspaper readers.

Radio and television broadcasting

Radio emerged in the early decades of the twentieth century, essentially an experiment encouraged and influenced by the government after the British Broadcasting Corporation was set up in the mid-1920s. Among its tasks, the BBC sought to educate and inform its listeners and was often seen as an arbiter of what was deemed to be good taste by its first general manager, John Reith. For many years there were only three BBC radio channels.

Not until the 'swinging' sixties, and the pressure from 'pirate' radio stations like *Radio Caroline* broadcasting pop music, was there a significant change as stations were renamed and Radio 1 began broadcasting. BBC radio and television broadcasts were, and continue to be, financed mainly from an annual licence fee (although the BBC has an increasingly lucrative commercial arm selling such products as DVDs of BBC programmes), which all television viewers under 75 must pay or risk prosecution.

Listening to the radio in the 1930s

Increasingly, 'commercial' radio stations emerged as rivals to the BBC, deriving their income from payments made by advertisers.

Television barely existed before the start of the Second World War in 1939 and only came into more general use as the technology improved in the 1950s. As with radio, the BBC had a broadcasting monopoly until 1955, when independent commercial television began. All programmes from the two channels were broadcast in black and white but people were captivated, especially after seeing the live broadcast of Queen Elizabeth's coronation in 1953. A second channel, BBC2, began in 1964 and it was the first channel to broadcast in colour, in 1967. Channel 4 (and its Welsh language equivalent S4C) began broadcasting in 1982.

In the 1980s, with the deregulation of the UK television and radio market, reflecting the move towards privatisation and freer markets, the BBC faced more intense competition from the commercial sector and from Channel 4 (a hybrid advertiser-funded public service broadcaster). In recent years, satellite, cable and digital television have become more widely available to viewers and listeners. There are also many local radio stations, some run by the BBC and some by commercial interests.

The ITV company Thames Television was the first to introduce 24-hour broadcasting, in 1987, but Rupert Murdoch's company, Sky, has been a major innovator in recent years. In 1989 it launched a four-channel service using the Astra satellites, and its first pay-to-view programme (a boxing match between Frank Bruno and George Tyson) was transmitted in 1996. Two years later, Sky digital was launched.

The BBC is a public service broadcaster that is required to be free from commercial and political influence — although politicians, through Parliament and with the close attention of the Treasury and the Department of Culture, Media and Sport, determine the level of its annual licence fee, which is its main source of income. In broad terms, it is a public corporation, incorporated under a Royal Charter that is reviewed every 10 years. In 2007, after the BBC Charter was last reviewed, its Board of Governors was replaced by the BBC Trust and its public service role was redefined. The BBC should seek to:

- sustain citizenship and civil society
- promote education and learning
- stimulate creativity and cultural excellence
- represent the UK and its nations, regions and communities
- bring the UK to the world and the world to the UK (BBC Radio operates a World Service financed by the Foreign Office)

- help deliver to the public the benefit of changing technologies, including playing a leading role in the gradual move from analogue to digital television

The effective delivery of the BBC's public duties, within the framework set by the BBC Trust, is the responsibility of its Executive Board, headed by the BBC's Director-General.

Many thought that, in an age of widescreen digital television and the iPod, radio would be either forgotten or confined to an elderly audience clinging to the past. However, the digital revolution that led to a huge range of television channels also applied to radio. Estimates suggest that in 2007 16% of radio listening was via digital forms and 4.4 million people (with a large proportion in the 15–24 age range) listened to radio on their mobile phone following the launch of Virgin's 3G mobile phone in 2005. Similarly, nearly 3 million listen to podcasts downloaded to iPods or other MP3 players.

It is digitalisation, mobile phone technology and iPods that, far from leading to its demise, have created new opportunities for radio. Digital technology has also given opportunities to a number of BBC and commercial stations, although GCap's The Jazz was short-lived after initial optimism.

Numbers listening to digital-only stations rose sharply to over 6 million people in 2007, according to the industry audience research body, RAJAR (Radio Joint Audience Research). By way of contrast, the podcast market remains dominated by the BBC, which also has the popular 'listen again' facility on its website. Overall, the BBC has just over 50% of the radio listening market, with commercial stations accounting for nearly all the rest.

It is not radio as many adults remember it, but digital radio (increasingly known as DAB — digital audio broadcasting), and listening to radio via digital television and the internet, suggests that many more people of all ages are seeking access to a wide choice of radio channels and clear reception. Certainly the digital revolution is not confined to television.

Controlling the media

Potentially, the mass media can have a considerable impact on public opinion. Radio and television programmes presented by the BBC are subject to the requirements of the BBC Charter, which requires them to be impartial. The 1954 Television Act and the 1981 Broadcasting Act require ITV to maintain 'balance, accuracy and impartiality' in programmes. Since 2004, Ofcom (Office of Communications) has been the single broadcasting regulator.

As the courting by politicians of the world's most influential media figure, Rupert Murdoch (the owner of News International), suggests, newspapers are not required to be impartial. All newspapers are likely to demonstrate some degree of political bias and to select, edit and structure some of their articles in a way that reflects the thinking and policies of the political parties that they support. However, newspapers are limited in what they can print by the laws of libel and must be mindful of people's right to privacy under the Human Rights Act.

Newspapers are also subject to the Press Code — a voluntary arrangement that seeks to set out some basic rules such as:

- offering a right of reply if they print something inaccurate
- correcting inaccuracy and, if appropriate, offering an apology
- avoiding prejudicial references, e.g. to someone's colour or sexual orientation
- not using clandestine devices (hidden cameras, phone tapping etc.) to gain information
- restricted reporting if children under 16 are involved
- not making payments to criminals and witnesses in criminal trials
- journalists having a moral duty to protect confidential sources of information

Compliance with the Press Code is the responsibility of an independent Press Complaints Commission with 17 members. In 2006 the Commission dealt with 3,325 complaints, mostly concerning allegations of inaccurate reporting.

Viewpoints

Do we need newspapers?

No	*Yes*
■ Tabloids are biased.	■ They are informative.
■ They try to persuade us to vote in a particular way.	■ They are entertaining.
■ Tabloids are obsessed with trivia. Broadsheets are boring.	■ We buy those that reflect what we are thinking.
■ They rarely tell the truth.	■ We are capable of drawing our own conclusions.
■ They have a total disregard for the privacy of the individual.	■ The Press Code protects us.
■ We can use other media.	■ If they get things wrong, newspapers have to print apologies.

Ask the examiner

Q **I don't read a newspaper. Will this put me at a disadvantage in the General Studies examination?**

A Many students do not read a newspaper, at least not regularly. Questions in all four units, at AS and A2, use newspaper extracts as sources, so the more familiar you are with them the more confident you will be.

Libraries often carry a wide selection and, wherever there are university students in large numbers, there are usually newsagents who sell broadsheets at around 30p instead of the usual cover price of around 80p. Looking at newspapers occasionally will give you an idea of how different newspapers cover the same stories and help you to spot bias. Don't ignore tabloids with their very different journalistic styles.

Remember that newspapers, even broadsheets, are rarely impartial, nor are they under any obligation to be so.

Practice questions

The following four paragraphs are part of a longer passage typical of one that might be used for Section A of Unit 1. Eight objective-type (multiple-choice) questions are asked on these four paragraphs. In a normal exam there will be 30 multiple-choice questions based on the whole passage and, in all cases, there is only one correct answer.

Courting danger

(1) When alive, she was revered as the most photographed women of modern times, but the inquest into the death of Princess Diana has shown what a double-edged sword publicity can be. In public there could be few private moments as a pack of photographers chased and harried, anxious for the one shot that might make them wealthy. Everyone felt the pressure in the circulation war. Editors had their discretion tested to the limit. The public displayed a voracious appetite for royal news. Quick to condemn the paparazzi and their methods, perhaps most of us ought to feel a tinge of hypocrisy.

(2) In the final analysis there is no statutory limitation on what newspapers deem fit to print, although they need to be mindful of the law of libel, which, if transgressed, could lead to substantial damages being paid out. The Press Complaints Commission does its job and mostly does it well, but there is a degree of incestuousness in its membership, with editors looking after the interests of other editors. But what's the alternative? New privacy laws that fill the pockets of expensive lawyers? Endless litigation? Yet another dose of unpleasant medicine from the nanny state?

(3) Fascinated as we are by celebrity culture, perhaps we're not entirely sympathetic to the celebrities concerned. Of course we rush to buy all those celebrity magazines with their inviting colours and bold headlines. Of course we want to read about the indiscretions of celebrities. And they feed off the publicity. Bolder, bigger and brasher, lest our voyeuristic tastes become jaded. More outrageous in their behaviour. And we're envious of the stars, of the WAGS and their handsome husbands. Yet we like to see the cellulose and the wrinkles, the signs that even celebrities are human.

(4) Diana's death was a terrible tragedy and how it came about may always be elusive. Yet we are still fascinated by stories about the royals. Informing us about Charles and Camilla is in the public interest. It's what we feel we should know about the successor to Queen Elizabeth. It's the same with Prince William. There's still a lot of love for the monarchy, and not just among older people. It represents continuity at a time when so much is changing — and not always for the better. People love a bit of pomp and ceremony and a touch of nostalgia. You don't get much of that with a republic.

1
The opening sentence of paragraph 1 is best described as
A   factual.
B   verifiable.
C   objective.
D   speculative.

2
The 'voracious appetite' referred to in paragraph 1 is one that
A   comes and goes.
B   cannot be satisfied.
C   must be condemned.
D   is a medical condition.

3
In paragraph 1 the author states that 'perhaps most of us ought to feel a tinge of hypocrisy' because
A   everyone is a hypocrite at some time in their life.
B   we support the paparazzi and Princess Diana's lifestyle.
C   we criticise the paparazzi but look at their work.
D   we envy Princess Diana and wish to copy her lifestyle.

4
According to the author in paragraph 1, newspaper editors
A   might have to wrestle with their consciences.
B   could no longer exercise discretion.
C   would use any methods to increase sales of their newspapers.
D   would never refuse a revealing picture of a celebrity.

5 **'Voyeuristic tastes' (paragraph 3) are based on**
A   fantasising about others.
B   envying others.
C   identifying with others.
D   watching others.

6 **Made famous by celebrity magazines, WAGs and their partners are most likely to be associated with**
A   tennis.
B   *Big Brother.*
C   football.
D   *The X Factor.*

7 **According to paragraph 4, the monarchy is popular for each of the following except**
A   it brings back pleasant memories of the past.
B   many people are fond of its rituals.
C   it has a number of engaging characters.
D   it helps to give people a sense of stability.

8 **In a republic**
A   the powers of the monarch are retained.
B   the president is chosen by the monarch.
C   a president rules without reference to parliament.
D   a president is the head of state.

The internet

Ideas for an 'internet' — a global link-up of computers — first emerged in the USA in the 1960s, largely in the context of potential developments in the scientific and military fields. Known initially as ARPANET, it first began to emerge online in 1969, initially connecting computers at four American universities. It was designed to provide a communications network for the country if a military attack disabled the existing communications system. At the time, there were no home or office personal computers and it was a very complex system to use. The word 'internet' was not used until 1982.

After 1989 Tim Berners-Lee began to develop a new technique for distributing information on the internet and called it the World Wide Web. By 1994 the American government had begun its own website, **www.whitehouse.gov**, and commercial sites had begun to become established. Opportunities increased as entrepreneurs realised the potential of the web and dial-up internet access.

One entrepreneur who became a dominant figure in the computer industry was Bill Gates. He quickly came to dominate the home computer market through his Microsoft organisation, achieving initial success in 1981 with his DOS (Disk Operating System). Microsoft Mouse was released in 1983 and in 1985 the first retail version of Microsoft Windows appeared, marking the start of the transition from DOS. Microsoft Office was introduced in 1989 and, in 1995, Windows 95 became a new version of the company's flagship operating system, with its new user interface and novel start button. This was later updated.

By 1998 Google opened its first office in California and in 1999 an American college student called Shawn Fanning developed Napster, a computerised method that allowed users to swap music over the internet. By 2005 E-commerce had become a buzzword as internet shopping accelerated into a major retail force that is overturning more traditional shopping patterns.

Increasingly, perhaps illuminating the overwhelming desire for speed in modern communications, dial-up was deemed by many to be too slow, and it also occupied a phone line. Broadband services, offering headline speeds of 8 megabits per second, spread quickly from 2004; and by 2007, Ofcom reported, more than 50% of UK adults had broadband at home (a figure seven times greater than that of 5 years earlier) as technology improved and competition between major providers such as BT, Talk Talk, Virgin, Orange and Tiscali slashed prices from £40 to as little as £10 per month. 'Packages' combining broadband with 'free' phone calls and line rentals are now available for less than £20 a month.

Blogging

Weblogs, commonly known as 'blogs', began to emerge as an increasingly popular form of internet communication in the late 1990s, but the identity of the 'first blogger' is disputed in the blogging community. (Jorn Barger was perhaps the first to describe sites with short posts as 'weblogs' before Peter Merholz shortened the word to 'blogs'.) They spread rapidly after the Blogger.com website was established in 1999 and the terrorist attack on the USA took place in 2001.

Since then, opinion about their worth has polarised, with blogging both hailed and damned. It was estimated by Technorati.com in 2008 that there were 70 million blogs (often referred to as the 'blogosphere') in existence. As many as 1.5 million a day are written, with the medium dominated by English-speaking people and the Japanese. Most sites are small and read by a limited group of friends.

Almost every subject has bloggers writing about it. Blogging is used increasingly by politicians and political commentators, even in countries like China where public criticism of the government is rarely tolerated. Blogging has created there an additional channel of political communication, even though cyber dissidents face imprisonment for making their thoughts publicly available. Much of the information about the uprising led by Burmese monks in 2007 came from bloggers before the internet was disabled by the Burmese government.

Supporters of blogging praise its openness and the fact that entry is unrestricted. It offers scope for the personal voice that is rarely available elsewhere. Politicians are unable to manage news in the way that they seek to do for newspapers and television because anyone can make comments on a blog. However, while this can extend democratic debate it also means that the uninformed and the obsessive can gain a forum, adding little to our culture but rumours and even establishing a cult of the ordinary — although sometimes the amateur can be smarter than the professional.

Consequently, critics claim that blogs are likely to be ephemeral, trivial and unreliable. The same might be said of social networks such as MySpace and Facebook and the video-sharing website YouTube — a celebration of the cult of personality rather than the cult of celebrity. However, the fact that anyone can publish almost anything is itself also enabling and liberating. It redefines the link between the individual and the wider world of mass publication — assuming there are enough people out there sufficiently interested in reading blogs.

Social networking

Facebook

Facebook was established in 2004, in California's Silicon Valley, by Harvard dropout Mark Zuckerberg — a typical young IT entrepreneur. It began as a site where university students could keep in touch with friends electronically (not unlike the British site Friends Reunited, established to keep old school friends in touch) but its purpose became wider and by 2007 there were thought to be 5 million members in

Britain alone and 65 million members worldwide. Facebook was estimated then to be worth $10 billion, and it was so attractive as an investment that it interested Yahoo, Google and Bill Gates's Microsoft, which already had a contract to supply display advertising.

YouTube

YouTube emerged in February 2005 and is a video sharing website where users can upload, view and share video, movie, television, music and amateur content clips. It is among the top five websites visited in the world and was named as *Time* magazine's Invention of the Year in 2006. Protection of copyright can be an important issue; but its potential was shown in 2007 when eight Democrat contenders for the US presidency faced video clip questions via YouTube. YouTube has been a subsidiary of Google since 2006.

The mobile revolution

Though it is difficult to believe, not long ago mobile phones were the size of house bricks and confined to a few daring or misguided individuals. Comparable two-way communication in the form of radiophones existed in ships, planes and police cars, but hand-held cellular mobiles have been available only since 1983, following pioneering work by Martin Cooper of Motorola a decade earlier.

Mobile phones are now considered both essential and a fashion item

The Finnish firm Nokia is the main manufacturer of mobiles — one of the top five (Motorola, Samsung, Sony Ericsson and LG) that control 75% of the market. A similar position exists in mobile phone networks, where the five dominant groups involved are 3, 02, Orange, T-Mobile and Vodafone. In two decades, mobile phones have gone from an exclusive to a mass market, outnumbering land-line telephones in some countries and more popular than the latter with many younger users.

As the functions of mobile phones have expanded (texting began in 1993), possession of one is seen as both an essential and a fashion accessory. Camera phones are now commonplace and internet access from mobile phones has become increasingly important. Some countries, including the UK, now have more mobile phones than people and, with the saturation of markets in many Western countries, the main growth potential is in Africa and India.

In 2003 the status-hugging BlackBerry (a hand-held mobile phone also used for sending e-mails, developed by the Research In Motion firm of Canadian Mike Lazaridis) was only just emerging from a laboratory prototype to what many saw as a short-lived rich person's plaything confined to North America. By 2007, there were over 8 million subscribers around the world, incorporating rapidly growing markets in countries such as Saudi Arabia and India.

Similarly, the phone company Orange revealed that its 15 million customers use their mobile phones not only for calls and texting but also as entertainment centres for music, videos and games. Many new mobile phones can access the internet as well as downloading games, ringtones and video clips. Most phones can download wallpaper, which is frequently changed and often features images of scantily clad women. Music downloading is increasingly popular and movie trailers and sports are often favoured clips.

Viewpoints

Are mobile phones a good or a bad thing?

Good

- They are a relatively cheap, immediate and accessible form of communication.
- They help parents keep in touch with their children.
- They are convenient, especially compared with the alternatives.
- They are useful in parts of the world where land-line access and infrastructure are limited.
- They are a major industry, providing many jobs.
- They are important for providing police evidence. (In the EU the communications of every mobile phone user are recorded.)
- They allow speedy notification of emergency situations.

Bad

- Calls can be expensive.
- Parents are often pressurised to keep up with the latest fashions.
- Mobiles are an easy target for petty criminals.
- Health fears have been raised.
- There is potential for improper use, e.g. by terrorists to detonate bombs.
- They are intrusive in public places.
- They can lead to accidents if used by drivers (and the use of hand-held phones while driving is now illegal).

Free media in a democratic society

Freedom of expression is a right that gives an indication of how democratic a democracy really is. However, as with all freedoms, there is general acceptance that in certain circumstances, when people need to be protected, it has to be curtailed. If newspapers make accusations or allegations against someone they must be able to substantiate them. If the accusations are unwarranted and defamation has taken place, the individuals concerned can take action for libel. Similarly, the law defines what might be considered obscene, and different forms of censorship exist to protect sensibilities, for example the age classification for films.

Key terms

free media: newspapers, broadcasts etc. that are allowed to comment freely, within certain legal guidelines, and to criticise others including the government and politicians.

democratic society: a social system in which people have human and legal rights and responsibilities, and are able to vote for competing candidates or political parties in secrecy and without fear of reprisal.

Newspapers represent a difficult area. Celebrities court publicity, which many newspapers provide because it helps to boost sales. Yet the same celebrities often complain that their rights to privacy are being infringed, perhaps by photographers seeking salacious, or otherwise intrusive, pictures. Similarly, readers do not wish to read lies and offensive statements. Yet we also wish to speak of a 'free press' and are particularly concerned by any hint of 'state censorship' — something associated with non-democratic governments (although the UK government uses defense advisory guidelines — D-Notices — to prevent reporting of details that might threaten national security).

In an ideal world, we might wish facts (which can be proved according to agreed criteria) and opinions (which may or may not be correct and accurate depending on the values and beliefs of those concerned) to be clearly separated so that we can make up our own minds without being unduly swayed one way or the other. In the real world we tend to accept that life is not like that.

What we get, through the press or broadcasts, is reporting. Broadcasters have a legal obligation to be balanced in their coverage, but there are important editorial decisions to be made about the ranking of reports, what pictures are to be shown and how the editing should be done. It is very difficult to be wholly impartial — to stand back and take an objective, detached look. Indeed, if everything were 'neutral' life might quickly get boring.

Despite accusations of phone rigging on certain television game shows, the broadcasting media tend to be trusted more than the press. Yet broadcasters have considerable advantages. Thanks to the modern technology that global satellites represent, broadcasters have immediate access to stories — hence the increasing use of the phrase 'breaking news'. We can be whisked away to different parts of the world and 'shown the action' in colour and via our increasingly digitalised and high-definition receivers. We see it 'as it happens'.

For newspapers, 'breaking news' almost inevitably means 'yesterday' and the medium of print, although much changed in recent years, lacks the versatility afforded to the broadcast media. As their circulation continues to decline, newspapers must battle hard to make an impact. Their advantage is that they have greater freedom than the broadcast media. They can be bold, brash, eye-catching — and not necessarily impartial. In that sense, they probably reflect what many of their readers want to read.

Just as politicians and their advisers are often accused of 'spin' — trying to present news in the best possible light for their parties — newspapers will often slant many of their news reports to support a particular party stance or viewpoint. The high-selling *Daily Mail* (over 2 million copies daily) is often described as 'the voice of

Middle England'. The identity of 'Middle England' is not entirely clear but the phrase seems to suggest a stereotype of a lower-middle-class Conservative voter living somewhere in the southern half of England. The paper itself invariably takes a pro-Conservative stance — which, again, might be what many of its readers wish to see.

An avowed opponent of the *Daily Mail* is the *Guardian* columnist, Polly Toynbee. It is a 'compact' rather than a tabloid. Its circulation is much smaller than the *Daily Mail*'s but it is an influential newspaper among the 'chattering classes'. Again, it is never quite clear who the 'chattering classes' are — the stereotype is of university-educated, faintly left-wing, middle-class people gathered round the dinner table in fashionable areas of London.

Relatively speaking, the *Guardian* is more impartial than the tabloids tend to be, but we should be under no illusions. Its articles are well written and persuasive but it has a political stance, mostly taking a liberal, left-of-centre position, probably in line with the political thinking of many of its readers. The *Independent*, another compact paper at the serious end of the market, claims to take a genuinely 'independent' stance in news reporting. To some extent it does, but its striking front pages suggest that it also tends towards a left-of-centre position. The *Daily Telegraph*, which remains a broadsheet, is unswervingly right of centre in the way that it presents the news.

Political processes and goals

The British political system

The British political system is often spoken of as a **two-party** system. This does not mean that there are only two parties, but that there are only two parties (Labour and Conservative) with a realistic chance of winning a general election with a majority over all other parties. (For a while until the 1920s it was more of a three-party system, as what was then the Liberal Party had a chance of winning.) Some features are:

- The British political system extends beyond general elections and the Parliament at Westminster.
- In Great Britain there are elections to the Scottish Parliament and the Welsh Assembly.
- Northern Ireland is included in the United Kingdom and has its own system of government.
- There is an extensive system of local government. Although there are some independent councillors, local government is also dominated by political parties. The Liberal Democrats play a more significant role in local than in national politics.
- Using the **first-past-the-post** system, UK general elections are almost always won outright by one party. However, if that did not happen, a **third party** could hold the balance of power and play a role in a coalition government.
- Because of the absence of coalitions in which several parties might work together in government, British government is often referred to as an **adversarial system**, with the two main parties (officially Her Majesty's Government and Her Majesty's Opposition) facing each other in the House of Commons.

In **local government**, councillors are elected for 4 years but elections for a proportion of seats are held each year. Local issues may be important but national issues tend to dominate, and voters may use a local election to register a 'protest vote' against the government. Turnout for local government elections is often low and a number of candidates may be elected unopposed. However, because local electoral areas are small and party loyalties less established, smaller parties and **independents** have more opportunities, and situations of 'no overall control' are not unusual.

Sinn Féin leader, Gerry Adams

Ian Paisley, Democratic Unionist Party leader from 1971–2008

Key terms

proportional representation: a voting system where there is a close match between the number of votes cast and the number of seats allocated to the political parties concerned.

devolved powers: powers transferred by the UK Parliament at Westminster, so that separate bodies for Northern Ireland, Scotland and Wales are granted powers that apply only to the inhabitants of those individual countries.

Outside England, the system is complicated by the inclusion of nationalist parties competing in just one specific country. In **Northern Ireland** the system is further complicated because local elections use a system of **proportional representation** known as the single transferable vote to elect the 108 members of its Assembly. The two major parties are the Democratic Unionist Party, supported mainly by Protestants who favour the union with England, and Sinn Féin, led by Gerry Adams, supported mainly by Catholics sympathetic to the Irish Republic.

Scotland has devolved powers in the form of a Scottish Parliament with limited powers. Of the Members of the Sottish Parliament (MSPs), 73 are elected to single-member constituencies using the first-past-the-post system; the remaining 56 are 'top-up' members from party lists, elected according to the votes cast for each party in the eight regions. This system allows smaller parties such as the Scottish Green Party to gain representation, and it was the Scottish National Party (SNP) that formed a government after the 2007 elections.

The 'additional member system' is also used for elections to the **Welsh Assembly**, where 40 members are elected in single-member constituencies via the first-past-the-post system, with a further 20 chosen via the additional member top-up system for five multi-member constituencies in proportion to the total votes cast. Deprived of an overall majority after the 2007 elections, Labour formed a coalition with the Welsh Nationalist Party, Plaid Cymru.

Between 1979 and 1994, UK elections to the **European Parliament** were based on the first-past-the-post system using single-member constituencies. Isolated as the only European country not using a proportional voting system, the UK switched after the election of a Labour government in 1997 to a closed-list system of proportional representation, with regional constituencies electing between three and ten Members of the European Parliament (MEPs) according to the size of their populations. (Northern Ireland's three MEPs are elected via the single transferable vote to ensure representation across the Protestant and Catholic communities, in a country in which religion still plays a significant role in voting choice.)

The role of the monarchy

Although the United Kingdom lacks a written constitution, it has what is known as a 'constitutional monarchy'. The Queen acts as head of state but the responsibility for passing laws is Parliament's, even though the monarch gives the royal assent to each bill that becomes an act of Parliament. (This is a purely formal power and refusal would provoke a constitutional crisis.)

In the absence of a written constitution, the rights and duties of the monarch are governed by conventions — non-statutory rules which are seen as binding. The Queen cannot make legislation and acts on the advice of ministers, most notably the prime minister, whom she is formally responsible for appointing as head of 'Her Majesty's Government'. Politically, the Queen must remain neutral and above party politics.

The Queen at the State Opening of Parliament, November 2007

In broad terms, the Queen acts as both head of state and head of the nation. Among the Queen's main constitutional responsibilities, she:

- formally appoints the prime minister (by convention the leader of the majority party in Parliament) and meets with him or her on a regular basis
- represents the UK across the world; she is head of the Commonwealth, receives foreign ambassadors and heads of state and has a special role to play in the Channel Islands and the Isle of Man, which are dependent territories of the English Crown
- acts as a focus for national unity and identity, especially at times of national celebration or tragedy

- performs ceremonial and official duties, which are kept separate from party politics
- represents continuity and stability (she has reigned for over 50 years and dealt with 11 prime ministers)
- acts as patron to many charitable and voluntary organisations
- recognises success through honours, awards and visits
- acts as 'Defender of the Faith' in her role as Supreme Governor of the Church of England

Viewpoints

Do we need a monarchy?

Yes
- The monarch is above politics.
- The monarch still performs important duties and acts as a figurehead.
- Many people support the monarchy and have particular respect for the Queen.
- The monarch is an important figure as Head of the Commonwealth.
- The Queen is a world figure and helps to maintain the UK's reputation.
- The royal family gives good value for money, making many visits and supporting many charities.
- The alternative (the UK as a republic with a president) has many potential weaknesses.

No
- The monarchy is an outdated institution.
- It is undemocratic because it relies on an accident of birth.
- It is a symbol of inequality.
- Only formal and ceremonial responsibilities remain.
- It is a waste of money.
- The Commonwealth is an outdated institution and individual countries make their own decisions.

Processes and powers of government and Parliament

We are often taught that the UK Parliament (particularly the House of Commons, which, unlike the House of Lords, is wholly elected) is the centrepiece of the British system of democracy. In broad terms, the main functions of Parliament are to:
- pass legislation
- make the government accountable
- act as a representative body

- offer a forum for national debate
- provide the source of recruitment for future ministers

In reality, the freedom of MPs to vote according to their conscience or to reflect the wishes of the majority of their constituents is often very limited. There are relatively few 'free votes' (free from the instructions of the party 'whips' who are responsible for maintaining party discipline). Some MPs from the majority party may be more rebellious in their voting habits than others, but they are likely to remain on the backbenches during their parliamentary career and may think twice about rebelling if a government made up of their own party members comes under serious threat.

MPs who might not wish to rebel, or opposition MPs, can do effective scrutiny work through membership of the select committees that oversee the work of government departments; in parliamentary debate with a minister; at the weekly prime minister's question time; or through written questions, with answers being recorded in *Hansard*, the official record of parliamentary debates. There have been radio broadcasts from Parliament since 1975 and television coverage of the Commons since 1989, after trials in the Lords.

The prime minister

The executive is at the centre of government and is chiefly concerned with how policy is decided and implemented. The government is a large body containing a number of junior ministers and totalling about 100 members. At the heart of the executive are the prime minister and the senior ministers, who are chosen by the prime minister as members of the cabinet.

The prime minister is the head of the government, chairing the cabinet, providing leadership and being the government's national representative. He or she can be a powerful figure because of the following functions of the job.

Authority

Much depends on individual personality, but the prime minister sets both the tone and the agenda for cabinet meetings, appointing its members and those of cabinet committees.

The prime minister also appoints senior civil servants, whose influence 'behind the scenes' is often considerable, and decides on the structure and naming of government departments.

Party leadership

The prime minister is the leader of the largest party in the House of Commons, usually being elected by a combination of party members and MPs. If he or she is to avoid a leadership challenge, it is important to retain party support and confidence. Strong party support enhances the position of the prime minister.

Patronage

The prime minister is responsible for many appointments. In addition to ministers and most senior civil servants, this extends to life peers in the House of Lords, senior judges, diplomats representing British interests overseas and senior members of the Church of England.

Policy making

The prime minister has the freedom to be involved with any aspect of government or policy making. Most prime ministers take a particular interest in both economic and foreign policy, although this can bring them into conflict with two key ministers, the Chancellor of the Exchequer and the Foreign Secretary.

Public recognition

One of the few politicians likely to be recognised by members of the general public is the prime minister. This is because of constant media exposure both nationally and globally. In a sense, it has brought the cult of personality, even celebrity, to politics and has led to suggestions that prime ministers might cultivate a more 'presidential' style. In many respects, Tony Blair sought to use this to his, and his party's, advantage. Gordon Brown, coming from a very different background and with a different personality, takes a more measured approach.

Recent prime ministers

The prime minister's office in 10 Downing Street has grown significantly in recent years and has a staff of nearly 200, including some important civil servants and special advisers appointed from outside government. A prime minister's leadership style is vital. Margaret Thatcher's forceful, decisive and domineering style apparently involved little cabinet discussion; eventually her ministers struck back, most notably Geoffrey Howe in a powerful speech to the Commons.

Her successor, John Major, used a more conciliatory approach. He had a much smaller Commons majority, however, and was said to lack both force of personality and clear vision — although the task of uniting pro- and anti-Europeans in his own party would have taken an act of political genius.

Tony Blair was a charismatic figure and his more 'presidential style', though less forthright and strident than Margaret Thatcher's, did not accord a significant role to the cabinet as a whole. As his party's parliamentary majority was significantly reduced after the 2005 election, Blair's authority decreased. Few were surprised when he decided to step down in 2007 after 10 years as prime minister and an often stormy relationship with Gordon Brown, the man who served throughout as Chancellor of the Exchequer and was Tony Blair's successor as prime minister.

Tony Blair, prime minister from 1997–2007

The cabinet

The full cabinet, which usually meets once a week for between 1 and 2 hours, consists of the senior members of the government, who hold the title Secretary of State, with a membership of between 18 and 25. Most cabinet ministers are heads of government departments. They must be Members of Parliament, to which they are accountable, and nearly all are drawn from the House of Commons. Ministerial behaviour is governed mainly by convention (what might be expected from a senior public figure), but there is also in existence the *Ministerial Code: A Code of Ethics and Procedural Guidance for Ministers*.

The cabinet remains an important body, bound by the principle of **collective responsibility**, although its influence has probably waned and much use is made of cabinet committees. Cabinet business is organised and regulated by the Cabinet Secretariat, located within the Cabinet Office. The Secretary of the Cabinet attends cabinet meetings and is usually close to the prime minister. Procedure is formal, although under Tony Blair first names rather than official titles were used.

> **Key term**
>
> **collective responsibility:** a convention that, whatever their personal feelings, all cabinet ministers must take responsibility for cabinet decisions and present a united front in public.

The cabinet's main functions are:

- approving government business in Parliament
- discussing major policy issues and reaching a decision on them
- ratifying major decisions taken elsewhere ('rubber stamping', according to critics)
- receiving reports on key issues and policy developments
- helping to settle disputes that might arise between government departments

Electoral procedures

For many people elections are their only form of participation in the democratic process. In a liberal democracy
like the UK where different political parties each present
a **manifesto**, elections should offer a meaningful choice
with an easily accessible and secret voting process. It is
through this process that the winning party derives a
mandate to govern, and governments are accountable
to the electorate for their record in office.

The sort of direct democracy that allowed many citizens
in ancient Greece to agree on decisions directly is no
longer realistic, so we now have representative democracy with voters seeking to choose their representative.
Referendums are rare. The first national referendum
was held in 1975 to help decide whether the UK should
remain a member of the European Union.

Key terms

manifesto: a statement of
party policies and beliefs
usually drawn up at election
time.

mandate: the party with the
most seats after an election is
deemed to have a 'mandate'
— the consent of those who
voted for it — to carry out its
manifesto promises.

referendum: a national
vote on a specific question
or issue that may or may
not be binding on the
government.

General elections to choose the 646 MPs who sit in the House of Commons must take
place at least once every 5 years, on a date chosen by the sitting Prime Minister and
his or her advisers. MPs are elected in single-member constituencies with an average
of 70,000 voters. (Constituency boundaries are determined periodically following a
review by the Boundary Commission, which is independent.)

The UK also elects 78 Members of the European Parliament (MEPs) (to be reduced
to 72 for the 2009 Euro elections) every 5 years. Voters in the respective countries
choose members of the Scottish Parliament and the Welsh and Northern
Ireland Assemblies. Local councillors are elected for 4 years. By-elections take
place if a seat becomes vacant through the death or resignation of the existing
representative.

In 1928, when the voting age for women was reduced from 30 to 21, all UK adults
(with a tiny number of exceptions) were given the right to vote if they registered to
do so (in 2005 there were 44 million names on the electoral register, although only
61% actually voted). In 1969 the minimum voting age was reduced to 18.

Traditionally, elections are held on a Thursday, with thousands of local polling stations
open between 7 a.m. and 10 p.m. Voting has been private since the 1872 Ballot Act.

Ballot papers for general and local elections in Great Britain are straightforward, with candidates listed in alphabetical order together with party identification. Voters place a single x in the box of the candidate they prefer. Postal votes have become more common since 2001, but trials of electronic voting have been limited because of concerns about postal fraud.

The main functions of elections are to:
- provide an opportunity for political participation
- allow registered electors to vote for a candidate to become their representative if he or she receives the most votes in the **constituency**
- help to choose a party to form the government
- help to choose the party with policies most in line with people's preferences
- call the government to account for its record
- give legitimacy to the democratic process through free and fair elections

> **Key term**
>
> **constituency:** the geographical area represented by each Member of Parliament (MP).

Electoral reform

The first-past-the-post (FPTP) system tends to favour the two main parties in British general elections. It is simple to understand — the winner needs to gain only one more vote than the next highest candidate to become the representative of a single-member constituency. Usually it produces a quick and clear outcome. Almost invariably, one party (either Labour or Conservative) wins a parliamentary majority over all the others and goes on to form a strong and stable government that becomes both responsible and accountable.

However, critics of FPTP argue that it:
- is unfair because the number of seats won by each party is not in proportion to the number of votes they receive (see Table 8.1)

Table 8.1 Distribution of seats and votes in the 2005 general election

Party	Seats won (%)	Votes gained (%)
Labour	55.1	35.2
Conservative	30.5	32.2
Liberal Democrats	9.6	22.0
Others	4.8	10.6

- disadvantages small parties with thinly spread national support and unfairly advantages the two main parties
- requires winners only to gain a plurality of the votes cast rather than a majority — 66% of MPs elected in 2005 did not gain a majority of the votes cast
- means that votes are of unequal value because constituencies vary in size and most seats are 'safe' (almost impossible for any party to win other than the one that has held the seat for many years)
- offers only limited choice, especially as candidates are chosen by political parties
- tends to divide voters geographically, with many Conservative voters in the south of England and rural areas and Labour voters concentrated in the north, Scotland, Wales and the cities. (In 2007 the major city councils of Manchester and Liverpool did not have a single Conservative councillor, effectively disenfranchising Conservative voters.)

Examples of alternative electoral systems

Alternative vote (AV)

Under the AV system as used in Australia, the winning candidate needs to achieve an overall majority of the votes cast (50% + 1). Electors vote by ranking candidates in order of preference (1, 2, 3 etc.). If no candidate secures an overall majority the lowest-placed candidate is eliminated and his or her second preferences are transferred to other candidates. This process continues until one candidate gains an overall majority.

Using the AV system means that MPs are elected by a majority of those voting, and it retains the link between MPs and single-member constituencies. However, it does not offer proportional representation.

Single transferable vote (STV)

The STV is another form of proportional representation that uses multi-member constituencies. Electors show their preferences from what is likely to be a long list by marking 1, 2 etc., voting for as many or as few candidates as they wish. To be elected, a candidate must achieve a quota and any votes in excess of the quota are redistributed.

The quota is calculated according to the following formula, known as the 'Droop quota':

$$\frac{total\ votes}{total\ number\ of\ seats\ + 1} + 1$$

If no candidate achieves the quota on the first count, the lowest placed candidate is eliminated and his/her second preferences are redistributed. This process continues until the required number of seats is filled. It is a system used for local and European Parliament elections in Northern Ireland.

This is a broadly proportional system that is likely to ensure that votes are of equal value. The winning party or coalition requires more than 50% of the votes cast, and voters have a wider degree of choice from a range of candidates. However, it is less accurate in matching seats to votes than list systems; it uses large multi-member constituencies; and it tends to lead to coalitions, where minor parties can hold the balance of power.

The additional member system (AMS)

The AMS is a mixed system, with a proportion of the seats elected by using the first-past-the-post system in single-member constituencies, with additional members chosen from a party list. Electors have two votes: one for their preference in a single-member constituency and one for their favoured party in a multi-member constituency. Additional members are allocated to parties to ensure that the total number of seats is proportional to the number of votes gained. This 'topping up' system is based on a mathematical formula known as the 'd'Hondt formula'. It is used in Germany on a 50/50 split between constituency and additional members, but a political party must reach a threshold of at least 5% of the popular vote because the German constitution seeks to guard against extremist parties. It is also used in elections for the Scottish Parliament and the Welsh Assembly.

This system leads to broadly proportional representation, uses single-member constituencies and enables electors to vote both for a candidate and the party of their choice. However, there are two types of representative elected, one without a distinct constituency base; parties have control over lists used to elect additional members; and small parties may remain under-represented, especially if a threshold is used.

Overview

Electoral reform of the Westminster Parliament still seems unlikely. Periodically, for the last 150 years, campaigns have taken place to secure a closer link between votes cast and seats won in British general elections. The most significant move was by the Plant Committee in the 1990s, which recommended AMS for the Scottish Parliament and a regional list system for European Parliament elections. It also proposed a supplementary vote system for the Westminster Parliament, but there was far less agreement about this and the proposal was not adopted. Neither was the recommendation of the alternative vote + additional member system by the Jenkins Commission set up by the new Labour government in 1997.

The Liberal Democrats, the 'third' and most disadvantaged party under the present system, have continued to campaign for electoral reform using a system of proportional representation, most likely to be STV. FPTP favours the two major parties and neither is likely to press hard for a system that reduces their political dominance. Voters generally show little interest in electoral reform, perhaps because the present system of FPTP seems simple to understand and almost invariably produces a decisive outcome rather than a coalition.

Table 8.2 Summary of voting methods used

Representative body	Type of voting method
British general elections	FPTP
British local elections (not Scotland, Northern Ireland & Greater London Assembly)	FPTP
Greater London Assembly	FPTP + AMS
Scottish Parliament	FPTP + AMS
Welsh Assembly	FPTP + AMS
Northern Ireland Assembly	STV
European Parliament (except Northern Ireland)	Closed regional party list
European Parliament, Northern Ireland only	STV
Directly elected mayors	SV

Party politics in the 2000s

In the 1990s 'New Labour' emerged as very different to Labour of 1945, and Tony Blair won the 1997 general election with a large majority — a success repeated in 2001 and 2005, albeit with a smaller majority in 2005. 'New Labour' was no longer 'left wing', moving to a more central political position similar to the Social Democratic parties of Europe. It rejected nationalisation; was closer to the private sector; distanced itself from 'tax and spend' policies; was less close to the trade unions, which provided much of its funding; and took a more conciliatory line on Europe. It remained committed to the welfare state but took a strong line on law and order.

Under Margaret Thatcher the Conservative Party had moved sharply towards 'the right', but by 1997 this seemed to be less attractive to many voters. Labour had, effectively, shifted towards the 'one nation' policies once associated with the Conservatives, while the Conservatives themselves remained divided in the way Labour had once been. There were sharp divisions on key issues such as immigration and Europe.

Some Conservatives aligned themselves with more traditional and recognisable Conservative policies, but it was an ageing party that underwent several changes of leadership after 1997. David Cameron, a young and photogenic Old Etonian, became leader with a modernising agenda after the party's failure in the 2005 general election — an agenda that made it even more difficult for voters to recognise differences between the Conservatives and Labour.

Ultimately, elections are often about how voters perceive the parties, their policies and, increasingly, their leaders. (Charles Kennedy was popular with many Liberal Democrat voters but some of his MPs had reservations about what were alleged to be his drinking habits. His replacement, Sir Menzies Campbell, was in his mid-60s. Some thought he was a victim of ageism when he stood down and was replaced by the photogenic Nick Clegg.)

David Cameron, who became Conservative leader in 2005

The key issue at election time is likely to be how the voters perceive the economic competence of a particular party, because the success of the economy has a major impact on personal living standards. Other major issues of recent elections have been law and order, health, education (for Tony Blair it was 'education, education, education') and taxation. Occasionally, foreign policy can be important. Victory over Argentina in the Falklands certainly contributed to the 1983 Conservative victory, while Labour, although winning in 2005, lost support because of intervention in Iraq with the USA following claims concerning the existence of 'weapons of mass destruction'.

Q I know nothing about politics. It's dull and boring and doesn't affect me.

A Many young people feel that politics does not affect their lives, yet it almost certainly does. Politicians do squabble and our adversarial system of Labour versus Conservative with the occasional intervention of smaller parties can seem childish at times.

However, we elect our politicians to act as our representatives and we are free to do far more than just cast our vote every few years. Politicians are responsible for spending huge sums of money and for establishing priorities. Education policy is one of the most important areas of politics and it helps to determine school funding, how A-levels are shaped and structured, and changes in university fees — to name but three areas that affect young people directly.

Q But aren't politicians all the same — just out for their own ends?

A There are similarities among politicians, partly because extremes rarely seem to appeal to British people. From time to time, there are exceptions. In recent years, the news reporter Martin Bell was elected as an independent MP for Tatton, defeating the sitting Conservative on an 'anti-sleaze' ticket, as did Dr John Taylor who stood on the sole issue of saving his local hospital. George Galloway was elected as MP for Bethnal Green in 2005 for his newly founded Respect Party, which campaigned against British involvement in the Iraq War.

Contrary to what many people believe, MPs in the UK are almost never corrupt and most do their best to serve their constituents. They may not always do what we would wish and, like everyone else, they make mistakes. They may like the power and the status, but no system is perfect and theirs is a difficult job.

Citizenship

Politicians have long been concerned about growing apathy among electors (**electoral turnout** fell to a general election low of 59% in 2001, edging up only to 61% in 2005, while voting in other kinds of election is often appreciably lower than this). Young people are often said to be both uninterested in politics and also lacking in knowledge about it. Often, frequently fuelled by the media, the alleged antisocial behaviour of many young people has come under the spotlight.

> **Key term**
>
> **electoral turnout:** the number of people who actually vote as a percentage of those registered to do so.

Another dimension is the changing nature of British society and the extent to which it is becoming more ethnically and culturally diverse. In some parts of the country, notably in some of the Lancashire former cotton towns, this has contributed to social tension, leading to occasional disturbances and providing fertile ground for the election of councillors belonging to the British National Party. 'Citizenship tests' have become increasingly associated with immigration policy, with unresolved debates about multiculturalism and the concept of 'being British'.

Owing much to the work of Professor Bernard Crick, and the enthusiasm of the then Labour Education Secretary, David Blunkett, citizenship became a compulsory part of the school curriculum in 2002. In its early stages, teaching of the subject has not been an unqualified success in an already overcrowded curriculum, and reports from the Office for Standards in Education (Ofsted) have often been critical.

The key elements of the citizenship curriculum are:
- legal and human rights and the operation of the civil and criminal justice systems
- diverse national, regional, religious and ethnic identities and the need for mutual respect and understanding
- the work of Parliament, the government and the courts
- playing an active part in the democratic and electoral process
- how the economy functions
- opportunities for individuals and voluntary groups to bring about social change
- the role of the media in providing information and affecting opinion
- the rights and responsibilities of consumers, employers and employees
- the UK and the European Union, the Commonwealth and the UN
- global interdependence and responsibility, including sustainable development and Local Agenda 21

Without doubt these are important themes that will all impinge on the life of individuals and the nation. Sometimes, however, the subject is met with indifference if not hostility by some older students, who see it as 'compulsorily doing good' and involving excessive adult moralising and lectures. It need not be so if properly taught and resourced.

Teachers, few of whom may have specialist qualifications given the 'newness' of the subject, have not always had the time or other resources to teach the many elements involved. There are rarely separate citizenship lessons and often the distinct parts of the subject are lost in a wider Personal, Social and Moral Education course that also dips into careers, drugs, health and sex education, often in no more than an hour a week and with limited funds for support materials.

Working towards a national qualification offers an incentive, particularly in terms of coursework that provides opportunities for participation and involvement outside the classroom, although in the initial years only a 'short course' GCSE has been available with no progression beyond the age of 16. This is due to change following further national curriculum reform in 2009.

Ask the examiner

Q **Will compulsory citizenship teaching produce more good citizens?**

A Like the rest of the national curriculum, citizenship is not compulsory in independent schools. While aspects of practical citizenship coursework have proved popular among some students, it must be admitted that the introduction of the subject has not been an unqualified success.

Teachers are required to teach a lot of different aspects of citizenship in a minimal time slot and with limited resources. Students do not like what they sometimes see as being 'preached at' or compelled to become a 'goody goody'. Teenagers are naturally rebellious and do not always react positively to what they see as adult direction.

Some would argue that parents ought to teach the values associated with being a good citizen and that teenagers are likely to be more influenced by the outlook and attitude of their peers. They often see the subject as less important than more established subjects and sometimes approach it negatively. Nevertheless, the efforts of teachers are unlikely to be entirely wasted.

CULTURE AND SOCIETY
Chapter 9

The relationship between law, society and ethics

Values and ethical issues which affect social interaction

If all people shared the same values, and those values reflected patterns of good rather than antisocial or criminal behaviour, social interaction would be different. Social scientists disagree about the causes of what they sometimes call 'deviant' behaviour, and the 'nature versus nurture' debate is often cited. There are those who consider that, perhaps for psychological reasons, some people will behave badly whatever their surroundings and degree of material comfort. Others put more emphasis on an individual's surroundings, or the extent to which they may suffer from emotional deprivation, or have got caught up in a cycle of poverty and deprivation from which it is impossible to escape.

'Social interaction' is a difficult term to define. It conjures up an image of people who are confident and who are good mixers. Life exists in a sort of ideal state of helping others and working effectively with them. Arguments, if they exist, are quickly settled and the natural state is one of harmony and good humour. Family life involves friendly cooperation rather than discord. This is, of course, a utopia.

Many people interact quite well on a superficial basis and live, broadly speaking, in a manner that acknowledges the code of ethics that guides 'right thinking people'. If they break the law it is in a relatively minor way. Some people interact less well — they may be more introverted, preferring to 'mind their own business'. At the other end of the scale there are 'problem families' who might be responsible for noise, vandalism and a range of criminal activities, which an ASBO (Anti-Social Behaviour Order) may or may not curtail.

Interaction involves conflict, much of which might be readily resolved. It also involves cooperation, where people genuinely find it possible to coexist with their fellow beings more or less in harmony. We are all individuals with different backgrounds, thoughts and values. Very few of us can exist in near-total isolation, although this is not to say that older or disabled people, or those without close family ties, may experience little interaction; they may be exceedingly lonely.

Politics

Politicians do not enjoy great public confidence or respect. Opinion polls suggest that they are widely mistrusted and that their integrity is frequently called into question. This is almost certainly unfair. It cannot be denied that some people enter politics with a measure of self-interest or the desire to exercise power. That is not to say, though, that they are corrupt and operate with disregard for ethical codes.

There have always been politicians who have fallen from grace. The work of a Member of Parliament can be very demanding, despite apparent 'long holidays' when Parliament is in recess. MPs in Westminster are frequently away from homes and families and, although late sittings are rarer than they were, conscientious MPs have many demands on their time, especially if they secure promotion and eventually reach the rank of cabinet minister.

Politicians — at local and national level — are not necessarily role models but, as public figures, they are expected to set a good example. A notable scandal was the Profumo affair of 1963, when John Profumo, the Secretary of State for War, resigned after lying to the Commons about his involvement with a woman whose favours were allegedly shared with a Russian. Generally such scandals were rare until the 1990s when, between 1993 and 1994, four Conservative ministers resigned — Michael Mates following allegations of improper links with a foreign businessman, David Mellor because of an extra-marital affair, and Tim Smith and Neil Hamilton who were caught up in allegations over 'cash for questions' in the House of Commons.

Prime Minister John Major, having advocated a 'back to basics' campaign harking back to a never-was era of lost Victorian values, was severely embarrassed by accusations of 'sleaze'. These confirmed for many the assumption that MPs were prone to misdemeanours and willing to abuse their positions of public trust. His response, in 1995, was to set up a Committee on Standards in Public Life, chaired by Lord Nolan. Among its recommendations was an ethical framework for public office holders to demonstrate a combination of 'selflessness, integrity, objectivity, accountability, openness, honesty and leadership'.

The extent to which anyone can demonstrate all these qualities consistently is open to question, although the aims are laudable. Major's successor, Tony Blair, was felt to be a prime minister of considerable integrity. Yet he too was caught up in 2007 in allegations that he might have known about claims that some of those close to him tried to augment party funds by recommending honours ('cash for peerages') to those involved in making donations. After extensive police investigations, no charges were brought but, once again, the image of politicians was tarnished.

Afghanistan, the poppy fields, the opium trade and addiction

The Taliban lost control of Afghanistan in 2001. Their Muslim fundamentalist regime was deeply conservative and highly oppressive, but they had the poppy fields of Afghanistan under control. Since then, according to a downbeat UN report, the land under cultivation for poppies has increased from 8,000 to 165,000 hectares. Between 2006 and 2007, poppy production in the country rose by 49%, and it is estimated that the country accounts for about 90% of the world supply of opium, a poppy derivative and the raw material for heroin. Much of the poppy cultivation is in one single province, Helmand, where some 7,000 British troops are currently based to support reconstruction and development.

The dilemma is obvious but complex. In an effort to contain the influence of the Taliban and terrorist supporters of al-Qaeda, Afghanistan is occupied by UN troops, including a large British contingent. It is a desperately poor country with a rugged terrain suitable for the production of very few crops — except poppies. Poppies are the only reliable source of income for the subsistence farmers and can earn them ten times as much as a cereal crop. More than 12% of Afghanistan's population are engaged in poppy production. The poppy harvests of Afghanistan will eventually put heroin on the streets around the world and Helmand is now the world's single largest source of illegal drugs, although in the north of Afghanistan the number of drug-free provinces has doubled to 13.

Poppies are the only reliable source of income for subsistence farmers in Afghanistan

With a heroin epidemic at home, cutting opium production was one of the main reasons for British involvement in Afghanistan, a mountainous and inhospitable country subject to extremes of temperature, where few foreign armies have enjoyed any sustained success. In an effort to reduce the amount of heroin finding its way to Britain, almost all of which comes from Afghanistan, the British government took responsibility for overseeing Afghanistan's anti-narcotics programme in 2002. In this deeply religious Muslim country, drug taking is frowned upon, yet it is estimated that there may be as many as 70,000 addicts in Helmand province alone. There is one British-financed drug rehabilitation clinic in a country where opium has the economic significance of oil.

Without viable and sustainable alternatives to offer the farmers, Britain is in a difficult position. Fighting between UN and Taliban forces is already frequent and Taliban resurgents exert considerable influence in the drugs trade, using the funds that it raises to support their resistance. (This represents something of a moral and religious somersault by the Taliban who, a few years earlier, condemned opium as 'un-Islamic'. Consequently, under their repressive regime, the crop was virtually eliminated. Now, desperate for funding to sustain their resistance, Taliban fighters protect Helmand's opium-growing farmers and skim off their profits. Just as the Taliban were effective in controlling opium in earlier years they have proved equally good at promoting it.)

The total value of Afghanistan's poppy harvest is estimated at £1.5 billion, which is about 50% of the country's entire gross domestic product (GDP). It also accounts for about 90% of exports. Removing the poppies would lead to economic collapse and serve only to increase conflict. Aerial crop spraying with herbicide, advocated by the USA, has so far been rejected because of the threats it might pose to health and to crops that are grown legitimately. Forced eradication — hitting the poor the hardest — would damage the 'hearts and minds' campaign essential in maintaining some support among the general population.

Growing, processing and selling opium dominates the Afghan economy. Poppies could be grown legitimately for the production of morphine, but both the US and Afghan governments are opposed to the licensing of opium for medical use because it would be difficult to regulate and control in areas where there is little infrastructure and there are no real powers of law enforcement and few safe areas, and where bribery and corruption at all levels are rife and the chances of detection negligible.

Although the principal figures in the drugs trade are well known, no major drug smuggler has been arrested in Afghanistan since 2001.

Without the rule of law, good government and an alternative to poppy growing, Afghanistan is more likely to become a narco-state than to contain an already desperate situation. It is, according to the British Foreign Secretary, David Miliband, 'a long haul'.

Practice question

The following source is typical of those that will be used in Section B of the Unit 1 AS examination paper. A question follows this source.

Every effort has been made by Britain since the occupation to stop Afghan farmers growing poppies. These poppies, which grow in abundance in Afghanistan, are used to produce opium, which eventually finds its way onto the world drug market. Yet for the farmers, nothing else can be planted in the barren and inhospitable land that would bring in the income that the poppies guarantee.

Opium dominates the Afghan economy and probably accounts for 60% of the country's income. There are even stories that some of the farmers who fall into debt have been forced to hand over their daughters to drug traffickers who lent them money to buy seeds. If they somehow find the money to pay off debts, their daughters are returned to the farmers. If not, who knows what will happen to them?

Once, when they controlled Afghanistan, the Taliban made some effort to control the poppies because drug taking was against the country's religion. Now there are rumours that the Taliban who are fighting the British and other troops in their country are siding with corrupt politicians. Those who control the trade can make big profits, and terrorism is costly to finance.

The Afghan government cannot get a licence from the UN to produce opium legally because it cannot guarantee that the drug will not end up on the black market. Since 2002 almost 5 million Afghans have returned to their country from neighbouring states like Pakistan and Iran. Most live in dire poverty and in the cold winters children die from exposure. They are used to war and religious extremism. What they need is more recognition and support from their own government and the international agencies.

Examine the political, moral and economic issues connected with the presence of British and American troops in Afghanistan since 2001. *(15 marks)*

Crime and punishment

Crime is a contentious area. It represents law breaking, and also antisocial or what is commonly called 'dysfunctional' behaviour. It is politically sensitive and voters appear to wish politicians to take a 'strong stance' on law and order. A 'strong stance' places considerable emphasis on prison and punishment, and the size of the prison population has risen sharply to over 80,000 since Labour came to power. Anything less than a prison sentence is seen as being 'soft on crime', but re-offending rates among ex-convicts are as high as 80%, and the cost of keeping someone in prison is high.

There is widespread agreement that those who break the law need to face sanctions and that the streets will be safer if serious offenders lose their freedom to walk them. Because there are different methods of compiling crime statistics, the extent to which crime is rising or falling is often disputed. Often it is more effective to look at figures for different types of crime because there can be significant variations.

The enduring problem for politicians is how people perceive crime, and their fear of it. Many are worried about gang culture, said to be particularly common in parts of London and Manchester, where young people appear to have easy access to guns and be prepared to use them. Such incidences remain rare but are highly publicised. Most people are more worried about lower-level but persistent crime and antisocial behaviour in their own areas; again, there is some intergenerational conflict.

Practice questions

The following three sources are typical of those that will be used in Section B of the Unit 1 examination paper. In each case, a question is based on the source and the candidate's own knowledge of the theme used, which in this example is crime and punishment.

Source 1

Prison works and that's a matter of fact. There will always be people who break the law and these days there are a lot more of them. It was a sad day when capital punishment ended in this country. The Americans have still got it and it's proved effective. Serious crime needs serious punishment. Once people fear prison it becomes a real deterrent. 'An eye for an eye' is what the Old Testament teaches us and that should be the basis of the way we treat serious criminals.

Question
Develop two arguments in favour and two arguments against the above viewpoint.

(9 marks)

Source 2

There's no doubt that binge drinking is a real issue and that a lot of young people are involved. A lot will be breaking the law because many of the drinkers are young — in their early teens or younger — and research shows that under-16s are drinking twice as much as they were in the 1990s. It gives them status and 'respect' among their friends and a lot of the new-style pubs are attractive. There are over a million incidents of alcohol-related violence every year and those are just the ones that get recorded.

The government has relaxed licensing hours so that it's possible to drink all night. That might just be an encouragement to drink more or, it might help because there isn't the wild rush to down lots of drinks near to closing time and the drunks don't all get tipped out on the streets at the same time. Whatever the case, a lot of drunks end up in Accident and Emergency on Friday and Saturday nights and hospital staff get assaulted.

At least you don't see as many signs now for 'happy hours', when the drinks are much cheaper. There are more security staff on the doors and they have to be better trained. Perhaps the days aren't far away when brewers have to follow the lead of cigarette manufacturers. As with cigarettes, television advertising that gives drinking a sexy image could become a thing of the past. One thing's for sure. If the industry can't police itself, the government will do it for them.

Question

Using both information from the source and your own knowledge, suggest a strategy that the government might use to tackle the problem of alcohol-related crime and anti-social behaviour among young people.

(11 marks)

Source 3

Speeding is a real problem. If there is one law that we all break it's probably exceeding the speed limits. We live life in the 'fast lane' as people say and modern cars have a lot of power. It's often difficult to stay within the limit, especially when the maximum speed is 30 miles per hour. Sometimes there are limits on roads that hardly seem to justify them. Maybe a law that so many people break is not a very good law and perhaps Britain's motorways should be like Germany's autobahns, where there are no speed limits.

Then there's the question of speed cameras. They seem to be everywhere and you can never be sure that they have been set properly. Once the police traffic control could exercise a bit of discretion but cameras can't do that. Are the cameras there to protect the public or are they just an easy way of hitting the motorist in the pocket once again? A lot of people feel that they are just an easy way of collecting money for the police.

Yet what would happen if we didn't have speeding laws and they weren't fully and fairly enforced? Discretion is never fair or consistent. Speed leads to accidents and we need those television adverts to remind us. They're horrific and they shock. They are all stark reminders of what happens when we exceed the speed limits. It's a simple message. Speed kills. If drivers don't obey the law they will learn the hard way.

Question
Discuss the legal, moral and social issues that might arise when trying to decide whether or not speeding and methods of enforcing the speeding law are acceptable.

(15 marks)

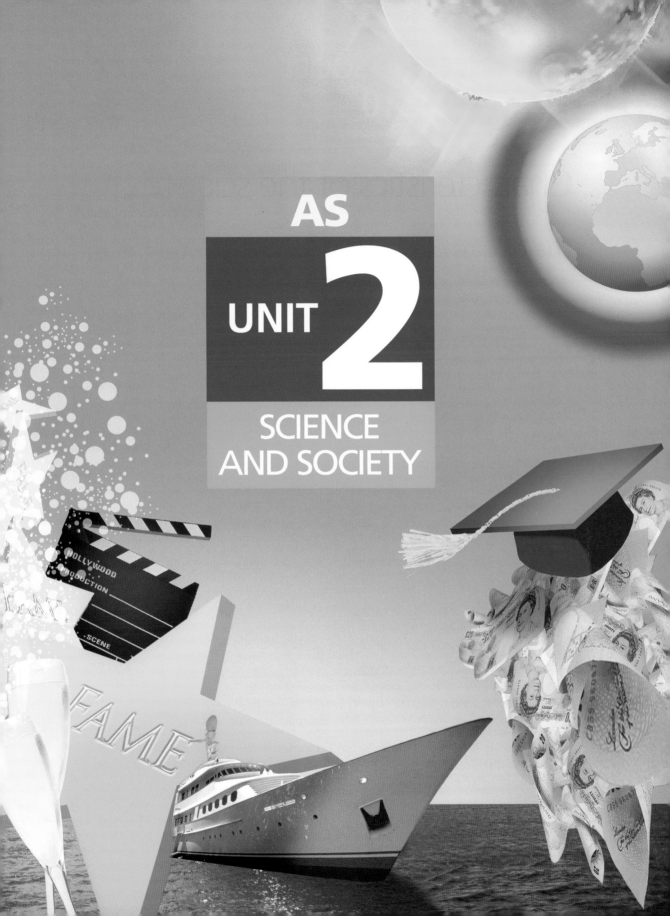

AS

UNIT **2**

SCIENCE
AND SOCIETY

Characteristics of the sciences

The origins of the universe, space and matter

There are some fundamental questions that most people ask about **the universe**:

- How old is it?
- How was it created?
- What has changed over time?

Unfortunately, nobody knows the answers to questions such as these and it is very unlikely that anyone ever will because, whatever hypothesis scientists may start with, they need evidence either to confirm or reject it.

Three of the main branches of science are:

- biological sciences (e.g. biology and biochemistry), which investigate the organic (living) nature of the universe
- Earth sciences (e.g. geology), which investigate the physical nature of the planet Earth
- physical sciences (e.g. chemistry and physics), which investigate the inorganic nature of the universe

In terms of evidence, scientists may consider:

- the Earth's geology and its oldest rocks and fossils
- computer models of the atmosphere and ocean
- techniques of molecular biology to study the relationship between life forms, perhaps with a view to identifying common ancestors
- undertaking laboratory experiments relating to early life forms
- studying life and survival rates under the most extreme conditions

Astronomers have succeeded to some extent in narrowing the gap in knowledge about the origins of the universe through their studies in cosmology. Of particular interest to cosmologists (astronomers who study and research the origin, structure and space–time relationship of the universe) are:

- an understanding of how galaxies have evolved from the distant past to the present
- a greater understanding of the scale of cosmic distances
- the testing of theories of the expanding universe

For a long time it was believed that the Earth was flat and even as late as the Middle Ages there were those who were afraid of falling off the edge, although as early as the fourth century BC the Greek philosopher Aristotle had suggested that the Earth was a sphere. Ptolemy developed Aristotle's ideas 500 years later, and put forward the view (the geocentric system) that the sun, the stars and all the planets revolved around the Earth in circular orbits.

In the sixteenth century, the Polish astronomer Nicolaus Copernicus changed the way we think about the solar system when he published *On the Revolution of the Heavenly Spheres* in 1543. Copernicus realised that the reasoning behind Ptolemy's model was wrong and put forward an alternative model (the heliocentric system), which placed the sun at the centre of the universe with all the planets, including the Earth, revolving round it. This challenge to the more established theory of Ptolemy was much disputed, especially by the Catholic Church, and the book was placed on the Church's Index of Forbidden Books for over two centuries.

Eventually, the invention of the telescope, and its use by Galileo, resulted in the end of Ptolemaic theory and confirmed the Copernican model. By the early seventeenth century, the German astronomer Johannes Kepler had developed the heliocentric model further by demonstrating that planets have elliptical, rather than circular, movements, giving us the laws of planetary motion.

Kepler's ideas on elliptical orbits were confirmed in the late seventeenth century by Isaac Newton, who used mathematical calculations to underpin his law of universal gravitation. Newton was concerned by his own belief that, because the stars of the universe attracted each other, they would eventually collapse into each other. We now know that this is not the case because the universe is not as static as Newton believed and gravitational collapse is prevented because the cosmos is in a state of expansion.

The issue of whether the universe has boundaries in time and space has been much debated. Some claim that the universe has existed for ever, whereas others claim it was created and there was thus a beginning in space and time. Enter the Big Bang theory.

Q **What is the Big Bang theory?**

A This is the dominant scientific theory about the origin of the universe and seeks to explain what happened around the time the universe began. According to this theory the universe was created anything between 10 and 20 billion years ago (probably between 12 and 15 billion years ago).

It is unlikely to have been the result of a big explosion as some originally thought, but scientists are unable to look back before the Big Bang began. For most scientists, the Big Bang was the instant when the universe started, when space and time came into existence and all the matter in the cosmos started to expand.

Most scientists believe that our universe began as a result of what some call a 'singularity' — something that was extremely small, intensely hot and highly dense — a 'fireball' or some sort of cosmic event. It took one second for the singularity to expand and cool, still intensely hot but cooling sufficiently for protons and neutrons to synthesise and form helium and hydrogen nuclei — building blocks for the formation of other elements. It is estimated that the Big Bang was over after 30 minutes.

Ironically, the name 'Big Bang' was said to have been popularised by the eminent scientist and science fiction writer Fred Hoyle, who disputed the claim that the cosmos was created some 12 billion years ago and who used the phrase 'Big Bang' dismissively in 1950.

The creation versus evolution controversy

- How did we get here?
- Did we evolve or were we created?
- Were we produced by some purposeful intelligence?
- What does the evidence say?

The Big Bang theory is the most widely believed by scientists. However, cosmogony (the study of the origin of the universe) brings together science and theology. If the universe had a beginning, is it possible that there was a master architect or intelligent designer? Put simply, religious believers ask: 'what role did God play'?

There are two competing theories relating to the origin of the universe and of life: evolution and creation (sometimes refined into what has become known as intelligent design). The creation versus evolution debate is ongoing and demonstrates wide differences in thinking about the origins of the Earth, life and the universe. Creationists take a primarily religiously based position while evolutionists tend to reflect the scientific consensus, where there is overwhelming support for evolutionary theory. However, it would be an oversimplification to see this as a science versus religion debate.

The theory of creation reflects a belief in a divine Creator of the world and its life forms. Evolution stresses the natural descent of all living creatures from a common ancestor that originally evolved from inorganic matter.

The debate has many dimensions.

- In the USA, especially in the more southern states (the 'Bible belt'), Republican supporters are more likely to have creationist beliefs. In the UK creationists and evolutionists are not linked to particular political parties or drawn from identifiable geographical areas.
- In the USA there is also more controversy about what should be taught in schools, because the separation of church and state is an important part of the US constitution.
- Much of the debate is over what constitutes good science as opposed to belief, and what constitutes scientific evidence and research rather than theorising.

Evolution

- Early ideas of evolution (the idea that complex organisms have developed gradually from simpler ones over geological time) began to emerge after the late eighteenth century, mainly as more knowledge emerged about geology and fossils. However, public debate was rare because of the threat to contemporary religious teaching.
- The original 'evolutionist' was almost certainly the Frenchman Jean Baptiste de Lamarck, with his idea of what he called 'transformation'. Lamarck believed that an individual who had acquired characteristics during a lifetime could pass them on to an offspring to aid its survival. What he lacked was supporting evidence.
- It was Charles Darwin who made the vital breakthrough. As a 22-year-old interested in geology, Darwin joined *HMS Beagle* as a naturalist in 1831 when it set sail on a 5-year surveying expedition to South America and the South Pacific. His job was to keep records of everything he observed — which included thousands of species of organisms and a wide variety of fossils.
- *The Beagle* spent 5 weeks in the Galapagos, charting the archipelago and making careful observations about both the geology and biology of the islands, including their birdlife. Darwin began a notebook on evolution in 1837, and in 1845 a general account of his travels and research was published in *The Voyage of the Beagle*.

- By then, Darwin had developed his early thoughts on what he called 'natural selection' — that those individuals born with characteristics that make them best suited for their environment are the ones most likely to survive and produce offspring.
- In 1859, and by then an eminent scientist, Darwin published *On the Origin of Species by Means of Natural Selection*. By that time, Darwin had received an essay from another scientist, Alfred Russel Wallace, who was living in the Malay archipelago and who advanced very similar ideas to those of Darwin. The first print run of Darwin's book sold out in a day. The controversy was intense but Darwin's meticulous and detailed approach, over many years, gave great scientific credibility to the theory of evolution, although many Christians still opposed the idea.
- What Darwin was doing, however, was calling into question the creation story of the Bible, that God created the world in 7 days. His idea of natural selection, based on genetic characteristics, went against any form of divine plan.

Creationism

- Creationism is the belief that the universe was created literally according to the Bible's account, contained in the book of Genesis; as it has evolved over the past 80 years, it is sometimes known as Creation Science.
- Creationists tend to be fundamentalist Christians.
- As public education expanded in the USA in the early twentieth century, some began objecting to the teaching of scientific evolution based on Darwin's theory of natural selection because it explains the origins of life without mentioning God.

There are different interpretations of the creation stories, but creationists are usually divided into three groups:
- **New Earth creationists**. They believe that the Earth and its life forms were created by God in 6 days about 10,000 years ago, and that since then only very minor changes to species have happened.
- **Old Earth creationists**. They also believe that the physical universe was created by God but use a less literal interpretation of Genesis. Old Earth creationists tend to follow the timelines favoured by astronomers and geologists but question evolutionary theory.
- More recently, **neo-creationists** have tended to separate themselves from both New and Old Earth creationists, favouring the term 'intelligent design' (ID).

Science and religion

The scientific community has remained sceptical of what seems to be more a claim than a scientific theory. Science always requires proof, and this is difficult for religion to offer. Creation of the Earth by God or any other divine force does not offer a concrete scientific explanation of life's origins. It is the Bible versus Darwin's *Origin of Species*.

It is widely believed that science and religion are diametrically opposed and cannot be reconciled, because they represent separate categories of thought that ask different questions and use different methods to answer them. One is based on data and the other is part of a belief system. For many scientists, intelligent design does not represent what they understand as scientific research and is essentially creationism under a more attractive-sounding and neutral name. For supporters of ID, evolution is a theory in crisis with barely concealed divisions between scientists.

In the USA the creationist and ID movements are very well organised and funded, with support groups and research foundations across the country. They have a particularly large following in some states, and the mixture of religion, science and politics has often proved highly inflammable.

In 2005 a poll for CBS News showed that over 50% of Americans rejected the theory of evolution. In addition, while the Creation Museum in Cincinnati had no difficulty in raising £3 million in donations, insufficient sponsors came forward to support an exhibition celebrating the life of Darwin at the American Museum of Natural History in New York, because they were reluctant to be accused of being pro-evolutionist.

The position in the UK

- In the UK, similar divisions exist but the debate has been much more restrained. UK schools are required to offer teaching in religious education; and the science curriculum has, in broad terms, used evolution with minimal criticism.
- The Royal Society, the UK's national academy of science, has declared firmly in favour of evolution as 'the best explanation for the development of life on Earth'. It stated that, although there were many things that science could not explain and young people should be encouraged to explore scientific and other beliefs, they were not well served by attempts to 'withhold, distort or misrepresent scientific knowledge and understanding in order to promote particular religious beliefs'.
- Similar views have been expressed by the Association for Science Education, a body for teachers of science. It stated that, when compared with the rationale used

to distinguish between 'good' and 'bad' science, 'ID has no grounds for sharing a platform as a scientific "theory"'; and that 'creationism, like ID, is not based on scientific evidence and, as such, is not scientific theory'.

- The Royal Society has criticised supporters of intelligent design for using evidence selectively and for treating any gaps in knowledge as if they were evidence for a 'designer'. It sees evolution as supported by the weight of scientific evidence and intelligent design as not.

- Nevertheless, by the end of 2006 some schools were using creationist teaching materials deemed by the government to be 'not appropriate to the science curriculum'. Teaching packs, including two DVDs, were sent to heads of science in all secondary schools by an organisation called Truth in Science.

- Of the 89 schools that returned the feedback postcard, 58 responded positively. Truth in Science claimed that its main intention was to encourage schools to look critically at Darwinism, and that supporters of intelligent design believed that there was empirical evidence for a 'designer'.

- Many schools, and even university departments, might teach creationism to show an alternative to Darwin's theories, although many scientists prefer a science curriculum based on science rather than faith and prefer scientific fact to what others argue is biblical fact.

- Nevertheless, the government has made it clear that 'neither intelligent design nor creationism are recognised scientific theories and they are not included in the science curriculum'. Phil Willis MP, a former teacher and chair of the parliamentary Science and Technology Select Committee, described the teaching of a creationist approach to science alongside Darwinism as a development that was 'deeply worrying'.

- The controversy goes on and has been re-awakened in the Catholic Church. In 2006 a group of scientists and philosophers visited the Vatican to discuss intelligent design with Pope Benedict XVI, a former theology professor, and it is felt that he is increasingly sympathetic to the creationist position.

- Because the theory of evolution and its mutations over hundreds of thousands of years cannot be fully proved, it cannot entirely exclude a role for God. However, the Pope has not yet endorsed the views of creationism or intelligent design about life's origins.

- Ultimately, the rational and methodical approach of science cannot answer all our questions, which is why some people turn towards philosophy or theology or faith, or to the belief that God created the conditions which led to evolution or that a 'creative force' was ultimately responsible for the universe.

Practice questions

The following source and questions are typical of those that will be used in Section B of the AS Unit 2 examination paper.

Darwin's theory of evolution caused a considerable stir. It showed that science, and scientific methods, had the potential to explain things which previously had puzzled many people. It also shocked many people and challenged the thoughts and beliefs of people in Victorian society.

Yet, the theory of evolution has stood the test of time and scientists recognise that the work of Charles Darwin involved careful research and scientific methods, which made evolution an essential part of science teaching. Creationism and intelligent design are interesting theories but they rely more on faith and belief than methods that can be recognised as scientific.

Questions

(1) For what reasons is Darwin's theory of evolution important in helping to explain the origins of life? *(17 marks)*

(2) Discuss the view that creationism and intelligent design should be included as part of a science programme teaching about the origins of life. *(18 marks)*

Explanation of human behaviour

Characteristics of human and social behaviour

Instincts

We sometimes say that we carry out an action or behave 'instinctively'. Basically, 'instincts' are not learned. They may be inherited patterns of responses or reactions to certain types of stimuli, but human beings have the ability to reason and instinctive behaviour is more likely to be observed among animals, perhaps in rituals of courtship or fighting. In Darwin's theory of evolution, the members of a species whose instinctive behaviour makes them most likely to compete successfully will have improved chances of survival.

Early psychologists in the late nineteenth century tried to identify what they considered to be human instincts, but as psychology developed in the twentieth century it became less common to use instinct as a way of trying to explain human behaviour. By the 1960s no human behaviour appeared to meet the sort of criteria that were being used to define instinct, although a few psychoanalysts have tried to link instinct to what they consider to be human motivational forces, or instinctual drives, such as sex and aggression. Others continue to argue that humans do not have any instincts that cannot be overridden.

Ask the examiner

Q What is free will?

A The issue of free will has long been debated by philosophers, although most people are convinced that they have free will. They feel they have the capacity, unique to humans, to control their actions and to choose a particular course of action; they do not feel they are coerced to take a particular course of action. What this actually amounts to is far less clear. Perhaps the two key questions are: 'In what sense are we able to act, or choose to act, freely?' and 'In what sense are we able to be morally responsible for what we do?'

The link between free will and moral responsibility has obvious importance. Without free will it would be difficult to claim that someone is morally responsible for a particular action. Particularly in what many see as our 'blame culture', the issue of moral responsibility is very important. Of course, it is possible for somebody to take a very bad action that amounts to a serious criminal offence because they suffer from a mental illness that leads to 'diminished responsibility'.

Similarly, there is the issue of the age of criminal responsibility — the age at which the law considers a child is old enough to know that the action he or she is taking is wrong and possibly against the law. Clearly, young children have only a limited grasp of right and wrong. In England the law states that the age of criminal responsibility is ten, but this is contentious and the age is set lower than in many European countries. Critics argue that ten is too young and that support for children at that age is more appropriate than punishment.

More contentious is the nature versus nurture debate — whether certain people are in some way predisposed towards certain actions, or how far an individual's environment influences their behaviour.

Q **What is determinism?**

A This is the view that everything that happens is a result of what has gone before, so that nothing can happen in a way other than it does. Because everything is somehow pre-determined, nothing new can come into existence. Thus all events are simply effects of other prior effects. Consequently, it can be argued that because all events in the future are unalterable, the freedom that humans are said to have is really an illusion; we seem to become almost non-autonomous, without the power to change the direction of our lives.

Determinists are, however, divided about the relationship between determinism and free will. Incompatibilists suggest that determinism implies that there is no free will, while compatibilists suggest that the two might not be mutually exclusive.

Genetic determinism is linked to the genes in our **DNA** (deoxyribonucleic acid, a chemical found in the nucleus of cells). Our genetic make-up may lead to certain forms of mental or physical disease. Some genetic determinists argue that our behaviour is determined by our genes, so that any attempt to alter our behaviour patterns is doomed to failure unless we discover, and are permitted to use, ways of changing our genetic make-up. For such genetic determinists, nature (in the form of biology and genetics) is more important than, say, the influence of our environment.

Marriage and the changing role of the family

For many people over 60 there is a clear picture of family life as it used to be portrayed. There were rituals of courtship and the teaching that sex before marriage was wrong. A proposal of marriage took place: after a suitable period of courtship — usually measured in months if not years — the father of the bride-to-be would be asked by the future bridegroom for permission to marry his daughter. Formal engagements were common and marriage eventually took place, in a church, with great ceremony.

The aim of the immediate postwar generation, many of whom had experienced the poverty of the 1930s, was security. In a sense, that was what marriage brought. During the Second World War many more women than before worked and achieved some measure of economic independence. They worked, though, while the men were away in the services. In postwar Britain, the continuation of work for women could not be guaranteed, and there was an expectation that the husband would be the 'breadwinner' while his wife would 'keep house'.

A 'happy family' in the 1950s

Home was important and newly married couples were usually keen to establish some measure of independence by having a home of their own. This might be rented — and large numbers of council houses were built after 1945 — or purchased by those who could afford a deposit and monthly mortgage repayments and who had aspirations to consolidate or assume a middle-class role in society.

Family life was fairly predictable. Children were still expected to be 'seen and not heard' and those who weren't were warned to 'wait until your father gets home'. Meals were taken together, at the table, and often with a measure of formality. Distractions such as television were not so common in the 1950s and family entertainment might be based on church or chapel attendance, visits to the cinema, a holiday of a week or a fortnight in a British seaside resort, and card games such as the aptly named 'Happy Families'.

It was expected that children would be part of the family and marriage was very much a heterosexual (male–female) partnership. Typically, there would be a husband, wife and an average of 2.4 children — large families were less common than they had been as contraception improved and more people aspired to higher living standards, which demanded smaller families.

The minority of children who passed the 11 + examination during their final year at primary school were rewarded with a much-coveted place at the local grammar school — the route to a secure, white-collar occupation with a pension. It was a process described admirably by Richard Hoggart in *The Uses of Literacy* and Brian Jackson and Dennis Marsden in *Working Class Community*.

Divorce was rare. It was expensive and difficult to obtain. There was also a considerable social taboo attached to being divorced (as there was to illegitimacy and the unmarried mother) and where relationships became strained, couples were expected to 'work on them' or to 'put up with it'. Couples were expected to 'stick together for better or worse' and extra-marital affairs met with considerable moral indignation. Divorce was, of course, always available to the rich because they could afford it.

Perhaps such a picture was an over-romanticised generalisation based on stereotypes. There must have been many exceptions to this pattern of family life, but it did not seem the case at the time, and reading books were based on the structure of the tightly drawn 'nuclear' family outlined above. With limited social and geographical mobility, the 'extended' family was also common, and aunts, uncles and grandparents were drawn into the wider family structure.

If change took place it may well have dated from the late 1960s, the result of factors such as:
- the emergence of the teenager as a social phenomenon
- a less deferential society, more willing to question the values of an earlier generation
- more relaxed social attitudes associated with the 'swinging sixties'
- the declining influence of the church and its values
- greater economic and social freedom for women
- more liberal divorce laws
- the development of the contraceptive pill

The end of marriage?

For the prophets of doom, 'family breakdown' was symptomatic of a slacker age where little thought was given to marriage vows and divorce was the answer to any marital problems that emerged, although old taboos died hard, and single parents (and it was almost always single mothers who were left with the family responsibilities) were demonised. Media focus and expressions of concern are almost always directed towards family breakdown and dysfunction rather than the number of family networks that survive and flourish.

Marriage rates in the early years of the twenty-first century are at their lowest since records were first collected in 1862; on the basis of figures from the Office for National Statistics (ONS) (the ONS became the United Kingdom Statistics Authority (UKSA) in 2008), there were nearly 237,000 marriages in England and Wales in 2006 (down significantly from the 352,000 marriages in 1981 and 307,000 in 1991).

Marriage rates may also be affected by recent legislation designed to limit the number of 'sham marriages' used to secure British nationality for one partner. Another possible explanation is that more British couples are getting married overseas and these marriages do not feature in ONS figures. More likely is the growing acceptability of cohabitation and the growing proportion of women in full-time work, which reduces their dependence on men for economic security.

According to a 2007 report by the ONS, there were 17.1 million families of all types in the UK in 2006. Using detailed government data on family life, the report, titled *Focus on Families*, gave these statistics for the period 1996–2006:

- The number of married-couple families fell by 4% to just over 12 million.
- The number of couples cohabiting (which might include those preparing to marry, those who have no wish to marry, and those testing the durability of their relationships before deciding whether or not to marry) rose by 65% from 1.4 million to 2.3 million.
- Younger people were more likely to cohabit, and half of cohabiting couples in 2001 were headed by a person aged under 35. Over 30% of teenagers now are likely to cohabitate rather than marry.
- The number of single parents increased by 8% to 2.6 million. London has the highest proportion of lone-parent families (22%), although this was as high as 48% in Lambeth and 47% in Islington.

The ONS also suggests the following:

- Marriage is associated with better health, especially for men.
- Lone parents are significantly more likely to suffer a long-term illness.
- Children are more likely to develop long-term illnesses in non-traditional family groups.
- Children in traditional family groups are more likely to be in education at 17 than their counterparts in non-traditional families.
- The majority of unpaid care is family care; and over 90% of care provided for 20 hours a week or more is provided to relatives, most notably partners and parents.

- Cohabiting couples are the fastest growing family type in the UK, and some estimates suggest that married couples may be in a minority by 2014. There has also been a sharp rise in childless couples, up from 855,000 to 1.3 million in a decade; the actual figure may be higher than this because same-sex couples are only counted voluntarily.

Using research relating to the Conservative Social Justice Policy Review Group headed by former party leader Iain Duncan Smith and based on a 200,000-word report, it has been suggested that unmarried couples are five times more likely to break up than couples who are married and that social problems (debt, drug addiction, alcohol abuse, reliance on social benefits, poor school achievement, teenage pregnancy, crime) were more likely to affect those who had been the victim of family breakdown than those who had not.

It is part of the UK's 'breakdown society' and, perhaps with good reason, Duncan Smith has turned his attention to the remarkable Beveridge Report, published in 1942 and used by the Labour government in its postwar reconstruction of the welfare state during the 1940s. Time has moved on and our welfare state is more comprehensive, but Beveridge's 'five giants' — want, squalor, disease, ignorance and idleness — are just as relevant.

A 2007 report by the United Nations Children's Fund (UNICEF) placed the UK at the bottom of a table that sought to assess the well-being of a nation's children. This could not necessarily be attributed to the UK's high rate of single-parent families. Sweden, with a similar level, came top of the table, but the Scandinavian country used its high tax rates to fund more generous social benefits, available to all parents irrespective of whether they were married, cohabiting or single. Marital breakdown is certainly an issue, but an even greater one might be family poverty, which tends to hit lone parents more than families with two adults.

Family structures

Family structures have changed considerably in the last two decades. Families might now be:
- 'traditional first-marriage' nuclear families, of married heterosexual couples who may be childless or who may have (usually a relatively small number of) children
- heterosexual married couples, of whom one or both partner may have been previously married, with children of their new and/or former relationships
- heterosexual couples where the partners live together but are not married to each other (the taboos surrounding illegitimacy having long since disappeared)

- single parents, usually mothers, who retain responsibilities for child-rearing after the break-up of a previous marriage or relationship
- same-sex couples who may in some cases also be raising children

Greater geographical mobility may have reduced the role of extended families (although not in all cultures, and grandparents may play an important childcare role as more mothers work full-time).

In addition, children's lives have changed dramatically, not least because of commercial pressures. They have more outside interests and for both them and their parents, friends have tended to become more important than relatives. Meals have become less formal, snacking and convenience foods are more common, and the internet is the modern medium of communication, with computer games increasingly occupying the time of younger males and teenagers.

Research by the Equal Opportunities Commission based on a survey of nearly 30,000 families confirmed that the division between 'breadwinner male' and 'home-maker female' has long gone. It found no links between women who work and developmental problems in children, not least because of improvements in childcare facilities and the greater use of grandparents (who may have retired earlier and be in better health).

Politicians usually like to be seen as promoters of marriage, and even David Cameron, the 'modernising' leader of the Conservative Party, has made it clear that he is a traditionalist on the subject of marriage. When addressing Conservatives, he referred to marriage as 'a great institution' while emphasising his view that if divorce rates came down and more people stayed together as man and wife society would be better.

In short, Cameron is backing the traditional family, and critics accuse him of stigmatising lone mothers and their supposedly delinquent children and trying to impose standards of morality. It probably does little for the very poor families who live in a state of chronic poverty or the deeply dysfunctional families who make life a misery for those in their neighbourhoods.

Labour's emphasis is, perhaps, slightly different. Both David Cameron and the Labour prime minister, Gordon Brown, are happily married with children. Brown is certainly not 'anti-marriage', but it seems that the Labour Party is more inclined to offer support to all families rather than to make judgements about the status or way of life of different kind of families. Health minister and cabinet member

Alan Johnson has spoken out strongly in favour of single parents, using his own experience as a child brought up by his mother and sister. The government is a microcosm of society in that it is made up of married, remarried, divorced, gay and single people.

Single parents

The number of lone parents has been growing steadily. In 1961 there were 500,000; by 1988 the figure had reached 1 million; and this figure continued to rise into the twenty-first century, easily exceeding 2 million. Lone-parent families are at a high risk of poverty as mothers or fathers try to combine work with childcare. About 800,000 lone parents are currently on income support, and Britain has the highest proportion of single mothers in the European Union (EU).

Periodically, there are political initiatives to get single parents off benefits and into work as politicians seek to reduce the 18% of the working population now on benefits of one sort or another. Once again, the issue of making judgements is raised, not least because 70% of young offenders come from lone-parent families and voters tend to look down on single parents irrespective of the cause of the lone-parent status.

Many lone parents would undoubtedly be happy to be given the opportunity to work, to increase their income and to raise the living standard of their family, although Britain does have some of the highest benefit rates for lone parents in the EU. A major obstacle, however, is often the absence of affordable childcare. Another problem is the reduction in the time that working mothers can devote to their children. The reality, according to the pressure group One Parent Families, is that most lone parents with older children are working. However, there are threats that lone parents may lose some of their benefits unless they look for work once their youngest child reaches the age of 12 instead of the present age of 16.

Children

Early in 2007, the international charity UNICEF published a report (*Child Poverty in Perspective: An Overview of Child Well-Being in Rich Countries*) on the well-being of children in a number of different countries. UNICEF used 40 separate indicators, grouped in six dimensions, to measure well-being. These dimensions were:

- poverty and inequality
- health and safety
- education
- family and friendships
- sex, drink and drugs
- happiness

Many people were shocked to read that the UK, the fifth largest economy in the world, was ranked 21st out of 21 countries measured. (The top three countries for the well-being of their children were the Netherlands, Sweden and Denmark. The bottom three countries were Hungary, the USA and the UK. British children came last in three of the six categories measured.)

The following were the main findings of the report:
- Over 30% of children aged 11, 13 and 15 in Britain said they had been drunk at least twice. In the country with the lowest number, France, this applied to only 8% of the age groups.
- The proportion of children in the 15-year-olds age group having sex was also the highest, at 38%. Britain had the third highest rate of teenage pregnancy in the countries surveyed and the highest rate in Europe.
- British children often said that they felt lonely and did not always enjoy friendly or supportive relationships with peers and parents. In terms of family, friendships and relationships, British children came lowest of the 21.
- British children were among the least likely to enjoy school or to describe themselves as happy. Of those surveyed, 22% described their physical and mental health as 'fair or poor'.
- British children suffered above-average rates of bullying and a high proportion had been involved in a fight in the previous 12 months.
- Britain was near the bottom of the rankings for material well-being. When it came to the proportion of children living in households where the income was less than 50% of the national average, only the USA was below Britain.
- British children did reasonably well on assessments of reading, maths and science, but the country had a poor record on the number of those remaining in education or training beyond the age of 16.
- British children were less likely to die in an accident than children in any other country surveyed, with the exception of Sweden.

Further research later in the year in the form of a Primary Review (*Community Soundings*) headed by a former education professor, Robin Alexander, seemed to endorse the UNICEF findings among younger children. The research was based on detailed interviews with 700 children, their parents and teachers. It indicated that many 7–11-year-olds reported feeling stressed and anxious about:
- national tests
- global warming
- terrorism
- friendships and peer acceptability

Q Are children in the UK really as unhappy as this?

A There are fewer certainties in social science research than in scientific research, but concerns have been expressed about the extent to which young people in the UK are involved in antisocial behaviour, binge drinking, drug taking and casual sex. The true extent is unknown. Parents are blamed for not exercising sufficient control over their children. Schools are blamed for neglecting their responsibilities for the teaching of personal, social, moral and spiritual education. Both are convenient scapegoats. Young people today are exposed to many media influences and are aware of world issues that concern both them and adults.

Divorce

Just as marriage rates appear to be falling, so too are divorce rates, perhaps because more people are not getting married until later (the average age for a first marriage is 31.7 for men and 29.5 for women), which often allows them to know their partners better and to bring more experience and emotional maturity to the marriage. Divorces are currently at their lowest level since 1984, with 133,000 couples divorcing in 2006. The average marriage lasts for 11.6 years and the average age at divorce is 43 for men and 41 for women. Remarriages are increasing, but the number of second-time divorcees has risen from 1 in 10 in 1981 to 1 in 5 in 2006.

Figure 11.1 Divorce law timeline for England and Wales

1857	Prior to this date divorce was difficult to obtain even for very rich people because it was in the hands of church courts. Now a new court independent from the church was set up for divorce, although it remained extremely expensive. Men could obtain a divorce if their wife had committed adultery. Women needed to prove 'aggravated adultery' — usually adultery and cruel or perverse behaviour.
1923	Men and women could now divorce on equal terms.
1937	The Herbert Act of 1937 was passed at the time when Edward VIII abdicated and married the twice-divorced American, Wallis Simpson, in France. 'Fault' remained an integral part of the grounds for divorce but these were extended to include cruelty, desertion (after 3 years) and prolonged insanity. In 1937 there were nearly 6,000 petitions for divorce. In 1938 there were over 10,000.

(continued)

1949	Legal aid became available for divorce.
1969	The Divorce Reform Act, which was operative from 1971, established the 'irretrievable breakdown of a marriage' as the basis for divorce. A judge was likely to accept this if one of the following had happened: **a** adultery **b** unreasonable behaviour (formerly cruelty) **c** desertion (after 2 years) **d** living apart for a minimum of 2 years (if both parties consented to the divorce) **e** living apart for a minimum of 5 years if one party contested the divorce The Act was important because of its central premise of 'irretrievable breakdown of marriage' as determined by a judge (either 'fault-based' — **a–c** — or 'non-fault' — **d–e**). Together with the 1973 Act, this Act still forms the basis of modern divorce law. 'Fault-based' divorces can often lead to bitter battles between husband and wife.
1973	The Matrimonial Causes Act developed the law to make decisions about the welfare of children involved in a divorce central to a settlement, and to allow a 'clean break' so that neither party in a divorce would have future obligations to the other if a 'clean break' was agreed as part of the settlement.
1996	The Family Law Act was an extremely ambitious attempt both to support the institution of marriage and to establish the principle of 'no fault' divorces. Underlying it was the desire to support marriage; to promote reconciliation and mediation services in an effort to save the marriage; to encourage good relationships and some continuity in parenting if divorce did take place; and to protect anyone involved in a divorce from violence. Much of the legislation was either never implemented or repealed.
2005	The 2005 Family Law Act reduced the 2-year 'living apart' clause to 1 year and the 5-year period to 2 years, but it applied only in Scotland. For many couples there is a 'no fault' divorce after 1 year's separation.

Divorce law is clearly a complex area and it remains politically sensitive. The church and many politicians wish to support the institution of marriage and wish to see two-parent families, arguing that more liberal divorce laws undermine these goals. Critics say that our laws were framed in a different age and that the reasons for marriage breakdown are complex. If couples try to maintain a marriage that has effectively broken down this is not good for their physical or mental health or that of their children.

Ask the examiner

Q **Is divorce too easy today?**

A Legally, divorce is easier to obtain and it can be argued that people enter into marriage too easily and are not sufficiently committed to making it work. In the past, people might have been more inclined to stay together 'for the sake of the children', but this might not have been a positive experience. Divorce can be expensive, it hits the living standards of all concerned and usually results in emotional distress. If a marriage has broken down 'irretrievably', making divorce more difficult to obtain is not likely to change the situation and can have equally undesirable results.

Practice questions

The following source and questions are typical of those that will be used in Section B of the AS Unit 2 examination paper.

The family always used to be important in bringing up children and giving them a sense of security. Families ate together and children learned how to behave properly, so that discipline wasn't a concern. Then there were the 'swinging sixties' and it all started to change — for the worse.

Now we are witnessing the death of the family as an institution and this is threatening our way of life. People enter into marriage far too easily and do not try hard enough to make it work. Divorce is easily available and religion plays a less important part in the lives of most people.

(1) **For what reasons have attitudes to marriage changed since the 1960s?**   *(17 marks)*

(2) **To what extent do you agree that we are now witnessing 'the death of the family'?**   *(18 marks)*

Race and race relations

In debates about immigration, we often forget how many different tribes initially colonised the British Isles before the Romans arrived around 250 AD. They brought an army that included a contingent of black legionaries drawn from parts of their African empire; but there were few non-white faces in Britain at least until the slave trading of the sixteenth century and after. Jutes, Angles and Saxons all came to more southern parts of Britain and the Vikings settled in the north and East Anglia. 1066 is a date we usually remember for the Battle of Hastings, but it also brought the Normans from France.

It was estimated that there were some 17,000 black people in England by the late eighteenth century. In 1807 the slave trade (though not slavery itself) was banned by parliament, and in 1833 all slavery in the British empire was finally outlawed. Increasingly, wealthy families brought black servants to England and both black and Chinese sailors began to settle. Particularly in the 1840s huge numbers of Irish people arrived to escape poverty and starvation in their own country. As early as 1892, Britain's first non-white MP was elected, the Indian Dadabhai Naoroji.

There were no rules on immigration but there were examples of racial prejudice and some of the earliest race riots took place in 1919. Many non-whites fought for Britain in both world wars and, when the Second World War ended in 1945, immigration increased to meet labour shortages. In a parallel situation to the recent expansion of the European Union, many Poles settled in the UK. In 1948 the *Empire Windrush* docked in London bringing hundreds of men from the West Indies — the start of what some saw as an age of mass immigration and the beginning of a period of unease, as new arrivals brought their own beliefs and cultures.

Immigrants tended to settle where other immigrants had settled, especially in major cities such as London and Birmingham. It was London that saw the Notting Hill race riots and serious disorder of 1958, as racial prejudice intensified and calls grew to restrict the immigration of people from the **British Empire** and **Commonwealth**.

Jamaican immigrants on board the *Empire Windrush* arriving in Britain in 1948

Key terms

British Empire: Britain was one of several countries that, as a result of voyages of discovery in previous centuries, colonised and controlled a number of countries around the world, primarily for trade purposes.

Commonwealth: a shorthand term for 'the British Commonwealth' or 'the Commonwealth of Nations', the successor of the empire and dating back, initially, to 1884. The Commonwealth today is a voluntary association of 53 countries, many of which were former British colonies, containing 2 billion citizens. Queen Elizabeth is Head of the Commonwealth.

They could enter the UK freely because they carried British passports. Racial discrimination in all walks of life was commonplace for ethnic minorities in the UK in the early 1960s.

A new Labour government was responsible for the first Race Relations Act (1965) which:

- made it unlawful to refuse access to anyone on racial grounds to public places (such as cinemas or hotels) or public transport
- prevented landlords from refusing to rent out accommodation to people because of their race
- made incitement to stir up racial hatred a criminal offence
- set up the Race Relations Board — the forerunner of the Commission for Racial Equality, later incorporated in the Equality and Human Rights Commission
- in an amendment of 1968, outlawed discrimination in areas such as employment and goods and services

In 1965, BBC Television began the screening of a comedy called *Till Death Us Do Part*, which introduced Warren Mitchell's brilliant portrayal of Alf Garnett, an older working man from the East End of London who exhibited many of the typical prejudices of the day. Writer Johnny Speight meant it as a **satire**, but many people identified with Alf Garnett's racism and **xenophobia** and, for many in the audience of 20 million, he said what others were afraid to say. Few saw it as deeply embedded prejudice or recognised the irony of the anti-Semitic Garnett being played by a Jewish actor.

> **Key terms**
>
> **satire:** a literary or dramatic technique that uses ridicule or scorn in a witty or humorous manner.
>
> **xenophobia:** the irrational fear or hatred of foreigners or strangers.

Enoch Powell and the years of conflict

In 1968 the Conservative MP Enoch Powell warned of the dangers of mass immigration and predicted that increasing discord would lead to 'rivers of blood'. He was promptly sacked from the shadow cabinet but won much popular support and London dockers marched to demonstrate their approval for such views. Legislation followed; by 1972, British passport holders born overseas could only come to the UK on a permanent basis if they had a work permit and could prove that one of their parents or grandparents had been born in the UK.

By 1970 it was estimated that there were about 1.4 million non-white residents in the UK. There was a wave of immigration from Uganda in 1972 when General Idi Amin expelled 80,000 African Asians, many of whom were British passport holders. In 1976 the Commission for Racial Equality was set up by the government to tackle racial discrimination, and the 1976 Race Relations Act strengthened the law, making direct and indirect discrimination unlawful and providing more effective redress for those discriminated against through the courts and employment tribunals. An amendment in 2001 required public bodies, including the local authorities and the police, to ensure that their policies were directed to achieving equal treatment for all.

Britain's first black newsreader, Sir Trevor McDonald, has become a much-revered public figure

In 1973 Trevor McDonald became Britain's first black newsreader; he eventually became a greatly revered figure. In 1978, after appalling examples of racist behaviour in the form of monkey chanting and throwing bananas onto the pitch against the few black footballers in professional football, Viv Anderson became the first black footballer to play for England amid great publicity. By 1993, the fact that a black player, Paul Ince, became England's captain seemed far less remarkable and, in 1999, the Indian-born Nasser Hussain captained England at cricket.

There were more serious race riots in 1981, most notably in the Brixton area of London, the Toxteth area of Liverpool, the St Paul's area of Bristol and the Harehills area of Leeds, all communities with a high proportion of African-Caribbean residents. It was widely believed that black youths were unfairly targeted by the police, and the subsequent report by Lord Scarman revealed the extent of distrust, discrimination and prejudice in many parts of the UK.

Four non-white Labour MPs (Diane Abbott, Paul Boateng, Bernie Grant and Keith Vaz) were elected in the 1987 general election. The bungling investigation of the brutal and unprovoked murder of the black teenager Stephen Lawrence in 1993 led to a public enquiry under Sir William Macpherson, which led to the police being labelled 'institutionally racist' — a far more severe indictment than Lord Scarman's judgement of a few 'bad apples'.

By the end of the twentieth century a new dimension to racial prejudice had emerged, with a rapid growth in applications to enter the UK made by asylum seekers from African and Asian countries. There was a further rise in racial tension and there was growing controversy concerning the government's plans for new immigration legislation and citizenship tests. Serious disturbances took place in 2001 in the declining northwestern towns of Oldham and Burnley and the Yorkshire city of Bradford, all with high proportions of non-white families in some areas.

In the 2001 census there were five ethnic groupings, although these groupings have attracted some criticism because of their 'colour coding' (and it remains to be seen if 'black' and 'white' will be used in the next census, due to take place in 2011):

- white (British, Irish or any other white background)
- mixed (white and black Caribbean; white and black African; white and Asian; or any other mixed background)
- Asian or Asian British (Indian, Pakistani, Bangladeshi or any other Asian background)
- black or black British (Caribbean, African or any other black background)
- Chinese or other ethnic groups

The 2001 census indicated that 87% of the population of England and Wales (96% in Wales itself) gave their ethnic grouping as white British with the highest proportions (over 95%) in the southwest and northeast of England. London has the highest proportion of people from ethnic minority groups and the most ethnically diverse part of the capital is Brent. The most ethnically diverse place outside London is Slough.

In some parts of the country there are high concentrations of particular ethnic groups:

- Although less than 3% of the population of England and Wales are Indian, the proportion in Leicester is nearly 26%.
- Similarly, although only 0.5% of the population of England and Wales are Bangladeshi, the proportion in the London borough of Tower Hamlets is 33%.
- In Frizinghall, Bradford, 73% of the population are Pakistani.
- In Rusholme, Manchester, 25% of the population are black Caribbean.
- In Broughton, Salford, 49% of the population are Jewish.

Of people living in England, 87.4% gave England as their country of birth and 3.2% named other parts of the UK. Again, there were marked variations between London (where only 72.9% of people said they were born in the UK) and the County Durham areas of Easington and Derwentside (where the proportion was nearly 99%, making these areas the least ethnically diverse in England). Nearly 97% of the population of Wales were born in the UK (75% in Wales and 20% in England).

Multiculturalism and 'Britishness': integration or segregation?

Britain is increasingly an ethnically mixed society, and the issues of both multiculturalism and 'Britishness' are keenly debated. There appears to be no agreed definition of the term 'multiculturalism', which is, in some respects, an ideology. It certainly applies to cultural pluralism and also, to some degree, tolerance. The key issue is the extent to which different ethnic, racial, religious and cultural groups can coexist in harmony in a single country rather than with limited tolerance, and to what extent they retain their differences.

Increasingly, there is an element of inclusion of minority cultures into mainstream culture, even though some cultures appear more exclusive with little openness and interactivity. There are both diversity and shared common values (although there are occasions when the two appear to be mutually exclusive).

Another way of looking at multiculturalism, although far less acceptable to mainstream integrationists, is to put greater emphasis on diversity, where people co-exist but retain their own cultural beliefs to a greater extent. A common thread of Britishness or some form of occasional mutual identification helps to hold things together. People have different cultures and we may need to accept this, although it can lead to voluntary segregation and the surfacing of periodic mistrust.

Somehow, multiculturalism must do the impossible — allow for a measure of individuality, pluralism and diversity while at the same time establishing common bonds and a shared sense of national identity.

We were reminded once again of the tensions and potential for conflict between ethnic groups when, in 2001, there was serious, and sometimes violent, rioting involving mainly young white and Asian males in Burnley, Oldham and Bradford. The inevitable enquiries identified some key issues:

- All three areas had high degrees of segregation in housing and schooling between white and non-white people so that different communities lived 'parallel lives'. There had been years of deep-rooted segregation between communities.
- Local councils had not done enough to address the causes of racial tension.
- High levels of poverty and deprivation were often evident, with high rates of unemployment, poor housing, drug abuse and petty crime.

- Fear grew from ignorance and prejudice about other communities, often something that was exploited by extremists, with the British National Party taking full advantage of the discord.
- Single-faith schools were criticised because they tended to result in deep community divisions.
- It was felt to be advantageous if a meaningful definition of citizenship could be found.
- Immigrants might take an oath of allegiance making clear their 'primary loyalty to the nation'.

Citizenship and a challenge to multiculturalism

There was clearly a need for greater community cohesion, economic regeneration and more dialogue between white and predominantly Asian groups. Consideration needed to be given to more integrated housing and education policies, and local councils and voluntary groups needed to promote more dialogue between different ethnic and religious groups. The debate needed to centre on identity, shared values and the concept of citizenship. Professor Sir Bernard Crick became a key figure in bringing compulsory citizenship studies to the school curriculum and in advocating education in language and citizenship for immigrants.

Crick saw no incompatibility between multiculturalism and Britishness, and was confident that Britishness must be part of multiculturalism. His call for 'mutual engagement and learning about each other' and his emphasis on the need for 'respect, tolerance and understanding' are admirable sentiments, but not necessarily those shared by large numbers of the population, even though he stressed that these did not necessarily mean having a single culture.

Perhaps surprisingly, Trevor Phillips, head of the former Commission for Racial Equality (and now head of the Equality and Human Rights Commission formed in 2007 to cover issues of inequality, disability and racial discrimination) used a newspaper interview in 2004 to question the meaning of multiculturalism, seemingly calling for the concept to be abandoned because it suggested 'separateness' and belonged to another era. This led to accusations that Phillips was taking up a 'right-wing' position, stressing strands of Britishness and indirectly targeting Muslims. His defenders suggested that second and third generation immigrants, often born in the UK, felt excluded and alienated and that a different approach was needed.

In many ways the debate continues and intensifies simply because there is no real agreement about what multiculturalism means. The controversy ignited again towards the end of 2007 when the Chief Rabbi, Sir Jonathan Sacks, wrote a book (*The Home We Build Together: Recreating Society*) calling for the end of multiculturalism. Like Trevor Phillips, Sir Jonathan also thought it had run its course since it first emerged as a positive force in the 1970s.

Sacks argued that the concept of multiculturalism no longer gave enough people a sense of belonging and therefore of responsibility. For Sacks, multiculturalism has led less to integration and more to separation. However, he was far less clear about what might replace it, together with the moral certainties that he thought had disappeared and been replaced by the identity politics of the aggrieved.

Increasingly, multiculturalism seems to be used to explain some of the growing divisions between ethnic groups and growing prejudice, discrimination and racist behaviour. Young Muslims may increasingly face discrimination in education and employment and the Muslim world and Islamic beliefs are sometimes demonised. Ethnic-minority groups are more likely to live in economically deprived areas.

Criticisms of multiculturalism may or may not be justified but, often unintentionally, they help to provide a more persuasive framework for people who have never acknowledged what multiculturalism may have achieved, and who may never have wished it to work.

Ask the examiner

Q **Should the government do more to make communities more integrated?**

A In an ideal world many people would support the principle of people of different ethnic groupings and religions living peacefully and cooperatively in the same communities. In reality there are those who prefer, or feel more secure, living in communities dominated by a particular ethnic group. Mixed communities can create tensions because of suspicion, ignorance or prejudice.

However, separate communities can make disadvantage between ethnic groups more pronounced or, in extreme cases, lead to 'no go' areas for members of other ethnic groups.

Britishness

The Act of Union brought together England and Scotland in 1707. That might offer something of a starting date for Britishness, although it was not a peaceful union and there is often intense rivalry between the two countries — so much so that international football matches between them have been discontinued. Even prior to devolution, some differences between England and Scotland remained, not least in the Scottish education and legal systems. Perhaps there never has been a homogeneous British population, and we may need to acknowledge that there may be different paths to some notion of Britishness.

It is unlikely that many people talked about Britishness in the 1940s and 1950s when British society was less ethnically diverse. The situation seemed less secure by the 1960s when there was a growing sense of flux. By the early years of the twenty-first century, the Home Secretary, David Blunkett, urged people from ethnic minorities to develop a 'sense of belonging'. He admitted that racial prejudice was deep-seated in many parts of the country, not least in areas where there was limited ethnic diversity. Blunkett also pointed to two particular practices, arranged marriages and genital mutilation, which he did not consider part of Britishness.

How, though, can we define Britishness? Suggestions might be:
- being born in Britain
- living in Britain
- working in Britain
- being educated in Britain
- identifying with 'the British way of life'
- being able to acknowledge and support 'national symbols'
- recognising certain democratic traditions

Norman Tebbit, the former Conservative minister and close ally of Margaret Thatcher, thought that immigrants should consider what became known as 'Tebbit's cricket test'. This equated support for the England cricket team, when they had opponents such as India, Pakistan, Bangladesh and the West Indies, with British patriotism; the point was identification with the 'home' country rather than what might have been the country of origin.

At a time when the Conservative Party was increasingly divided over the relationship between Britain and the European Union, John Major (Thatcher's successor as prime minister) evoked a country characterised by warm beer, dog lovers, shadows on cricket grounds and ladies of an indeterminate age cycling to Holy Communion through the morning mist. It all seemed a long way from the experience of a great many people of all ethnic backgrounds.

One of the dangers of trying to define Britishness is that such definitions often resemble Englishness, and often the Englishness of the southeast of England. Scotland has its popular symbols such as the kilt, the thistle, whisky and the saltire (the cross on the Scottish flag), as does Wales (rugby, the Welsh language, male voice choirs and the dragon).

Research suggests that it is mainly the English who see themselves as British, whereas many of those who live in Scotland, with its Scottish Parliament and Scottish National Party, see themselves as Scottish. Similarly, many of those who live in Wales (with its Welsh Assembly and Plaid Cymru party), see themselves firmly as Welsh, particularly if they were born there. With Northern Ireland a country traditionally, and often bitterly, divided by religion, national differences and devolution seem to emphasise a measure of separateness in all four countries of the United Kingdom.

There are many who want to preserve a national identity, even if they cannot define it readily, and there remains a residual suspicion, and even fear, of foreigners and foreign cultures. This almost certainly contributes to the relative success of political parties such as the United Kingdom Independence Party in the European Parliament.

Positions may have grown more polarised in recent years, not least since the 9/11 events of 2001 and the killing of over 50 people by suicide bombers on London transport in 2005. There is more suspicion of Muslims, bordering in some cases on **Islamophobia**, indicating how successful terrorists have been in implanting fear in the public mind. MI5 has warned of a number of plots, often with links to **al-Qaeda** in Pakistan. Such warnings are necessary but fill people with trepidation, and suspicion may fall upon law-abiding members of Muslim communities.

Key terms

Islamophobia: the fear, dislike or hatred of Muslims and their beliefs and culture.

al-Qaeda: an international terrorist network opposed to the USA and its allies and to Western beliefs and values.

On the other hand, the extent to which national identity, patriotism, jingoism and xenophobia can be separated is less clear. We are not far removed from views that state, or imply, that 'there are too many immigrants in Britain' and suggest that racism, which is illegal, is acceptable.

At the centre of the debate is the question of how far diversity can allow multiethnic communities rather than what appears to be voluntary self-segregation to develop; the latter might result in ghettos. The question highlights a range of issues such as:

- religion
- other cultural beliefs and values
- language
- food and diet
- leisure pursuits such as sport and music

Addressing the Trades Union Congress in 2007, Gordon Brown (a Scot by birth) used the words 'Britain' or 'British' 45 times. After becoming prime minister that year, one of his first actions to encourage Britishness was to order that the Union flag should fly from government buildings, and to emphasise qualities such as liberty, fairness and a sense of responsibility to unite the British people. He has backed the historian David Cannadine's idea for a new Institute of Britishness.

In the future there may be a national British Day, perhaps modelled on Australia Day (or 4 July in the USA or Bastille Day in France); a citizenship pack for every first-time voter (perhaps at 16 as in the Isle of Man rather than 18); greater emphasis on volunteering; and migrants being accepted as British citizens only if they can demonstrate an appropriate knowledge of the language, good behaviour and evidence of a willingness to integrate. People will have to earn their citizenship, and every test brings passes and failures.

It is clear that the prime minister will make it a priority to identify ideals and principles that might bind the country together, and that these will form part of wider proposals for constitutional change and a more developed sense of citizenship. Brown clearly wishes to go beyond political rhetoric. The present atmosphere of suspicion and mistrust might make it difficult for him to do so, but the issue is increasingly how to keep the United Kingdom together, and this has made the issue of Britishness all the more important.

It may be a subtle and long-term process, and efforts to impose Britishness are unlikely to achieve the desired results. Few, though, would disagree that Britishness is a nebulous concept that needs to be redefined and that there is no place in society for ill-disguised bigotry and racism.

More contentious might be resolving the paradox between what appears to be growing enthusiasm, not least on the part of politicians, for faith schools, and the extent to which these might inhibit, rather than promote, greater religious understanding and tolerance. The pace of change in the twenty-first century has been rapid and in some respects destabilising, and there are no gains in an increasingly suspicious and more divided society.

Practice questions

The following source and questions are typical of those that will be used in Section B of the AS Unit 2 examination paper.

As more and more immigrants, mostly from countries of the Commonwealth, have come to Britain to work since the end of the 1940s, race relations have at times been uneasy and this has sometimes led to social conflict. Changes in the law have been important but we also need changes in attitude, and that is more difficult to bring about.

We need to learn more about other cultures and to ensure that people are more tolerant of others and that racial discrimination is a thing of the past. It is possible for people of different ethnic groups to live in harmony and this can be more easily achieved if people live in ethnically mixed communities. Then it will also be easier to encourage feelings of 'Britishness'.

(1) For what reasons might it be difficult to make people more tolerant of other cultures and to eliminate racial discrimination?   *(17 marks)*

(2) Discuss the difficulties of reaching agreement about what 'being British' and 'Britishness' mean.   *(18 marks)*

Social and economic trends and constraints

Economic issues on a national scale: the workings of business, commerce and industry

It has been said, many years ago, that 'money makes the world go round' and that 'money is the root of all evil'. Part of the reason why we seek to pass examinations and go on to higher education is the hope that, if we get good qualifications, we are more likely to find employment that pays a high salary or good wages. We need money not only to satisfy our basic needs for food, clothing and shelter but to get a good lifestyle.

Just as individuals and families need money, so does the national and international economy. The provision of financial services by various institutions is a major contributor to the success of the British economy. The Treasury is the most important government department, not least because it has to approve the spending plans of other departments. The Bank of England, established in 1694 as the government's banker and debt manager, has been responsible since 1997 for setting interest rates, which are important in helping to determine rewards for saving and the cost of borrowing.

Internationally, globalisation has raised the importance of the world economy and of financial institutions such as the World Bank and the International Monetary Fund. In terms of **gross domestic product (GDP)** per capita, the richest countries are in Europe (Luxembourg, Norway and Switzerland), although in terms of total GDP the USA

Key terms

the World Bank: set up as the International Bank for Reconstruction and Development, it promotes economic development in the world's poorer nations.

the International Monetary Fund: an international organisation with 185 members, first established in 1944. It acts as the main instrument of international monetary management, providing short-term assistance to stabilise currency exchange rates, or correcting difficulties in balance of payments.

gross domestic product (GDP): a measure of economic performance based on the value of all goods and services produced within a nation in a given year.

would lead. Using GDP per capita, the poorest countries, are all in sub-Saharan Africa (Burundi, Democratic Republic of Congo and Ethiopia).

In terms of the economy, everybody is a consumer of goods and services, and many people are likely to be producers of goods and services through their full- or part-time employment. These people may work for a business in the private sector that may be owned by individuals or by shareholders who leave the actual running of the company to managers. Their key goal is to make a profit, which can be used to:

- meet costs such as wages, rent and the purchase of stock
- invest in the development of the business to ensure that more branches can open or the most modern production methods can be used
- reward, through the payment of dividends, the shareholders, who took a risk when they bought shares in the company, the value of which may go up or down

Competition is central to the private sector, with each firm striving to be the most efficient and most competitive in the market place. In the last 20 years, some firms have given a higher priority than before to social responsibility (perhaps helping with community schemes) and environmental awareness.

The other key sector of the economy is the public sector, which is run wholly or mainly by the government or local councils. The public sector includes important areas in public life such as the fire service, policing, education, social services and the National Health Service. Such services will not be able to make a profit but, increasingly, governments and local councils have used strict financial controls to prevent overspending.

Some public services work together with private sector providers and this is an increasing trend in the National Health Service and the prison service. Transport, increasingly in the hands of the private sector, is also a public service. There are often government and council subsidies to keep down fares (helping to encourage the use of public transport and thus limit other traffic on the roads) and to ensure that rural areas, which could never generate sufficient profits, are not left without any public transport service.

The Department of Trade and Industry first emerged in 1970 but underwent a series of changes of name and responsibility, often having a wide range of responsibilities covering business growth, company law, consumer law, employment law, energy, innovation, regional economic development, science, and trade. It was replaced in 2007 by the Department for Business, Enterprise and Regulatory Reform.

The north–south divide

During the industrial revolution of the eighteenth and nineteenth centuries, industries tended to set up close to sources of power and, sometimes, raw materials. Coal was found mainly in parts of northern England, south Wales and the Scottish lowlands, and coal mining was a major industry in these areas until the harsh and violent battles between politicians, the police and miners in the 1970s and 1980s. Both steel and shipbuilding were major industries, typically located in the same geographical areas, and the textile industry centred on parts of Lancashire and Yorkshire.

By the twentieth century, as improvements took place in the supply of gas and electricity, industries were less dependent on an immediate proximity to power, and newer industries often located closer to population centres in the midlands and southeast of England. Foreign competition had intensified by the 1920s and economic depression hit traditional industrial areas, with their scarred landscapes, very badly in the 1930s, although there was some recovery after 1945.

As the UK became less dependent on secondary manufacturing industries and more dependent on freely locating tertiary service industries, there was a greater polarisation between the north and south.

The geographical dividing line between north and south is disputed but it may traditionally be drawn from the River Severn, some way north of Bristol in the west, to the Wash in Lincolnshire in the east. (Quite where the midlands stands has never been entirely clear.) Despite its eligibility for regional aid, the north retains some of the less desirable features of its industrial heritage, although the trend for city-centre living among young professionals has seen the transformation of many city centres, Manchester being one of the most notable, as old buildings are converted into expensive flats.

Manchester's innovative cityscape

The divides are, in fact, cultural, social and political and some may depend to a degree on stereotypes and caricatures. Not least is the picture of northerners of another age with their flat caps, whippets, racing pigeons and black puddings. In the north:

- house prices tend to be cheaper, despite pockets of affluence in parts of Cheshire and North Yorkshire and southern pockets of poverty, particularly in parts of London
- average life expectancy is lower
- voters are traditionally more inclined to support the Labour Party
- wages, prices and the cost of living tend to be lower
- academic achievement tends to be lower and there are fewer independent schools
- problems associated with high alcohol consumption are more extensive
- it is often colder and wetter

Ask the examiner

Q **What is meant by inflation?**

A Inflation is basically a measure of how quickly prices for goods and services are rising. (It uses the consumer price index to produce an average but this does not include mortgage payments.) Such rises often relate to a cycle involving growing demand, expanding businesses, rising costs of resources such as labour because of greater competition for them, rising costs as higher wages and rents are paid, and higher prices then being passed on to consumers, who may or may not wish to buy at those prices depending on the commodity concerned. Price stability is important to ensure economic growth at a sustainable pace and to provide a stable level of employment.

Rising prices may affect people unevenly. (The average increase may be 3% but some people may spend a higher proportion of their income on goods and services where prices are rising more rapidly.) Those who rely on savings will see the value of their savings fall. The lower paid are likely to see prices rising faster than wages. Anyone with a mortgage will feel the impact of rising interest rates quickly. If inflation rises too fast, governments or central banks may seek to take corrective action. Similarly, if prices are stagnant, business confidence might fall and the economy may move towards a more depressed state.

Taxes and National Insurance

Taxes were brought to Britain by the Romans, although income tax as we understand it was introduced in 1799 to meet the escalating costs of war with Napoleon's France. It ceased in 1816, soon after the war ended, but returned on a permanent basis in 1842. Table 12.1 shows the taxes that the government hoped to raise money from in the Budget for 2007–08 (the tax year runs from 6 April in one year to 5 April in the next).

Table 12.1 Tax levels according to the 2007–08 Budget

Tax	Amount raised (£bn)	%
Income tax (workers usually have an income tax allowance on which no tax is paid. There are two progressive tax levels after the allowance: 20% basic rate; 40% higher rate)	157	28.4
National Insurance contributions (most employers, employees and the self-employed pay compulsory NICs, nominally as a contribution to social benefits relating to sickness and unemployment)	95	17.2
Value added tax (a consumer tax charged at 17.5% on supplies of many goods and services, with a 5% rate on some others. A few goods and services are 'zero rated' for VAT)	80	14.5
Corporation tax (charged on the profits and chargeable gains of companies)	50	9.1
Excise duties (charged on goods such as motor fuel, vehicles, alcohol and tobacco)	41	7.4
Council tax (charged by councils on local residents, whose rented/owned properties are put in price bands)	23	4.2
Business rates (charged by councils on business premises)	22	4.0
Other	84	15.2

By comparison, Table 12.2 shows the planned government spending for 2007–08.

Table 12.2 Government spending according to the 2007–08 Budget

Spending area	Amount spent (£bn)	%
Social protection	161	27.4
Health	104	17.7
Education	77	13.1
Public order and safety	33	5.6
Defence	32	5.5
Debt interest	30	5.1
Personal and social services	28	4.8
Housing and environment	22	3.7
Industry, agriculture, employment and training	21	3.6
Transport	20	3.4
Other	59	10.1

The £35 billion gap between anticipated income and planned expenditure is made up by public borrowing and adding to the National Debt.

Credit cards and personal debt

The first **credit card** was issued by Diners Club in 1951 and was accepted by a small number of New York restaurants. The American Express charge card, first introduced in 1958 to cover travel and entertainment charges, was much more widely used, and Barclay's Barclaycard became the UK's first general credit card in 1967. By the 1970s, other British banks had combined to issue the Access credit card, and the Bank Americard, developed in 1958 as the first multi-purpose credit card, became Visa. In 1987 Barclays introduced the first **debit cards**. In 2003, chip and PIN (Personal Identification Number) trials began for greater security, and gradually customer signatures were phased out and replaced by PIN numbers.

Credit card issuers are regularly accused of:

- reckless lending, offering credit to people who will not be in a position to repay what they have spent
- charging excessively high interest rates to people who fail to repay what they have spent within the specified period

Viewpoints

The advantages and disadvantages of credit cards

Advantages of credit cards

- They can offer interest-free use of funds providing debt is repaid by the specified date.
- They are more convenient to carry around than cash.
- They provide a means of payment for goods bought over the internet or telephone.
- There is less chance of being robbed.
- They can help people to build up a good credit history, which is advantageous when seeking to borrow money or secure a mortgage.
- Some banks donate a percentage of each individual's spending to a charity.
- They are widely accepted around the world, and are more secure than travellers' cheques.
- They usually have some sort of protection against fraud.

Disadvantages of credit cards

- Debts quickly accumulate.
- Cardholders are likely to spend more.
- High interest rates mean that they cost more than many other forms of credit if debts are not repaid on time.
- Although security is improving with developments like chip and PIN, the danger of fraud is always present.
- They have complicated terms and conditions.
- Credit ratings are easily damaged if payments are late or debts accumulate.

For the first time, the free and independent advice charity Citizens Advice reported in 2007 that debt was the leading source of enquiry, even ahead of welfare rights and benefits. A declaration of bankruptcy, despite its implications for the future, is increasingly becoming the main escape route from pressing creditors. Other people get caught up in a labyrinth of loans, often at punitive interest rates, so that they can meet day-to-day living costs. The consumer society we live in invariably creates more accute problems for the lower paid, especially those in less secure forms of employment, or for those already burdened by debts accumulated while students.

Impact of political and economic issues on science, society and the environment

The nuclear power debate

Substances are made up of a large number of very tiny particles known as atoms. Some substances, such as hydrogen, oxygen and uranium, consist of only one kind of atom. Such substances are known as elements. Other substances contain two or more kinds of atom joined together in groups (in the way that water contains atoms of hydrogen and oxygen joined together). Atoms themselves are collections of even smaller particles — electrons, protons and neutrons. In the structure of an atom, the neutrons and protons are packed together in the atom's central part, the nucleus, which the electrons orbit around.

The ability to change one substance into another eluded scientists for many years. The breakthrough was made by Nobel Prize winner Ernest Rutherford after the end of the First World War. It was observed that if a radioactive material such as radium was placed in a sealed box of air, small amounts of hydrogen would appear.

Rutherford realised that in the presence of powerful radioactive rays, nitrogen turns into hydrogen and oxygen.

Alpha particles produced by the radium embedded themselves within the nuclei of nitrogen atoms while expelling single protons. What remained was an oxygen nucleus. The protons were nuclei of hydrogen. What was needed was for the nuclei to build up the necessary number of electrons and they would become atoms of the respective gases. Now the capacity to change one element into another through such nuclear reactions is regarded as routine.

Viewpoints

Against nuclear power

Nuclear power has a controversial record for four main reasons:
- It is a powerful and deadly weapon of war, capable of causing great damage to any of its targets.
- It is associated with potential accidents, although few have been on the scale of Chernobyl in Ukraine in 1986. There a combination of a poorly designed reactor and operational errors led to a steam explosion, and fire released at least 5% of the radioactive core into the atmosphere. This resulted in 28 deaths in a short period from radiation or thermal burns, and sent a radioactive cloud over Europe.
- It is difficult to deal effectively with nuclear waste.
- An attack on a nuclear power station as a terrorist target could have a devastating impact.

The first nuclear power plant to generate electricity was located at Obninsk in Russia, but the first commercial nuclear power station opened at Calder Hall in Cumbria in 1956. The UK now has a number of nuclear power stations, but most are quite old and there are concerns about their safety, especially as it is predicted that cracks in fuel moderator bricks will threaten the safety functions of the graphite cores in stations such as Hinkley Point and Hunterston in Scotland. According to British Energy, cracking has also occurred in boiler tubes at Hinkley Point, although repairing these is a less challenging engineering problem.

Both stations were closed temporarily in 2006. Both of them are over 30 years old — a period usually looked upon as the lifetime of a nuclear power station. However, the plants provide 6% of Britain's electricity and, with demand continuing to rise, and the stations generating large amounts of revenue for the company, British Energy is hoping for a 10-year extension. In 2005 only one of British Energy's eight nuclear power stations was fully operational. (Other plants are managed by the state-owned British Nuclear Fuels.)

Nuclear power: the clean fuel for the twenty-first century?

There is support for the construction of a new generation of nuclear power stations in the UK — not least from British Energy, which may join up with its French equivalent, EDF (with companies like E.ON UK and RWE also said to be interested) — particularly in view of:

- the rapidly ageing existing capacity
- the insatiable demand for electricity
- the key fact that nuclear-generated electricity does not produce climate-damaging CO_2
- increasing threats of stricter EU controls on CO_2 emissions

Gas and coal generate 70% of UK electricity but produce much more CO_2 than the nuclear option (leading to more global warming), and this is a key political factor in the debate. France generates about 75% of its electricity from nuclear sources, and in the USA nuclear power is the second most used source after coal. It is estimated that nuclear power produces nearly 20% of the world's electricity and the USA has about 25% of the world's nuclear power plants.

Although the 2003 energy White Paper had promised 'the fullest public consultation' prior to any decision to develop nuclear power further, a recent government energy review was successfully challenged by Greenpeace (one of many diverse interest groups with a wide range of views on how best to secure future power supplies) on the grounds that it was heavily predisposed to the nuclear power option. In a scathing High Court judgement, Mr Justice Sullivan quashed the government's plans for a new generation of nuclear power plants as 'unlawful' and ruled that the consultation exercise was 'seriously flawed'.

Insufficient information was made available to potential objectors, especially in key areas such as financing the new stations and disposal of waste. A new White Paper is expected to set out the UK's future power generating plans and may take a more diverse approach, perhaps placing more emphasis on renewable sources such as wind, wave and tidal power and biomass (plant matter used for biofuel), but even these have proved controversial, particularly in the case of wind power.

Unquestionably, the planning process needs speeding up. Objectors can use public enquiries to delay projects for years (as they did with Sizewell B), especially as the problem of the long-term disposal of high-level waste remains unresolved. Even if the approval process can be streamlined, it is unlikely that the first of the new plants, which will be water-cooled rather than gas-cooled as at present, will emerge before 2017, although potential power shortages are anticipated from 2015 or earlier.

The construction of Sizewell B nuclear power station took 7 years before its completion in 1995

Early in 2008, after 4 years of argument, it was reported that the cabinet had backed plans to invest in a new generation of 10 nuclear power plants. The aim is to reduce dependency on imported gas and oil and to generate more than 20% of Britain's electricity from nuclear sites. Even with planning permission, nuclear power stations take many years to build. It seems likely that, in future, the government will seek to limit inquiries into the safety or economics of nuclear power, but continued opposition from the anti-nuclear lobby seems inevitable.

Disposing of nuclear waste

Radioactive waste is generated by the use of radioactive materials in medicine and industry, and by controlled fission in nuclear power stations. It may also be produced by Britain's nuclear weapons or by nuclear-powered submarines. Radioactive waste comes in three forms: high-level, intermediate-level and low-level. Deep disposal of high-level waste has been on the political agenda for at least 30 years without a satisfactory solution emerging, and the government is currently looking for a site for a deep storage bunker. The difficulty of dealing with nuclear waste is one of the major obstacles to its further use and development.

It is estimated that current amounts of high-level waste fill a volume of about 80,000 cubic metres and weigh about 100,000 tons. However, because of anticipated decommissioning of some of the older power stations, it is estimated that the volume will increase significantly in the twenty-first century.

High-level waste is particularly problematic because its temperature can rise significantly because of radioactivity. It comprises waste products from the reprocessing of nuclear fuel, which must be converted from a liquid to a solid by a process of vitrification.

At present there is no coherent disposal plan and temporary measures are in place involving short-term storage and shallow disposal of low-level waste. Predictably, the level of public opposition to any sites identified by Nirex was so fierce that they were abandoned. It was a classic example of the NIMBY (Not In My Back Yard) syndrome.

In 2003, the government appointed a committee made up of representatives from a number of organisations, including the pressure group Greenpeace which is opposed to nuclear power. In 2007, the committee published its report, which contained a list of 15 disposal options. These included launching the waste on rockets and burying it in polar ice sheets — a less feasible possibility given the likely impact of global warming. The most likely option remains some form of deep burial.

Nuclear power offers many possibilities, but there remain huge obstacles for politicians in terms of:
- the operation of the NIMBY syndrome
- memories of the horrors of Chernobyl
- fear of a terrorist strike
- the availability of relatively plentiful alternative power-generating sources such as gas and electricity
- the possibilities offered by renewable sources of energy generation
- cost and the long time span involved in developing nuclear facilities

Viewpoints

The advantages and disadvantages of nuclear power

Advantages
- Nuclear power stations do not burn fossil fuels to produce electricity so they do not produce smoke or carbon dioxide, therefore they do not contribute to global warming.
- They produce significant amounts of energy from small amounts of fuel.
- Nuclear power is reliable and less subject to interference or interruption by other factors.

- Supporters claim that nuclear power is environmentally friendly and clean and, with world demand for electricity rising rapidly, nuclear power is one of the few ways of protecting the environment.
- It reduces reliance on oil from suppliers in politically unstable parts of the world.
- France has helped to show that it is worth investing in a large-scale, strategic programme to produce much of the country's electricity from nuclear power.

Disadvantages

- Difficulties of storing nuclear waste have not been overcome.
- A lot of money has to be spent on safety factors.
- Nuclear power does not always enjoy public confidence and backing it may not be a popular political option.
- There is a fear of serious accidents and potentially serious consequences if radiation leaks.
- Politically unstable countries might acquire or develop nuclear weapons and could use them to create global instability.
- The investment required is considerable and it takes a long time to build modern nuclear power stations.

Practice questions

The following source and questions are typical of those that will be used in Section B of the AS Unit 2 examination paper.

In France, nuclear power is widely used for the generation of electricity. In the UK, governments have been more cautious. Using nuclear power is a complex process and not without its risks, but it does not lead to the emission of harmful gases in the way that burning fossil fuels does.

The horrors of Chernobyl live on, but that was a one-off. The reality is that the demand for electricity is increasing rapidly and we cannot carry on polluting the atmosphere by continuing to rely on using coal and gas to generate increased supplies. The answer is to ignore the objectors and generate more electricity by investing in the cleaner and more efficient use of nuclear power.

(1) Outline the process of using nuclear power to generate electricity.   *(17 marks)*

(2) Explain why the use of nuclear power in the UK leads to protests and objections.   *(18 marks)*

Understanding of scientific methods, principles, criteria and their application

The nature and use of scientific method and investigation

Scientific method involves a series of logical and rational steps that allow scientists to organise their thoughts, to test them and to reach conclusions. Definitions of what constitutes 'scientific method' may vary, but it is likely that the key stages will include the following:

- Everyone must have a starting point based on the area of science involved and the particular interest of the scientist concerned. This will be narrowed down so that a question in the relevant area of science can be defined. Preliminary research will then take place using whatever sources are available, ideally using as many as possible.

- Scientists, or a group of scientists, need to formulate a logical hypothesis that can be tested using experimental methods — and here their skill, experience or innovative thinking may be a key factor in helping to shape scientific advance. The hypothesis is a way of setting out what the outcome of an experiment might be, perhaps expressed in a single sentence that might be a question.

- Scientists must approach and carry out scientific tasks in an objective manner to reduce the likelihood of bias in the methods, thinking or results. The key principle is that scientific knowledge should be value-free. Scientists may have a preference for a particular outcome and must seek to ensure that the preference does not bias their interpretation.

- Scientists design experimental studies to test hypotheses. The experiment is central to scientific method, and scientists may seek to perform as many different experiments on their subject as possible.

- Researchers collect data through observation and experimentation. This will be done in a systematic and careful manner, measuring relevant quantities where appropriate. Measurements might be undertaken in a controlled setting, perhaps in a laboratory, with measurements properly tabulated and recorded; specialised scientific equipment might be used. The data collected will need to be interpreted.

- The steps are repeated in order to predict future results from evidence and to reach a conclusion that may support or reject the original hypothesis. This might be done to test the prediction further and to see how far the hypothesis is matched by results, bearing in mind that time and other resources will inevitably be limited.

- The findings are published so that data and methodology can be shared with, and scrutinised by, other members of the scientific community with similar interests. This allows peer review to take place, which gives other scientists an opportunity to identify research flaws or mistakes in the findings.

- Scientists accept that scientific research is an ongoing process. They constantly seek refinement and perhaps allow for more accurate and comprehensive models to be formulated.

Millions of people use homeopathic medicines worldwide

Is homeopathy good science?

Controversy always surrounds different forms of complementary, or alternative, medicine. One of the most fiercely contested areas is homeopathy, which has existed for at least 200 years. It follows the work of Dr Samuel Hahnemann in Germany, who was looking for an alternative to radical and ineffective practices such as bloodletting. Supporters now claim that many more people are turning to homeopathic methods when they feel that conventional medicine has failed, perhaps because of side effects, or because they prefer what they consider to be a more 'natural' approach to treatment.

There are about 4,000 registered homeopaths in the UK and five homeopathic departments in hospitals funded by the National Health Service (NHS). Homeopathy is said to focus as much on the individual as the disease. It was estimated that in 2006 over 20% of people in the UK bought homeopathic or herbal remedies; millions of people use homeopathic remedies worldwide. While some NHS doctors are broadly supportive of alternative medicines, others are more sceptical or dismissive.

Unlike conventional drugs, homeopathic remedies use raw materials from the plant, animal or mineral kingdoms. They are used to treat a variety of illnesses, and patients are given small, diluted doses. The theory is that these tiny doses will help to stimulate the body's own healing powers — tiny dilutions of the 'problem' help the body to produce its own cure. Crucially, this may take place without the unwelcome side effects of many conventional medicines.

Viewpoints

The critics and supporters of homeopathy

Critics

Although homeopathy has many supporters, it also has a number of critics:

- There are doctors and scientists who are sceptical because conventional medicine relies on stronger, more concentrated doses. Homeopathic remedies are so diluted that it may be difficult to see how they can be effective.
- They are critical of the lack of clinical data to support the homeopathic case. Conventional medicines are subjected to rigorous safety trials, often referred to as controlled clinical trials, before they are licensed; and the results of the trials are published and subjected to critical scrutiny. Homeopathy cannot be explained precisely.
- Doubt is expressed over the qualifications of some of those involved in homeopathic medicine, and the possibilities of fraud are often raised.
- It is widely argued that the 'placebo effect' (sometimes described as a psychobiological phenomenon) is important (those given a harmless and ineffective treatment at the same time as others are given the approved homeopathic remedy might still claim that the treatment has worked in relieving or removing their symptoms). It is claimed that scientific reviews of homeopathy repeatedly conclude that homeopathic remedies do not produce outcomes that are significantly different to those of placebos. Patients may improve but for reasons unconnected with the homeopathic medicines recommended.

Supporters

Supporters of homeopathy make the following claims:

- Homeopathic remedies are available at relatively low production costs, and the cost of dealing with side effects is avoided. (St John's wort is often compared to conventional anti-depressants, many of which have undesirable side effects.)
- Conventional medicine does not sufficiently address the wider needs of each individual.
- Homeopathic remedies are unlikely to be dominated by global drug companies with a powerful vested interest in raising profits.

- Drug companies are often involved in financing biomedical research and may seek to use their power, influence and resources to influence the media to report sceptically or adversely, perhaps portraying complementary remedies as 'quack medicine'.
- Drug companies claim that the costs of their products are high because they require intensive research and development. However, they may also seek to keep costs artificially high, increasing their profits while giving the NHS higher bills.
- The real nature of the placebo effect is unknown and it is common practice to use placebos in controlled clinical trials.
- The placebo effect is overstated because homeopathic remedies may work on babies or animals. It is difficult to explain how either would be conscious of being treated at all.
- Bias or vested interest may still play a part in what are said to be objective and controlled clinical trials. Emphasis may be placed on more positive outcomes. Some drugs that are marketed have to be withdrawn later because of harmful side effects.
- Controlled clinical trials (CCTs) cannot guarantee the safety of drugs that are being tested. A CCT may not show how individual patients might react to a particular drug or course of treatment.
- Homeopathy is more likely to be beneficial to patients emotionally as well as physically.

Technology in contemporary society and description of underlying scientific principles

Mobile phones

Mobile radio telephones were brought into use in vehicles used for emergency services in the 1940s, but the first cellphone, developed by Martin Cooper of Motorola, did not emerge until 1973. Cellphones, commonly known as mobile phones, are radio telephones that contain a radio transmitter for sending radio signals and a radio receiver for incoming signals from other phones.

Cellphones route their calls through a network of masts linked to the main telephone system. Early mobiles used analogue technology (in which vibrations produce an analogy of a voice). Modern cellphones use digital technology (turning voice sounds into a pattern of numbers, or digits, which are beamed through the air). Digital technology means that computerised data can be sent or received — hence the development of multi-system mobiles.

- Whereas land lines are based on a direct, wired connection between two handsets, cellphones use electromagnetic radio waves — a type of electromagnetic field (EMF) — to send and receive calls.

- A tiny microphone in the handset converts voice sounds into a pattern of electrical signals. A microchip then converts these signals into strings of numbers.
- The numbers are aggregated into a radio wave and beamed out from the phone's antenna (sometimes called 'base station'). The radio wave moves at the speed of light until it reaches the nearest cellphone mast.
- Cellphone masts are important because the radio transmitters and receivers cannot send their signals very far as they are not sufficiently high-powered. Cellphone masts are very high-powered and can route calls from cellphones onwards to their intended recipient.
- Geographical areas are divided up into smaller areas, known as cells (hence the term 'cellular'), each having its own mast. Each cell has a transmitter and receiver station.
- Each mobile phone communicates with a cell station by sending out a microwave signal in the radio frequency end of the spectrum. An uploader at the station sends information to another station once a connection has been made.
- Because radio waves only reach limited distances, a network of many base stations has to be established, each providing radio coverage for a particular area (base stations are more numerous in urban areas to deal with the volume of calls).
- The cells enable the system to handle a great many calls at once because each cell uses the same set of frequencies as neighbouring cells.
- The mast receives the signals and passes them to an exchange. Calls made to a cellphone on a different network or to a landline have to be routed in to the main telephone network.

Viewpoints

Advantages of mobile phones

They:
- provide instant communication in a fast-moving society
- assist safety, in communicating between parents and children or with road assistance or emergency services
- frequently provide a wide range of communication services (e.g. radio, e-mail)
- are a fashion accessory for many young people
- are relatively inexpensive — competition has brought down prices
- are easily recycled and many charity shops accept unwanted mobiles
- develop new industry, helping to provide additional employment
- are helpful in less economically developed countries where there is a limited infrastructure of landlines
- can be used, through call records, as criminal evidence in police investigations

Disadvantages of mobile phones

- There are unconfirmed health concerns linking the use of mobile phones to the development of brain tumours.
- Masts can be unsightly and are also associated with possible health hazards.
- Some mobiles are particularly desirable, and this may lead to increased crime rates in terms of theft and assaults.
- Calls are expensive compared to the cost of landline calls.
- They can be irritating when used in public places such as railway carriages.
- There is uneven coverage in some parts of the country.
- There is a growing incidence of text bullying.
- Drivers are tempted to use hand-held mobiles when driving, although this is illegal.
- Phones are frequently discarded for newer models, leading to problems of disposal.

Practice questions

The following source and questions are typical of those that will be used in Section B of the AS Unit 2 examination paper.

Not many people realised the potential of mobile phones. The early ones were not always reliable and were expensive, cumbersome and heavy. Yet technology developed quickly and what was once a curiosity has now become almost indispensable.

In 20 years, mobile phones have gone from luxury to necessity and their spread has been nothing short of remarkable. It has brought convenience and advantages to the world, making communication between people easier and faster. However, the disadvantages associated with the fast-growing technology cannot be ignored. These problems not only affect people personally but they also have wider implications for society.

(1) Describe how mobile phones work.   *(17 marks)*

(2) Discuss the advantages and disadvantages of the rapid spread of the use of mobile phones.   *(18 marks)*

The nature of scientific objectivity and the question of progress

Scientific research and development

Scientists are human beings rather than boffins hidden away in a laboratory and, as human beings, they are subject to the same influences as non-scientists. They will have their own beliefs and values, perhaps believing in a particular set of religious teachings, or supporting a political party, or following the fortunes of their favourite sports team. Scientists will also experience emotions in the same way that non-scientists do, and all these factors may play some part in what they choose to research.

- To avoid the dangers of a subjective approach or interpretation, scientists may seek to use standardised measuring tools or instruments, expressing the results in an agreed, scientific way.

- The testing becomes independent from the scientist and the aim is to seek results that are both verifiable and have reproducibility in ways that can be recognised and understood by other scientists.

- Scientists like to move from a tentative and untested explanation (hypothesis) to an experiment, perhaps repeated several times under specified conditions, and then to a theory that makes reliable predictions based on their observations.

- Theories are the best explanations available and will need to be demonstrated to fellow scientists for close scrutiny.

- Theories might be overturned by further critical experiments so that new theories are advanced. In this way, scientific progress takes place as better and more reliable theories emerge and, in some way, the lives of people may be improved.

Scientists pursuing the same objective may end up with different sets of data

- In experiments, scientists may observe and measure different variables and then seek to establish the extent to which there might be correlations between them. In that way, the number of cigarettes smoked and the time period over which smoking had taken place was used to show a correlation between smoking and lung cancer (or the extent to which the lungs can recover if an individual stops smoking).
- In other experiments, a scientist might change one variable (the independent variable) so that the effect of that change can be measured.
- Scientific enquiry depends on reasoning. Most people distinguish between two types of reasoning, deductive and inductive:
  - Deductive reasoning is often summed up as moving from general principles to specific conclusions: the process of reasoning logically from given premises to a conclusion.
  - Inductive reasoning is usually summed up as moving from the specific to the general, often based on experience or observation.
- Observation and recording are always important in scientific method but scientists have to make initial decisions about the parameters of their study and the most appropriate form of methodology.
- Scientists may be called upon to make assumptions or interpretations, and scientists pursuing the same objective may end up with different sets of data. In this way, scientists debate their findings with their peers and legitimate controversy may arise.
- Much may depend on whether a scientist is seeking to support or add to a theory or to challenge it. Often results may be inconclusive so that interpretation becomes important and, though scientists may have made every effort to conduct their work objectively, it is not impossible for a scientist's own beliefs and values, consciously or otherwise, to play a part in that interpretation.
- Research may be costly and it is always important to ask if there is any degree of vested interest in seeking a particular outcome and if this might be a threat to the integrity of the research.
- Peer review, where other scientists pass judgements on research, might be intense or it might be limited by time pressures or limited funding. Perhaps the reviewers are colleagues of the scientist concerned. Perhaps they are competitors. Their decisions might help or hinder publication of the work in a particular scientific journal.
- Errors may occur at any stage and are likely to be unintentional. It is always possible that deliberate falsification of results might take place and that the scientist concerned will, if the fraud is detected, become completely discredited.

- The motives for such falsification of results might include some form of financial gain or the hope that the scientist concerned will gain the acclaim of other members of the scientific community if undetected.
- Our knowledge of the extent of any malpractice is confined to the very few occasions when falsification is discovered.

Ask the examiner

Q

Can we trust scientists?

A

Just as questions are asked about the relationship between political parties and those who donate money to help fund them, questions will be asked about the extent to which scientists depend on pharmaceutical companies to fund what is often extremely costly research that, if successful, might be of considerable benefit to the companies concerned.

Scientists cannot predict the final result of their work. They have a hypothesis and they are aware of the direction that they wish to go in but, until they have gone through some rigorous research practices, they cannot reach conclusions. Genuine errors are always possible and falsification, or the selective use of evidence, cannot be ruled out. However, scientists are only as good as the integrity used to produce their work and the reputations that they build. If they are discredited they are ruined professionally.

It is probably impossible that anybody can fail to be influenced by some part of their life or upbringing, but scientists strive for objectivity in their research methods and are aware that, if they do make what appears to be a significant breakthrough (say, in the treatment of a disease), their work and research methods will be scrutinised rigorously by their peers.

Developments in computer technology

- Put at its simplest, a computer is a programmable electronic device that can store, retrieve and process data. In the first half of the nineteenth century, the Englishman Charles Babbage is credited with the design of the first prototype computer, but the building stage never got beyond a few parts.
- Much of the inventiveness of the succeeding years was directed towards various forms of calculators, with American inventors well to the fore.
- A century after Babbage another Englishman, Alan Turing, was exploring the nature and potential development of human and computer intelligence.
- The first commercially successful electronic computer (UNIVAL), designed to handle both numeric and textual information, did not appear until after 1950 and, by the mid-1950s, it was unlikely that there were more than a few hundred very large computers in the world, used largely for scientific and military purposes.

- Between 1959 and 1964, what were known as second-generation computers emerged. These were based on transistors (tiny devices which amplified electronic signals) and printed circuits (small boards).
- The so-called third generation of computers is usually associated with Jack St Clair Kilby's invention of the integrated circuit (microchip), which had begun to appear in computers by 1963. This led to the development of the minicomputer.
- In the early 1970s, Marcian Hoff's invention of the microprocessor (which placed all the circuits on a silicon chip) heralded the fourth generation of computers, and the more efficient use of chips enabled computers to be even smaller and faster than before.
- Home computers began to be more common in the 1970s, especially with the release of Apple II in 1977, accompanied by the emergence of specialist computer magazines. By the 1980s IBM had entered the personal computer market, and in 1984 Apple launched the Macintosh.
- It was in the early 1980s when the internet — a network connecting many computer networks — was first established to allow academics in some of the world's universities to share data. The system was transformed through the work of Tim Berners-Lee and his colleagues at CERN, the European Centre for Particle Physics in Geneva. Berners-Lee launched his proposal for a global hypertext project to be known as the World Wide Web, operating over the internet, in 1989.
- By the end of 1992 there were only some 50 websites in the world. Berners-Lee was particularly anxious that the web should be available for all users and, in 1994, decided that the World Wide Web should be available to users free of royalties.
- The CD-ROM emerged in 1982, allowing computers to use digital sound and video images. Increasingly it took on a wider multimedia purpose as desktop computers with built-in stereo speakers became more common. Microsoft's Windows 3.0 operating system appeared in 1990, to be superseded by Windows 95 5 years later.
- By the end of the twentieth century more personal computers included USB (Universal Serial Bus) ports for easy connection to digital and video cameras, printers and scanners and, soon afterwards, DVD players.
- Other new developments included WiFi (Wireless Fidelity — a method of transmitting data over a wireless network allowing connections to the internet at broadband speeds without cables) and LCD (Liquid Crystal Display) monitors.

Few could have anticipated the massive impact that constantly developing information technology would have for data storage, retrieval and dissemination, advertising, leisure and the computer games industry, social networking, financial transactions and retailing. Although the so-called 'dot-com boom' between 1999 and 2001 was short-lived, some names are almost as prominent in the public mind as those of the major supermarkets. These include the Google search engine, the Ebay auction site, Amazon retailing, the social networking sites YouTube, Facebook and MySpace, and the phenomenally successful Bill Gates, whose Microsoft Company, which developed the Windows system, is now 30 years old.

The homeworking/teleworking revolution

Traditionally, since the industrial revolution, people have travelled to work. For those who work in London this has often meant commuting long distances, either by car or public transport, because of the price of housing. As ever more people have equipped themselves with personal computers in their own homes, and particularly with the wider availability of high-speed broadband connections, an increasing number of people work from home for either the whole or part of the week. It is estimated that over 10% of the UK workforce operate from home, many of whom are teleworkers who are able to connect to a corporate network by using smartphones, personal digital assistants (PDAs) and laptops. Numbers are growing rapidly.

It is estimated that over 10% of the UK workforce operate from home

Viewpoints

Advantages and disadvantages of homeworking for employers

Advantages

- It may be easier to recruit workers who have the option of being able to work from home for some, or all, of the week.
- It may be easier to retain workers, particularly those with childcare responsibilities.
- Employees may be more productive away from the distractions of the workplace.
- Staff might be better motivated, leading to less time off for illness.
- There might be savings on office space, equipment and other facilities.
- It is relatively easy to arrange video conferencing.
- Employers can allow employees to maintain social contacts via sites such as Facebook.

Disadvantages

- It may be more difficult to manage and monitor the performance of employees.
- Employers do not always trust homeworkers.
- Health and safety responsibilities may be more difficult to exercise.
- Home computers may be less secure than an office-based system, especially if sensitive information is not encrypted.
- Communication is more difficult.
- Homeworkers may become less motivated.
- Homeworkers are no longer part of a team-based approach.
- Homeworking may result in the deterioration of an employee's skills and work quality.

Advantages and disadvantages of working at home for employees

Advantages

- Working at home can be far less stressful and tiring, especially if commuting to a workplace entails a long and frustrating journey.
- Physical and mental health may improve as a result of eliminating the strains of commuting and less contact with employees who may be suffering from illnesses that are easily spread.
- Not having to travel to work can mean more time with the family.
- There is potential saving on hidden costs associated with going to work, such as more formal work clothes, fares or petrol costs, parking, possibly childcare arrangements.
- There are far fewer distractions working from home.
- The working environment can be personalised.
- Work hours can often be more flexible and work can be arranged around family commitments. Homeworkers are able to work at their own pace. Home-based employers can be more productive.
- Homeworking can be advantageous for disabled workers.

Disadvantages

- Many homeworkers begin to feel isolated and lonely when they withdraw from the office environment. They miss the everyday contact, camaraderie, gossip and inter-action with colleagues. Loneliness can turn into depression.
- Homeworkers are divorced from work developments and may find it more difficult to gain promotion.
- Those still working in an office environment may be envious, sceptical or even hostile to colleagues who have an 'easy life' working from home.
- Fewer opportunities to meet people may reinforce the sense of isolation.
- Homeworking requires considerable self-discipline and personal motivation. Not everyone can work to their own timetable and homeworkers can end up doing too much or too little work. Independence also involves responsibility.

- There may be different sorts of distractions at home — perhaps from young children or an elderly relative.
- Working uses up space in the home and can make a house feel either smaller or more cluttered.
- It is not always easy to separate home from work. Homeworkers might be inclined to break off for socialising, shopping, cooking and cleaning.
- Less skilled workers in particular may be underpaid and exploited, often working below the current adult minimum wage of £5.52 per hour.
- People working at home usually have to meet energy costs.

Practice questions

The following source and questions are typical of those that will be used in Section B of the AS Unit 2 examination paper.

Much has changed in recent years about the way data is collected, stored and received. Space, and time-consuming paper files have gone. Rapid developments in technology have transformed the situation. Computer files dominate the ways in which information is stored and it can be retrieved at the touch of a keyboard.

Yet increasingly, many people are concerned about the amount of personal information that is stored and its possible loss and misuse. There is talk of the emergence of a 'surveillance society', almost as if technology has developed at a quicker rate than humans are dealing with its consequences.

(1) **Examine the ways in which developments in information technology have changed the ways in which businesses and government agencies can use and store information about individuals.** *(17 marks)*

(2) **How far do you feel the existence of a 'surveillance society' is justified?** *(18 marks)*

Data collection and the surveillance society

Ever since George Orwell's warning about 'Big Brother' in his 1948 novel *Nineteen Eighty-Four*, concerns have been raised about the extent to which the agencies of the state should legitimately gather and hold information about individual citizens.

However, it was widely assumed that surveillance and 'intelligence gathering' was limited to the military and that 'phone tapping' by the police or security services was rare and carefully regulated. The world of state informers was often associated with the apparatus of totalitarian spying regimes and state bureaucracies associated with countries such as the former East Germany before the downfall of the Eastern Bloc — and shown so effectively in the highly acclaimed 2007 film *The Lives of Others*.

Things have changed, partly because of the fear of terrorism and other forms of serious crime and partly because of rapid and sophisticated advances in technology. Methods of surveillance have increased and a mass of personal information is held on government databases, and the level of surveillance looks set to rise and become even more pervasive.

The right of access to information and the conditions under which it can be acquired, stored, shared and disposed of are governed largely by the 1998 Data Protection Act and the Freedom of Information Act of 2000. These Acts are now the responsibility of the Ministry of Justice and the Information Commissioner, who heads the UK's independent supervisory authority reporting directly to Parliament. The Commissioner also promotes access to official information.

In 2004 the Commissioner warned of the dangers of 'sleepwalking into a surveillance society'. By 2006, in launching the highly detailed and informative *Report on the Surveillance Society* from the Surveillance Studies Network, he felt we might be waking up to one. The report raises important questions about the balance between security and essential information on the one hand and personal freedom and privacy on the other.

Surveillance techniques

Closed-circuit television (CCTV) cameras are used to monitor buildings, city centres, parking areas, shopping malls, residential areas and roads. There are no statutory safeguards relating to CCTV cameras but it is estimated that there are over 4 million in Britain and that, in some areas like city centres, a person can be captured on camera several hundred times per day.

Digitisation has led to automatic CCTV systems that can recognise vehicle number plates. Speed cameras, regularly criticised as an easy device for raising revenue rather than a means of promoting safer driving, raise over £100 million per year in fines.

Geographical information systems can track the movements of people, often by using radio-frequency identification (RFID) chips, the Global Positioning System (GPS) or the triangulation of radio signals transmitted by mobile phones — all of which have potential advantages for law enforcement. Electronic monitoring (tagging) is used as part of early-release or parole schemes that might ease the pressure on prison places, and RFID has also been used more recently in schemes to microchip animals and pets.

Databases

Once there was an overwhelming reliance on files and other paper-based systems. The spread of the computer database has completely revolutionised the ways in which information can be gathered, stored and cross-referenced, allowing for much speedier access in both the public and private sectors.

DNA database

The 2003 Criminal Justice Act allowed the police to take both the fingerprints and a DNA sample from anyone arrested. The records, accessible via the police national computer, will remain on the DNA database irrespective of whether or not the person concerned is charged. It is estimated that the database contains over 3 million samples, with a disproportionate number being of African-Caribbean origin. The DNA database was not discussed in Parliament. Police databases are also used for criminal record checks, which are compulsory for those seeking jobs involving the care of the young or vulnerable.

Driver and Vehicle Licensing Agency (DVLA)

The DVLA has a database of vehicles registered for use on the road and of the estimated 42 million driving licence holders. By maintaining a database of drivers and vehicles, the DVLA can help to promote road safety and enforce the law. In addition it collects vehicle excise duty (road tax). In 2007 the Transport Secretary, Ruth Kelly, disclosed that a computer disk containing the names, addresses and phone numbers of 3 million driving test applicants had gone missing. It was lost by the Iowa-based Pearson Driving Assessments, a contractor to the Driving Standards Agency.

National Health Records

The government plans to develop an IT system that will allow for the transfer and uploading of each individual's medical records to a national database; the NHS programme, *Connecting for Health*, is the largest in Europe. Plans for electronic patient records represent an extremely ambitious scheme, which has led to concerns being expressed about data security and rights of access to potentially sensitive information. Richard Jeavons, director of IT implementation for the NHS, admitted to the House of Commons Home Affairs Committee that no system could offer complete protection against the activities of 'the wicked'. The loss of personal health records by nine separate health trusts and hospitals, revealed at the end of 2007, only served to create further concerns.

The Home Office

This government department operates the world's biggest DNA database (covering over 5% of the population) and it is also responsible for the Identity and Passport Service with its passport database, which holds the travel details relating to passport holders.

HM Revenue and Customs

The Customs Service and the Inland Revenue merged to form this department, which is responsible for the nation's taxation records. In November 2007 a major potential information breach occurred when two disks disappeared in transit between HM Revenue and Customs and the National Audit Office. The two disks contained the names and personal details (including bank accounts) of everyone in receipt of child benefit — over 7 million families and 25 million individuals. It is thought that one of three carriers might have been used but, despite extensive police searches, the whereabouts of the disks remains unknown. Should the disks fall into the wrong hands, the potential for fraud seems unlimited.

Consumer databases

Each time we use items such as credit and debit cards or the loyalty cards distributed by major supermarkets such as Tesco and Sainsbury's we provide data on our spending and shopping habits. Marketing profiles are easily built up by combining this with other data (e.g. post codes indicating what sort of area we live in). 'Desirable' targets (high spenders in affluent areas) can be targeted and 'undesirable' targets (poor credit risks in high-crime areas) can be filtered out. The extent to which this sort of information is shared is uncertain and the explosion in internet shopping has exposed many more people to identity fraud.

Biometrics and ID cards

Biometric identifiers (iris scans, digital fingerprinting, facial scans, voice **biometrics** and hand scans) have all been identified with more secure systems of passports or identity cards to meet concerns about credit card fraud, illegal immigrant labour, border controls and, particularly, terrorism. Certainly biometrics are central to government plans, announced by Tony Blair in 2005, to reintroduce identity cards, used during the Second World War as protection against German spies but abandoned by the Conservatives in 1952. They were tolerated in wartime but felt to be unnecessary in peacetime.

Timetable

December 2008 — compulsory ID cards launched for foreign nationals from outside the EU entering the UK.

December 2009 — ID cards available for some UK citizens involved in 'sensitive' occupations, e.g. airport workers.

December 2010 — ID cards available for young people and public sector workers in a position of trust.

2011–2012 — wider implementation based on details of all passport renewals are entered on national ID database.

Viewpoints

Arguments for ID cards
- They can be a deterrent to terrorism and other serious crimes. Terrorists frequently depend on false identities, as do drug traffickers and those involved in international money-laundering activities.
- ID cards would make it easier to identify illegal immigrants. They would make it easier to check whether a job applicant is legally entitled to work. The same would apply to entitlement to social security.
- They would help to protect against the rapidly growing problem of identity fraud, which currently costs the UK economy £1.3 billion a year.
- They would give people a greater sense of security and might help to promote a shared feeling of citizenship and belonging.
- The government is responding to wider global trends involving the use of biometric techniques in the development of ID cards.
- There are potential cost savings, by reducing spending on dealing with illegal immigration and benefit fraud.

Arguments against ID cards

- They would signify a major change in the relationship between citizens and the state.
- They infringe civil liberties. It needs to be established under what circumstances ID cards can be checked by the police or other authorities. They might increase discrimination against minorities.
- Both production costs and the cost of the cards to individuals are likely to be higher than the original estimates. The money might be better spent on alternative policies.
- Biometric techniques are not always totally reliable.
- There is a lack of political consensus — both the Liberal Democrats and Conservatives are opposed to ID cards.
- Public opinion is divided. While many people want greater national security, they don't necessarily want ID cards for themselves; or they are concerned about reliance on databases and 'function creep' as more individual information is stored electronically.
- Having to attend a local passport office to be photographed and fingerprinted is inconvenient.
- The fraudulent use of ID cards is likely to encourage crime as international criminal gangs seek to copy the cards illegally.
- Vulnerable people may lose their cards and be denied access to essential services.
- In countries that already have ID cards, such as Spain, terrorism has not been eliminated.
- Unscrupulous employers may not bother to check ID cards so that they can continue to employ illegal immigrants cheaply.

Privacy and security

Following the disappearance of the disks from HM Revenue and Customs, the powers of the Information Commissioner were extended to enable his office to carry out spot checks on databases held by public-sector organisations — despite the fact that the government had rejected a request by the Commissioner for this to happen only a month earlier. In addition, the Cabinet Secretary, Gus O'Donnell, was instructed by Gordon Brown to instigate security checks on all government departments to ensure that data were adequately protected.

At issue are two twenty-first century fundamentals:
- the nature of the relationship between the state and the citizen
- the balance between privacy and national security

People are very much aware of the terrorist threat and expect the government to take all possible steps to identify and apprehend terrorists. Equally, protection of personal data is of the utmost concern. Although the Data Protection Act sets out a clear, if somewhat limited, framework for how organisations should process and manage personal information, concerns about day-to-day management errors and unauthorised access to information are widespread, and the Information Commissioner has called for tougher penalties for major breaches of the law and wider access to data held by private organisations. Ultimately, the main problem with even the best system is people.

There are also contradictions in the approach of many people to the protection of personal details. There is no shortage of people willing to parade themselves publicly in programmes like *Big Brother* or *I'm A Celebrity…Get Me Out Of Here* and millions reveal personal details on internet sites such as YouTube or MySpace.

Ask the examiner

Q **How dangerous is the surveillance society?**

A It is a concern, but few people would want to go back to a system of paper records and files. Technology is constantly changing, often to the advantage of a country's citizens. It is impossible to calculate all the benefits of the age of the computer, many of which we now take for granted.

We cannot always anticipate all the consequences of change and perhaps that is why many people are suspicious of it or resist it. Others embrace it enthusiastically. We look to politicians and legislatures both to maintain our freedom and to protect us against undesirable actions. Laws are passed to this end but they are not always observed.

We know that CCTV can have positive outcomes, not least in helping to deter wrongdoers or to identify offenders. Yet we do not like to think, whenever we go to a town centre or railway station, that we are being watched — even if it might ultimately be for our own good.

Similarly, access to the benefits of a personal computer has transformed the lives of millions. We have the convenience of being able to shop online and to avoid long queues in banks by transferring money or paying bills from our accounts. Yet we worry, quite rightly, about the dangers of identity fraud. Databases can be extremely helpful, but confidential information does not necessarily remain confidential.

Unless we are going to turn our backs on new technology — something that is all but impossible — we have to be as vigilant as we can, taking care not to make the task of the information criminal any easier. We also have to be critical in the way we view change, asking questions of those who would see us all issued with identity cards, comparing the arguments and reaching our own conclusions. We should not blame others if we are reluctant to take responsibility ourselves.

The nature of objectivity in social sciences

Research in social science and its contribution to society

Natural scientists are connected with research in areas such as biology, chemistry, geology and physics, where areas of predictability are generally more secure than in the areas we often associate with the social sciences, such as economics, politics, psychology and sociology. There are similarities. Both natural scientists and social scientists depend, to a greater or lesser degree, on gathering data. Both may use **quantitative methods** to produce primary data — perhaps weighing and measuring for the natural scientist, and compiling questionnaires and surveys, or analysing census data, for the social scientist. Often, not least in connection with A-level study, natural sciences are seen as being more demanding and rigorous while social sciences are dismissed as being easy.

Key terms

quantitative methods: methods based on the use and analysis of numerical data. An experiment using these methods normally involves a number of cases with only a few variables; such methods may be useful in helping to describe social phenomena on a larger scale.

qualitative methods: methods involving the use and analysis of wider, non-numerical data, perhaps of a personalised nature. They usually involve few cases but a larger number of variables; such methods may help to describe and explain in more detail but on a smaller scale.

Scientists conduct experiments and repeat them several times. However, although psychologists may conduct limited experiments, social scientists also have to rely on forms of evidence produced by **qualitative methods** that emphasise personal experiences and interpretation. The evidence might take the form of historical records, reports or participant observation. The findings and conclusions of social scientists are likely to be more tentative than those of natural scientists. Social science research, mostly involving work with people, is often less precise, even if approached scientifically, than, say, research in chemistry or physics, although some areas of social science, such as branches of economics, have adopted a more quantitative methodology.

Just as we might have the image of a scientist based on the stereotype of an eccentric in a white coat who almost lives in a laboratory, we think of social scientists as being:

- long-haired, left-wing academics whose main objective is to use some limited social science research to support their particular ideological outlook
- pseudo-scientists who spend a considerable amount of time in determining something that most people might argue is fairly obvious from the outset
- people seeking a degree of respectability for their subject by using specialist vocabulary that is so reliant on jargon that it is unintelligible to almost everyone else

In reality, if their work is to be accepted and valued, social scientists have to approach their work in a way that means they can be trusted and respected. Central to this goal is the question of how far work in the social sciences can really be value free — the product of an objective rather than a subjective approach. This can be very difficult because social scientists are likely to work with people. People have values. Social scientists are people. They have values too.

Research in action

The Economic and Social Research Council

The number of UK universities increased in the 1960s and, in particular, in the teaching of social science. The Social Science Research Council began life in 1965 as an independent organisation established by royal charter and covering 14 different social science disciplines. It was restructured in 1983 as the Economic and Social Research Council. Most of its funding comes through one of the government's two main departments responsible for different branches of education, the Department for Innovation, Universities and Skills. The Council had a budget of over £180 million in 2007–08, a third of which helps to train social scientists of the future who are working at postgraduate level. The six main research areas established after reorganisation were:

- economic affairs
- education and human development
- environment and planning
- government and law
- industry and employment
- social affairs

These have been further modified and refined to take into account developments in society, politics, the economy and world affairs in recent years.

The resources of the state

Some of the most important data gathering and reporting is undertaken by the UK Statistics Authority (UKSA), the government department which is responsible for the collection and publishing of official statistics relating to the UK's economy and society. Two of its most important functions are the national census and *Social Trends*.

The national census

Since it began in 1801, the census has been carried out every 10 years with the exception of 1941, which coincided with the destruction and disruption brought about by the Second World War. The census is a major statistical exercise that requires much detailed and meticulous planning and provides essential information on population changes, particularly in relation to public service needs such as education, health and housing.

Planning for the 2011 census began in 2002. It was concluded that, despite the growth of alternative methods of information gathering, traditional methods would be retained in 2011 in order to safeguard the quality of the information gathered. In response to calls from the Treasury Select Committee, the UKSA produced a detailed case to demonstrate how far the census and the information it provided to those responsible for budgeting billions of pounds of public money could be justified in cost–benefit terms.

Social Trends

This is an annual publication that, through the UKSA, uses a range of data from government departments to identify trends and to indicate in what ways aspects of British society may be changing. The main theme in the 2007 edition of *Social Trends* was changes taking place in the lives of children and young people, highlighting issues such as changing family structures, young people and communication technology, opportunities for participation in sport at school and educational participation. The 13 chapters cover: crime and justice; education; environment; expenditure; health; households; housing; income and wealth; labour markets; lifestyle and participation; population; social protection; and transport.

Mass Observation

Mass Observation was a large-scale investigation of the people of 'Worktown' — the Lancashire town of Bolton. It was the idea of three young men — Charles Madge,

Humphrey Jennings and, in particular, Tom Harrisson, an anthropologist. Madge and Jennings had been involved in a London-based plan that sought to use a national panel of volunteers to reply to questionnaires on a number of matters.

The survey began in 1937, shortly before the outbreak of the Second World War, and, although some of the observers and investigators were working-class people from Bolton, others were Oxford and Cambridge students. In an effort to understand more about what 'ordinary people' thought and did it was decided to watch and record, often in minute detail, their daily lives, mainly without their knowledge. Their work was supplemented by a national panel of volunteer diarists who wrote down their day-to-day observations and who were asked to respond to 'directives' to investigate particular subjects. The reactions of those studied, and sometimes photographed, in Worktown were not always favourable.

After the outbreak of the Second World War, Mass Observation was used by the Ministry of Information to gauge public opinion and monitor the effectiveness of the government's public information campaigns. The work of Mass Observation continued after the war ended. In 1981 the Mass Observation Archive, located at the University of Sussex, began a new project to study everyday life. It recruited a self-selecting national panel of predominantly women volunteers who have agreed to respond to 'directives', writing subjectively in whatever form they feel is appropriate and offering their insights into everyday life.

Practice questions

The following source and questions are typical of those that will be used in Section B of the Unit 2 AS examination paper.

Most people trust scientists and the research methods they use. They recognise that scientific research is important whether it be for medical purposes or to improve technology, which plays an increasingly important part in our lifestyles.

The same cannot be said of the research of social scientists. They are much more subjective in their research and are considered to be far less trustworthy. The general consensus is that they are usually either trying to prove the obvious or seeking to promote change and unrest in society.

(1) **Compare and contrast the reliability of research methods used by scientists and social scientists.** *(17 marks)*

(2) **Using specific examples to support your answer, discuss the potential advantages of research in *either* medical science *or* social science.** *(18 marks)*

Mathematical and scientific reasoning and its application to the Unit 2 passage

For the new specification, Unit 2 has become Science *and Society* and there is no longer a separate section containing mathematics questions. Although the passage will retain a primarily scientific theme, there will be 30 objective-type questions (instead of 25) and approximately seven of these will reflect the social and political dimensions of the new Unit 2.

Passage 1

The following actual AQA exam passage is reproduced in its entirety to show the length and nature of a passage that might be used in Unit 2, Section A. The passage is followed by nine objective type questions; in the exam there will be 30.

Demographic difficulties

(1) The world's human population has been growing significantly during the last century, and at present is continuing to do so at a significant rate. This growth cannot continue indefinitely, however, and this passage considers some of the issues associated with the size of the world's population in the future.

(2) If organisms do not reproduce they will become extinct within one generation. For reproduction, all organisms use a proportion of the energy they have available to them. They may use this energy to produce large numbers of fertilised eggs, which are then left to develop on their own, or they may produce fewer offspring at a more mature stage, and use more energy to rear them. We describe these alternative reproductive styles as 'r-strategy' — where many offspring are produced; and 'k-strategy' — where the energy is used in rearing. R-strategists tend to be plants, or animals which are both aquatic and cold-blooded, since an aquatic environment will provide nutrients, support and a constant temperature.

(3) K-strategists vary in the number of offspring. For instance, ground-nesting birds often have larger numbers of offspring that are at a more developed stage (i.e. able to run about and feed themselves on hatching) than do tree-nesting birds. Parent tree-nesters spend many hours providing food for their relatively undeveloped young.

(4) For all organisms, however, whether r-strategists or k-strategists, in a perfect and limitless environment population size increases exponentially, but in practice when populations reach a certain size environmental pressures prevent further growth. Births and deaths then balance and the population stabilises. The size of this stable population is known as the carrying capacity.

(5) Human beings operate a k-strategy, and human infants have a long period of dependency on their parents. The natural gap between offspring is in the region of 2 years, which implies that each woman is capable of producing in the region of 15 living offspring. Very few women, however, ever used to reach that maximum and even fewer do so now. In primitive societies the population grows only slowly because of high infant and high maternal mortality, both of which result in the mean number of living offspring per woman falling well short of the maximum. However, even small improvements in public health can cause a rapid population rise as fewer infants and mothers die.

(6) Globally, the human population does not yet seem to have reached its carrying capacity. Estimations of the world's carrying capacity have varied from 1 billion to 1,000 billion. Currently the world population is approximately 6,300 million and it is estimated that this will rise to about 9 billion by 2050.

(7) This 'global picture' masks huge variations in population patterns across the world. In many developed countries (including the UK) birth rates are now below replacement levels. Populations are still growing only because people are living longer — they have undergone a demographic transition. The ageing of the population in developed countries has been referred to as a 'demographic time bomb'.

(8) Elsewhere, in societies dependent on subsistence agriculture, children are able to contribute to the family welfare from a very young age, and to provide a net gain to the family from the age of puberty. In developed countries, however, the period of dependency of children has been artificially extended. Prolonging the period of dependency increases the demand on k-strategy reproducers and the biological response is to have fewer offspring. This implies that any action that increases the period of dependency, for instance raising the school-leaving age, will result in a lowered birth rate, and that this effect will occur before the later-leaving students themselves reach reproductive age.

(9) Consequently, in recent years most of the world's population growth has come from the less economically developed regions, particularly from China, Africa and the Indian sub-continent. While China has responded with the 'one child' policy and India has used many strategies to encourage the use of birth control, in much of Africa little or nothing has been done.

(10) Is it likely that the world population will increase by almost 50% in the next 50 years? The greying of the population in developed countries will reach its natural halt long before 2050 — all the evidence seems to indicate that while many more people will reach very old age (90+), the maximum length of life is unlikely to be greatly extended. Demographic predictions assume that there is no increase in death rates and that the determinant of population size is the birth rate. However, across sub-Saharan Africa the AIDS epidemic is raging unchecked; in Zimbabwe it is estimated that 30% of the population is HIV positive. Many lethal diseases are developing resistance to the drugs used to treat them, and there is always

the possibility of the evolution of a new and untreatable disease. The head of the United Nations Population Division reduced his 2002 estimate of 9.3 billion by 400 million in March 2003, and it may yet need to be further reduced. He also stated that 'fertility rates will be below replacement level in three-quarters of the world by 2050'.

(AQA AS exam, June 2006)

Each of the questions below consists of a question or an incomplete statement followed by four suggested answers or completions. You should select the most appropriate answer (A to D) in each case.

1 **What is the meaning of 'cold-blooded' (paragraph 2)?**
A   colder than the environment.
B   temperature varies with the environment.
C   warmer than the environment.
D   always at the same temperature.

2 **Which of the following correctly describes properties of the two different strategies (the r-strategy and k-strategy) referred to in paragraph 2?**

	r-strategy	k-strategy
A	rear their young	have few offspring
B	large number of eggs	do not rear their young
C	do not rear their young	offspring quite mature
D	most mammals	most birds

3 **Which of the following must be true when the carrying capacity of a human population is reached?**
1   the birth rate is equal to the death rate.
2   environmental pressures prevent further growth.
3   existing medical knowledge cannot reduce mortality rates.
4   people are generally living longer.

Answer
A   if 1 and 2 only must be true.
B   if 1 and 3 only must be true.
C   if 2 and 4 only must be true.
D   if 1, 2 and 3 only must be true.

4 **The head of the United Nations Population Division has reduced the estimate of the world's population from 9.3 billion to**
A   9.1 billion
B   9.0 billion
C   8.9 billion
D   6.3 billion

5 **If fertility rates are below replacement level in 75% of the world by 2050 (paragraph 10) it implies that**

A   the other 25% will be reproducing rapidly.
B   population growth will slow.
C   famine will increase.
D   demand for clean water will reduce.

For each of the next three questions you are given an assertion followed by a reason. Consider the assertion and decide whether, on its own, it is a true statement. If it is, consider the reason and decide if it is a true statement. If, and only if, you decide that *both* the assertion and the reason are true, consider whether the reason is a valid or true explanation of the assertion. For each question, choose your answer from the A to D table.

	Assertion	Reason	Argument
A	True	True	Reason is **a correct** explanation of assertion
B	True	True	Reason is **not a correct** explanation of assertion
C	True	False	Not applicable
D	False	—	Not applicable

6 **Human reproductive style is described   because   a lot of energy is used in
as following the k-strategy   the rearing of offspring.**

7 **According to paragraph 8, more young   because   they will be dependent
people going to university will increase   on their parents for
the birth rate   longer.**

8 **The writer implies (paragraph 10)   because   a high proportion of
that the world's population will rise   people will survive AIDS.**

9 **How is the overall conclusion of the passage best summarised?**

A   Urgent measures to increase birth control should be adopted.
B   The world's population may not grow as quickly as earlier predictions suggested.
C   People will live longer and longer.
D   The carrying capacity will soon be reached.

The social, ethical and environmental implications of scientific discoveries and technological developments

The environment and global warming

In recent decades there has been an increase in the world's temperatures, and temperatures in Alaska, western Canada and eastern Russia — traditionally among the coldest parts of the world — have risen by 4°C in the last 50 years. Scientists, using observation satellites, estimate that the Arctic is losing its sea ice because it is warming twice as quickly as the rest of the Earth, and this acceleration is causing scientists, environmentalists and politicians great concern. In Siberia, where the peat bogs are thawing, harmful methane is being released into the atmosphere. In the UK, the four hottest months on record have all come in the last 23 years.

Ice melting in the Arctowski Peninsula, a worrying sign of global warming — the effects of climate change are expected to be more pronounced nearer the poles

The UK has the benefit of detailed records kept by the Meteorological Office from its information base of 500 weather stations. These weather stations record temperature inside a box (the Stevenson screen) with ventilation slats that make it look like a beehive.

The Central England Temperature (CET) records. The records, dating back to 1659, have been vital in calculating how the weather has changed. They suggest that, although temperatures have always fluctuated, a warming trend began to emerge towards the end of the 1800s and started to accelerate in the 1970s.

Ask the examiner

Q What is the greenhouse effect?

A We often talk about 'the greenhouse effect' but the term has two meanings.

- The first is the **'natural' greenhouse effect** that keeps the Earth's climate sufficiently warm to be habitable. Without that, temperatures would be far too low to maintain life. The Earth's warmth comes from the rays of the sun. Most of the heat energy passes through the Earth's atmosphere while some is reflected back into space. As the Earth's surface warms, infrared energy is radiated back into the atmosphere. This energy has a different wavelength to that coming from the sun and some is absorbed by gases in the atmosphere.

- Four naturally occurring gases are responsible for the greenhouse effect — water vapour (the most important of the greenhouse gases but human activity has little direct impact on it), carbon dioxide (CO_2), methane (CH_4) and nitrous oxide (N_2O). As these gases absorb energy, gas particles vibrate and radiate energy, sending about 30% back towards Earth. Consequently, the Earth's average surface temperature is maintained by this blanket at about 15°C.

- The other greenhouse effect is known as **'man-made'** or 'enhanced', caused by human actions such as the increased consumption of coal, oil and natural gas by domestic users, industry and motor vehicles (and to a lesser extent by methane which is released through the digestive processes of animals).

- Plants absorb CO_2 as part of the process of photosynthesis and thus reduce the concentration of CO_2 ; but when land is cleared, perhaps through deforestation (forests also absorb CO_2), the situation is worsened because of clearance, burning or decay.

- This is increasing the concentration of greenhouse gases, particularly carbon dioxide, in the atmosphere, which intensifies the blanket effect, preventing more of the heat from escaping.

- Many scientists have warned about the potential dangers of the 'enhanced greenhouse effect', which contributes to what has been termed 'global warming' — as the enhanced greenhouse effect continues the world's climate will change.

- The effects of climate change will vary but are expected to be more pronounced nearer the poles than the equator. In some areas rainfall will increase, while in others drought is more likely.

Ozone depletion

Ozone (O_3) occurs naturally in the highest levels of the stratosphere (upper atmosphere). A problem sometimes linked to the greenhouse effect is ozone depletion, which concerns the destruction of the ozone layer. It is the ozone layer that absorbs the potentially harmful ultraviolet (UV) radiation from the sun. Too much UV exposure can increase the danger of eye damage and the development of skin cancer, already a growing health problem. It can also cause damage to plants. (At ground level, ozone is a pollutant and can contribute to smog.)

Ozone depletion is caused by a group of chemicals known as halocarbons (the most well-known being chlorofluorocarbons — or CFCs). UV radiation breaks down CFCs in the upper stratosphere. This releases chlorine. The ozone molecules are destroyed while the chlorine catalyst reforms.

CFCs were, in the past, commonly released by aerosols, refrigerators, fire-fighting chemicals and cleaning solvents, but it was not until the 1970s that concerns were expressed about potential dangers. In 1985 scientists discovered a hole in the ozone layer over Antarctica, and by 2000 the hole was larger than North America, although since then it has been shrinking. Ozone layer damage has also extended across the globe.

Since the dangers of halocarbons became evident, steps have been taken to phase them out, but production in the UK continued to 2000. Phasing-out measures emerged after the signing of the Montreal Protocol on Substances that Deplete the Ozone Layer in 1987, with several revisions since. However, it is estimated that it will take between 50 and 100 years to bring about the full recovery of ozone levels.

The effects of climate change

The following are some of the ways in which the changing climate is likely to alter the planet:

- The world's ice is melting; for example, one of the best-known mountains, Mount Kilimanjaro in Tanzania, has had an ice cap for 100,000 years. Over 80% has melted in the last 20 years and within another 20 years it is all likely to have gone.
- For the first time, polar bears have been found drowned in the Arctic. Normally good swimmers, the bears have been finding that melting ice leaves them too far from land. They are also far less likely to catch seals, which might normally surface through cracks in the ice.

- It is predicted that sea levels could rise between 5 and 12 metres over coming decades. About 270 million people live in coastal areas will be threatened by a 5-metre rise. Bangladesh and Vietnam are likely to be worst hit.
- Continuing deforestation, in areas like the Amazon rainforest, will increase the amount of carbon dioxide circulating in the atmosphere.
- Mosquitoes will thrive, making malaria more common, particularly in Africa.
- An increasing number of land species will be threatened by extinction.
- Expanding deserts are a growing worry, and not just in parts of the world which, historically, have had very little rainfall. Spain might be among those countries threatened by increasing desertification.
- Warmer temperatures are increasing evaporation from the oceans, causing atmospheric concentrations of water vapour. This powerful greenhouse agent is said to have increased by 4% over the sea since 1970.
- Coastal erosion has been a problem for some years on the English North Sea coast, affecting places such as Skipsea in the East Riding of Yorkshire and Suffolk's Bawdsey coast in particular. As sea levels rise the problem will be even greater. The UK government has now developed a blueprint to work with the 92 coastal local authorities responsible for coastal erosion work to help improve national protection for people and property.
- Extremes of weather — in the form of prolonged droughts and heatwaves such as the one seen in Australia in 2007, violent storms and hurricanes and unpredictable monsoons — are becoming more common. Even in the UK, the summer of 2007 was the wettest for 300 years and 11 of the 12 warmest years since 1850 have occurred since 1995.
- Flooding in areas like Bangladesh is washing away low-lying homes and refugees are on the move. In 2006, 37 inches of rain fell in Mumbai, India, in one day. Severe floods hit Hull and the East Riding (where over 15,000 homes were flooded), parts of south Yorkshire and Gloucestershire in the summer of 2007. In total, nearly 50,000 homes and 7,000 businesses were flooded. Thirteen people lost their lives.

Jane Buekett

Thousands of homes were flooded in Britain in the summer of 2007

- Because of drought, particularly in large parts of Africa, crops are failing and starvation is widespread. It is estimated that between 145 and 220 million people in parts of Africa and southern Asia could fall below the $2-a-day poverty line. Around 800 million people (over 10% of the global population) are currently at risk from malnutrition.

The Kyoto Protocol

- In 1992, a number of countries adopted the Framework Convention on Climate Change in an effort to make a coordinated attempt to tackle the problem of greenhouse gas emission.
- In 1997, after over 2 years of negotiations, they went further, moving from encouragement to commitment with the signing of the Kyoto Protocol at a conference in Japan.
- The Kyoto Protocol — an international agreement setting targets for industrialised countries to cut their greenhouse gas emissions — was considered to be the most far-reaching international agreement on the environment and sustainable development. It became legally binding in 2005, soon after it was ratified by Russia.
- The agreement requires developed countries to reduce their greenhouse gas emissions below levels specified for each of them within a clear time span, running from 2008 to 2012, when the first commitment ends.
- To provide flexibility, countries were allowed to earn and trade emissions credits, allowing them to buy and sell agreed allowances of greenhouse gas emissions. High-polluting countries can buy unused 'credits' from countries that do not use all of their allowance because they have taken emission-cutting measures.
- The Kyoto Protocol was ratified by over 50 countries, and Australia signed up in 2007 after a general election brought in Kevin Rudd's Labor government.
- In 2001 the USA pulled out of the Kyoto Protocol on the grounds that complying with it would damage the global competitiveness of the American economy. The USA, with 4% of the world's population, is responsible for about 25% of harmful emissions.
- One argument used by the USA is that the agreement does not require developing countries to make any commitment to reduce the output of dangerous gases. Two rapidly industrialising countries and potential competitors fall into this category — China and India — although both have ratified the Protocol safe in the knowledge that it does not require them to make any binding obligations.

- Critics have argued that the overall target of each nation reducing emissions by 5% of 1990 levels are modest and that targets must be much more ambitious to be effective. Of European Union countries, the UK has a good record on reducing emissions but progress across the EU is variable.

Perspectives on the potential dangers of global warming

Politicians and voters

- In the UK, environmental debate has entered the political mainstream. Labour, in power since 1997, is undoubtedly sympathetic but the party in government has to face political reality, and the cost of change, far more readily than parties in opposition.
- David Cameron has certainly provided a greener edge to the Conservative policy.
- The Liberal Democrats, whose main hope of influencing policy is likely to be as a partner in a coalition because the two main parties lack an overall majority, have a long-standing commitment to the environment.
- Because of the heavy reliance on fossil-based sources of energy across the world, politicians have to proceed with caution. They are anxious to show their concern yet at least some of this is inevitably rhetoric.
- Major changes of policy, with much more emphasis on the use of renewable energy sources, are fraught with danger. Jobs are threatened and so is economic growth.
- Cheap, large-scale electricity generation from renewables is not yet possible because the technology is not sufficiently developed. Kyoto has proved that international agreements, though important, are insufficiently inclusive.
- Voters almost certainly remain ambivalent. Most are likely to accept that the climate is changing. The UK has had a sequence of warmer summers, with an unusually wet one in 2007. Snow is far less common than it once was and it is widely felt that the weather has become stormier, with high, potentially damaging, winds.

Individuals are probably more committed to energy-saving measures and are being asked to make sacrifices for future generations. Sacrifices are likely to be expensive. Separating household waste and recycling glass, drinks cans and newspapers is laudable but, to take just one example, efforts to encourage more people to use public transport, thus reducing the number of individual vehicle journeys, has had very limited success. People prefer the convenience and personal mobility that comes with their own cars. Air travel has become much cheaper, making it affordable for many more people. Foreign holidays are enjoyed by millions, but it pollutes the atmosphere and additional green taxes are deeply unpopular with voters.

At the end of 2006, the Stern Report was published in the UK. The report, probably the first really comprehensive view of the economics of climate change, was commissioned by the Treasury and conducted by Sir Nicholas Stern, the former World Bank chief economist. The 600-page report suggested that global warming could shrink the global economy by 20% of its output, with millions fleeing flooding and drought.

According to Stern's stark report, speedy international action would cost the equivalent of £184 billion annually — 1% of world gross domestic product. Though dealing with carbon emissions would cost a lot of money, failing to do so, according to Stern, would cost between five and 20 times more. Opponents were quick to dismiss the report as 'junk economics' just as they sought to dismiss Al Gore's predictions in his film *An Inconvenient Truth*, as 'junk science'.

For Stern, three crucial actions would involve:
- putting a price on carbon emissions
- increasing low-carbon technological development
- encouraging people to change their behaviour

Scientists
- Scientists are not unanimous on climate change and the contribution of greenhouse gases to global warming.
- Researchers are constantly collecting data in an effort to make their hypotheses more convincing or even conclusive.
- The overwhelming majority of scientists are now convinced that human activities have had a major impact on climate change in the last 50 years and there is growing consensus that urgent action is necessary.
- A small minority of scientists, mostly in America where they are often well organised and funded, but including British figures such as David Bellamy, have been more sceptical. They argue that evidence supporting theories of global warming is inconclusive and that the incidence of global warming has been exaggerated.
- Sceptics also claim that there is no reliable way of predicting how temperatures will change in the future, and that climate change is complex and difficult to predict with any degree of scientific accuracy.

- The overwhelming majority of scientists are convinced that increases in the concentrations of greenhouse gases in the atmosphere have enhanced the greenhouse effect, leading to extra warming.
- That carbon dioxide strongly absorbs infrared radiation is a matter of fact. Carbon dioxide is the most dominant human-influenced greenhouse gas and is responsible for much of the warming arising from changes in atmospheric concentrations.
- Records suggest that carbon dioxide has increased since industrialisation began after 1760, and most noticeably in more recent years as more countries have increased the scale and pace of industrialisation, burning more fossil fuels and increasing the rate of deforestation.

In particular, the melting of the sea ice in the Arctic is one of the clearest and most worrying signs that the process of global warming might be accelerating. Studies by the American space agency, NASA, using satellite monitoring technologies, seem to point to this. One shows that Arctic sea ice that usually remains during the summer shrank by 14% in 12 months between 2004 and 2005, reducing the ice cover by some 280,000 square miles. A second study indicated that during the winters of 2004 and 2005 the perennial ice melting rate, which had averaged 0.15% a year since satellite observation records began in 1979, had increased to 6% a year. If such trends continue, the Arctic ice could be gone by 2070.

Early in 2007, the world's scientists were indicating that climate change was even worse than they thought. In an intensive study of climate change undertaken over 6 years by 2,000 of the world's leading climate scientists, the fourth report of the Intergovernmental Panel on Climate Change (IPCC), it was indicated that global temperature rises of between 2 and 4.5°C are almost inevitable. They concluded that there is now overwhelming evidence that human activity is responsible for accelerating the pace of key climatic changes; and the message to politicians, 17 years after Kyoto, should be clear.

Following a meeting attended by 173 Kyoto Protocol countries in Bonn at the end of 2007, a 10-day meeting of the United Nations Framework Convention on Climate Change took place on the Indonesian island resort of Bali. This brought together scientific and political representatives of over 180 countries, with the aim of taking the first steps towards negotiating a new international agreement to succeed the Kyoto Protocol when it expires in 2012. According to the UN, the IPCC report made clear 'beyond doubt that climate change is a reality'.

At the end of the Bali meeting, the position of the USA was far from clear. American diplomats did their best to sound as if the USA wanted to be part of the solution to the problems presented by global warming. James Connaughton, senior environmental advisor to President Bush, insisted that the USA would be seeking national commitments from countries most responsible for greenhouse gas emissions — the USA and China being the two biggest contributors.

The UK's chief environmental minister, Hilary Benn, leader of the delegation to Bali, talked of a 'historic breakthrough'; he claimed that all the world's nations had agreed to negotiate a deal by 2009 and that countries would adopt a shared vision for the future. We must hope that Benn's optimism was justified and that the 'roadmap' he envisaged will result in international agreement on measures that will reduce dangerous emissions and deforestation.

Yet few believed that radical change was likely, and while the Bali meeting was going on President Bush's chief scientific advisor, John Marburger, offered a much more sceptical view to 15,000 scientists meeting in San Francisco. He questioned the wisdom of trying to compel growing economies to accept emissions limits, emphasising again high costs and global economic competition. Democrats in the American Congress accused President Bush of manipulating climate change and misleading policy makers for years. Much depends on the new American president elected in 2008; and politicians of both parties are acutely aware that the USA must reduce its dependency on imported oil.

Practice questions

The following source and questions are typical of those that will be used in Section B of the AS Unit 2 examination paper.

There may still be a few doubters but, as the Stern Report has confirmed, most scientists are deeply worried that rates of global warming are accelerating to such an extent that there are major threats to future generations.

Increasingly, politicians are taking action, but it is important that everyone does something, as an individual, to save energy in the home and to reduce their own carbon footprint.

(1) **Examine the ways in which many scientists are predicting that global warming will damage the planet.** *(17 marks)*

(2) **Discuss the effectiveness of the contribution that individuals can make to becoming more energy-efficient and to reduce their carbon footprint.** *(18 marks)*

Q **Is it too late to do anything about climate change, and is it worthwhile for individuals to make the effort?**

A It is not too late and we have seen that restrictions on the chemicals responsible for ozone depletion can have an impact. Individuals can make a contribution, especially when the contributions of each individual are added together. It is difficult to bring about significant change because nobody can afford to ignore the costs of a major switch to cleaner fuels and because key world organisations like the United Nations cannot force the government of a sovereign country to commit itself to an international environmental agreement. There is no doubt that a lot of the options that might make a significant impact will be uncomfortable, both for politicians and voters. Some of the options are listed here.

Individuals
According to the Department for Environment, Food and Rural Affairs (Defra), individuals are responsible for more than 40% of the UK's CO_2. There is an official government website that enables individuals to work out the size of their carbon footprint and take action to reduce it: **www.direct.gov.uk/ActOnCO2**.

Individual actions might include:

- installing cavity wall insulation/solar energy
- turning down the house thermostat by 1°C
- insulating pipes and hot water cylinders
- only boiling the amount of water needed rather than a full kettle
- turning off lights when not in the room
- not leaving electronics on standby
- buying energy-efficient A-rated kitchen appliances such as washing machines and refrigerators
- buying more fuel-efficient cars
- making greater use of public transport
- taking fewer foreign holidays involving air travel
- recycling more household waste
- being prepared to accept more green-based taxes
- buying more locally produced food
- cycling or walking to work or school

Politicians
Actions from politicians might include:

- accepting that it is a global problem that requires concerted action by all countries
- setting annual targets for emission reductions
- reducing industrial emissions

- making more determined efforts to curb motor vehicle and aircraft pollution — aviation fuel is currently untaxed
- investing in green transport
- encouraging the development of greener homes
- increasing the drive for a renewable energy policy
- encouraging more carbon trading schemes
- restricting/prohibiting sales of non-essentials such as incandescent lights/garden flood-lights

Even a selection of these measures requires people to do things that have previously been done only by a minority. Governments are unwilling to commit themselves to detailed change, partly because the technology does not exist for them to do so but mostly because change is expensive and will involve a change in lifestyles and living standards. Opinion polls consistently suggest that British people are now convinced about the dangers of global warming but either are not sure what to do to work against it or have decided to ignore the issue, not least because they see green taxes as a cynical ploy by the government to gain an extra source of revenue.

Politically, no government likes to risk losing votes by threatening the status quo that underpins the economy. The fuel lobby is extremely powerful and oil underpins the global economy; decreased dependence would threaten the power of OPEC and destabilise the balance of power in a way that might give an advantage to religious fundamentalists. In broad terms, the intentions of the UK government are clear in its energy White Papers and climate bills. A coherent, commercially viable and politically acceptable strategy may prove more elusive.

Key term

OPEC: the Organization of Petroleum Countries (OPEC) founded in 1960. It now has 13 members from Middle Eastern, African and South American countries. It seeks to coordinate oil production policies to help stabilise world oil supplies and prices, while securing a reasonable return for OPEC member countries. Critics see it as more of a cartel — a price-fixing group for world oil supplies.

Health, fitness and a balanced diet

In recent years, increasing concern about the weight and fitness of the population has been expressed by doctors, politicians and sports scientists. The main focus of concern has been on:

- the low status in the curriculum of physical education and the extent to which it is disliked by many young people
- the extent to which school playing fields have been sold for private development, usually leading to the diminution of sporting facilities in the schools concerned

- the unhealthy nature of school dinners (highlighted by *Jamie's School Dinners* television campaign for healthier school meals by the celebrity chef Jamie Oliver, which led to an improvement in the quality of school meals but a fall in their take-up)
- the poor quality of packed lunches, with a preponderance of fatty foods and fizzy drinks
- the unhealthy products dispensed by school vending machines, which are now subject to closer control
- the lack of regular exercise and participation in sport throughout the population
- the extent to which young people prefer more sedentary leisure activities such as computer games
- the increasing reliance on ready meals and fast food outlets — foodstuffs that often have a high sugar and salt content

Jamie Oliver picking up an award for his television series of *Jamie's School Dinners*, which highlighted the unhealthy nature of school dinners in the UK

- the excessive marketing of junk food to children despite controls on television advertising
- the growing levels of obesity throughout the population

Diet

According to the British Medical Association there may be as many as 1 million obese British children, and obesity levels for both boys and girls have risen sharply in the last 15 years. Adult obesity rates have quadrupled over 25 years and over 60% of UK adults are said to be overweight. It is feared that, unless drastic action is taken to reverse the trend, this will lead to more people developing type 2 diabetes and heart disease, or even cancer, at an earlier age, adding significantly to the cost of healthcare. According to the National Audit Office, obesity can reduce life expectancy by up to 9 years.

Conversely, teenage girls in particular have become obsessive about their weight, often influenced by very slim models on the catwalk and the craze for a 'size 0' figure. Eating disorders such as anorexia nervosa and bulimia nervosa have become more common.

A healthy diet needs to centre on eating the right amount of food (supporting a more active lifestyle) in the right balance. A balanced diet should include a combination of carbohydrates (for energy), fats (for fat soluble vitamins), fibre (for the bowels), minerals, proteins (for body growth and repair) and vitamins. There are five basic food groups and a healthy diet is based on eating a variety of foods, in the correct proportions, from each of the groups: (1) bread, potatoes, pasta and rice; (2) fruit and vegetables; (3) milk and dairy foods; (4) meat, fish and poultry; and (5) food containing fats and sugars.

Exercise

A balanced diet should be complemented by regular exercise, which can:

- use up extra calories to help control weight
- boost the immune system
- promote bone density to guard against osteoporosis
- help to produce healthy blood sugar levels, thus protecting against or helping to control diabetes
- increase HDL ('good cholesterol') levels, thus reducing the likelihood of heart disease
- help to reduce blood pressure, lessening the risks of heart disease and strokes
- help to keep joints, tendons and ligaments flexible
- improve self-confidence and self-esteem by helping people look better
- improve mental health and help to guard against depression (exercise helps to release chemicals like serotonin in the brain, which reduce anxiety and stress)
- improve sleep patterns

More exercise can come from:

- walking (briskly for at least 30 minutes five times a week), jogging, aerobics, cycling and swimming
- walking or cycling to school and the shops rather than going in the car
- participating in energetic sports — joining a club or a team can also extend social opportunities
- visiting a local gym or leisure centre regularly

Because of extensive publicity, many people are aware of what constitutes a healthy diet, why it is important and the need for exercise; yet obesity continues to increase. There can be many reasons for this:

- habit — old habits die hard
- inertia — people make promises, especially in the form of new-year resolutions, that they are unable to keep
- fatty foods are often the most appetising and tasty
- dependency on alcohol
- inability to find the time to exercise because of work and family commitments

- limited facilities for exercise, especially in rural areas
- the cost of gym membership
- fears about personal safety when exercising outside
- poor weather — people seek comfort foods and are less inclined to leave the home
- the need to vary activities to avoid boredom and maintain motivation

Often there is conflicting advice about what foods and drinks are or are not healthy. Reductions in weight and improvements in fitness are often longer-term goals and require a generous measure of dedication, deprivation and self-discipline. Recent London University research in genetics has pointed to the existence of genes that predispose certain people to higher weight, meaning that some people have to work harder at dieting and exercising because of their genes. Irrespective of that, the basic message of 'eat less and exercise more' is not one which many people find palatable.

Such is the urgency of the situation that obese people will be rewarded for losing weight under a £372 million incentive scheme designed to make Britain the first country in the world to reverse rising obesity levels. This proposal is based on a scheme used in the USA that offers obese adults cash incentives for losing weight. With 25% of adults already estimated to be obese, the figure could grow to 60% by 2050 if nothing is done, and an original target of halting the rise of child obesity in Britain by 2010 has been put back to 2020.

Ask the examiner

Q **Science has taught us about the benefits of a balanced diet and exercise, so why is there so much concern about an obesity epidemic?**

A We do not always make logical and rational choices and people do not always like being told what to do by the government, which can stand accused of trying to run a 'nanny state'.

Plenty of people do pay close attention to their diet and also take regular exercise. Many do not for a variety of reasons: some feel that they do not have the time; some lack the money; the self-discipline to exercise on a regular basis is difficult; unhealthy foods, often because of their sugar and fat content, are appetising; advertising techniques can be powerful; and people prefer to make individual choices about their lifestyles.

All the evidence shows that obesity is growing rapidly, and the National Health Service is already expensive to run without making extra demands through increased rates of cardio-vascular disease and diabetes. As the proportion of older people in the population increases and new treatments are devised, costs will increase. Everybody wants high-quality healthcare but it comes at a cost, and that cost often includes higher personal taxation.

Scientists, doctors and nutritionists have given us a clear message, showing us how we can increase our life expectancy. We may or may not wish to follow the advice, just as people continue to smoke and drink alcohol or try to give up one or both. Often it is a matter of inertia or habit rather than conscious choice. In the end we are human beings. If we are ill we often know that there are medicines that will make us better, yet if those medicines are unpleasant we may decline to take them.

Practice questions

The following questions are typical of those that will be used in Section B of the AS Unit 2 examination paper.

Jamie Oliver's campaign to improve the quality of school dinners by introducing healthy alternatives and reducing the choice of food and drink with high quantities of saturated fats, salt and sugar had both supporters and opponents.

The least healthy foods are often the tastiest and the most tempting. As most people take little or no exercise, they quickly put on weight and become obese, increasing the risk of heart disease and diabetes.

(1) Examine the social and scientific reasons that support the call made by both medical professionals and politicians for a varied and balanced diet.

(17 marks)

(2) Discuss the difficulties involved in reducing the number of obese people in the United Kingdom.

(18 marks)

The moral responsibility of scientists

The atomic bomb

With war against Nazi Germany seeming inevitable by the end of the 1930s, intelligence sources believed that German scientists were working on an atomic bomb. Otto Hahn, Lise Meitner and Fritz Strassmann's discovery of **nuclear fission** led to the real possibility that the Germans — with their vast industrial base and chemical engineering industry, heavy-water plant and increasingly high-grade uranium compound — would be first to develop a nuclear bomb.

One of the scientists involved, an Austrian Jew called Lise Meitner, fled to Sweden, where she continued her work on fission with Otto Frisch. This was reported by the Danish physicist Niels Bohr, leading to the possibility that it could be used to construct the ultimate weapon of destruction — the atomic bomb.

- Scientists have the training, skills and knowledge which are essential to all weapons research, but the implications of their talents and discoveries may not always be immediately apparent.
- Scientists also have the responsibility to consider that their work might be used for non-peaceful means — by politicians in their quest for national security, terrorists fighting for their particular cause or criminals seeking financial gain.

Shortly before the outbreak of the Second World War in 1939 the eminent scientist, Albert Einstein, was prompted to write to the American president, Franklin D. Roosevelt, to inform him of efforts being made by German scientists to purify uranium-235, which could be used as the basis of an atomic bomb. In 1941, the British opened up their atomic research facilities to the Americans who were to set up the Manhattan Project — a research programme that led to the development of an atomic bomb for use by the Americans.

The major problem was producing sufficient amounts of enriched uranium (the only natural element whose atoms can be split relatively easily) to sustain a chain reaction, as uranium-235 was difficult to extract and to separate from uranium-238, which was chemically identical.

Under the physicist Dr J. Robert Oppenheimer, who directed the scientific team, research prior to the explosion of the world's first atomic bomb is said to have cost over $2 billion. Many were apprehensive about the potential effects of the bomb test — that it might fail, or about its potential impact on the upper atmosphere and the possibility of radioactive fallout. Testing of what was code-named the 'Gadget' took place in the mountains of New Mexico in the summer of 1945. The light of the explosion turned orange as the atomic fireball shot upwards, producing what was to become the characteristic mushroom cloud of radioactive vapour at 30,000 feet. Several of the observers, watching inside a shelter, were blown flat by the blast.

- On witnessing the explosion, its creators are said to have had mixed reactions. Oppenheimer, though delighted by its success, talked of the danger of 'the destroyer of worlds' and admitted that 'we knew the world would not be the same again'. Ken Bainbridge, the test director, told Oppenheimer that 'now we're all sons of bitches'.
- A brilliant scientific achievement, capable of being used for good, also meant that a monster had been unleashed — the most powerful destructive force ever created — and some of the participants in the test realised this.
- For many of the scientists concerned it was essential that the killing of Americans, and the wider threat posed by the Japanese, were brought to the quickest possible end. Szilard and Einstein were writing again, this time to warn the new American president, Harry S. Truman, of the bomb's potential dangers.
- The atomic bomb has only been used twice as a weapon of war. The Americans were fearful that the war with Japan would drag on, at great cost to American lives. Consequently, on 6 August 1945, on the orders of President Truman, a 9,700 lb uranium bomb, referred to as 'Little Boy', was dropped from an American B-29 bomber, the *Enola Gay*, and exploded on the city and military centre of Hiroshima.
- It is estimated that between 66,000 and 130,000 people were killed immediately and thousands more were injured. It is said the site of the explosion reached a temperature of 5,400°F after an explosion of 15 kilotons — the equivalent of 15,000 tons of TNT. Less than 10% of Hiroshima's buildings survived without damage.
- The impact of the release of x-ray energy, the thermal radiation, the atmospheric blast and the movement of longer-term radiation mean that both the early impact and the longer-term after-effects are catastrophic.

- After warnings from the Americans that they 'were in possession of the most destructive explosive ever devised by man', a more complicated plutonium bomb referred to as 'Fat Man' was dropped 3 days later on Nagasaki, devastating an area of 2 square miles, killing an estimated 40,000 people and injuring over 25,000. A few days later, the Japanese emperor told his people that they must 'bear the unbearable' and surrendered.

- After 1945, as scientists in the Soviet Union (the USSR) also developed an atomic bomb, relations between the two 'super-powers', the USA and the USSR, cooled and the latter began its own nuclear technology programme.

- By 1952, the Americans had tested an even more powerful bomb — a hydrogen bomb relying on the release of thermonuclear energy by the condensation of hydrogen nuclei to helium nuclei. Oppenheimer, so instrumental in the development of the atomic bomb, became increasingly concerned and suggested that the United Nations should be central to further nuclear development.

- The threat of nuclear war was uppermost in the minds of many, particularly as the USA ('defenders of the free Western world') and the Soviet Union ('leaders of the Eastern communist bloc') faced each other in what became known as the Cold War, which ran from the end of the 1940s to the end of the 1980s.

- Both sides claimed that their weapons would only be used for defensive, rather than aggressive, purposes and both kept extensive arsenals of nuclear weapons to counter possible attack despite the enormous costs involved.

- Safety, it seemed, could only be safeguarded by the threat of retaliation. It could be argued that nuclear deterrence is effective, because no nuclear weapons have been used in warfare since 1945.

The mushroom cloud that rose 20,000 feet above Nagasaki after a plutonium bomb was dropped on the city in August 1945

- In 1969, the Strategic Arms Limitation Talks (SALT) were an acknowledgement of the need for the super-powers to show restraint, although negotiations leading to limited disarmament were still a long way off, materialising only in the later 1980s and becoming less significant with the break-up of the USSR and the demise of Eastern bloc communism in the 1990s.
- While nuclear weapons held by the USA, Russia, the UK, France and China are almost legacies of the past, both India and Pakistan, fierce historical rivals and neighbours, are known to possess limited nuclear possibilities.
- In 1996, the International Court of Justice declared that the use of nuclear weapons was contrary to the established rules of law, but rumours persist about Israel, Iran and North Korea, where such rules are unlikely to be held in high regard.
- While nuclear weapons continue to exist so do suspicion, antagonism and the danger of further escalation and an ensuing arms race.

Chemical and biological warfare

- Biological warfare is one of the most feared weapons of modern war and terrorism. It involves the use of biological pathogens — bacteria, viruses and toxins (poisonous compounds produced by organisms) — to kill or severely injure one's opponents.
- It is not new, and early warfare involved such things as arrow heads dipped in poisonous animal faeces, plague-infected corpses, smallpox-ridden blankets and highly poisonous snakes.
- The science of germs and how diseases are transmitted was not understood until the later nineteenth century following the work of Louis Pasteur and Robert Koch.
- Modern biological warfare probably dates from the First World War when, though illegal under the Hague Convention on the rules of warfare, poison gas used by the Germans on their Eastern and Western Fronts was responsible for an estimated 100,000 deaths.
- **Biological weapons** are based on naturally occurring organisms that cause disease. Common examples are:
  - the bacteria *Bacillus anthracis* (anthrax spores that can lie dormant in soil and can enter the lungs if inhaled)
  - *Clostridium botulinum* (the highly poisonous botulism), which produce toxins
  - smallpox (a highly infectious viral disease thought to have been eliminated 30 years ago after a worldwide vaccination campaign but kept as cultures in both the USA and Russia)

- **Chemical weapons** are poisons and two of the most well-known are mustard gas and sarin (a colourless, odourless gas that attacks the nervous system).

- In 1928 the Geneva Protocol sought to limit the production and possession of biological weapons but there was no provision for inspection. It was signed by over 100 nations, although they mostly agreed just to outlaw the first use of such weapons, and it was not ratified by the USA until 1974.

- It is thought that the Japanese experimented extensively in several areas of biological weapons research in the 1930s and beyond, with over 3,000 scientists and technicians working in Unit 731 in Manchuria.

- Inhumane experiments were undertaken during the Second World War by the Germans, who deliberately infected prisoners in Nazi concentration camps with bacteria.

- No country wanted to be the first to use biological warfare against another country between 1939 and 1945 for fear of retaliation, however, and some scientists might have believed that what appeared to be cruel research may have led to advances in the knowledge of human physiology.

- Britain also had a secret biological warfare plan based on anthrax, and Gruinard Island, in Scotland, was chosen as a test site. However, an outbreak of anthrax in sheep and cattle occurred in 1943 on the Scottish coast and attempts at decontamination proved impossible, as spores of anthrax had become embedded in the soil.

- The terrifying potential of biological warfare was indicated when *Bacillus subtilis* — laboratory-produced in a form said not to be harmful to humans — was released in the New York subway in 1966. It showed that, as a result of prevailing winds and the vacuum created by passing subway trains, one station could infect all stations in the network.

- By 1970 the USA had terminated its offensive bio-weapons programme and the only permitted research was for defensive purposes. By 1972 there was a United Nations Convention on bacteriological and toxin weapons, which was then ratified by member nations.

In contemporary form, biochemical strikes can be attempted through:
- fine particle distribution via aerosol sprays
- explosives (perhaps using missiles or bombs which are detonated)
- contamination of food or water supplies
- absorption or injection into the skin

Viewpoints

Advantages of bio-weapons to those who produce them	Disadvantages of bio-weapons
■ Such attacks may not be immediately detectable. ■ A single microbial bio-weapon can reproduce in the host. ■ Disease can continue after its release as secondary infection spreads to affect many more. ■ Biological toxins are extremely toxic. ■ Bacterial agents and equipment may not be difficult or necessarily expensive to produce using hidden or mobile facilities. ■ Large quantities of bio-weapons can be produced in a relatively short time.	■ It is difficult to protect those involved in the handling, production and transport of bio-weapons, especially if those concerned have little expertise or scientific training. ■ There is a danger of unintended release into the environment. ■ Delivery targeting may be difficult: ultra-violet light will destroy a number of biological materials, the wind can blow spores in unexpected directions and rain is another hazard. ■ Storage difficulties can easily arise. ■ They are difficult to control if used in warfare and the country's own troops might be infected.

Biological and chemical weapons can be used to target individuals, and in 1978 a Bulgarian journalist who worked for the BBC, Georgi Markov, died from ricin (a toxin derived from the castor bean) poisoning 3 days after being pricked, possibly by an umbrella, while waiting in a London bus queue.

In a much-publicised case in 2006, a former member of the Russian Federation's Federal Security Service, Alexander Litvinenko, who had defected to Britain, was poisoned with a rare and highly toxic radioactive isotope, polonium-210, perhaps after drinking contaminated tea.

Bio-terrorism hit the USA in 1984 when a cult known as the Rashneeshee contaminated some salad bars in Oregon, causing a widespread outbreak of salmonella poisoning. Another cult, an extreme Buddhist sect known as Aum Shinri Kyo, were responsible for an attack on the Tokyo underground in 1995 using the deadly nerve gas sarin. Fifteen stations were affected, 12 people were killed and over 5,000 injured. This group had also attempted to produce an anthrax spray and had tried to collect samples of the Ebola virus. In another US attack, letters containing anthrax spores killed five people in 2001.

During the time of Saddam Hussein, UN specialists confirmed that Iraq had used mustard and nerve gases in the 1980s in the war against Iran. In 1988, Iraq used chemical weapons against the Kurdish minority and threatened to use chemical weapons against Israel — which also possessed them.

SCIENCE AND SOCIETY
Chapter 19

The relationship between technology, science, society and ideology

Consumption of the Earth's resources

There are many forms of energy but two of the most important are:

- kinetic energy, associated with movement
- chemical energy, which is stored in fossil fuels or food

Central to the development of society has been the ability of humans to convert various forms of energy, enabling them to adapt their environment to best advantage. They began this pattern by converting the energy of wood into fire, which provided a means of both keeping warm and cooking.

The industrial revolution of the eighteenth and nineteenth centuries harnessed energy on a large scale. Initially, water was used widely to power mill wheels; and the chemical energy of coal was used to turn water into steam and eventually into the kinetic energy that by the late 1820s powered steam locomotives. Michael Faraday did much of the early pioneering work in electricity, inventing both an electric motor and a transformer. The internal combustion engine emerged in the second half of the century and a petrol engine was available in the 1880s.

As society has become more industrialised and transport systems have become more sophisticated and expensive, the world demand for energy has risen sharply. Changes in lifestyle, the quest for higher living standards, greater emphasis on consumerism and the speed at which fast-growing and heavily populated nations like China and India are industrialising mean that the amount of energy used globally is constantly increasing.

This trend is expected to continue, increasing carbon emissions and increasing the dangers associated with global warming, although the European Union is seeking to reduce energy use by 18% by 2020. Conversely, the International Energy Agency predicts a 50% increase in world energy demand by 2030, with much of the increase coming from carbon-based fossil fuels. Much will depend on the ability of scientists to find ways of using fuel more efficiently, reducing carbon dioxide and other harmful emissions and developing the technology to allow large-scale and commercially viable ways of using renewable sources to generate electricity.

Non-renewable fuels

Energy resources tend to fall into two categories: **renewable** and **non-renewable**. Nearly all the energy needed to support a modern industrial economy, often to generate electricity or for transport, comes from non-renewable fossil fuels formed from the organic remains of prehistoric animals and plants. These **fossil fuels** have a negative effect on the environment because they release harmful carbon dioxide emissions — the most prevalent and harmful of the gases known as 'greenhouse gases'.

> **Key term**
>
> **fossil fuels:** fuels found within the rocks of the Earth's surface, having been formed millions of years ago from dead animals and plants. Once they are used they cannot be replaced.

Oil and natural gas

Oil and natural gas are made from both plant and animal remains and are chemicals made from molecules containing just carbon and hydrogen. Natural gas and oil can be found in many parts of the world. When they burn they produce mainly carbon dioxide and water, releasing energy. Oil comes from crude oil, which is a mix of hydrocarbons with some oxygen, nitrogen and sulphur impurities. The main source of crude oil reserves is the Middle East. Refined oil is widely used in transportation as well in the production of plastics, tyres and pharmaceuticals.

Oil is usually recovered by drilling wells, often through nonporous rock barriers. It then has to be processed. The refining process separates crude oil into different hydrocarbons, through fractional distillation. Impurities such as nitrogen and sulphur are removed. As a liquid, crude oil can be brought to the surface under pressure and much of it can be transported to a number of its destinations via pipelines.

Natural gas is the gas component of coal and oil formation and it is used for heating, cooking and as a fuel for electricity generation. Natural gas reserves are greatest in the USA, Russia and parts of the Middle East. Wells for natural gas are usually drilled in underground reservoirs of porous rock. The natural gas can then be pumped to a processing station or stored until it is needed. Pipelines are the main methods of transporting natural gas. World demand for gas has increased by 75% in the last 20 years.

An off-shore oil rig, Saudi Arabia

Coal

Coal is an abundant fossil fuel, found in many parts of the world. It consists mainly of carbon atoms originating from plant material from former swamp forests where the water prevented the plant material from decaying completely. Layers of peat built up and heat from below the Earth's crust eventually turned this into coal. It is widely used for the production of electricity and as a heating fuel. The most energy-efficient forms of coal are the bituminous and, particularly, the anthracite forms. Coal contains impurities such as sulphur (which can lead to sulphur dioxide pollution where coal-burning plants are used for electricity production). Coal also produces carbon dioxide when it burns.

Viewpoints

Advantages of fossil fuels

- Very large amounts of electricity can be generated, relatively cheaply, from small amounts of fuel.
- For historical reasons, the infrastructure is well-established and fossil fuels are readily available — changing the infrastructure would be extremely expensive.
- Transporting oil and gas to power stations, using an extensive network of pipes at source, is relatively easy.

- Coal, natural gas and oil are still, in the shorter term, abundant.
- Gas-fired power stations are very efficient.

Disadvantages of fossil fuels

- Environmental pollution is a major disadvantage because of the extent to which the burning of any fossil fuel produces harmful carbon dioxide.
- Once burnt, fossil fuels cannot be renewed so will eventually run out.
- Oil reserves in the Middle East are particularly vulnerable to political unrest and this can both affect supply and make prices unstable.
- Exhaust gases such as nitrogen dioxide released from vehicles can be damaging to health, especially in high-traffic-density parts of urban areas.
- Oil can enter the sea and cause considerable ecological damage.
- Burning coal produces more carbon dioxide than burning gas or oil and can also produce sulphuric acid, which contributes to acid rain.
- Coal mining is difficult and dangerous, especially in parts of the world where working conditions are largely unregulated.
- Coal-fired power stations need to be supplied with large amounts of bulky fuel, often necessitating extensive road and rail links.

Nuclear power

The extended use of nuclear power to generate electricity has some support, not least because supplies of uranium will not be exhausted for a long time and the process does not lead to the emission of harmful gases. Opponents, however, point to the cost and length of time it would take to modernise the UK's nuclear power plants; the problems of disposing of radioactive waste; the dangers to life and the environment of leaks; and the possibility of targeting by terrorists.

Renewable fuels

Because of the finite nature of these non-renewable resources and fears about global warming, much more emphasis is being placed on renewable energy resources — such as wind, solar and various forms of water power. These offer considerable potential, not least in environmental terms, but their use so far has been limited and the UK government has targeted a significant increase in the amount of electricity generated from renewable sources.

According to a report by the Energy Saving Trust, British people were among the worst offenders in Europe for wasting energy. Common ways of wasting energy were:

- leaving electrical appliances on standby:
- boiling more water in kettles than was needed

- leaving chargers plugged in
- failing to turn off lights in empty rooms
- using cars for short journeys and leaving the engine running when stationary
- washing clothes at unnecessarily high temperatures
- keeping the central heating thermostat too high

The trust estimated that householders could save £11 billion by 2010 by avoiding such wasteful habits. Rapidly increasing oil, gas and electricity prices may provide a sharp incentive.

Hydroelectric power

Hydroelectric power (HEP) is created by the flow of water — a system that has been used in less advanced ways for centuries, although its use in the generation of electricity dates only from the 1920s. Turbines are placed in the flowing water and are driven by its kinetic energy; the turbines then drive a generator that converts mechanical energy into electrical energy. The sites are concentrated in the Scottish highlands.

Although noise and emissions are low, HEP schemes might involve the flooding of associated areas, and dams are not always felt to be visually attractive. Opportunities for further development of large-scale generating sources are limited by the lack of commercially viable and environmentally acceptable sites, although small-scale developments remain possible. Less than 2% of the UK's electricity is generated in this way.

Tidal/wave power

The harnessing of the natural movements of tides, which are predictable and contain huge amounts of energy, produces tidal power. Tidal power stations require the construction of an expensive tidal barrage and can only generate power when the tide is flowing in or out. Offshore turbines are cheaper to build.

There are plans in Cornwall, which has limited gas supplies to many areas and 300 miles of coastline, to develop the largest wave-power project in Europe at a cost of £21 million, using a site some 10 miles off the north Cornwall coast and linked to the shore by an undersea cable. However, according to the Carbon Trust, wave power is up to ten times more expensive than windpower.

Wind generators

Like water power, the use of wind power to drive windmills has been utilised for centuries and the UK has considerable potential, because of climatic conditions, for the development of turbines grouped into wind farms, the first of which opened at

Delabole in Cornwall in 1991. These are environmentally friendly in terms of the absence of emissions and have no fossil fuel costs. They can also be sited in remote, windswept areas.

Some cooperatives, such as the Baywind Renewable Energy Cooperative in Cumbria and the Westmill Wind Farm Cooperative in Oxfordshire, have secured community support and local investment, overcoming the opposition of objectors. In Scotland, after a 5-year planning battle, work started in 2006 on Europe's biggest onshore wind farm, Whitelee, a 3-year project on moor and forest land south of Glasgow. 16% of Scotland's electricity comes from renewables compared with 4% across the UK as a whole, and there are outline plans to build the world's biggest wind farm near Stornoway in the Scottish islands.

Wind powered generators in the Fenlands

Increasingly, however, the development of wind farms has met with resistance on the grounds that they are visually intrusive, noisy for nearby residents, a potential danger to the bird population and have to feed into the national grid at its margins where it is at its weakest. Securing planning permission in the face of often concerted and well-orchestrated opposition from local NIMBYs ('Not In My Back Yard') and an anti-wind pressure group known as the Renewable Energy Foundation is proving ever more difficult.

Offshore constructions, such as North Hoyle off the coast of North Wales — one of the five offshore sites already in operation — might offer some potential for development. Planning permission is less likely to be resisted, winds blow more strongly at sea and projects can be bigger. However, siting wind farms at sea is technically more difficult than on the land and power generation is more expensive. The world's largest offshore wind farm is likely to be the London Array in the Thames estuary, planned to occupy a site of 90 square miles off the Kent coast. At an estimated cost of £2 billion, it could supply 25% of London homes with clean power from 2010.

Solar energy

The sun is extremely powerful and solar energy can be harnessed from the sun's rays. There are many types of solar power applications, from calculators to plants capable of generating electricity on a large scale. Central to solar power is the 'photovoltaic' (PV) cell.

In the UK, solar panels containing PV cells are sometimes used on the roofs of houses and these can absorb the light coming from the sun. The DC electricity from the solar panels enters an inverter which converts it to AC power that can be used in the home. (Alternatively, buildings can be designed in such a way that they are able to collect the sun's heat.)

Predictably, there is greater potential in parts of the world that have high sunshine totals and the UK is behind many other countries in the development of solar power technologies. The USA, particularly in the 'sunshine state' of California, has seen extensive solar power development, and considerable inroads have been made in countries such as Japan and Germany.

A solar electric generating system in the Mojave Desert of southern California

The Spanish have recently developed a new solar thermal power plant near Seville, using a 40-storey solar tower surrounded by a field of 600 steel reflectors (heliostats) which direct the sun's rays to a heat exchanger (receiver) at the top of the tower. Solar energy from the heliostats is converted by the receiver into steam, which is used to drive turbines that will supply electricity to homes in the area. Unfortunately, the process is three times as expensive as conventional methods.

Another possibility is investment by European governments in solar power stations along the coasts of North Africa and the Middle East, which could generate electricity that would be transmitted by undersea cable to Europe. Relatively cheap land in North African countries could be utilised to build concentrated solar power stations using giant mirrors to focus the sun's rays onto a pillar, vapourising water it contained and using the steam to drive turbines. Such stations might also have a dual use as desalination plants capable of providing fresh water in areas where it is relatively scarce.

As well as the vagaries of the weather, costs remain a considerable obstacle, and it is likely to be at least 10 years before photovoltaic cells are competitive in price with more conventional non-renewable electricity-generating sources.

Biofuels

Biofuels are any kind of fuels made from living things or from the waste they produce. This can include wood (widely used in Sweden), straw, biogas (methane) or liquid fuels made from plant material or waste oil. Increasingly, cellulosic ethanol is being developed using fermentation techniques as a potential substitute for petrol. In the UK, sugar beet is being used to create ethanol for a petrol mix and, in the USA, maize is a widely used raw material in ethanol production. The USA and Brazil (where sugar cane is widely used) are the world's leading producers of ethanol.

At present, no bioethanol is on general sale in the UK, but there are a few outlets for biodiesel, which can be produced from recycled waste vegetable oil and oil crops such as rapeseed. (Such ideas are not new. Over 100 years ago, when Rudolf Diesel developed his new engine, he claimed it would run on peanut oil.) Burning the fuels does release carbon dioxide but growing the plants absorbs a comparable amount of atmospheric gas.

Biofuel supporters have criticised what they consider to be the British government's timid and largely unfocused approach to the use of biofuels. According to the House of Commons Environment, Food and Rural Affairs Select Committee, five different government departments are involved in various aspects of bio-energy policy.

However, the nitrogen fertilisers used to stimulate the growth of crops used for biofuels may have been produced in factories burning fossil fuels that pump carbon dioxide into the atmosphere. More plants for biofuels may mean less for foodstuffs — which may have a considerable impact on the starving millions in areas like sub-Saharan Africa. More intensive cultivation can threaten wildlife habitats according to the Royal Society for the Protection of Birds. Nevertheless, Britain is committed to what seems a highly ambitious target of 5% total fuel sales being biofuels-based by 2010 even though an increasing number of British scientists are arguing that biofuels may do more harm than good because of their impact on food prices and greenhouse gas emissions due to deforestation.

Viewpoints

Advantages of renewable energy sources
- They can greatly reduce the emission of the harmful gases that contribute to global warming.
- Solar, wind and water energy need no fuel and produce no waste or pollution.

Disadvantages of renewable energy sources
- Current methods of producing bioethanol for blending into petrol are fairly expensive, can lead to intensive farming of specific plant resources and have tended to increase world food prices.
- Solar and wind power are dependent on the weather.
- Solar cells cost a great deal in relation to the amount of electricity they are able to generate and are most appropriate for low-power applications.
- Tidal and hydroelectric power have high start-up costs.
- Wind turbines often meet with opposition because they can be noisy and visually intrusive.

How the UK government sees it

- Towards the end of 2007, it was announced that a new agency was being established to manage Britain's commitment to the development of biofuels.
- Starting in 2008, the Renewable Fuels Agency will be responsible for the daily running of the Renewable Transport Fuels Obligation.
- By 2010, it is planned that 5% of all fuels sold in the UK should come from biofuels.

- The direction of the government's overall strategy remains unclear. Fossil fuels are still readily available and represent the cheapest short-term option for the generation of electricity.
- The expansion of nuclear power will help to cut harmful emissions, but modernisation and rebuilding is a slow and costly process and there remains public uncertainty about the safety of nuclear power and the difficulties of disposing of nuclear waste.
- Ideally, the government would like to see the greater use of renewable energy forms and has set a target of 10% of UK electricity to be generated from renewables by 2010 (and 20% by 2020); but opportunities for large-scale sustainable generation at prices attractive to consumers remain limited.
- At present, only 2% of the UK's total energy comes from renewables. On current policies — and much could change in the next decade — civil servants estimate that the UK will produce only 5% of its total energy from renewables by 2020. By comparison, Germany has 200 times as much installed solar power and 10 times as much wind power.

Ask the examiner

Q **Why is it taking the government so long to produce a clear and strategic policy for energy?**

A Governments have to balance a lot of interests. Jobs are at stake, yet people are much more aware about environmental issues and the potential dangers of global warming. 'The environment' is now more prominent on the political agenda.

The cost of fuel over the short term is probably of most interest to most voters. Despite significant price rises in the cost of oil, gas and electricity, conventional fossil fuels are still the cheapest, and renewable alternatives remain largely undeveloped in large-scale commercial terms.

Pressure groups generate a lot of publicity, but the dangers are mostly in the longer term and governments have a short life. Some longer-term planning and target setting is inevitable but most people are more concerned about themselves than about future generations.

We cannot safely predict future scientific and technical developments, so perhaps of more concern is the possibility of financial and political collapse. The threat to American banks because of the 'sub-prime' mortgage lending crisis in 2007 — and even the run on Northern Rock in the UK when investors felt threatened — sent tremors around world financial markets. Politically, the rise of Islamic fundamentalism presents a significant threat to the stability of the Middle Eastern countries with significant oil supplies and reserves.

Consensus plays a large part in political decision making. Put crudely, governments have to secure as many votes as they can to remain in power. Nuclear power is clean and efficient but will be expensive to modernise and is associated in the public mind with danger. Renewables have their attractions but production costs remain relatively expensive and objectors have slowed up development. Maintaining the status quo is cheaper, but no political party in the twenty-first century can be seen to endorse environmentally damaging methods. It is a conundrum that even the best brains are unlikely to master.

Waste and its disposal

Waste is essentially what we discard when we no longer need it. It takes many forms, all of which require disposal and most of which can be environmentally damaging. The production and disposal of consumables uses up valuable resources and energy and can add to environmental pollution.

Waste can come from domestic, manufacturing, commercial and agricultural sources and, for every tonne of household waste produced, commerce and industry produces another six tonnes. It can also involve the production and disposal of hazardous substances — perhaps chemicals or medical waste — and includes sewage treatment. Litter, often the scourge of our streets and countryside, has been a problem from even before the foundation of the Keep Britain Tidy campaign more than 50 years ago.

Packaging and plastic bags

Consumer groups have shown increasing concern about the amount of packaging used by retailers. Food packaging comes in a variety of forms (such as boxes, cans and bottles) and includes a variety of materials, most notably paper, cardboard, glass and plastics. For fresh foods, packaging is often non-biodegradable to prevent contamination by other foods. Packaging is necessary for:

- the physical protection of food products, which are often sent thousands of miles to meet demand all the year round for what were once seasonal fruits and vegetables
- protection from contamination from parasites and pathogenic bacteria
- the inclusion of essential information such as price, weight, sell-by date, cooking instructions, ingredients and the extent to which saturated fats, sugar and salt might be included
- selling purposes in terms of presenting an attractive design to potential customers

It is estimated that between 8 and 10 million plastic bags are issued each year. The taxing of non-recyclable plastic bags in the Irish Republic led to a significant reduction in their use but few supermarkets in Britain charge for their plastic bags. Other places are planning to follow the example of Modbury, in Devon, which became the first place in Britain to ban them from its mostly independent shops. (Bangladesh was the first country to ban plastic bags, in 2002, because of the extent to which they contributed to flooding by blocking drains.)

In 2000, the Waste Strategy for England and Wales was produced as part of an EU initiative. Much more attention has been paid to **sustainable development** and a 'waste management hierarchy' that emphasises, in order of priority, waste reduction, re-use (as with plastic bags, clothing, furniture, computers and spectacles), recovery (through recycling, composting or energy recovery) and disposal.

> **Key term**
>
> **sustainable development:** a way of securing social and economic development by meeting contemporary needs in a way that does not exhaust a country's natural resources to the detriment of future generations.

Agenda 21 was established during the 1992 United Nations Conference on Environment and Development — the so-called 'Earth Summit' held in Rio de Janeiro to demonstrate a commitment from individual countries to sustainable development and its promotion at local and regional levels. The conference focused on conservation and the preservation of natural resources and the environment in an effort to tackle such problems as air pollution, energy consumption, waste production and disposal, deforestation, biodiversity loss and transport issues.

- Of the estimated 36 million tonnes of municipal waste generated in the UK about 90% is collected from households; this household waste represents a problem partly because it contains large quantities of organic waste as well as materials such as plastics that are not biodegradable.
- Typically, over 50% of household waste comprises garden waste, paper and board and putrescible waste such as kitchen waste.
- Figures from the Department for Environment, Food and Rural Affairs (Defra) indicate that household waste per person increased by 14% between 1995–96 and 2005–06, with each individual producing an average of more than half a tonne of household waste each year.
- Historically, our response to residual waste is usually to dispose of it either in landfill sites or through incineration.
- Certain forms of clean and unmixed waste can be recycled and garden waste can be composted.

- UK **recycling** rates are far below those of many other European countries, such as Switzerland, the Netherlands, Austria, Germany, Norway and Sweden.

Under the Environmental Protection Act, local councils are obliged to collect and dispose of rubbish, primarily on health grounds; but each council can make its own decisions on the methods and timing of waste disposal — hence the plethora of different-coloured disposal sacks, wheelie bins, other bins and containers. Many councils have made efforts to separate waste, with separate containers for paper, glass and garden waste, and there is currently a heated debate on whether household collections should be made weekly or fortnightly. The cost of collection is met from the local council tax.

The slow and variable pace of recycling is another contentious issue, and the government has set targets for councils to recycle/compost proportions of household waste and to recover a proportion of its value. Consequently, local recycling banks and household waste recycling centres have proliferated.

Waste disposal methods

Landfill

Landfill is the technical term used to describe filling large holes in the ground with waste. In Britain 75% of municipal waste is sent to landfill sites, compared to the EU average of 43% and to landfill disposal rates below 20% in the Netherlands, Denmark, Belgium and Sweden. Landfill sites may be specially created for the purpose or may be old workings such as quarries or mine shafts. Such sites have been the most commonly used disposal method, and over 100 million tonnes of waste finds its way to some 2,000 landfill sites in the UK annually. However, there are problems with this:

- Suitable sites have increasingly been used up (existing sites are unlikely to last beyond the next 10 years).
- It is estimated that 1.5 million tonnes of methane — a particularly harmful greenhouse gas, and one that might also present dangers by burning underground — is released annually from landfill sites.
- Leachate fluids from decomposing waste may pollute underlying water, although they can be contained by containment landfills (modern landfill sites are usually separated into cells and lined and capped).

- Some items of waste such as plastics will not rot away and others may take a long time to do so.
- Landfill sites are often unpopular with nearby residents because, without proper control, the sites can create a nuisance through the emission of unpleasant smells, flies, rodents, maggots, dust, wind-blown litter or noise.

As a deterrent, waste going to landfill sites is increasingly taxed by central government; in 2004 the landfill tax was raised from £1 to £15 per tonne, with further rises after that date. For the 2007–08 financial year, the tax was £24 per tonne, set to rise by £8 per year for the following three years. By 2010, councils will have to pay £150 for each tonne above their quota which goes into landfill sites.

A landfill site in Belfast, one of 2,000 tips in the UK

Incineration

Incineration is the combustion of waste at high temperatures. Smaller proportions of waste are incinerated, but this consumes energy and can give off hazardous air pollutants, which has drawn criticism from pressure groups such as Friends of the

Earth and Greenpeace. Modern incineration plants can use waste energy to generate electricity, although many do not.

Although methods of incineration have improved significantly in recent years, incineration is still often viewed as a 'dirty' technology and incinerators tend to be located on the edges of industrial estates or in more remote areas. Despite tight environmental controls there is a fear that toxic emissions such as dioxins (an accidental byproduct of the chlorine industry which might be present in pulp and paper) can enter the atmosphere as a result of incineration. Consequently, applications for planning permission to build new incinerators almost invariably meet concerted local opposition.

Recycling

Recycling involves the separate collection (and often cleaning) of items such as newspaper, cardboard, glass, plastics (thermoplastics melt when heated and can be remoulded) and aluminium drink cans. Through recycling, both raw materials and energy consumption can be saved but, though the UK recycles over 30% of its glass, the proportion of waste recycled is much lower than in many other European countries. About 20% of discarded tyres are re-treaded and re-used.

According to Defra, the government's target to recycle and compost 25% of household waste in England by 2005–06 was exceeded by 2%. However, regional rates for recycling vary. Northeast England showed a significant improvement in 2005–06, leaving London as the area with the lowest rate of recycling at 21%, compared to rates of 33% achieved in the east midlands.

By 2006–07, the east, southwest and east midlands all had recycling/composting rates above 35% (with the top councils of North Kesteven and Rushcliffe both reaching 50%), but the rate for London had risen only by 1%. London and the south-east fared far better in recovering value from their waste, although both were some way behind the 58% recovery rate of councils in the west midlands.

With councils facing severe fines, recycling rates are likely to improve further, although Paul Bettison, chairman of the Local Government Association's environment board, has said that Britain is still 'the dustbin of Europe', throwing more rubbish into landfill than any other country in the EU.

Composting

Food and garden waste can often be composted (biological decomposition using a combination of open air and high temperature conditions, killing pathogens) as, in a matter of weeks, organic waste breaks down into a humus-rich mulch that can be used as fertiliser. This method, commonly used by gardeners, is now being applied on a wider scale by newly developed civic amenity sites, and there is a target to recycle and compost 33% of household waste by 2015.

Anaerobic digestion

Anaerobic digestion is a biological process in which organic material is broken down by the action of micro-organisms. Unlike composting, the process takes place in the absence of air. The residue remaining can be used as a soil conditioner. Only a few such plants exist in the UK. Waste decomposes in an enclosed chamber and digestion takes place in an oxygen-free environment. This sustainable disposal method is forecast to increase and is more widely used in a number of other countries.

The UK government and local authorities

In 2000 the government set recycling targets for each local authority and this policy is reviewed annually, taking into account landfill regulations and requirements for disposing of electrical goods. The aim is to drive local authorities towards more extensive methods of waste reduction, re-use and recovery, and the best way to deal with waste is not to produce as much of it.

Government thinking is set out in *Waste Strategy for England 2007*. Its key objectives are to:

- decouple waste growth from economic growth
- place more emphasis on waste prevention and re-use
- meet Landfill Directive diversion targets for biodegradable municipal waste between 2010 and 2020
- increase diversion from landfill of non-municipal waste
- secure better integration of treatment for municipal and non-municipal waste
- secure investment in improved infrastructure relating to waste management and disposal
- secure the best possible benefit from recycling of resources and recovery of energy from residual waste, using a mix of technologies

Getting tough

Although many people support 'green' ideas, the proportion of waste going for recycling in the UK remains stubbornly low in most areas. This may be because of inertia on the part of individuals, because councils do not have sufficiently wide arrangements for individual householders to separate their waste prior to collection, or because some people lack the mobility to reach Neighbourhood Recycling Centres.

Some councils have experimented with fortnightly rather than weekly waste collections (often involving the collection of non-recyclable waste one week and recyclable waste the next), but these have usually proved unpopular because of the smells that circulate in hot weather and the potential threat to public health due to rodent infestation and the increasing presence of foxes in urban areas. For many residents, the collection of rubbish is one of the few council services that are immediately visible and, as council taxes rise, householders often feel they are being offered an inferior service.

However, the Local Government Association claims that the 40% of English and Welsh councils that are using this system succeed in recycling a lot more waste. The ten English councils with the highest recycling rates all operate a system of fortnightly collections.

Inevitably, computer technology has come to waste disposal in the form of hidden chips placed in wheelie bins in some areas. As the bin is emptied the chip passes across an antenna fitted to the lifting system. An individual serial number is read and a computer inside the truck records the weight of the contents. At the depot the information for each household is downloaded to the council's computer. This might then enable the council to make an additional charge, perhaps for non-recyclable waste, to the council tax already paid by local residents, although councils claim that the chips are to improve efficiency and recycling rates to help meet the EU Landfill Directive. The schemes are rarely publicised by the councils concerned.

For critics, it is yet another example of a Labour government 'stealth tax'. The German firms principally involved, Sulo and Delster Electronic, already operate wheelie-bin sensor systems across Europe. Once again, data collection is involved and the media has substituted 'Bin Brother' for 'Big Brother'.

Practice questions

The following source and questions are typical of those that will be used in Section B of the Unit 2 examination paper.

It is often said that we live in a consumer society and we buy things that are over-packaged, we drink more from bottles and cans, we read more magazines and make far greater use of plastics and use plastic bags.

We don't usually think about their disposal, but it is becoming increasingly difficult for local councils to undertake this task and some are having to take drastic measures to change people's habits.

(1) **For what reasons is waste disposal a growing problem in the United Kingdom?** *(17 marks)*

(2) **Discuss the difficulties that the government and local politicians face in changing people's habits in disposing of household waste and recycling.** *(18 marks)*

UNIT 3

CULTURE AND SOCIETY

An understanding and appreciation of the changing nature and importance of culture

Liverpool: European Capital of Culture

It is sometimes said that London, as England's capital city, is also its cultural centre. The sheer size of London and its attraction for tourists tends to mean that it dominates many of the more traditional aspects of culture. Competition for the title of England's 'second city' is intense, with Birmingham and Manchester usually the main contenders. Liverpool, the European Capital of Culture for 2008, achieved some measure of fame in the 1960s as the home of a number of pop groups, most notably the Beatles, who played at the city's Cavern Club. The group's two surviving members, Sir Paul McCartney and Ringo Starr, have been involved in the year-long programme. Liverpool is equally well known as the home of two famous football clubs, Liverpool and Everton.

40,000 people gathered on St George's Plateau on 11 January for The People's Opening of Liverpool Cultural Capital 2008

The idea of a European Capital of Culture first surfaced in 1985, when Athens was the designated capital. Until Liverpool was chosen to be Culture Capital in 2008, the only other city in the UK to be accorded the honour was Glasgow in 1990 after its 'Glasgow's Miles Better' campaign. Little is known about how much the chosen capital benefits in social and economic terms, but usually its image is enhanced by the publicity generated. Liverpool One is one of Europe's largest city centre retail developments.

It is perhaps no surprise that the famous musical *West Side Story*, with its feuding Jets and Sharks, is being reinvented as *North-West Side Story* featuring rival Scousers and Mancunians. As a curtain raiser to 2008, the 2007 Turner Prize exhibition took place at Tate Liverpool rather than in London for the first time in its 23-year history.

'Highbrow' music

Classical music has long been looked on as 'highbrow' — the preserve of a knowledgeable elite with the education and experience to appreciate sometimes long and difficult musical compositions. Concerts given by well-known regional and national orchestras are seen as something for older and socially exclusive audiences. In broadcasting terms, Radio 3 (formerly the Third Programme until 1967) was for years the only source of nationally broadcast classical music, and it was accepted that its appeal would be limited to a small minority audience.

A radical challenge came with the establishment of Classic FM, a commercial radio station playing classical music and rising to become one of the five most listened-to national radio stations. For Radio 3 this challenge came in an age when increasing notice was taken of the size of audiences. For Radio 3 devotees, Classic FM was an imposter, playing only snippets of the most popular pieces of classical music. Radio 3 was a serious broadcasting station, not shirking from broadcasting full works that might be obscure and challenging. For the devotees, classical music could rarely, if ever, be popular and challenging at the same time.

What Classic FM offered was, for its critics, background music, in bite-sized pieces and accompanied by friendly and informal presenters. But doing nothing while Classic FM flourished was not an option for the controller of Radio 3. Though primarily a classical music programme, it also had wider musical aims at a time when the market for 'serious' classical music recordings, and the 'high art' that it represented, was small and shrinking. The only way that Radio 3 could compete was by what some people saw as 'dumbing down'. Was this, however, a snobbish reaction, a feeling that 'real' classical music could only be appreciated by 'true' music lovers, the traditional elite? The presence of new audiences might not be appreciated.

There is no doubt that Radio 3 has made strenuous efforts to vary its output in recent years — to the detriment of its responsibilities to classical music, many of its critics would argue. It would be a mistake to see it as a radio station that broadcasts only classical music, and its website (**www.bbc.co.uk/radio3**) is illuminating in this respect:

> *BBC Radio 3 makes available a broad spectrum of classical music, jazz, world music, drama and arts discussions...Radio 3 plays a role in shaping the national cultural agenda through its promotion of musical performance; its commissioning of music; and through its drama and ideas programmes.*

Ultimately, though, 'classical music remains at the heart of the schedule, and new partnerships with UK orchestras in Birmingham, Bournemouth and Manchester have ensured a greater range of classical music on the network'. However, by the middle of 2007, after its most radical programme shake-up since 2003, RAJAR (Radio Joint Audience Research) figures indicated that it had an audience of 1.78 million listeners — its lowest figure for a decade.

Classic FM began broadcasting in 1992 and Nick Bailey, who opened the broadcast then with Handel's *Zadok the Priest*, is still one of the station's presenters. Within 5 years, the station had over 4 million listeners tuning in each week and has won the Sony Awards Station of the Year three times. The figure is now closer to 6 million — a figure that does much to satisfy its mission statement, which is very different from that of Radio 3.

Classic FM talks of the daunting task of making music composed a long time ago 'relevant to the twenty-first century', whereas many Radio 3 listeners might prefer to keep it in the historical and cultural context in which it was written. A prime aim of Classic FM, based on its own research, is to use classical music 'to help cope with the stress of modern life' and to 'improve the mood of the listener by providing an environment to relax, find balance and stir emotions' — something the station sees as 'a mental breath of fresh air, restoring mind, body and spirit' (see **www.classicfm.co.uk**).

Classic FM certainly does not have either the range or the depth of programmes broadcast on Radio 3. It focuses wholly on music: 'familiar music alongside less well-known pieces, all chosen to uplift, soothe and stir the emotions'. This represents an approach 'designed to make classical music as accessible to as many people as possible...regardless of age which is why the station starts young with music education in schools an important part of its work'. (The station has an estimated 400,000 children among its listeners.)

The battle between the two stations represents far more than a skirmish between two broadcasters:

- It focuses the underlying tension between the duties and responsibilities of a public service broadcaster (Radio 3) and a commercial broadcaster (Classic FM) dependent on revenue from advertisers.
- It highlights a central argument in the arts about the nature of high culture and popular culture, and the extent to which at least some of the arts remain exclusive while others have the 'inclusivity' and 'accessibility' favoured by the Labour government.
- It focuses on the role of the arts in challenging their audience by making them think and work hard; in being something more than mood music in the background as an accompaniment to other tasks.
- It reflects the therapeutic role of the arts in a society where the emphasis is often on pace and long hours of work.
- In terms of classical music, what is the ultimate goal? Classic FM has undoubtedly done much to revive interest in classical music; but in doing so, does it misrepresent its original purpose, thus diluting its quality? Or are the purists too inflexible, unwilling to acknowledge social dynamics and the different demands that they make?

Ask the examiner

Q **Do I have to like classical music?**

A Nobody should feel that they are being forced to like anything. A lot of people feel they have to like it because it is expected of them — in the same way that most adults are thought to be dismissive of pop music. Try listening to Classic FM with its bite-size musical excerpts. If you find composers or works that you like, ask yourself what it is you like about them and use the internet for a bit of research and extra listening.

Beyond music

Similar questions concerning inclusivity and exclusivity are asked about other areas of the arts. Often it is a question of image and perceptions. Sadler's Wells in London may be associated in the minds of many with classical performances yet, over the year, it covers a range of dances including hip-hop.

The same applies to the Royal Opera House. This grand venue has run an educational outreach programme, Chance to Dance, for 16 years. Its aims are to take ballet to young people who wouldn't normally experience it and to spot talent that may otherwise be concealed. The programme is widening perceptions and helping to change long-held stereotypes, and it has given more than 20,000 children from the primary schools of the London boroughs of Lambeth, Southwark, and Hammersmith and Fulham opportunities and the chance to learn skills that many would not have dreamt of.

From the youngsters come a small percentage destined to become ballet dancers, including some who will take dance out into the community and increase diversity, encouraging dancers from a variety of ethnic groups.

Potentially, dance is extremely popular, even if much of that popularity is confined to the Christmas/New Year period when performances of *Sleeping Beauty*, *Swan Lake* and the *Nutcracker Suite* are usually guaranteed sell-outs. *Strictly Come Dancing* has proved a successful television series, the more so with celebrities involved. Although still predominantly female, dance has the potential to bring in people from both genders and to cut across age groups and traditional cultural borders.

Dance has a number of benefits:
- It is a physical activity that fits in well with current calls for more health and fitness. Dancers have to be strong, fit and healthy.
- It provides opportunities for involvement and participation.
- It teaches a range of skills and requires learning and concentration to do well.
- It encourages innovation, creativity and experimentation in the arts, both in groups and individually.
- It keeps young people together and helps to give them a sense of identity, especially when different ethnic groups share their dancing cultures.

The film *Billy Elliott* (2000) is still popular. Its central character — and hero — was, unusually, not only a boy but a working-class boy, and not from London but from the northeast of England, traditionally a stronghold of macho culture. It was an interesting and welcome portrait, because boys who dance are likely to get teased and bullied; training is arduous, long and expensive; provision beyond London and major cities is limited; and ballet dancing is predominantly middle-class.

Does art have to be dumbed down to be popular? Not necessarily. In the period between April 2006 and April 2007 the Tate had 7.7 million visitors, over 5 million of whom visited Tate Modern, which became the second most visited tourist attraction in Britain (the most popular, by cultural contrast, was Blackpool Pleasure Beach).

Working-class boy Billy Elliott (Jamie Bell) with his teacher played by Julie Walters

Practice question

This is typical of a question that might be asked in Section B of Unit 3.

'There is a declining interest in arts and culture in the UK but this could be reversed if there was more arts coverage on television at peak time. This would raise awareness, stimulate interest and encourage more people to attend exhibitions and go to the theatre.'

To what extent, and for what reasons, do you agree with this viewpoint? *(25 marks)*

Creativity, innovation and aesthetic evaluation

Creativity, innovation and artistic style

Most people undertake creative artistic activities, from the simplest at nursery school to the hobbies that people might develop as adults and the work that some produce as professional artists. To be creative we develop ideas and use our imagination. The creative instinct might be applied to any art form and the end product is of variable quality.

Innovation is rather more demanding because it suggests something that is new — something different to what has been created or experienced before. It can involve ideas, materials or techniques. An innovative film or drama might involve a new technique or a new insight; in the arts generally, innovation might lead to the development of a distinctive style, form or genre.

Names of artistic styles may be used to describe works of art with similar characteristics, ways of performing or aspects of design. In this way, artworks can be grouped together and labelled. Such labels are broad and may often be viewed in a historical context. We may refer to Elizabethan literature or war poetry — particularly the work of poets such as Wilfred Owen and Siegfried Sassoon in the First World War. Alternatively, written work may be categorised as crime fiction or science fiction. Films may be 'westerns' or 'art house'.

The Renaissance

The word 'Renaissance' was adapted from the French equivalent of the Italian word *rinascimento* meaning 'rebirth'. It was first used by Jakob Burckhardt in his book *The Civilisation of the Renaissance in Italy* (1860). The Renaissance represented a cultural rebirth and signified a revival in the arts and learning that began in Italy and spread throughout Europe.

Famous artists associated with the Renaissance are Leonardo da Vinci (an Italian painter, sculptor, architect and engineer whose paintings *The Last Supper* and *Mona Lisa* are universally known) and Michelangelo (an Italian Renaissance sculptor, painter and architect who was commissioned by the Pope to paint the ceiling of the Sistine Chapel in Rome between 1508 and 1512 and who had an unparalleled influence on the development of Western art).

Two important English composers of the Renaissance were Thomas Tallis, who served four monarchs from Henry VIII to Elizabeth I and was the pre-eminent church musician, and William Byrd, probably the foremost composer of the Elizabethan age and celebrated for his achievements in keyboard music and madrigals.

Leonardo da Vinci's *Mona Lisa*

Impressionism

'Impressionism' was a term first used in 1874 by a French art critic, Louis Leroy, in a derogatory way as criticism of Claude Monet's early painting *Impression: Sunrise* when it was shown in a Paris exhibition. Leroy was not alone as a critic who thought the style might be a disguise for poor technique. The forerunner of Impressionism is sometimes thought to be Joseph Turner's painting *Rain, Steam and Speed*, which he painted in the early 1840s.

The main Impressionist period is roughly 1860–1900, although sometimes it is not easy to distinguish Impressionist art and music from that of its predecessor, Romanticism. (Claude Debussy is widely considered to be the leading musical Impressionist but his famous composition *Clair de Lune* sometimes seems more Romantic than Impressionist.) The aim of Impressionist painters was to suggest rather than depict, and the use of light to transform the object it shines on was important. Everyday situations were often used as subjects for Impressionist paintings.

Monet became famous for his paintings such as *The Picnic* and remained a devoted and dedicated adherent of the movement, using the water garden in the grounds of his house in Giverny as the scene for his famous series of paintings, *Waterlilies*.

Le Moulin de la Galette (1876) by Auguste Renoir

Pierre-Auguste Renoir was responsible for some of the most well-known and commonly reproduced images in paintings such as *The Bathers, Luncheon of the Boating Party* and *Le Moulin de la Galette,* although he became less attached to the movement as his technique developed.

The Impressionist composer, Claude Debussy, like Monet, found some of his early work was quickly dismissed. Debussy was responsible for enduring compositions such as *Reverie* and *The Submerged Cathedral* but he was never happy with the term 'Impressionist music'.

Maurice Ravel was a great admirer of Debussy, using rich harmonies and new scales. He was interested in the music of other cultures, particularly Spain, and wrote orchestral music, two operas, ballets (including *Daphnis et Chloé* and *Bolero*), and songs with instruments (including *Sheherazade*). His most enduring composition for piano was most probably *Pavane for a Dead Princess.*

Pop art

'Pop art' was an obvious abbreviation of 'popular art' and used everyday objects to demonstrate elements of popular culture, particularly comic strips and images in advertising and on television. The term was first used in 1958 by an English critic, Lawrence Alloway, who made links with the consumerism and materialism that began to develop in the late 1950s and 1960s after a period of postwar austerity. It marked a move away from Abstract Expressionism. It rejected abstract painting because of its association with artistic elitism.

One of the prominent pop artists was Andy Warhol, who began as a commercial illustrator, then moved to comic strips and quickly achieved fame after his first exhibition in Los Angeles in 1962, which featured his *32 Campbell's Soup Cans.* Warhol also made silkscreens of cultural icons of the age such as Mick Jagger, John Lennon, Brigitte Bardot, Marilyn Monroe and Truman Capote. Later in his life, Warhol used Polaroid photographs as the basis for creating portraits of ten of the most famous sports stars of the age and, when they went on sale in 2007, the price tag was over £14 million.

Roy Lichtenstein was an American who achieved fame in 1963 with *Whaam!* In comic strip style, it featured a fighter aircraft firing a rocket into an enemy plane with boxed caption and a striking red and yellow explosion.

David Hockney is usually regarded as the father of British pop art. He learned his artistic skills in Bradford and London, where his work first featured in a Royal College of Art exhibition in 1961. Heavily influenced by a visit to Los Angeles in 1964, he established a base in California. His swimming pool paintings were among his best; and his portraits shown in London's National Portrait Gallery in 2006 resulted in one of the gallery's most successful exhibitions. Hockney's most recent landscapes include *Bigger Trees near Water*, a 40 x 15 foot tribute to the East Yorkshire landscape and the largest painting ever hung in the Royal Academy of Arts.

Participation and communication in the arts

The cinema

Until the mid-1950s, the cinema had no rivals. It was a relatively cheap form of popular entertainment for individuals and families. It was a place of action, adventure and romance — in the latter case both on and off the screen. Not for nothing were cinemas called 'picture palaces', with their finely upholstered seats, grand designs, warmth and usherettes at a time when home entertainment was very limited.

The death of the cinema has been widely predicted ever since television became more popular during the 1950s. Similar predictions were made when colour broadcasting came to television and when video and DVD players and even satellite television became more widely available, yet the cinema has not only survived but frequently flourished. However, a number of cinemas did become run-down and seedy as it became more and more difficult to generate revenue, and some were dismissed as 'fleapits'.

To its credit, the industry did not lie down and die, and the age of the multiplex instead of the single-screen cinema helped the cinema to revive; by the bumper year of 1971, 182 million people went through the doors. Walt Disney's *The Aristocats*, the film version of the popular television comedy *On the Buses*, and the western *Soldier Blue* (hailed for its brutal and realistic portrayal of relations between native Indians and settlers but condemned by some for its violence) were box office favourites.

When audience figures next approached the 1971 peak in 2002, the top four films (*The Lord of the Rings*; *Monsters, Inc.*; *Star Wars II*; and *Spider-Man*) were all visual extravaganzas combining fantasy, computer-generated images and stunning special effects. Box office takings reached £812 million.

There has been a marked, if sometimes uneven, upward trend in UK cinema-going since the mid-1980s. Over the period from 1997 to 2006, UK cinema attendance rose by 18.5% — a figure comparable to rises in France but much bigger than the 5% rise in Italian audiences and decidedly better than Germany, where there was an 11% fall. The year 2007 was another bumper one for the cinema, with *Harry Potter and the Order of the Phoenix*, *The Simpsons Movie* and *Transformers* proving very popular. The UK is now the world's number three cinema market.

Yet there are still battles to be fought as technology continues to advance. Challenges from lending chains such as Blockbuster have probably been seen off and piracy has been challenged rigorously. More people are buying wide-screen televisions as prices fall but it is thought that this trend is unlikely to present the cinema with a major challenge. The biggest threat is likely to be the extended use of the internet to show films and Jaman.com has spent millions of dollars developing a new method of enabling subscribers to download a film from its library (which it plans to increase to 10,000 films) to be stored on their own computers for 7 days in a fairly sophisticated 'high definition' form.

Various factors help to maintain the popularity of cinemas:
- Multiplexes are stylish and welcoming.
- Many different films can be show in the same venue because of the large number of screens.
- In recent years there has been a rise in the popularity of more intimate cinemas with fewer screens and rural cinemas, often maintained by local volunteers.
- Relatively speaking, cinemas offer good value in terms of admission prices.
- There is a large amount of publicity about films.
- The big screen continues to be an exciting experience, especially for young people who can gather safely in groups.
- Timings are flexible, thus suiting a wide range of tastes.
- Special effects in the cinema are exciting and multi-dimensional.
- Though the majority of cinema-goers are still young (nearly 50% are under 25), older audiences have returned to the cinema, with the number of over-45s doubling between 1996 and 2006.

- According to research commissioned by the Film Distributors' Association, 49% of young people say that cinema-going is their favourite overall activity.
- Hollywood films, in particular, have big production budgets and are often visually very exciting (although the most popular film of 2006, the James Bond movie *Casino Royale*, was British).
- The weather continues to play a significant role in cinema attendances. Figures drop during hot summers and rise in wet summers like 2007. (School holidays have a considerable impact on yearly figures.)

The theatre

Rightly or wrongly, the cinema is often associated with popular culture, although in some respects it appears classless. There seem to be no barriers to the cinema, perhaps because its prices are much cheaper than the theatre. Because the theatre can be expensive, with London tickets usually between £25 and £50, the theatre is more exclusive. People may still dress for the theatre in a way they feel no compulsion to do for the cinema, and cinema habits of coke and popcorn would draw disapproving looks among theatregoers.

The most detailed evidence available about London theatre audiences — and London inevitably has many more theatres than any other British city — comes from the West End Theatre Audience Report compiled by MORI and based on a survey of 6,615 theatregoers in 2003. Some of its main points are listed below:

- Nearly 75% of West End theatre audiences came from the UK, and half of those from London.
- Of the 25% who came from other countries, nearly half were from the USA or Canada. Other foreign visitors to the theatre came from 11 different, mostly European countries.
- There was a significant gender difference, seemingly long-standing, with a 2:1 ratio in favour of females; this difference was more pronounced among younger age groups.
- The breakdown of age groups was fairly even except for the over-65s, who made up only 10%.
- 67% of theatregoers were working full- or part-time, while 15% were retired and 11% were students.
- Audiences were overwhelmingly (92%) white — a figure almost identical with the proportion of people describing themselves as white in data gathered for the 2001 census.

- 20% of those surveyed earned in excess of £50,000 a year with 41% earning over £30,000 — although audiences for opera or dance productions were more affluent.
- Topping alternative leisure pursuits among theatregoers were visits to a museum or art gallery and the cinema.

In many respects, theatre audiences in London are buoyant. According to the Society of London Theatre there were record attendances in 2006, when more than 12 million visitors were attracted to London theatres. Theatres are usually associated with plays but London theatres are increasingly dominated by musicals, a number of which might be based on films or television programmes.

Is there sufficient serious drama? Is the theatre any longer innovative? Once again we cannot ignore the commercial realities of the arts, particularly if subsidies are small or non-existent. The central issue is how to combine quality with audience appeal and that begs the question of what we understand by 'quality'.

Musicals are a visual extravaganza that feed the imagination, entertain and offer a couple of hours of escapism. The names are familiar: *Les Misérables*, *Joseph and the Amazing Technicolour Dreamcoat*, *The Phantom of the Opera*, *The Sound of Music*, *Grease*, *Mamma Mia!*, *Mary Poppins*, *Hairspray*. These are productions that go on and on and cannot be divorced from public demand.

Context, taste and aesthetic judgement

It is probably unrealistic to try to appreciate works of art, in any form, without having some knowledge of the age in which they were created. An understanding of Elizabethan society would provide a backcloth for understanding the plays of Shakespeare, and the novels of Charles Dickens, though sanitised by musicals such as *Oliver*, grew out of conditions in Victorian England.

Creative artists both shape opinion and reflect it — certainly it would be impossible to live in total isolation. They probably also create for an audience or a patron with particular tastes and values, because that is the commercial reality of working as a full-time artist. It can be an inhibiting factor because audiences are less likely to favour highly original works with which they are unfamiliar and may well reject them entirely. Equally, a more liberal age such as the 1960s saw more radical developments including the emergence of pop art, the loosening of cinema taboos and the ending of the Lord Chancellor's role in theatre censorship.

Aesthetics concerns the study and appreciation of art. We may never be sure how far our taste is conditioned by what we are used to hearing, seeing or reading, or by cultural trends or nostalgia, or by the quality and range of our own experience. To a greater or lesser extent taste is open to external influences, and in a rapidly changing world with new technologies and fashions, judgements often become more difficult and less secure.

Individuals often make judgements based on personal tastes and preferences and may not readily be able to articulate the reasons for their reaction to a particular stimulus. Critics or 'experts' are unlikely to escape as easily with subjective reactions and must seek more defined criteria, although even these might be contentious. They might take the aspects below into account.

Age

The age of an object or creation may lend an air of reverence, in that the work in question has 'stood the test of time' (i.e. remained admired and popular). Something new may prove to be transitory and ephemeral. (For example, paintings classed as 'Old Masters' are almost beyond criticism. Finalists for the Turner Prize are routinely criticised for what many believe to be a lack of artistic merit in the more traditionally understood ways. Classical music is seen as better than pop music on a number of grounds, not least because it tends to rely on more skill in composition and delivery.)

Form and production method

A critic might consider the style, originality, skill of execution and complexity of the work.

- Works of art may be based on a recognisable style or follow generally accepted rules in the way they have been created.
- Although works of art are almost invariably creative, very few are highly original; those that are may not in fact be readily accepted or appreciated even by critics.
- Many creative artists — be they writers, painters, sculptors, actors, singers or dancers — may show a high degree of technical skill or be recognised craftspeople.
- Complexity is often a feature of an artistic creation — a film, play or artefact — especially if a measure of integration is required. (The films of Peter Greenaway, such as *The Draughtsman's Contract* and *The Cook, the Thief, his Wife and her Lover*, often backed by music composed by Michael Nyman, are often both visually striking and complex in form.)

Content

A common question we ask ourselves is what the creator of a work of art is trying to say. Alternatively we may ask if the artist has been successful in eliciting a reaction from the audience, particularly if the work seeks to offer a comment about a social problem. A classic example was Jeremy Sandford's *Cathy Come Home*, strikingly shot using 16 mm cameras in Ken Loach's innovative drama-documentary shown as part of BBC television's *The Wednesday Play* series in 1966. Based on homelessness and the separation of families, it drew a massive audience and caused outrage, leading to the foundation of the pressure group Shelter.

The series, and its post-1970 successor *Play for Today*, introduced innovative and original writers such as Dennis Potter (who later combined music and drama to great effect in *Pennies from Heaven, The Singing Detective* and *Lipstick on your Collar*) writer–directors like Mike Leigh with his improvised style (made famous by the play *Abigail's Party*) and campaigning director, Ken Loach.

Morality, the law and the arts

Some writers and directors are rarely far from controversy because of their politically committed stance. Jim Allen's television play *The Big Flame* (1969), featuring scenes of violent industrial unrest as workers fought to take over Liverpool Docks, was twice postponed, and Roy Minton's *Scum*, which took an uncompromising look at the life of young offenders in a borstal and was originally made for television in 1977, was banned until 1991.

Other controversial but challenging plays written for BBC television in the 1960s were Nell Dunn's *Up the Junction* (timed to coincide with the political debate on the Abortion Law Reform Bill, watched by an audience of 10 million and containing a graphic abortion scene), and Jimmy O'Connor's *Three Clear Sundays* (screened during the debate on the abolition of capital punishment). Loach, with his desire to mix fact with fiction and to take drama to the streets, bringing social realism into millions of households, was involved in both.

Alleged obscenity was always a likely reason for problems with the law and controversy over morality, although tastes change. Radclyffe Hall's 1928 novel *The Well of Loneliness* was banned for many years; perhaps, like Queen Victoria, many considered the topic of lesbianism impossible to contemplate. Following the passing of the 1959 Obscene Publications Act, Penguin Books was prosecuted for publishing

D. H. Lawrence's *Lady Chatterley's Lover* on the grounds that descriptions of the sexual relations between a gamekeeper and his employer's wife would 'deprave and corrupt'. After a 6-week trial, Penguin was found not guilty.

Between 1843 and 1968, the Lord Chamberlain's blue pencil ruled the theatre and led to the banning of one of George Bernard Shaw's plays, *Mrs Warren's Profession* (prostitution). After the demise of the Lord Chamberlain with the 1968 Theatres Act, the controversial American musical *Hair* came to London with its nudity, drug taking and desecration of the US flag in a protest about the Vietnam War.

In many respects, it seems that the battle for artistic freedom has been won, although criminal prosecutions remain possible if boundaries, though ever expanding, are transgressed. There were violent protests by Sikhs in Birmingham at the end of 2004 against the play *Behzti* ('dishonour'), written by the Sikh playwright Gurpreet Bhatti, on the grounds that it was disrespectful to Sikhism because of its depiction of sexual abuse and murder in a Sikh temple. The play was taken off by the Birmingham Stage Company on health and safety grounds.

According to Dalya Alberge writing in *The Times*, the 2005 Barbican production of William Marlowe's 1580s play *Tamburlaine* was cut to eliminate a scene featuring the burning of the Koran. The evangelical group *Christian Voice* had mixed success in its protests against the touring theatrical production of *Jerry Springer: The Opera* in 2006, but it helped to orchestrate 60,000 complaints after it was shown on BBC television in 2005.

Artistic achievement from a range of cultures

The Russian-American

Born in Russia in 1903, Mark Rothko moved with his family to New York as a 10-year-old. He had his first solo exhibition at New York's Contemporary Arts Gallery in 1933 and though often described as a practitioner of abstraction and expressionism Rothko was much more sympathetic to the latter. He achieved fame after a solo retrospective at the Museum of Modern Art in New York in 1961; towards the end of his life (he died in 1970) he painted murals for a new nondenominational chapel in Houston. In 2007 Rothko's abstract oil *White Center*, typical of his bold use of colour and uneven hazy divisions, sold for nearly $73 million at Sotheby's New York. For the first time, the electronically displayed panel of currency conversions included roubles, indicative of the growing power of Russian buyers.

Protest art

Disasters of war: *Francisco de Goya*

Napoleon's invasion of Spain in 1808 led to the torture of Spanish peasants by French troops and similar retaliatory action by Spanish fighters. In 1810, Goya began a graphic sequence of 82 prints showing the conflict between Spanish guerrillas and Napoleon's army during the Peninsular War.

Never before had an artist captured the horrors and atrocities of war with such scenes of violence, starvation, rape, mutilation and execution. The work was finished in 1820 but not shown until 1863.

Guernica: *Pablo Picasso*

Picassso's painting is one of the best-known works of art depicting the horrors of war. It commemorates the attack by German *Luftwaffe* bombers and planes from Italy's *Aviazione Legionaria* during the Spanish Civil War on the Basque market town of Guernica in 1937. The attack killed over 1,600 people and injuring many more. Only 1% of the town's buildings are said to have survived.

The raid prompted Picasso to change a canvas he was painting for the Paris Exhibition. Picasso started work on the vast mural about a week after the bombing had taken place. *Guernica* was exhibited later in the year in the Republican Spain pavilion at the Paris Exhibition. Picasso refused to let *Guernica* return to Spain during Franco's dictatorship. It did so in 1981 and hangs in Madrid's Reina Sofia Museum, having become an icon for anti-war protesters.

Guernica (1937) by Pablo Picasso

East–West exchange

In 2007 China's new Capital Museum in Beijing — one of the many new cultural buildings built in connection with the 2008 Olympics — hosted 'Aftershock: Contemporary British Art 1990–2006', the city's biggest exhibition of contemporary British art. It featured the work of artists such as Damien Hirst and Tracey Emin (her unmade *My Bed* of 1998 toned down to the neat and tidy *The Simple Truth*) and included the *Übermensch* sculpture by Jake and Dinos Chapman depicting the physicist Stephen Hawking perched precariously on top of a cliff. These artists, and Gilbert and George who exhibited in China in 1993, all influenced newly emerging Chinese artists. Meanwhile, Tate Liverpool exhibited the work of a new generation of 18 Chinese artists in 'The Real Thing: Contemporary Art from China', including a £100,000 commission for Ai Weiwei to build an 8-metre high, 2-tonne chandelier that will float in the city's Albert Dock.

With China undergoing both an economic and cultural revolution, and a number of settlements of artists emerging in Beijing and Shanghai, the work of Chinese artists such as Wang Guangyi, Zeng Fanzhi and Zhang Xiaogang continues to appreciate in value. The latter's 1993 work, *Tiananmen Square*, sold for £1.2 million in Christie's Hong Kong auction house in 2006 and Hong Kong has been a vital conduit in uniting curators and collectors (the latter including the leading British collector and patron Charles Saatchi, who has a website dedicated to Chinese art).

Venice Biennale

Every other June, thousands of artists, critics, curators, patrons, dealers and art lovers gather in Italy for the Venice Biennale. It has taken place for decades and draws artists from all over the world to compete for the much-coveted Golden Lion award. Of more than 60 contemporary art biennials, Venice remains pre-eminent. With its networking and partying it is one of the major events in the art calendar and it is often said to be the art world's greatest stage.

There are permanent national pavilions in the city's public gardens and the British pavilion is a classical tea room, which is much admired. Commissioned by the British Council, Tracey Emin was chosen to represent Britain in 2007 with her show *Borrowed Light*. In addition to the individual national pavilions (77 countries were involved in 2007, with Turkey and India there for the first time), there is also a central international exhibition coordinated by a prominent curator. Successful appearances at the Venice Biennale can have a major impact on the sales of artists' work, especially if it is shown in other exhibitions.

Practice questions

This is typical of a question that might be set in Section A of Unit 3.

> Study Sources A and B on Doris Salcedo's Tate Modern installation, *Shibboleth*, and then answer Questions 1 and 2.
>
> Use your own words, rather than simply repeating those used in the sources, to show your understanding of the points being made.

Source A: *Shibboleth*

Some remarkable things have appeared in the former power station that is now the Turbine Hall at Tate Modern. The latest in a long line of interesting installations is rather disconcerting — even alarming. And I don't suppose I'm alone in thinking this. Essentially, it's a 548-foot crack in the floor and it's certainly sufficient to feed the appetites of the doubters of modern art.

A number of questions come to mind, the most obvious being: how did it get there? There's also the issue of health and safety and I have to ask myself how dangerous it is and how many people might have fallen down there? Strange in these litigious days, where blame is apportioned on a pass-the-parcel basis ('no win no fee'). Finally I'd like to know what it means.

Part of one question is easily answered by reading a leaflet that provides a clear message for visitors: 'Warning. Please watch your step in the Turbine Hall. Please keep your children under supervision.' Luckily I'm not short-sighted and I don't have a little one clinging to my arm asking either for a new toy or to do something interesting.

Doris Salcedo's *Shibboleth* in the Tate Modern's Turbine Hall

The leaflet also tells me that the crack is the work of a Colombian artist, Doris Salcedo, and I have a vague memory of one of her other creations that featured a large stack of chairs. This one is called *Shibboleth* and the leaflet tells me that a shibboleth is 'a token of power: the power to judge and kill'. It's certainly meant to be symbolic. Part of the past that's been disregarded or marginalised. Or is it the darker side of racism? Whatever it is, it's brought in plenty of visitors.

I'm still wondering just how she did it because the crack is not small. In fact, it's very large indeed. As it starts it's barely noticeable — just the tiniest hairline fracture in the concrete floor that gets wider and deeper as it zigzags across the floor. At its widest point it can't be far short of twelve inches across and at its deepest it must go down three times that distance.

According to the artist it took her a year to create. The process of installation took about 5 weeks, but she has refused absolutely to reveal her precise method of construction, arguing that the meaning of her work is more important than how it was constructed. It is, she says, 'as deep as humanity'. A spokesperson for the Tate was equally tight-lipped.

Rumours are not always reliable and disagreement over technique fuels debate and forms part of the work's mystique. Whatever method it was, it involved an awful lot of cement and probably a measure of polystyrene moulding. At some stage there must have been plenty of labouring and no small amount of finishing.

For some people it will undoubtedly work and many will find it captivating, intriguing and evocative. Somehow it seems to capture the spirit of the physical environment and it allows us scope for interpretation. Others might be alarmed by the threatening nature of the crack, but perhaps that is part of the challenge. Risk, in a world that has become anodyne and almost risk-free. Truly innovative art should offer that sort of challenge.

Source B: What would the school caretaker have said?

Doris Salcedo built a mountain of old chairs at the Istanbul Biennial in 2003. It reminded me of my schooldays when, at the end of the summer term, there was a cull of old furniture. Grumbling and growling, the caretaker could be observed from a distance piling up all the rejected wooden chairs near to his hidey-hole in the boiler room. Climbing them was a temptation as the mountain grew, but he was a formidable character. We saw it as an adventure rather than a quest to find the meaning of art. For him it was firewood.

Now Doris Salcedo is at the Tate Modern's Turbine Hall, where she seems to have introduced a crack into the floor. I could imagine what our caretaker would have said: 'Wanton vandalism.' He wasn't a man to argue with or to discuss the finer points of modern art and its meaning. 'Art? Must have seen you coming.'

It's proved a very popular exhibition and will be showing for some months so there are obviously plenty of enthusiasts, and the Turbine Hall is quite selective about what it commissions. It wouldn't do it for the caretaker and, to be honest, I'm not sure that it does it for me either. He could never articulate the criticisms, but sometimes I wonder who does set standards in conceptual art and whether he wasn't right all along. 'Can't see it? Well there's nothing to see. It's just a crack in the floor. It ought to be filled in before somebody gets hurt.'

Questions
(1) **Assess the strengths and weaknesses of the comments made in the above sources about Doris Salcedo's work Shibboleth.** *(12 marks)*

(2) **How far do you consider such contemporary works to be worthwhile forms of art?** *(8 marks)*

Beliefs, values, morals and religions in a pluralist society

Key words in any world religion are 'worship' and 'belief', the belief representing faith in a supreme power. Most societies have religious systems, although belief in a religion is deeply personal. Some people are strongly committed to their religion and may even resort to violence against those who have different beliefs. Many believers are undemonstrative and may or may not participate in organised religion, agnostics are unsure, and atheists reject the idea of personal religious belief for themselves.

On the basis of a voluntary question on religious belief contained in the 2001 UK census, there are 42 million Christians (71.6% of the population). Muslims were the next largest religious group, with 1.5 million believers (2.7% of the population), although the 9 million who indicated that they had no religion made up 15.55% of the population. In total, more than 170 distinct religions were revealed by the census, indicating the extent to which Britain has become a multi-faith society.

There are local concentrations, as in the London borough of Tower Hamlets, where 36% of the population are Muslims, Harrow, where nearly 20% are Hindus, and Barnet, where nearly 15% are Jewish. There is a high concentration of Sikhs in Slough.

In reality the situation is likely to be very different and society much more secular than the census suggests, mainly because many people, when asked if they have a religion, tend to declare themselves 'Christian' or 'C of E' rather than agnostic or atheist, but they might not practise their religion or participate in worship.

Many of those who profess belief do not take part in organised religions and the two major Christian religions, the Church of England and the Roman Catholic Church, have suffered a significant decline in attendance in the last 30 years. (The only churches where attendance is increasing are the Greek and Russian Orthodox churches and churches attended by charismatic evangelical Christians such as the English Pentecostalists.) According to research by Tearfund published in 2007 (*Churchgoing in the UK*), based on interviews with 7,000 people in the UK aged over 16:

- 10% of the UK population attend church at least once a week
- 15% attend church at least monthly
- 26% attend church at least annually
- 59% never, or virtually never, attend church

As such polls tend to overstate the numbers involved, the actual number of regular attenders may be as low as 6%, and the *English Church Census* of 2004 revealed that half a million people ceased Sunday worship between 1998 and 2005 — although the large influx of Polish immigrants since the expansion of the European union, a number of whom are Roman Catholics, may reverse the trend.

Trends towards a more secular society are apparent in many other developed countries, with the exception of the USA, which remains a more noticeably religious country. The division between Protestants and Catholics is still pronounced in Northern Ireland, where schools and housing areas are often segregated.

There are several reasons why people might hold religious beliefs:
- family circumstances and socialisation
- the influence of school or peers
- a particular religious experience
- a wish to live life in a particular way based on the teachings of a specific religion
- personal conviction
- they offer support and comfort
- the promise of an afterlife or reincarnation
- tradition
- a sense of solidarity

Major religions usually have holy books that provide guidelines for believers, perhaps based on what are believed to be divine revelations. Often they combine teaching with instructions about how to behave, and the link between religion, moral codes and the law is often strong.

The place of religious and moral education

In the nineteenth century, when there was little or no state provision, churches often helped to fund the provision of elementary schools. That changed with the coming of board schools after 1870, but the 1944 Education Act ensured that churches continued to have a role in the running of both primary and secondary schools even if they provided very little of the funding.

- Some parents prefer to choose schools that have a more prominent religious ethos.
- Faith schools are expected to teach their pupils about other religions as well as their own.
- In 2001 there were about 7,000 faith schools (more than 25% of the UK total). Most faith schools are primary schools (35.6% of the total compared to 17.5% of secondary schools).
- They are predominantly state-funded but retain a high degree of autonomy. The faiths concerned are overwhelmingly Church of England and Roman Catholic. In addition there are over 30 Jewish schools and a very small number of Muslim schools.
- Voluntary controlled faith schools are paid for completely by the state but have few religious privileges.
- In voluntary aided schools, the religious body has to find 10% of building and repair costs but has many more religious privileges.

The central issue is often the extent to which religion and religious teaching of a particular faith should play a part in the educational system. Religious education (RE) is not part of the National Curriculum but the law requires all publicly funded schools to provide RE that meets the requirements of a locally agreed syllabus (which must not be designed to convert pupils or to press a particular religious belief), also taking into account 2004 guidelines from the Qualifications and Curriculum Authority (QCA) that encouraged the teaching of the tenets of Buddhism, Hinduism, Islam, Judaism and Sikhism. Schools with a religious character usually follow a diocesan syllabus. RE is intended to be for all pupils (including sixth formers in 11–18 institutions but not in sixth form colleges or further education colleges unless it is requested). However, parents have the statutory right to withdraw their children from some, or all, of RE.

There must also be a daily act of collective worship and the law requires that the majority of these occasions must be wholly, or mainly, Christian in character. Parents have the statutory right to withdraw their children from collective worship and, depending on the ethnic and religious mix of their schools, head teachers may apply, locally, for a 'determination' for some or all of their pupils. This removes the requirement that collective worship should be broadly Christian.

As part of the curriculum, RE should promote the spiritual, moral, social and cultural development of the pupils. As a subject, it does not occupy a high place in the traditional curriculum hierarchy of subjects, where English, science and maths are the most important. Often it is allocated only 5% of curriculum time, which means that a teacher sees each class for one period a week. In faith schools RE may occupy a more prominent position but many pupils, generally, view the subject negatively.

The recruitment of specialist RE teachers is often difficult as these are in short supply. Ofsted (the Office for Standards in Education) has indicated that the subject is often not taught by those qualified in the subject in secondary schools although the subject is increasingly popular at GCSE, particularly as approaches have broadened to include current affairs and moral issues. Frequently, short courses are followed in both RE and citizenship studies and the results of these are combined to form a 'full' GCSE. This allows schools to meet the legal requirements of teaching and assessing these two subjects.

Personal, social and moral education (PSME) is another curriculum area that is fraught with difficulties. Surveys reveal that British children are among the most unhappy in Europe, with high rates of alcohol consumption, drug taking and teenage pregnancies. Most secondary schools offer some form of programme, especially in Years 10 and 11, but the time and resources available are usually minimal.

Despite the apparent significance of the issues involved, PSME is another curriculum area that is not highly rated by many young people. As with RE and citizenship studies, few teachers have specialist qualifications and there is no incentive of an external qualification at the end of the course.

Viewpoints

In favour of faith schools
- They increase parental choice.
- Parents have a right to educate their children in the faith of their choice.
- Such schools recognise religious diversity and individual human rights.
- They are said to get better examination results.
- They serve the whole community — they do not discriminate and proselytise.
- They are said to have a better ethos.
- They help religious minorities to preserve their culture and beliefs.

In opposition to religious schools
- In a secular society, non-believers are denied choice.
- It is not the job of publicly funded bodies to instil a religious faith in children.
- Intake selection in faith-based comprehensive schools is on the basis of religion as well as ability.

- Such schools make integration more difficult because of their commitment to a particular religion.
- They lead to hypocrisy as parents seek to establish dubious religious connections to get their children into a faith school.
- The government supports inclusion but faith schools inevitably favour those who have links with their own faith.
- They result in religious segregation, which may lead to more discrimination.

Philosophical, moral and ethical problems

Abortion

The legal position

We have come a long way since the Ellenborough Act of 1803 introduced the death penalty for anyone carrying out an abortion after 16 weeks (later amended to apply to the whole of a pregnancy). Following Liberal MP David Steel's **private member's bill**, which had the support of the Labour government, abortion in Great Britain was legalised by the 1967 Abortion Act; although this has since been amended, the broad principles remain the same. (In Northern Ireland abortion is legal only if the mental or physical health of the woman concerned is 'at serious risk'.)

Key term

private member's bill:
bill brought forward by an MP as an individual rather than by the government, although such bills are rarely successful without government support.

A massive investment in school sex education has not yielded the dividends expected

Figures from the Department of Health indicate that 193,000 abortions took place in England and Wales in 2006, 20% of which involved girls aged 15–19. These figures highlight concern about teenage morality with inevitable references to binge drinking, drugs and promiscuity, and reflect disappointment that a massive investment in school sex education has not yielded the dividends anticipated. In response, representatives of the Family Planning Association have pointed to a resources crisis and the closing of clinics.

The following are the legal conditions for an abortion:

- Up to 24 weeks, two doctors must decide that the risk to a woman's physical or mental health (or that of the child) will be greater if she continues with the pregnancy than if she ends it.
- There is no time limit on abortions where two doctors (or one in a medical emergency) agree that a woman's health or life is gravely threatened by continuing the pregnancy or that the foetus is likely to be born with severe physical or mental abnormalities.
- To proceed with an abortion, a woman does not need the consent of her own doctor, partner or family.
- Girls aged under 16 can have an abortion and parental consent is not always necessary.

In reality, the overwhelming majority of abortions take place during the first 12 weeks of pregnancy and it is often less easy to arrange an abortion between the thirteenth and twenty-fourth week of pregnancy. The 'health risk' criteria are widely used and, although doctors make clinical judgements, they often have to take a subjective view of risk. Some doctors tend to follow the wishes of their patients and support the request for an abortion on health grounds. This often leads critics of abortion to argue that it is available 'on demand'. (In 2006, 97% of abortions that took place did so on grounds of 'health risk to the woman'.)

Religious views

No religion supports abortion but most accept that, in certain circumstances, it may be necessary (see Table 22.1). A few religions are totally opposed. Most believers try to balance their personal circumstances with the teachings of their religion and, in practice, may resort to abortion as a last resort — perhaps to limit family size or when contraception has failed.

The extent to which abortion generates strong feelings is illustrated by the comments made in a provocative sermon delivered in 2007 by Cardinal Keith O'Brien, head of the Roman Catholic Church in Scotland, who described abortion as an 'unspeakable crime'. Controversially comparing abortion with the massacre of children in a Scottish primary school in Dunblane in 1996, Cardinal O'Brien said: 'We are killing — in our country — the equivalent of a classroom of kids every single day', referring also to 'the wanton killing of the innocent'.

Cardinal O'Brien's words drew fierce criticism in response. His language was not dissimilar to that used by militant opponents of abortion in the USA, where those who offend pro-life fundamentalists by assisting in abortion might go in fear of their lives, and where abortion can be a significant election issue in some states.

Table 22.1 Attitudes to abortion of the different religions

Religion	Stance on abortion
Church of England	Many feel that there may be certain circumstances (threat to health) where abortion is justified.
Roman Catholicism	Teaches that sacred life begins at the moment of conception and that abortion is forbidden in all circumstances, punishable by excommunication from the church.
Islam	Usually felt that the life of the woman takes precedence over the life of the foetus if the situation arises. May also sanction abortion if a pregnancy results from rape.
Hinduism	Abortion only permitted to save a woman's life.
Judaism	Orthodox Jews only accept abortion if the mother's health and life are at serious risk. More liberal Jews may seek to take into account wider personal circumstances.
Sikhism	Does not support abortion but may take into account moral issues and the circumstances of the individual involved.
Buddhism	People are encouraged to act according to their conscience in seeking a decision that is right for them.
Jehovah's Witnesses	Abortion is unacceptable in all circumstances.

Ask the examiner

 Q **I am a Roman Catholic and attend a Roman Catholic school. My position on abortion is clear.**

 A Nobody would ask you to go against the teaching of your church on this controversial subject and you should put forward arguments in support of what you believe. Protecting the rights of the unborn child is very important, but you should try to understand the position of those who take other perspectives and why they take such positions. You do not have to agree with them but you do need to use counter-arguments.

Moral and ethical issues

Laws tend to be built on facts, such as the stage of development of the foetus when abortion might usually be permitted. Even then, the law has to be interpreted and people have to act according to their consciences. Often people believe that their personal view is right and that the views of their opponents are wrong, but beliefs are subjective reactions that cannot be proved or disproved by reference to objective criteria.

Measuring public opinion for or against abortion is fraught with difficulty. Much may depend on the credibility of the pollster, the structure of the questions that are asked and the willingness of the respondents to provide an honest view (or any view at all) on an intensely personal and sensitive subject.

Viewpoints

Opponents of abortion
- The position of the Roman Catholic Church on abortion — that all life is sacred and that every life is created by God in his own image — has been reiterated by its leader in England and Wales, Cardinal Cormac Murphy-O'Connor.
- Few could have envisaged how easily the 1967 Act would work and that the annual number of abortions carried out would approach 200,000. In 1988 Lord Alton, backed by 300 MPs, tried to have the limit reduced to 18 weeks, but his private member's bill was eventually unsuccessful.
- Anti-abortion campaigners were more successful in 1990, when the law was amended to incorporate the current 24-week time limit.
- In 2006 the government resisted pressure from the Catholic Church and some MPs to set up a parliamentary enquiry into abortion time limits.
- Roman Catholic MPs are in a difficult position. The teachings of their church are clear, yet all MPs must take into account their own conscience, the views of their party, and the opinions of their constituents — which may be very divided.
- We all originated as a foetus and the destruction of a foetus might contribute to the destruction of the human race. If humans were created in the image of God, the destruction of an embryo becomes a mortal sin.

Defenders of the right to choose
- The extent to which Roman Catholic priests, all of whom take a vow of celibacy, understand the position that some women find themselves in is questioned by pro-abortionists.
- One position, often adopted by feminists, is that a woman has absolute control over her own body.
- Pregnancy may be a result of rape or the life of the mother may be threatened.
- The foetus may be severely handicapped.
- Every child should be a wanted child.
- Men can withdraw from a relationship as a result of pregnancy. Women may not be able to cope without financial/emotional support.
- 'Back street' abortions are dangerous.
- Up to a certain stage, the foetus is only a potential human being.

Many people, not necessarily religious believers, may accept that human life is unique and should not be taken without good cause, and that an embryo, unable to protect itself, should receive protection from the state. It is argued that those seeking an abortion do not always have sufficient opportunity for counselling (for discussing all aspects of the process and its possible consequences), and guilt is often a neglected factor that can affect some women who choose to have an abortion for the rest of their lives.

Clearly, what is a crime in one country is a right in another. Sixty-nine countries across the world ban abortion, but nearly all are prepared to make exceptions if there is a threat to the mother's life. Only three countries — Nicaragua, Chile and El Salvador — ban abortion even if a woman has become pregnant because of rape or if her life is endangered by the pregnancy. These countries will prosecute any woman who has an abortion, and this places doctors in a difficult ethical position as they try to take into account the consequences of breaking the law and their duty to save a life.

Ultimately, in British politics, pragmatism rather than philosophy or dogma usually rules. While it is possible that the time limit might be lowered further, there is no chance that Parliament will be persuaded to vote for a measure that would significantly reduce the number of abortions. Abortion will not go away, and illegal abortions can be extremely dangerous. In countries where abortion is legal, the mortality rate of mothers is 0.2 per thousand, but in countries that do not permit abortion, illegal abortions lead to a maternal mortality rate of 330 per thousand.

Beliefs are often strongly felt and sincerely held, but moral questions rarely have a 'right' or 'wrong' answer. Individual beliefs are based on many influences: friends, family, media and personal experiences all play a part, as does religion. Ideally, we should be open-minded, receptive to different ideas and willing to hear them even if, ultimately, we reject them. We should not try to shout down opponents or simply walk away from the debate.

The following questions are often asked, if rarely answered:
- Whose rights are more important — those of the mother or the developing foetus?
- At what stage does life begin and when does a foetus become a person — at conception, a particular stage of foetal development, or birth?
- Even if there is a legal right to abortion in certain circumstances, can abortion morally be classed as murder?

- Is abortion justified to avoid passing on a genetic condition or if the baby is likely to be born with a severe handicap?
- What approach should be taken to gender abortions in countries where male children are more 'prized', economically, than female children?
- Is opposition to abortion justified if the pregnancy results from rape?

The law and religious belief

Blasphemy laws

Blasphemy laws have existed in the UK for centuries and date back to the time when the church was the main influence on the law. In the UK, blasphemy laws only protect Christians; blasphemous libel occurs when literature is published that is 'reviling' or 'scurrilous' to Christians or when 'ludicrous matter' relating to Christian concepts is published.

The laws are rarely used and efforts are being made to see them repealed. Between 1922 (when the last person was imprisoned for blasphemy) and 1977 there were no prosecutions. However, three legal judgements made since 1979 have been important:

- 1979 *R.* v *Lemon*: moral crusader Mary Whitehouse pursued a prosecution against *Gay News* following its publication of a poem about Jesus titled 'The Love that Dares to Speak its Name'.
- 1991 *R.* v *Chief Metropolitan Magistrate*: some British Muslims tried to invoke the law against the author Salman Rushdie, whose book *The Satanic Verses* was deemed to be insulting to Islam. The court's judgement was that the blasphemy laws did not apply to anti-Islamic blasphemy.
- 1997 *Wingrove* v *UK*: in 1997, the British Board of Film Classification banned the film *Visions of Ecstasy* on the grounds of blasphemy. The court rejected the director's claim for the right to free speech.

Promotion of religious hatred

Islam is a peaceful religion but Muslim extremists have sometimes taken the view that opponents and their religions can be condemned in extreme and often inflammatory terms. In 1988–89 there were widespread protests against Salman Rushdie after the publication of his book, *The Satanic Verses*. There were ritual burnings of the book and a fatwa was issued against him. Fearing for his life, Rushdie then spent many years moving between secret locations.

The rise of Islamic fundamentalism and subsequent increases in Islamophobia in the last few years have raised the profile of what constitutes 'religious hatred' and have generated a keen debate about what can be done to contain and prevent it.

Labour promised legislation in its 2005 election manifesto and, after much debate, the fiercely contentious Racial and Religious Hatred Act of 2006 created an offence of inciting (or stirring up) racial hatred (by threatening words, behaviour or written material on the grounds of their religion), although the Act is yet to be fully implemented.

What actually constitutes racial hatred is difficult to determine. In 2005, a Danish newspaper published 12 cartoons that depicted the prophet Muhammad. It is very unlikely that there was any intention to promote religious hatred but the portrayal was considered blasphemous in Islam. The cultural divide is considerable. *Jerry Springer: The Opera* brought many Christians out in protest. Poor taste, perhaps, but not deemed to be blasphemy.

People should be free to criticise because they have the right of free speech. Religion, which is not always a force for the good, cannot expect to be immune from criticism or debate, and the important principle of freedom of expression must be defended. Those who feel offended have the right to express their outrage in a peaceful manner.

It is not necessarily the role of government to punish publishers who offend certain sections of the community, but it is if demonstrable harm is done. When Nick Griffin, leader of the British National Party, was secretly filmed by the BBC saying that Islam was 'a wicked and vicious faith' he certainly offended Muslims, but it could not be proved that his intention was to stir up racial hatred. Many people are equally offended by Muslim practices of advocating death for apostasy (a change, or desertion, of faith) or the stoning to death of a woman for adultery.

There is a danger in seeking to outlaw what many see as legitimate criticism; the law is designed simply to stop those who intend to stir up racial hatred. Its intention is to ban only 'threatening' words and behaviour, not what is more likely to be critical, abusive or insulting. It remains to be seen how much the law will ultimately be used, particularly as any prosecutions would have to be approved by the Attorney General, the government's chief law officer.

Practice question

This is typical of a question that might apear in Section B of Unit 3.

'Whether it be disagreements between Muslims and Christians or Jews and Arabs, recent events have shown that people of different religions and beliefs are still unable to live in harmony.'

Examine this statement and discuss the main causes and consequences of religious conflict in contemporary society. *(25 marks)*

A2

UNIT **3**

CULTURE AND SOCIETY
Chapter 23

Media and communication

Media controversy, control and censorship

'Reality television' and shows that involve viewers in voting have proved popular for the main television channels. However, the alleged racist bullying of Bollywood actor Shilpa Shetty by some of the other contestants during the fifth series of *Celebrity Big Brother* resulted in an unprecedented number of complaints (10,000 to Channel 4 and 44,500 — three times higher than the highest number previously received — to the broadcasting regulator, Ofcom). It was a row that generated unwelcome headlines and even involved the Indian government, although one suspects that though it was morally wrong, it did no harm to viewing figures, as genuine controversies stimulate interest.

Bollywood actor Shilpa Shetty

In a not unexpectedly severe judgement, Ofcom ruled that Channel 4, which showed the series, had committed 'a serious error of judgement' and had breached its broadcasting code on four occasions. In the process of the enquiry, it emerged that there were also other, unbroadcast, incidents of racism. Channel 4's own review also concluded that it had failed to deal properly with the public's concerns or to recognise that offence might be caused even if it was not intentional. Its eventual interventions were felt to be 'too late or insufficiently forceful'. Channel 4 announced a 10-point plan to implement the recommendations.

Channel 4's chief executive, Andy Duncan, referred to 'a 24/7 media environment' and there is no doubt that broadcasters are under constant pressure, not least to improve ratings as audiences fragment — particularly important for commercial broadcasters in attracting advertisers. (Ironically, in one of the BBC's major television drama hits of 2007, the 1970s-based *Life on Mars*, developed further in 2008 as the 1980s-based *Ashes to Ashes,* the main character, Philip Glenister's DCI Gene Hunt, was very much a figure of 30 years ago and his behaviour — distinctly politically incorrect, being homophobic, misogynistic and racist, was deemed to be acceptable and was exceedingly popular. It was an indication of how much attitudes have changed in 30 years.)

Prior to the launch of the eighth series of *Big Brother*, Ofcom forced Channel 4 to schedule three on-air apologies for the previous incidents. Critics denounce reality television as a modern peep show, tasteless, devoid of any cultural significance and inviting viewers to look at the modern-day equivalent of freaks. It is something suitable for 'the masses', cynically trading on human discomfort and misery. But if reality television is designed to mirror the world that we live in — which might make us very uncomfortable in some circumstances — perhaps that is what it does. It is estimated that Channel 4 draws a quarter of its advertising revenue from *Big Brother*, and over 6 million people watched the first episode of series eight.

In the eighth series of *Big Brother*, it seemed that lessons had been learned when Channel 4 acted quickly by evicting a contestant after she used the word 'nigger' during the show. At the same time, a Channel 4 documentary, *Diana, the Witnesses in the Tunnel*, which showed photographs of the car crash that killed Princess Diana, resulted in over 2,000 complaints from viewers. Princes William and Harry had requested Channel 4 not to use the pictures in its programme and Channel 4 was faced with a difficult editorial decision, which some claimed put them under pressure to act as censors. It was pressure that Channel 4 resisted, and the programme was watched by over 4 million viewers.

Early in 2007, it was revealed that Channel 4's *Richard and Judy* programme had cheated callers out of £1 million by encouraging viewers to phone in when they could not win. Later in the year, the telephone operator behind Noel Edmonds's *Deal or No Deal* was fined £30,000 by the premium rate watchdog ICSTIS after it was revealed that callers phoned in live to win a prize even though the organisers had already selected the winner. This prompted Channel 4 to axe all premium-rate profit-making phone-in competitions. Also in 2007, Channel Five suspended phone-in shows after the quiz show *Brainteaser* was found to have misled callers. When no callers answered the quiz correctly, false names or names of members of the production team were used as winners. Five was fined a record £300,000.

The main channels did not have a good year in 2007 either. The ITV reality show *I'm a Celebrity, Get Me Out of Here* was accused of losing 30,000 phone votes for David Gest in November 2006 and *Dancing on Ice* also appeared to have missed 11,500 phone votes. It was also revealed that a phone-in competition for the BBC's flagship children's programme, *Blue Peter*, designed to raise money for the UN organisation Unicef, was rigged, and soon afterwards the BBC admitted that phone-ins had been manipulated in *Comic Relief*, *Children In Need*, *TMi* and *Sport Relief*.

As ever, the pressure is on producers to maximise revenues and to cut costs in a highly competitive market, and phone-ins have been popular among viewers, 18% of UK households indicating that they have watched call-in television quiz programmes. Many of the high-profile scandals have been blamed on errors of judgement by 'junior' members of staff, although the BBC claimed to have suspended several senior executives over the abuse of phone-ins.

What's wrong with television broadcasting?

For Mark Thompson, attacks on the BBC and tabloid headlines such as 'BBC CHEATS' (*Daily Mirror*) and 'BEAR FACED CHEATS' alongside a picture of Pudsey bear from *Children In Need* (*Sun*) were a rude awakening. Pressure on the balance between costs and revenue has led to more outsourcing of programmes and a greater reliance on freelances and independent companies, making monitoring more difficult. A great many of the people who make programmes for the BBC — or other television companies — do not actually work for them and many are employed only on a programme-by-programme basis.

> **Key term**
>
> **Hutton Report:** Lord Hutton's enquiry (August 2003–January 2004) into the death of Dr David Kelly. Dr Kelly was found dead in 2003 after being named as the source for BBC journalist Andrew Gilligan's claim that the government and its press secretary, Alastair Campbell, had exaggerated claims about Iraq's military capabilities and possession of weapons of mass destruction.

The BBC itself has often in the past been accused of taking too liberal a stance on many matters or exhibiting left-wing sympathies. In particular, questions were raised about the BBC's journalistic standards and the impartiality of its coverage of the Iraq war following the suicide of the government weapons inspector Dr David Kelly, which led to the **Hutton Report**. But most criticisms have remained unsubstantiated assertions, often made by those with their own agendas. Many newspapers that have been quick to criticise the BBC have not always maintained high standards of reporting themselves.

Another accusation made against the BBC is that it is too much of an upmarket service, and a far-reaching review called *Household Value* has sought to identify which social groups use the BBC most often. Inevitably, lower income families (especially in parts of northern England, Wales and Scotland) are less likely to have access to digital channels, to be able to listen to podcasts or to download programmes from the internet.

The licence fee brings in some £3.4 billion a year for the BBC and many liken it to a viewing tax, perhaps forgetting how much they are prepared to pay for privately owned satellite services. Plans are in hand to take some services away from high-cost centres in London to Salford, near Manchester. The projected rise in the licence fee between 2007 and 2012 is from £131.50 to £151.50 — little more than 10%, and not equal to the projected rise in inflation. Consequently, Mark Thompson announced a series of planned economies at the BBC, including 2,500 job losses from its staff of 25,000. Salaries such as Jonathan Ross's rumoured £18 million over 3 years are likely to become a thing of the past.

As cable and satellite services become more accessible, BBC shows need to be popular. Plots of audience pullers like *EastEnders*, with viewing figures usually below those of its great rival, ITV's *Coronation Street*, have to become more daring and exciting — not an easy task because of the impositions on adult content imposed by the 9 p.m. 'watershed'. Unlike ITV, BBC is also seen as a national institution that sets standards that many people say they want but can't necessarily reach in their own lives. Audience share and ratings are important, but the race for popularity can lead to the rule of the lowest common denominator. Popularity is not the same as quality.

Channel Five (now 'Five'), a commercial television station that began broadcasting in a launch by the Spice Girls in 1997, has also been the subject of criticism. It was set up in response to the Independent Television Commission asking for programmes 'of high quality' which would appeal to 'a wide variety of tastes and interests'. With an annual programming budget of £215 million (less than half that of Channel 4 and only a quarter of ITV's), Five is the least watched of Britain's terrestrial broadcasters, and between 2006 and 2007 its pre-tax profits fell by nearly 50% to £14 million.

It has, though, had success with its most popular show, *CSI: Crime Scene Investigation* (a US drama based on the work of five forensic scientists), and *House* (a US medical drama starring Hugh Laurie as a maverick anti-hero). By contrast, *Naked Jungle*, fronted by a naked Keith Chegwin, was voted the worst programme ever broadcast in a 2006 *Radio Times* poll, and it is argued that Five relies disproportionately on cheap programmes imported from America.

The extent to which any television channel can seek to occupy the high moral ground and to rely on serious, factual programmes is questionable. Channel 4 is criticised for relying too much on quiz and game shows in its afternoon scheduling (when it began broadcasting in 1982, its first programme was *Countdown*). Perhaps it provides what a number of viewers want to watch, but Channel 4 is awkwardly balanced between being a public service provider and commercially self-funding and small audiences do not generate the sort of advertising that Channel 4 depends on.

For Jeremy Paxman, the respected presenter of *Newsnight* and *University Challenge* and no intellectual lightweight, television needs to recover a sense of purpose. He agrees with Tony Blair that intense competition is at the heart of the issue. In his 2007 MacTaggart lecture (*Never mind the scandals: what's it all for?*) delivered at the *MediaGuardian* Edinburgh International Television Festival, Paxman made the following points:

- Instead of a handful of television channels there are now hundreds; and people are both more familiar with the medium and more sceptical about it.
- As, increasingly, people can watch programmes at a time and place they choose, the balance of power has shifted towards the audience.
- The decline of audiences (or the fact they are more thinly spread) has meant that no one programme or organisation has the authority conferred by dominance.
- The crisis of television is inextricably linked with the crisis of confidence in politicians.
- Too many people in the industry answer the question 'what is television for?' with 'to make money'.

In Paxman's view there has been a retreat from programmes once deemed to be in the public good and from children's programmes. Increasingly, commercial judgements have come to predominate. In a highly competitive environment more and more people rely on making an impact — whether crassly or outrageously, or simply by placing televisual newsreaders in front of the desk. Threatened by a new medium such as the World Wide Web, there is a danger that television might become marginalised, especially as its core audience gets older.

Jeremy Paxman

More people will have supported Paxman's conclusion that we should 'spend less time measuring audiences and more time enlightening them'. We must be clearer about what television is for in a globalised, multimedia age. The BBC, dependent on the licence fee and the trust of its viewers, has probably got most to lose if the question remains unanswered because, like the National Health Service, the BBC is a national institution created by royal charter, of considerable interest to politicians and a bulwark of national identity. It used to mean something. Perhaps it still does but, in the light of the scandals and malpractice involving the true identity of programme contestants and premium rate phone calls, there is much to prove.

Ask the examiner

Q

Can we trust television reporting?

A

Television is facing a period of unparalleled change as more and more channels appear and competition for viewers and advertisers becomes more intense. There have clearly been occasions when standards have slipped, sometimes unacceptably so in the case of interactive phone-ins.

Compared with newspapers, television reporting is more impartial and it is very unlikely that regulations to stop bias are seriously breached. Although presenters may have their own views, they are skilled professionals who would not wish to risk their careers.

Total impartiality and balance are probably impossible, however. News items have to be selected and edited. Decisions have to be made about headline items and how much time should be spent on different reports. It would be difficult to make such decisions totally value-free. Our own lives certainly aren't; and also viewers often see what they want to see rather than what is actually presented.

Q

Is there a future for public service organisations like the BBC?

A

Many more services of all kinds have been run privately since the 1980s and there is a feeling that the incentive of competition and the pursuit of profits means that businesses are likely to be run more efficiently.

The BBC has always been seen to be a public service with a wider role than simply providing the most successful and profitable programmes. BBC news, BBC websites and BBC products are widely used and plenty of viewers appreciate having programmes free from advertisements.

The BBC is able to cater for a wide range of interests and tastes, and run programmes for minorities. Considering the number of programmes available on both television and radio, the cost of a television licence does not seem to be excessive. There are always likely to be services that are run in the public interest, although the fact that income is guaranteed can sometimes lead to complacency and high costs.

Film censorship

The extent to which artistic freedom of expression should be subject to constraints has always been controversial, and as early as 1912 the British Board of Film Censors (BBFC) was set up by the film industry as an independent body. In 1984, following national concern about the release of gruesome 'video nasties', the Video Recordings Act required videos to be classified as films were. The BBFC became the British Board of Film Classification with powers that were extended to include DVDs. Classification of films is undertaken by the BBFC on behalf of local councils, which are responsible for licensing cinemas.

Films have been classified from an early stage — initially into U (universal and fit for all) and A (public, but more suitable for an adult audience). A third category, H, was added in 1932, with a minimum age of 16, when many councils were concerned about the growing popularity of horror films.

A more liberal approach to film censorship was evident by the 1960s, and in the 1970s Mary Whitehouse failed in a private prosecution brought under the Vagrancy Act against *La Grande Bouffe (Blow Out)*. A retired Salvation Army officer, Edward Shackleton, used the Obscene Publications Act against the 'publication' of *Last Tango in Paris*. His efforts were unsuccessful but in 1977 the Obscene Publications Act was amended to include the distribution and exhibition of films.

In 1982 films were re-classified:

U   universal admission

PG parental guidance (children can be admitted but parents are warned that a few scenes might not be suitable for young children)

15 passed for audiences aged 15 and over

18 passed for audiences aged 18 and over

R18 passed for screening only in specially licensed cinemas that exclude those aged under 18

In 1985 a similar classification was introduced for videos, with the sale of R18 videos being restricted to licensed sex shops.

In 1989 a further age band was introduced:

12A suitable for cinema audiences aged 12 and over but children apparently under that age had to be accompanied by an adult

Viewpoints

Should there be censorship?

Arguments against

- It is a dated concept and people are capable of making up their own minds about whether they wish to view or read something.
- Artists should be free to be creative without having to concern themselves with what might or might not be permissible.
- Judging what should or should not be censored is subjective and therefore subject to the whims of certain individuals.
- What is deemed unacceptable at one time becomes acceptable in another time so artists are never sure how much of their work will be accepted.
- The internet has led to much more freedom for individuals to display what they wish.
- Censorship is dangerous. It could be used to suppress freedom of speech and to stifle political dissent.
- It is impossible, in practical terms, to control innovations like blogging without setting up a complicated system of internet regulation which might be impossible to enforce.

Arguments for

- It is part of the function of government to act responsibly, and a responsible government will seek to set standards of propriety and decency.
- There are certain absolute standards of decency that are the signs of a civilised society.
- It is important that children should be protected.
- Even the internet is subject to certain safeguards.
- Human nature is such that without the action of external agencies, certain forms of behaviour that are unacceptable to the vast majority of people will take place and cause offence.
- No country in the world has abandoned all forms of censorship.

The power of language and images to transmit, persuade or distort

Shortly before stepping down as prime minister in 2007, Tony Blair made a powerful speech delivering a broadside against the media, and particularly the press, although, according to Blair, it was 'not a whinge about how unfair it all is'.

Stressing the importance of free media in a democracy, Blair sought to examine the relationship between the media, public life and politicians in a changing communication environment. This was perhaps fitting for a man who courted the media assiduously, was repeatedly accused of the excessive use of 'spin' and who acknowledged that the relationship between politicians and the media has always been fraught.

The media world is much more diverse and fragmented than before. Once the main BBC and ITV news bulletins could command a nightly audience of 8 million. Now, in the days of rolling 24-hour news and hundreds of television stations, it is half that. Newspapers battle on just to maintain their share of a shrinking market, and advertisers who might once have used newspapers now have the alternative of the internet. Bloggers abound and young people have few preconceived ideas about communication. It is not surprising that newspapers are investing heavily in forms of e-readership because news moves in real time. Politicians must somehow respond in the same way.

For Blair — and for politicians throughout the world — a major part of his job was 'coping with the media, its sheer scale, weight and constant hyperactivity', and at times 'it literally overwhelms'. To admit this is almost to admit weakness, yet it is real enough. Like most people, politicians sometimes struggle to keep up with the pace of modern life, and when they cannot the response is often cynical and dismissive. We live in a blame culture and our elected representatives can act as convenient scapegoats, especially if they have made rash promises to the electorate.

Much as Jeremy Paxman observed, the media is driven by 'impact' — by finding ways to make a bigger and better impression than a rival — and the danger is that standards of reporting will be driven down in the battle for sensation. Terms of anger and shock become paramount.

For Blair, the consequences of these developments are as follows:
- Scandal and controversy are more important than ordinary news reporting.
- Attacking someone's motive becomes more important than attacking his or her judgement.
- The media are driven by the fear of missing a story so hunt in packs, with the result that they become like 'a feral beast tearing people and reputations to bits'.
- There is a trend to provide a commentary on the news instead of merely reporting it.
- In turn this leads to a confusion of news (the factual element) with commentary (interpretation and opinion).

Ultimately, in the eyes of Blair, 'it is rare, today, to find balance in the media'. Although life is usually grey (and dull), media reporting is likely to come in bold shades of black and white (attention-catching, with positions polarised).

In calling for 'a rebellion against the press', the *Guardian* columnist Polly Toynbee identifies its most powerful figure, Rupert Murdoch, the owner of diverse global media organisations such as Sky and News International, which controls newspapers ranging from *The Times* to the highest-selling and politically influential tabloid, the *Sun*. According to her, 'downmarket is the direction Mr Murdoch knows' and the image of society developed by papers such as the *Sun* and the non-Murdoch *Daily Mail* is one 'where nothing works, everything gets worse, public officials are inept, public services fail, tax is wasted, lethal dangers proliferate, and everyone conspires to lie about it'.

Murdoch, a native Australian who first developed his media interests in that country (where his company has more than 100 newspaper titles), bought America's *Wall Street Journal* in 2007 — America's most famous and prestigious financial newspaper — paying over $5 billion dollars for it, to complement his ownership of the tabloid *New York Post*. He already owned the country's newest news channel, Fox News, which now has more viewers than CNN, and also controls the internet's MySpace social networking site, which his News Corporation bought in 2005 for $536 million. It is a giant, worldwide empire, with publishing interests extending to both Europe and Asia. It gives Murdoch almost unrivalled power and influence — he is said to have had a periodic hotline to Tony Blair when Blair was prime minister.

Are the regulators strong enough?

In his speech that identified the media as 'a feral beast', Tony Blair was of the view that the regulatory framework would at some point require revision. He certainly envisaged something more effective than the present system, operated primarily by the two main regulators, Ofcom and the Press Complaints Commission. Politicians themselves are of course guilty on occasion of spin and the burying of bad news.

The Press Complaints Commission

The Press Complaints Commission (PCC) has operated since 1990 when it succeeded the Press Council, which had been established some years earlier to safeguard the standards of ethics in journalism. Since then it has acted as a regulator of printed newspapers and magazines, although its remit was extended in 2007 to include the editorial and audiovisual material of newspaper and magazine websites. The vital question of regulating other online content remains unanswered, although views expressed on the internet are subject to such laws as libel and data protection.

It is funded by a charge to newspapers and magazines. They contribute to the costs of the PCC on a voluntary basis and adhere to its code of practice (drawn up and updated by editors) and rulings. Lay members of the PCC have a majority over journalist members. The PCC has no legal powers, which means that the industry is largely self-regulating, but it does offer a 24-hour service for complaints and its conciliation procedure has been widely complimented.

The main features of the code of practice, which was strengthened after the jailing of a *News of the World* reporter in 2007 for mobile phone bugging, are:
- accuracy of both written material and pictures
- providing an opportunity to reply to any inaccuracies
- privacy ('it is unacceptable to photograph individuals in private places without their consent')
- avoidance of intimidation, harassment and persistent pursuit
- sensitivity in cases involving personal grief or shock
- safeguards relating to children under 16
- not obtaining or publishing material gained by hidden cameras or listening devices, by intercepting mobile phone calls, texts or e-mails, by the unauthorised removal of documents or photographs or by unauthorised access to digitally held private information

Any member of the public may make a complaint to the PCC and the commission's members rule on whether the code of practice has been broken. Magazines and newspapers that infringe the code may have to print a factual correction or apology. Financial penalties for a breach of the code are not imposed.

In 2006 the PCC received over 3,000 complaints, the majority alleging factual inaccuracy and a growing number suggesting an invasion of privacy. Where complaints involve celebrities or prominent public figures, the complaints generate a lot of publicity. Recent successful complaints have been made by the singer and television presenter Charlotte Church for breach of privacy after the *Sun* printed rumours that she was pregnant. The actress Elle Macpherson had a similar claim upheld against *Hello!* magazine, which without consent published pictures of her on a private beach.

Prince William's girlfriend, Kate Middleton, has been a regular complainant, illustrating the fine line between safeguarding the privacy of the individual and what might be deemed reasonable reporting of a 'royal romance' — something for which many newspaper and magazine readers appear to have an insatiable appetite.

Prince William and Kate Middleton

In 2007 complaints against the allegedly over-zealous and intrusive paparazzi were generated after Prince William and Kate Middleton were pictured being driven away from a Kensington nightclub in the same week that the inquest opened on William's mother, Princess Diana, 10 years after her death in a Paris car crash after it was pursued by photographers. Photographers are not covered by the PCC and the paparazzi represent a difficult area given the rise in freelance photographers seeking to make large sums in a global market.

It was 'royal reporting' that resulted in the PCC's most prominent enquiry in 2007, following the trial and imprisonment of a *News of the World* reporter and a private investigator for illegally accessing voicemail messages on phones belonging to members of the royal household. After the jailing of the reporter, the *News of the World*'s editor, who maintained that he knew nothing about the bugging, announced his resignation. Ironically, the executive chairman of Rupert Murdoch's News International, which owns the *News of the World*, was also chairman of the PCC's code committee on this occasion.

The issue of how far the press must be allowed to be 'free' remains contentious, as does the question of the safeguarding of privacy — often of celebrities who sometimes do their best to court publicity. Newspaper sales may be falling by 4% a year, but an average of over 11 million national newspapers are still sold in the UK every day. The code of practice is clear and Sir Christopher Meyer, chairman of the PCC since 2003, has proved a skilled operator who has used his skills as a career diplomat to good effect. Whatever the weaknesses of the PCC and its code of practice, it does provide a regulatory framework and help to safeguard a free press. The alternative might be unworkable laws or the freedom of the bloggers — and a sharp decline in journalistic standards.

Ofcom

Ofcom emerged from the 2003 Communications Act when five previous bodies were merged to form the Office of Communications to act as the broadcasting and telecommunications regulator. Its board of up to ten members is appointed by the Secretary of State for Culture, Media and Sport. The position of Ofcom contrasts sharply with that of the Press Complaints Commission, in that Ofcom is a statutory body with a duty to promote competition and protect consumers.

Ofcom operates in an open and participative way, making wide use of public consultation. Its reports on trends in communications are detailed, comprehensive and informative, and it is unusual among public bodies in the efforts it makes to provide summary reports in plain English.

Under the 2003 act, Ofcom's specific duties are:
- ensuring the optimal use of the electromagnetic spectrum
- ensuring that a wide range of electronic communications services are available throughout the UK
- ensuring a wide range of television and radio services of high quality and wide appeal
- maintaining plurality (a range of providers) in the provision of broadcasting
- applying adequate protection for audiences against offensive or harmful material
- applying adequate protection for audiences against unfairness or the infringement of privacy

Ofcom deals with specific complaints from viewers and listeners and decides whether the broadcasting code has been breached. It also deals with the licensing of areas such as mobile phone transmissions and private communications networks. Ofcom was particularly active in 2007, investigating various examples of competition rigging in television phone-in voting and, in some cases — again in contrast to the Press Complaints Commission — imposing substantial fines for breaches of the broadcasting code. GMTV was fined a record £2 million for 'widespread and systematic deception' after up to 25 million viewers spent £35 million entering phone-in competitions they had little or no chance of winning.

Despite its work on behalf of the consumer, unfavourable comparisons have sometimes been drawn between Ofcom and another regulatory body, the Office of Fair Trading (which does not deal with media and communication). The latter is apparently more willing to act to enforce competition law than is the case with Ofcom.

Some of Ofcom's least publicised, but most valuable, work is to highlight key changes in how consumers are using new digital communications services in a wider social context. Using the telling headline 'UK benefits from communications any time, anywhere and at a lower cost', its 2007 Communications Market Report revealed the following:

- UK consumers spent 50 hours a week on the phone, surfing the net, watching television or listening to radio.
- Average household spending on communications services was £92.65 (representing both increasing use and falling prices, especially with the 'bundling' of landline, broadband, digital television and mobiles in a single package).
- Children aged 8–15 were changing what they do with their time noticeably because of the rapidly expanding range of services and devices now available to them. Over 75% of 11-year-olds now had their own television, games console and mobile phone.
- Older people were consuming more media in an age of 'silver surfers', with 16% of over 65s using the web.
- We were increasingly reliant on mobile phones, with double the number of mobile connections (69.7 million — a higher figure than the total UK population) than landline connections (33.6 million). Mobiles were used for far more than making phone calls: as digital cameras, as mini games consoles, for internet access and to listen to FM radio.
- Of UK homes, 80.5% had digital television with its wide range of stations — something that is changing what, when and how we watch television.
- Radio listeners had a much wider choice of stations than before (there are 389 radio stations in the UK, 169 of which are available on DAB) and ways of listening as a result of the proliferation of digital channels; 17.2% of UK homes had a Digital Audio Brodcasting (DAB) radio, although the over 55s was the only age group to increase its average listening time to radio between 2002 and 2007.
- Four of the five most listened-to radio channels were all provided by the BBC. The top five were Radio 2, Radio 1, Radio 4, Classic FM (commercial) and Five Live. BBC radio expenditure was £637 million compared with the £512 million spent by commercial radio.
- As television advertising revenue fell (and there were calls for a relaxation by Ofcom of the rules governing the amount of advertising per hour permitted on commercial television), revenue from online advertising was rising sharply.

Introduced at the start of the decade, by 2007 broadband coverage was available to 99.6% of the UK, and the speed of technological change was outpacing the capacity of policy makers and administrators to deal with it. Social networking had grown greatly via sites such as YouTube and Facebook. Nobody can predict with any degree of accuracy what future broadband needs will be as Ofcom tries to do the impossible by consulting the industry on what is needed for a digital future.

Practice questions

These questions are typical of those that might be asked in Section B of Unit 3.

(1) 'We should encourage artistic freedom and innovation and trust parents to protect their children from artistic excesses.'

Discuss the case for and against the censorship of the cinema and theatre.

(25 marks)

(2) 'They can't have it both ways. Public figures court publicity and they shouldn't complain if it's not always advantageous or flattering to them.'

Examine the position of public figures and celebrities in the media and discuss the effect that being a public figure or celebrity might have on a person's right to privacy.

(25 marks)

Websites

www.pcc.org.uk
www.ofcom.org.uk
www.uk.youtube.com
www.facebook.com

Ideologies and political processes and goals

Democracy or not? A world view

Russia

In 1993, President Boris Yeltsin used military force to dissolve parliament and a new constitution declared Russia a democratic, federative, law-based state. Executive power is in the hands of a prime minister and president although it rests principally with the latter. Elections are competitive and there is a 628-member parliament (Federal Assembly) based on two houses, the most important of which is the lower house, the Duma.

By Western standards, Russia has a rather tenuous claim to parliamentary democracy, and parliament is seen by some as an instrument of the Kremlin. President Vladimir Putin, who became acting president in 1999 and was then elected in 2000, is extremely powerful. Having served two terms Putin was constitutionally barred from the 2008 presidential elections. The new president, Dmitry Medvedev, won 70% of the vote as Putin's 'preferred candidate'. By Western standards the Russian electoral process offered only limited choice and media coverage was overwhelmingly biased towards Medvedev.

China

The People's Republic of China was proclaimed in 1949 by chairman Mao and remains a one-party state under the rule of the Chinese Communist Party. It is estimated that the party has between 58 and 74 million members in China and its currently nine-member Politburo Standing Committee is central to decision making and the approval of key appointments.

Although five religions (principally Christianity, Buddhism and Islam) are officially tolerated, China attracts widespread criticism for its position on human rights, and opposition to party policy is not tolerated. This was best demonstrated in 1989, when there were long-running student protests that led to the declaration of martial law. On 4 June tanks and Chinese troops entered Tiananmen Square (ironically 'The Gate of Heavenly Peace') in the Chinese capital, Beijing. Protesters were brutally suppressed and a number were killed, as one of the greatest challenges to the communist state was crushed.

Leaders were imprisoned and a key figure, Wang Dan, was sentenced to 11 years' imprisonment after a 4-hour secret trial. In 2007, with Chinese artists at the forefront of a surge in contemporary art prices, the Tiananmen Square-inspired *Execution* by Yue Minjun sold for nearly £3 million at Sotheby's — a London record for a Chinese artist.

Capitalism has helped to revolutionise the Chinese economy in recent years and the country is poised to overtake Germany as the third largest economy in the world after the USA and Japan. This comes at a cost, and it is estimated that as many as 750,000 Chinese a year are killed by the effects of pollution. However, President Hu's concept of 'scientific development' promises economic development with more attention paid to sustainability and the environment.

Beijing, every bit a modern and Westernised city, hosted the 2008 Olympic Games and China has promised a much greater degree of freedom to journalists than was hitherto the case as the Olympics become a showcase for a decade of Chinese achievement. However, it remains a communist state in which democratic activists and dissenting writers are briskly dealt with and may be sent to labour camps. With 30,000 foreign journalists in China covering the Olympics, there will be pressure from human rights organisations. Change, if it comes at all in China, will come only slowly.

Afghanistan

After the Islamic fundamentalists of the Taliban were overthrown towards the end of 2001, NATO (North Atlantic Treaty Organisation) forces took over security of the country in 2003. Hamid Karzai became the country's first democratically elected president in 2004 and parliamentary elections took place in 2005.

In reality, neither the president nor parliament enjoys wide powers and local government is plagued by corruption. Fundamentalist Taliban opponents remain strong in Helmand and around the Pakistan border; they are influential in the flourishing heroin trade that dominates Afghanistan's economy and is controlled by fearsome warlords.

Iraq

Prior to the overthrow of Saddam Hussein, Iraq was ruled by the Ba'ath Party and a nine-man Revolutionary Command Council, which enacted legislation by decree.

US forces invaded Iraq in 2003, citing links between Saddam and al-Qaeda and the existence of weapons of mass destruction.

Things were looking up for Iraq by the end of 2005 after elections in which all ethnic and political groups were invited to participate and a new constitution agreed by referendum had been put in place. The first permanent government emerged, with Shi'ites prominent and Prime Minister Nouri al-Maliki heading the 275-seat Council of Representatives.

After that, however, the country plunged towards civil war; Sunnis (many of whom boycotted the 2005 election) and Shi'ites continued to fight each other and al-Qaeda continued its campaign of terror. As British troops continued to make a strategic withdrawal, large numbers of US troops remained in the country. Between 2001 and 2007 over 50,000 people were said to have met violent deaths; and, according to the UN, over 40,000 people were in either Iraqi or US custody and over 2 million Iraqis were living as refugees.

Iran

Iran is a strongly Islamic country, with Ayatollah Ali Khamenei as Supreme Leader since 1989. It has a 290-seat national assembly (the Majlis) elected by popular vote every 4 years. According to President Bush, Iran is controlled largely by a small number of extremists, but the country has benefited from seeing the USA eliminate enemies in Iraq and Afghanistan.

President Mahmoud Ahmadinejad has proved to be a difficult and skilled strategist, exploiting his country's key role in the world oil market and its ability to cut off supplies from the Gulf. The former Mayor of Tehran was elected as president in 2005 and is unusual among world leaders because of his background in technology — Dr Ahmadinejad has a PhD in civil engineering.

Burma

Burma (Myanmar) remains one of Asia's poorest, most secretive and least democratic countries, where dissent is banned. It is subject to widespread international sanctions because of its denial of human rights. Military rulers have remained in power since 1962 and uprisings like the one in 2007 led by students and Buddhist monks have been put down with extreme severity.

Although the UN Security Council has censured the Burmese government, direct intervention in the affairs of Burma is considered unwise and, although a number of economic sanctions do exist, the more they are imposed the worse things will get for an already impoverished nation. There is widespread support for the opposition leader, Aung San Suu Kyi, but she has been kept under house arrest for much of the time since 1989. Her party won elections in 1990 but the military **junta** refused to hand over power.

> **Key term**
>
> **junta:** a group of people, often military officers, that controls a country after seizing power.

The only country with close contacts and political influence with the junta is Burma's neighbour and key trading partner, China, which also gave support to the UN Security Council. However, it is likely that countries such as China, Russia and India are still supplying the junta with weapons that are used to keep the regime of Than Shwe in power and to stifle dissent.

Somalia

Somalia emerged as an independent country in 1960 but by 1969 the first of many military coups had taken place. By the 1990s the country had descended into civil war and, in 1993, two US Black Hawk helicopters were shot down (the basis for the famous film *Black Hawk Down*), leading to the eventual withdrawal of US and UN troops.

Somalia is one of Africa's most unstable war-torn countries, with no effective central government since 1991. Areas of the country are ruled by different warlords and there is much inter-clan fighting, especially around the capital city, Mogadishu. The situation is one of lawlessness and chaos.

Somalia is a predominantly Muslim country and battles intensified in 2006 between Somali troops and the Islamic Courts Council, leading to victory for Somali troops and warlords, backed by Ethiopian troops and with US support. The situation remains unstable and a threat to world peace.

Zimbabwe

President Robert Mugabe came to power in 1980 following the country's first free elections and in 2007, aged 83, he retained absolute power in a divided country where his opponents and protesters were often met by violence with all public protests banned. A master technician, Mugabe has the political skills to outmanoeuvre other Commonwealth leaders and most international organisations. Millions of people have crossed the border to South Africa, but some still see him as a liberator against the previous domination of the country by a white minority (largely forced out of the country after land invasions in 2000).

Economically, Zimbabwe seems close to ruin, with inflation in August 2007 running at over 7,000%. Most people live in absolute poverty, and life expectancy, which had risen to 60 in 1990, was estimated at 37 in 2007. Wealth tends to be in the hands of a political elite and the Central Intelligence Organisation is comparatively well funded. Mugabe's ZANU-PF supporters exert considerable control over the work of the World Food Programme in the country.

Elections to the House of Assembly (parliament) were held in 2005, with ZANU-PF winning a comfortable majority. Of the 150 seats, 120 are elected. Mugabe nominates 20 and the chiefs decide on 10. Allegations of fraud and other forms of malpractice were widespread. Mugabe submitted himself for presidential election in 2008 but, even though it was believed that President Mugabe's party lost, the election result was disputed and he refused to relinquish power.

Aspects of government: the European Union

Table 24.1 Key dates: from European Coal and Steel Community to European Union

Date	Key development
1951	Six countries (Belgium, France, Italy, Luxembourg, the Netherlands and (West) Germany) form the **European Coal and Steel Community**. They aim to ensure peace and co-operation, 6 years after the end of the Second World War.
1957	The Treaty of Rome establishes a common market based on the six countries. Organisation now called the **European Economic Community**.
1973	The community expands to nine countries as Denmark, Great Britain and the Irish Republic join. Common policies are developed.
1979	First direct elections to the European Parliament.
1981	The first Mediterranean enlargement. Greece joins to take membership to ten.
1986	The second Mediterranean enlargement. Portugal and Spain join to take membership to 12.
1993	Completion of the single market.
1993	The Treaty of Maastricht establishes the **European Union**.
1995	The European Union expands to 15 as Austria, Finland and Sweden join.
2002	12 countries adopt a common currency, using euro notes and coins.
2004	Ten new countries (Cyprus, Czech Republic, Estonia, Hungary, Latvia, Lithuania, Malta, Poland, Slovakia and Slovenia) join the EU to increase membership to 25.
2007	Expansion of EU to 27 countries as Bulgaria and Romania join.

Figure 24.1 EU countries in 2007

A	Albania
B	Belgium
BO	Bosnia
C	Croatia
CZ	Czech Republic
L	Luxembourg
M	Moldova
MA	Macedonia
N	Netherlands
S	Slovenia
SE	Serbia
SL	Slovakia
SW	Switzerland

EU countries

Non-EU countries

Key institutions and decision making in the EU

The political system that makes up the European Union continues to evolve as the EU increases in size. There is a decision-making triangle, with the Council of the European Union (Council of Ministers) at its apex.

Table 24.2 The decision-making triangle of the EU

EU institution	Composition and functions
The Council of the EU (Council of Ministers)	This is the main decision-making body in the EU and represents the 27 member states, which take it in turns to hold the presidency for a period of 6 months. Which ministers attend depends on the subject under discussion. Under the Maastricht Treaty the European Council initiates major policies and votes are allocated in proportion to the member country's population.
The European Parliament	The European Parliament and its 785 MEPs are elected by voters in each member country every 5 years to represent the EU's citizens. The EPs' work takes place in Brussels and Strasbourg and it shares some decision-making powers with the European Council. It also shares equal responsibility with the Council for the EU budget.
The European Commission	The European Commission is the main executive body of the EU. It has the right to propose legislation and it must ensure that EU policies are properly implemented by the EU's member states. Members of the European Commission are appointed for 5-year periods and there is one commissioner for each member state. The Commission is responsible to the European Parliament and is assisted by a civil service based mainly in Brussels and Luxembourg.

Table 24.3 Other EU institutions and bodies

EU institution	Composition and functions
The Court of Justice	Based in Luxembourg, it is made up of one judge from each member country, appointed for a renewable term of 6 years. Its role is to ensure that EU law is complied with and that its treaties are interpreted correctly and applied in member states.
The Court of Auditors	Based in Luxembourg, it has one member from each country, appointed for 6 years. Its main role is to check EU income and expenditure and that the EU budget has been properly managed.
The European Economic and Social Committee	A consultative body representing economic and social interest groups and appointed by the Council for 4 years.
The Committee of the Regions	Consists of representatives of regional and local government proposed by member states and appointed by the Council for 4 years.
The European Investment Bank	Based in Luxembourg, it provides loans for the EU's less developed regions.
The European Central Bank	Based in Frankfurt, the ECB is responsible for managing the euro and the EU's monetary policy.

Features of the European Parliament elections of June 2004 in the UK

Table 24.4 Elections to the European Parliament, 2004: UK results

Party	Votes	Percentage of votes cast	Seats in EP
Conservative	4,397,087	26.7	27
Labour	3,718,683	22.6	19
UKIP	2,660,768	16.2	12
Liberal Democrat	2,452,327	14.9	12
Green Party	1,028,283	6.2	2
British National Party	808,201	4.9	0
Respect	252,216	1.5	0
Scottish National Party	231,505	1.4	2
Plaid Cymru	159,888	1.0	1
Others	749,645	4.6	0
Total	**16,458,603**	**100**	**75**

- There was a turnout of 38.2% from an electorate of 43,084,598.
- Following expansion of the EU, the number of UK seats in the European Parliament was reduced from 87 to 78.
- As in 1999, the d'Hondt quota system was used in Great Britain to allocate seats on a regional basis across 11 regions (including the whole of Wales and Scotland). The twelfth region, Northern Ireland, allocated its three seats by single transferable vote.
- For the first time, Gibraltar was included in the South-West region.
- The Conservative Party won the most seats, but it lost 8 seats and its share of the vote fell by 9% in comparison with the 1999 European Parliament elections.
- Labour, who won the second highest number of votes, lost 6 seats and its share of the vote fell by 19% in comparison with the 1999 European Parliament elections.
- The United Kingdom Independence Party (UKIP) won 12 seats and its share of the vote increased by 9%. The British National Party (BNP) polled over 800,000 votes, an increase of 5%.
- Turnout was higher in 2004 than it was in 1999, especially in the four regions that piloted all-postal ballots.

The debate continues

UK membership of the European Economic Community and, later, the European Union, has always been contentious since joining under the pro-European Conservative prime minister in 1973. In the early days the issue divided the Labour Party, and a referendum on whether to continue with membership was held in 1979, which produced a large 'yes' majority. In more recent years, the Conservative Party has been ambivalent about membership and a minority of members have been strongly Eurosceptic.

The United Kingdom Independence Party was founded in 1993, with its principal aim being the withdrawal of the UK from the European Union (and giving devolved powers to Northern Ireland, Scotland and Wales). It attracted many from the anti-European wing of the Conservative Party. It now has some local council seats, and it held two seats on the London Assembly until its members defected to follow the former Labour MP and chat show host Robert Kilroy-Silk, who resigned from UKIP in 2005 to form his own, short-lived, Veritas party.

UKIP undoubtedly benefited from the proportional representation voting system used in the European Parliament election. The party did less well in the 2005 general election, where the more traditional first-past-the-post system operated. UKIP gained 618,000 votes, equating to 2.8% of the total votes cast — a much better performance than in the 2001 general election but still not one that gained UKIP any seats in the Westminster Parliament.

Viewpoints

Arguments against continuing British membership of the EU

■ The EU is too expensive and does not work. Much more is paid into the EU than is received from it. The enlargement of the EU, with a number of poorer countries, will make this worse.

■ By ceasing to pay levies to the EU, public spending could be increased and taxation reduced.

■ According to UKIP, corruption is more common in EU politics and administration than it is in the UK, where corruption is rare.

■ The Common Agricultural Policy (CAP) is particularly expensive and is used to subsidise small and inefficient farmers. British farming is more efficient and productive than farming in most other countries.

■ Originally set up as an economic organisation, the identity of the EU has changed and it is now too powerful in political terms, particularly since the signing of the Maastricht Treaty.

- British people are subject to far too many EU regulations, many of which are unnecessary and intrusive.
- The EU is undemocratic, with too much power in the hands of the Council of Ministers or unelected Commissioners and the EU bureaucracy. The democratic element, the European Parliament, has relatively few powers.
- The EU is based on the principle of supranationalism and undermines national sovereignty. Its laws override those of individual countries.
- The free movement of labour has led to wage undercutting and pressure on services in some parts of the UK.
- The absence of effective border controls has made it easier for smugglers and those involved in people trafficking.

Arguments in favour of continuing British membership of the EU

- Since it was fully set up in 1993, the single (or 'internal') market has brought many benefits to industry, businesses, employees and consumers as a result of EU policies. It is the world's largest single market. The total population of the EU is now over 500 million (200 million bigger than the population of the USA).
- Border controls have been abolished, cutting costs to businesses and speeding up the physical movement of goods and people across the EU. It is much easier for EU citizens to travel, live and work in other EU countries without border controls or paperwork.
- Up to 3 million British jobs are linked to exports to the EU.
- The EU has been able to tackle many anti-competitive practices since 1993, especially monopolies and cartels. (An investigation into UK price fixing resulted in large price reductions in replica football kits; deregulation allowing advertising and more competition among opticians has widened choice and cut prices; the price of books has fallen sharply since the ending of the Net Book Agreement.) Contrary to popular belief about a 1-year guarantee, EU law protects consumers against faulty goods for 2 years.
- In 2004, it was the EU that banned animal testing on finished cosmetic products.
- Common technical standards have allowed the EU to become the world leader in the manufacture and use of mobile phones.
- In global markets, the size and resources of the EU mean that it can compete more effectively with big countries like the USA and China.
- The EU has allowed more than 2 million young people to study in another member country.
- Politically, the EU has a more effective voice in world affairs than that of individual countries.
- The EU is a unifying force and it has ensured that there has been no war between its member countries for nearly 60 years.
- The EU is the biggest donor of aid for development around the world (€47 billion in 2006).
- EU regional aid has helped to raise living standards in poorer regions of Europe and has been particularly important in economically disadvantaged parts of Wales, Scotland, Cornwall and northern England.
- The EU is a leading force in action to protect the environment and promote sustainability.

Q Is it really worth the UK continuing to be a member of the EU?

A Ever since joining, the UK has never quite had the full commitment shown by most other countries, and there have been fierce arguments about issues such as the EU's costly Common Agricultural Policy, EU influence over British law and the freedom of access to the UK for workers from poorer EU countries.

There are valid arguments on both sides, but the EU is a large and complex organisation that few understand fully. The issue generates great passion and rather less detached analysis. However, it is not easy to see an obvious alternative in terms of helping to sustain the UK's political influence and economic performance.

Practice question

This is typical of a question that might be asked in Section B of Unit 3.

'The benefits are such that the United Kingdom must continue to remain an active and supportive member of the European Union.'

Discuss the arguments for and against this viewpoint. *(25 marks)*

The individual and the state: terrorism

Terrorism has existed for centuries. It was used in England in the 1970s by Irish republicans unhappy with the political situation in Northern Ireland, which seemed to discriminate against the Roman Catholic minority in favour of Protestants who favoured continuation of the union between Northern Ireland and Britain. Bloody battles took place in a number of towns in Northern Ireland, with British troops caught between the warring factions. Attacks on the British mainland were rare but sometimes devastating.

> **Key term**
>
> **terrorism:** the unlawful threat or use of violence against people or property to intimidate governments and create a climate of fear in order to achieve political or ideological goals.

Terrorists ruthlessly promote a cause even though the possibility of winning might be remote or non-existent. They want what Margaret Thatcher called 'the oxygen of publicity', even if this is based on what others condemn as atrocities. They seek to put fear into the population by striking without warning and with disregard for the lives of others.

The 9/11 air attacks on buildings in New York in 2001 were unexpected in a country that seemed almost immune from such attacks. The July 2005 London tube and bus attack was also unexpected, violent and shocking. In response to the al-Qaeda-inspired strike on New York, the USA embarked on a 'war on terror' — renamed the 'long war' by the Pentagon in 2005.

The fear of terrorism is such that most people support the anti-terrorist measures taken by Parliament, but human rights lawyers and pressure groups such as Liberty and Amnesty International have highlighted the potential that legislation has to restrict human rights. The problem often relates to the reliability of the evidence that leads police to suspect individuals of being engaged in terrorist activity; only a minority of those detained are ever charged. The most publicised and tragic example of injustice was the case of Jean Charles de Menezes, an entirely innocent Brazilian shot dead by a CO19 officer at Stockwell tube station in July 2005 because he was a suspected suicide bomber.

Terrorism has changed over the past decade in some ways:
- Explosives are more widely available via the world's illegal arms trade.
- Terrorists are more mobile because of the development of air travel.
- Technology has become more advanced and weaponry more terrifying.
- Religious fundamentalism, and the promise of paradise, has led to a significant rise in suicide bombers.
- Possible access to biochemical material has led to the fear that a terrorist group will produce a 'dirty bomb'.
- There are concerns that terrorists will make a strike on a nuclear power generating plant.

The worldwide impact of terrorism since 2001

- **11 September 2001, USA** Nearly 3,000 people died when fundamentalist terrorists hijacked four passenger aircraft in the USA, crashing two into the twin towers of New York's World Trade Center and one into the Pentagon. Another plane crashed into a field in Pennsylvania after passengers resisted the hijackers. Shortly afterwards a UN resolution demanded that the Afghanistan Taliban surrender the al-Qaeda leader Osama bin Laden; the Taliban refused.
- **7 October 2001, US and UK forces began bombing Afghanistan.**
- **12 October 2002, Bali** Over 200 people, including 25 British tourists, were killed when three bombs exploded in Bali.

Ground Zero, New York — the aftermath of the attack on the World Trade Center, September 2001

- **20 March 2003 The USA and its allies invaded Iraq.**
- **27 February 2004, Philippines** A television set filled with TNT exploded on a ferry leaving Manila and 116 people were killed.
- **11 March 2004, Spain** Shortly before a Spanish general election, 190 people were killed and over 2,000 injured by bombs placed on commuter trains in Madrid.
- **7 July 2005, England** Three suicide bombs exploded on the London underground and one on a bus during the morning rush hour, killing 52 people. (On 21 July a repeat attack on London transport failed.)
- **23 July 2005, Egypt** Bomb attacks in the seaside resort of Sharm el-Sheikh killed 88 people.
- **11 July 2006, India** Bombs on the railway system in Mumbai killed 207 people.

- **18 October 2007, Pakistan** A suicide bomber in Karachi attempted to assassinate the opposition leader Benazir Bhutto when she returned to Pakistan after 8 years of self-imposed exile; 138 people were killed and many were injured.
- **27 December 2007, Pakistan** Benazir Bhutto was assassinated when campaigning in Rawalpindi.

Anti-terrorist measures in the UK

While armies fight in many parts of the world, counter-terrorism is now a crucial part of the defence of many countries and in the UK much of this counter-terrorism work is undertaken by the security service (MI5) and the Joint Terrorism Analysis Centre. A new system of assessing the threat levels of terrorism so that the public can be warned is now in operation and grades the terrorist threat at any one time on a five-point scale from 'low' (an attack is unlikely) to 'critical' (an attack is expected imminently).

Anti-terrorist laws that operated before 2000 were framed largely to counter the situation in Northern Ireland. As that threat declined in the twenty-first century the threat from other terrorist groups became much greater, and laws have changed to reflect this.

The Terrorism Act 2000

- It became illegal for certain 'proscribed' terrorist groups to operate in the UK.
- Police were given extended powers to stop and search and to detain suspects after arrest for up to 48 hours, with a possible extension of up to 7 days.
- A number of new criminal offences were introduced, allowing police to arrest those suspected of inciting terrorist acts or training terrorists in any way.

The Anti-Terrorism, Crime and Security Act 2001 (ATCSA)

Police powers were increased, mainly in an effort to:

- cut off terrorist funding
- improve data gathering and sharing among government departments and agencies
- make immigration procedures more vigilant
- provide greater security for nuclear and aviation industries
- improve the security of dangerous substances

The Prevention of Terrorism Act 2005

After the strengthening of legislation by the Anti-Terrorism, Crime and Security Act (ATCSA) in 2001 debate has increased about the balance between the powers available to law enforcement bodies to protect people from attack, and the freedom of individuals and the protection of their human rights. The 2005 Act came after a decision by the House of Lords Judicial Committee that certain powers under the 2001 Act (Section 4) were incompatible with articles of the European Commission on Human Rights. The Committee decided that parts of the 2001 Act were discriminatory because they applied to foreign nationals and not to British citizens and that they were not proportionate to the threat from terrorism faced by the UK.

Parts of the 2001 Act were repealed and a new system of 'control orders' was introduced that applied equally to UK and foreign nationals suspected of terrorism.

Control orders allow conditions to be imposed on individuals, including restrictions on association with named individuals, restrictions on movement or curfews. Normally, the Home Secretary must apply to the courts to impose a control order, and the maximum period for such an order is 12 months. The order may be challenged but breaching it is a criminal offence.

The Terrorism Act 2006

The extent to which anti-terrorist legislation needs to be strengthened reflects the growing threat that terrorism poses.

A number of new terrorist offences were created in the 2006 Act, involving terrorist planning; the incitement or encouragement of others to commit terrorism; the dissemination of terrorist materials; and terrorist training. The Act also:

- introduced warrants enabling police to search any property owned or controlled by a terrorist suspect
- extended police powers to detain suspects after arrest for up to 28 days (the period had been increased to 14 days by the 2003 Criminal Justice Act)
- extended search powers covering bays, estuaries and ports
- increased powers to proscribe groups that glorify terrorism

The forgotten world of Guantanamo Bay

Soon after the 9/11 terrorist attack on the USA in 2001, President George Bush gave a military order to detain non-American citizens suspected of having links with terrorist groups such as al-Qaeda. According to President George Bush, the prisoners held in Guantanamo Bay are 'unlawful combatants' because of their alleged links to al-Qaeda terrorists and thus are not subject to the normal protection of the Geneva

Convention. In some cases it is possible that they may never be put on trial and, as the war on terrorism is never likely to end, could be detained indefinitely.

The prison camp is symbolic of the USA's worldwide campaign against terror and it survives despite allegations of brutal treatment. A decision taken in 2004 by the US Supreme Court allowed prisoners to challenge their detention in the US federal courts; however, defence lawyers are military officers chosen by the Pentagon and parts of the trial can be held in secret. By 2007, nearly 150 detainees had been released, including five to the UK. It is thought that about 500 remain in the camp.

British resident Jamil el-Banna arriving in Britain on 20 December 2007 after being held captive for more than 4 years in Guantanamo Bay

The world becomes a more terrifying place

The Taliban lost control of Afghanistan following attacks by Western forces in 2001, and it was assumed that Iraq would soon be a very different place after its invasion by American and British forces in 2003. However, Taliban supporters regrouped, and terrorist acts continue on a daily basis in the unstable conditions that prevail in Iraq.

President Bush's 'war on terror' has not only been countered by fierce resistance but has also helped terrorist groups like al-Qaeda to increase their support. Terrorists accept that if they attack the Americans, other innocent people will die; each attack is likely to provoke a revenge attack. Violence becomes a daily ritual in countries like Iraq and almost loses its power to shock. In Afghanistan suicide bombings, never seen in the war with Russian troops in the 1980s, have risen dramatically since 2001.

Far from resulting in what President Bush called 'mission accomplished', Iraq in particular has proved the catalyst for a ferocious backlash, aiding recruitment to Islamist fundamentalism. It has helped to radicalise many Muslims and sometimes to polarise opinion between them and Christians. Once again, the role of new technology and the scope of global communications have proved crucial. Terrorist attacks are videoed and the footage is uploaded to the internet and shown to impressionable teenagers who might be groomed as future suicide bombers.

Practice question

'Modern terrorists use more sophisticated methods and are more difficult to detect than ever. Their influence is felt in many countries across the world.'

Discuss the problems caused by international terrorism. Explain why it is so difficult to tackle successfully. *(25 marks)*

The individual and the state: migrant workers

For a long time the issue of **asylum seekers**, illegal or genuine, made headlines in the tabloid press. As laws were changed to make it more difficult to be granted asylum in the UK, with applications falling to 23,000 in 2006–07, attention switched to migrant labour from the European Union. The EU expansion of 2004 brought in a number of eastern European countries, leading to an influx of workers onto the British labour market.

Key term

asylum seeker: a foreign national seeking permission to stay in another country, usually as a refugee, to avoid persecution because of nationality, religious beliefs, membership of a particular social group or political opinions.

Viewpoints

Importance of economic migrants

- In the 12 months up to June 2006, government figures suggest that over half a million people from the new member states registered for employment in the UK.
- The overwhelming majority were Poles, plus over 50,000 each from Lithuania and Slovakia.
- Despite well-publicised stories about Polish plumbers and bus drivers, most immigrant workers took jobs in offices, bars and catering and, more seasonally, in agriculture. In the same period, 385,000 EU migrants left.
- Most intended to stay for a year or two before returning home but some were looking for settlement in the UK on a longer-term basis. Over 80% of the new entrants were in the 18–34 age group.
- One of the favourite destinations was eastern England, with its vast acres of agricultural land and food processing factories, but migrants moved to all areas of the UK.
- For the most part the migrants were welcomed, not least by employers who had been unable to fill employment vacancies using British workers. Research by government

departments indicates that migrant workers contributed £6 billion to the UK's economic growth between June 2005 and June 2006 and that the migrants paid more in tax than they used in public services.

■ The most significant areas of settlement were the City of London and the borough of Westminster. In Cumbria, where over 100,000 workers help to sustain the tourist industry centred on the Lake District, it is estimated that 25% of the labour force is made up of migrant workers, helping to fill a major gap in the labour market.

■ Towns which have seen sudden and large increases in their populations because of the arrival of migrants include Boston, Peterborough and Northampton, together with the county of Cambridgeshire, all in eastern England.

Critics of economic migrants

■ Even though many of the migrant workers quickly gained a reputation for hard work and reliability the numbers were vastly in excess of estimates.

■ Pressure was placed on services such as health and education.

■ Too many economic migrants were undercutting wage rates and pushing up the cost of rents. Police translation services in Cambridgeshire were estimated to cost £1 million a year.

■ Nobody can say with certainty just how great the change has been because some of the new migrants are transient, but the pace of change has been rapid in some areas.

A tabloid campaign raising fear of the UK being 'swamped' by 300,000 new migrants led the government to impose more stringent conditions on workers from Romania and Bulgaria when those two countries entered the EU. Given that the gross domestic product per head in the UK was more than double that of Poland and well over three times the Bulgarian figure, it is not surprising that the UK proved an attractive location for many workers from east European countries.

Polish newspapers began to find a place in newsagents', banks used Polish language advertisements and shops specialising in east European food and drink began to spring up. There have been considerable economic benefits, with young people working for relatively low wages creating a mobile, flexible and productive pool of labour, helping to keep down inflation and interest rates. The extent to which these workers may have taken up jobs that could have been offered to young British workers is disputed. Young people leaving school with few or no qualifications might have had less difficulty finding work — assuming they were willing to take it. The proportion of migrants in the labour force has risen from 7.4% in 1997 to 12.5% in 2006.

Exploitation has taken place, especially in seasonal agricultural employment picking fruit and flowers and gathering vegetables. Contract labour in such areas is often undertaken by **gangmasters** involved in a labyrinth of subcontracting. Some have no regard for normal employment conditions, health and safety and rights in what is often a shadowland of harsh, brutal and illegal employment. Such conditions were tellingly shown in Ken Loach's film *It's a Free World*.

Cockle pickers at work on the tidal sands of Morecambe Bay

After 23 Chinese cockle pickers were drowned in Morecambe Bay in 2004, tighter regulations were introduced. The Gangmasters' Licensing Authority was established in order to offer greater protection to workers and to reduce tax evasion arising from 'cash in hand' payments. The GLA has nine inspectors and powers to revoke the licences of gangmasters.

Practice questions

Study Sources A and B on the impact of economic migrants coming to the UK after the expansion of the European Community in 2004 and then answer Questions 1 and 2.

Use your own words, rather than simply repeating those in the sources, to show your understanding of points being made.

Source A

There are a lot of migrants coming to this area and 'taking a chance'. Certainly the number of migrants registered as self-employed has risen in the past year, according to the latest figures. An official report into migrant work in the UK says they are more reliable and harder working than British-born workers. A Home Office report says the economic output of foreign workers has been considerable and that they have contributed around £6 billion to the UK economy.

Some will come to the UK for a while and then return to their home country, but more and more are predicted to make the move from overseas. In this region, local figures suggest that about 5,000 foreign workers have gained employment. Without them a lot of seasonal jobs would be difficult to fill and half the area's buses would be off the road. A council spokesperson said that the migrant workers in the town have helped boost its economic output. 'They pay their taxes and help boost demand in the local economy,' she said.

Immigrants now account for at least 4 million of the 37 million working age people in the UK. The latest Home Office study highlights the huge economic benefits of immigration but admits the numbers in work may be harming unskilled British workers. Employers on the coast benefit from the large influx of eastern Europeans; they work in the entertainment industry and in many leading hotels.

A manager of one of the biggest hotels said: 'The east Europeans have brought with them an excellent work ethic and have maintained it so that they can rise into the junior managerial positions if they wish. They add a real sense of industry and energy to the workforce. The main resorts have a number of Polish shops and bars and there are special Polish nights in some of our biggest nightclubs.'

Source: a council's local information booklet, 2007.

Source B

At first the government said that foreign workers had taken 800,000 jobs in Britain since 1997. Then, barely 24 hours later, the figure had risen to 1.1 million jobs and according to the Department for Work and Pensions, 52% of jobs created since 1997 have gone to foreigners. If the government can't produce reliable figures, who can? Do they just pluck them out of the air? The data on who is coming into the country and who is going out are totally inadequate.

Perhaps it's no surprise that the government is maintaining curbs on Romanian and Bulgarian workers who want to come here, at least until the end of 2008. Only 20,000 of these are able to come to the UK under special schemes for seasonal agricultural labour and food processing.

Now local councils are asking for an extra £250 million because they can't cope with sudden rises in the local population and the demands placed on services. The government is failing to address the serious pressures that these high levels of immigration are putting on housing, transport, schools and health services. Economic costs and economic benefits of migrant workers are just not distributed in the same way.

Just as worrying are the ways in which skilled immigration reduces the incentive for employers to train British workers. Who knows how many school leavers are left without work or training or how far wages are being forced down? It leads to tension and a lot of strain on community relations. At the end of the day nobody has any real grasp of where and for how long migrants are settling. The speed of change is breathtaking.

Source: letter to a local newspaper from 'concerned', 2008.

Questions

These are typical questions that might be asked in Section A of Unit 3.

(1) Explain the strengths and weaknesses of Sources A and B.
Give examples to support your answer.   *(10 marks)*

(2) Which sources do you support? Give reasons for your answer.   *(10 marks)*

The relationship between law, society and ethics

Usually, people take little interest in the machinery of politics — how Parliament and local government work and what goes on in Westminster or in town halls up and down the country. Politics becomes a matter of personalities, especially those deemed to have a wide televisual appeal, and policies. Some of the policies are complicated — especially those involving two of the most important areas of government, foreign affairs and the running of the economy — so the focus tends to be on 'issues' that seemingly can easily be identified.

One such issue is 'law and order'. Older people look back to an age of greater social rigidity, when social classes were more clearly defined and there was more respect for figures in authority. After the end of the Second World War young men in Britain were called up for 2 years of National Service (compulsory recruitment to the armed services), which provided them with discipline. At that time the death penalty was still in place for murder.

Society, though, is never static. There is conflict between generations and social values change. The 1960s were a period of dramatic change — abortion was legalised, capital punishment was suspended and then abolished and homosexual acts in private were legalised. Critics talked of a 'permissive age', and the development of the contraceptive pill revolutionised sexual relations.

Everyone is affected by crime. Petty crime is small-scale but not necessarily minor if it is constant. Antisocial behaviour is annoying, the more so if efforts to reduce it do not appear to work. There is great concern about violent crime and the easy availability of knives and guns.

Crime and punishment: 'prison works'

Prison is said to have four main purposes:

- to protect law-abiding citizens
- to punish offenders by depriving them of their liberty
- to act as a deterrent, discouraging other potential criminals
- to rehabilitate criminals by providing them with skills that will help to prevent them re-offending

Because many voters are influenced by the stance of the political parties on law and order, Labour and Conservative politicians have taken increasingly 'tough' lines, mostly underpinned by a former Conservative Home Secretary, Michael Howard's slogan 'prison works'. It does, in the sense that it keeps criminals off the street for a period — and many people are thankful for that — but the majority of those sent to prison re-offend and prison numbers have risen rapidly in recent years. Over 80,000 prisoners now fill all the existing prison spaces and spill over into areas such as police cells — which is said to cost the same as a night at the Ritz hotel.

Generally, ministers are terrified of the tabloid press and the images it sometimes creates of a lawless Britain at the mercy of violent criminals, dangerous sex offenders and uncontrolled gangs of young people. Projections based on current trends suggest that by 2012 the number of prisoners will exceed 100,000 and, despite the evidence, many people still believe that 'prison works'. The use of prison ships and ex-army camps is being considered until new prisons can be built and old ones extended. Words and phrases like 'a broken society', 'anarchy' and 'chaos' feature prominently among the headlines.

- Opinions are divided over the purpose of prison. Obviously prison is meant to be a punishment, and there are many who think prison conditions should be more basic to deter criminals from going back to a life of crime after their release.
- There is also the call for retribution — almost a sort of public revenge on those who break the law. Another purpose of prison is rehabilitation, to provide prisoners with the education and skills to help them to 'go straight', thus saving the taxpayer a great deal of money.
- The abduction and killing of the Liverpool toddler Jamie Bulger, by two schoolboys in 1993, was so appalling that it resulted in a widespread feeling that criminal behaviour could only be tackled effectively by depriving more offenders of their liberty, often for very long periods in the case of more serious offenders.

- Serious social problems have complex causes; but attitudes hardened and punishment was seen as more important than anything else. Politicians, always aware of the votes that keep them in office, are disinclined to take risks.
- The UK now imprisons many more people (150 per 100,000 of the population) than other European countries.
- The greater number of people sent to prison in the early years of the twenty-first century than before does not necessarily mean that there is more crime. Politicians have encouraged judges to use prison more often as a punishment — to the extent that prisons are desperately overcrowded. Full prisons often mean that there is less scope for rehabilitation.
- Home Office figures indicate that more than 50% of prisoners have committed crimes in order to buy drugs and there are many addicts in the prison population.
- The number of women in prison doubled between 1997 and 2007. Ten per cent of prisoners are said to be mentally ill and levels of literacy and numeracy are low.
- It is expensive to keep people in prison and prison has failed if the proportion of re-offenders is high. (Home Office figures indicate that 79% of those sentenced for theft will re-offend in 2 years.)

Crime is a difficult problem to quantify because of the way that data are gathered. There is no doubt that the prison population rose from 44,500 in 1993 to 73,600 by 2003, yet figures from the British Crime Survey suggested that reported crimes fell from 18.5 million to 11.7 million. Home Office figures for the period June 2006 to June 2007 indicate that crime recorded by the police fell by 7%. The sharpest falls were in criminal damage, theft from vehicles, more serious violence and sexual offences. The only category of crime to rise — quite sharply — was drug offences.

What, though, does that mean?
- Perhaps less crime is being reported to the police because people think that little or nothing will happen.
- Perhaps methods of recording crime have changed.
- Perhaps the police have gained new or simplified powers.
- Perhaps there are significant regional variations. Perhaps economic conditions have improved, with more scope for employment — a situation that can help to reduce crime in some categories.
- Often the key issue is how the figures are interpreted and, no matter what the data might suggest about crime levels falling, many people simply do not believe this and claim that crime has gone up. The British Crime Survey uses the views of

40,000 people each year and their experience of crime. It indicates this opinion clearly, together with falling confidence in the criminal justice system, especially in dealing with younger criminals.

The number of young people in custody has risen rapidly in recent years. Partly, this reflects an effort by politicians to convince voters that they and the courts are 'cracking down on young thugs' by delivering a 'short, sharp shock' — even though 80% are reconvicted. Seven times as much is spent on youth custody as on prevention schemes, and Britain seems to place a greater reliance on custody than on intervening at an earlier stage to help the damaged and the vulnerable, especially those coming from homes where violence and domestic abuse are commonplace.

Table 25.1 Young people in custody in the UK and elsewhere

Country	Young people in custody per 100,000 of population
UK	23
France	6
Spain	2
Finland	0.2

Politicians in particular use tough-talking rhetoric. Tony Blair was determined to be 'tough on crime; tough on the causes of crime' — although there seems to have been relatively little emphasis on the latter. Voters are also impressed by talk of 'zero tolerance' of minor crimes such as minor criminal damage, shoplifting, minor drug possession and public disorder.

There are ever more community support officers on the streets, especially in city areas, and more visible police controls, which are favoured by the public, but there is little evidence that they have a significant impact on crime rates. Labour's latest emphasis is on 'safety and security' and the UK has one of the highest numbers of surveillance cameras in the world.

Community support officers on the streets of London

Some estimates suggest that national crime figures fell by 35% between 1997 and 2007 but few voters are convinced by the statistics. Both knife and gun crimes have received much publicity, especially those involving young people. The killing in 2007 of the entirely innocent 11-year-old Rhys Jones, caught up in Liverpool gang warfare, was more shocking than many other stories reflecting the resurgence of gang culture and the ease of securing weapons of all descriptions. Whatever the figures might say, many people fear crime even if, statistically, the chances of it affecting them directly are remote.

- Underpinning all this is the complex issue of how, why and to what extent society has changed in the last 20 years. 'Desocialisation' is mentioned as often as 'socialisation', whether regarding family life or life in the community.

- Whatever we might say about the discipline of another age, the importance of the family, the role of the church and the work of voluntary agencies, we cannot move backwards in a technological age.

- There are few opportunities for those without the necessary skills (about 30,000 teenagers leave school each year with no GCSEs) or who might come from a social system where there are no longer any clear and coherent values.

- Inequalities are greater now than they have been for some time. Joining a gang can seem to offer a more comfortable, even exciting, life based on respect through imitating others in a gang culture that provides a sense of identity and protection.

- The gang culture is not a new phenomenon and newspapers of the 1950s and 1960s were full of stories of the dangers of teddy boys and clashes between mods and rockers. Those seeking a return to 'Victorian values' would presumably not wish to return also to the gangs of that age.

Inevitably, one route to a more comfortable life will be crime, and this might be more common among the poorly housed, poorly educated, poorly parented and poorly socialised. This does not answer the wider question of why, and with what effects, we imprison more people per head than other European countries that might be thought comparable. It seems unlikely that the British are innately more criminal.

Yet a change of policy is unlikely and it is estimated that an additional 10,000 prison places will be available by 2012. Few would deny that serious and dangerous offenders should be locked up, but a great many prisoners do not fall into those categories, and for them rehabilitation might work. We must think positively. If we have any answers, they are likely to be long-term, rather than political expedients, and will require a reallocation of resources in the fourth richest country in the world.

The alternatives to prison

- Community sentences or orders allow offenders to work in the community — 'paying it back' for their offences — under the supervision of the probation services, with the possibility of improving basic literacy and numeracy. Such sentences are appropriate for low-risk offenders and help to teach responsibility but many see community sentences as soft options, even though breaches can mean being sent to prison. There have been calls, so far rejected, that those on community sentences should be 'named and shamed' or should wear distinctive community service clothing.

- More use could be made of supervised early-release schemes, involving low-risk prisoners and using electronic tagging.

- Pressure on the prison population in 2007 was such that some 1,500 non-dangerous offenders were released 18 days before the end of their sentence simply to create more prison spaces.

- Pilot schemes exist for restorative justice orders that bring together victims and offenders. Early results suggest that victims report a high rate of satisfaction and there are low levels of reconviction.

- Anti-Social Behaviour Orders (ASBOs) have been widely used but there are many ways that they can be breached, leaving the offenders liable to imprisonment. In the subculture inhabited by some young people, ASBOs are badges of pride that can gain respect from peers.

- The ultimate goal — although it seems to be utopian — might be a smaller number of prisons, for those who present a serious danger to the public, with an increased number of specialist places for the high proportion of prisoners who are mentally ill or addicted to drugs. More opportunities could then be provided for raising literacy and numeracy levels and improving vocational education. In many respects these would be more cost-effective options but would meet with massive public opposition.

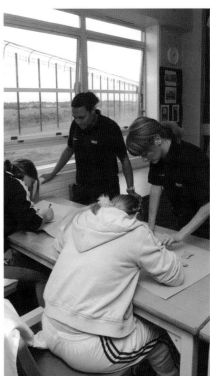

Young offenders attending an art class in a secure training centre

Viewpoints

Does prison cut crime?

Yes

■ Some statistics suggest that fewer crimes are committed when there are more people in custody.`

■ Prison is a deterrent that makes offenders realise that crime does not pay.

■ Crime is antisocial and prison allows law-abiding members of the community to satisfy their natural desire for retribution.

No

■ Community sentences are more effective in cutting re-offending rates.

■ Prison is becoming too costly, especially if it fails to cut re-offending.

■ Prison breeds crime as offenders learn new techniques.

■ Far too many prisoners need drug rehabilitation programmes or mental health support.

■ Prisons are overcrowded and ineffective, and bad conditions breed resentment.

Practice question

'It is important in a democracy that politicians must do as they say and be tough on crime and the causes of crime. That's the only way to bring crime figures down.'

To what extent, and for what reasons, do you agree with this statement?   *(25 marks)*

A2

UNIT 4

4

SCIENCE
AND SOCIETY

Explanation and evaluation of human behaviour

Social class and social mobility

Social class can be a perplexing topic, particularly since two recent prime ministers, John Major and Tony Blair (Conservative and Labour respectively) have made much of what they consider to be 'a classless society'. Unlike, for example, the caste system in India, social class in the UK has never been rigid and sociologists have found it difficult to reach agreement over a definition of the concept because society is not static.

Often shorthand terms are used such as 'working class', 'middle class' and 'upper class', but these are useful only in broad terms and can easily lead to stereotyping. In recent years, a number of sociologists have identified the growth of an 'underclass' — poor people who may exist on social benefits, often in 'sink neighbourhoods' of sub-standard housing, high crime and poor educational facilities with little or no chance of ever changing their situation. They are almost the equivalent of the 'undeserving' or 'indolent' poor from another age.

Similarly there are the 'chavs' of modern British society — potential troublemakers who hang around, lack fashion sense, aren't 'cool', take drugs, live on council estates and lack parental interest and support in their lives.

Traditionally, determinants of an individual's social class might include:

- a background determined by birth
- inheritance
- occupation
- income
- wealth
- housing
- education

For many people, incomes and living standards have risen in recent years. The traditional working class — often typified by men, as 'breadwinners', working in heavy industry, belonging to a trade union, reading tabloids, living in rented housing, having limited educational qualifications, and in certain parts of the country wearing cloth caps and keeping whippets or racing pigeons — is much diminished, not least due to economic changes. Many 'blue-collar' industrial and manufacturing jobs have disappeared, leading to what sociologists refer to as changing structural mobility. There is now much more opportunity for people who are aspirational to enter the ranks of the middle classes, not least as white-collar workers.

However, a research programme called 'the millennium cohort study' tracked the progress of over 15,000 children born between 2000 and 2002, recording differences in parental background and family circumstances. In its report in 2007, the study indicated that social class could form a dividing line as early as the age of 3, despite the efforts of the government's Sure Start programme launched in 1998 to counter this. (Previous studies concentrated on similar disadvantages at the ages of 5 and 7.) Children of graduate parents, even when very young, scored much more highly in vocabulary tests than those whose parents had few educational qualifications. Similar differences are seen on the basis of ethnic divisions, with Bangladeshi and Pakistani children often noticeably disadvantaged. The results of the millennium study reflect those of previous studies undertaken in 1958 and 1970.

One of Labour's key social policies from 1997 was to reduce rising levels of child poverty. And the situation improved through programmes like Sure Start, better childcare provision and tax credits. Child poverty has proved an intractable problem, though, especially for the children of single parents so often demonised by both politicians and sections of the popular press. Sure Start has been devolved to local councils and they have been ordered to expand it fivefold, but with limited funding that is not ring-fenced to ensure that it can be spent only on that programme.

Results from the 1958 and 1970 studies suggest that there has been a decline in UK social mobility, which was particularly evident for those growing up in the 1970s and 1980s. The trend of worsening social mobility is now less pronounced but, in comparison with many other European countries — especially Scandinavia — a much higher percentage of people in the UK (nearly 50%) stay in the same income group as their parents. The gap between rich and poor in the UK is similar to the gap that exists in the USA.

Key term

social mobility: the extent to which a child's social status and class can change during the course of his/her life. This may be a result of policies that provide equality of opportunity, although these do not necessarily lead to equality of outcome.

In a pamphlet published in 2008, former Labour minister (holder of three cabinet posts) David Blunkett warned of the dangers of more entrenched inequality and the continuing development of a significant underclass. He favours remedial action such as an increase in the child trust fund at key points in the lives of young people and extra state cash for poorer pupils, including payments for life mentors who would provide positive role models.

Continuing inequality

In terms of income and wealth, Britain is more unequal than for decades, with people whose incomes exceed £500,000 per year pulling even further ahead of those behind them. However, society is less deferential and Britain is probably rather less snobbish or prejudiced than might have been the case 50 years ago. There is much better legal protection against discrimination for women and ethnic minorities, although this may be less applicable to older people and the disabled, for whom legislation has been more recent.

Other indicators are more mixed:

- Selection for a grammar-school education by passing the 11 + examination was once a well-established route to social mobility for some working-class children.
- The Conservative Party has traditionally supported selective grammar-school education, but is now less keen because of doubts that grammar schools still encourage mobility — most pupils now already come from middle-class backgrounds.
- Slightly more children than before from the poorest families now obtain a university degree, but appreciably more do so from the richest families.
- Raising educational attainment at all stages among poorer children is felt to be of great significance. It is this educational gap that sets the UK apart from many European countries.

Immigrants to the UK have traditionally been downwardly mobile to begin with, typically taking relatively unskilled jobs at first irrespective of qualifications and previous experience. However, because of this, in some ethnic groups the children may be able to move into a higher class than their parents. Ethnic minorities are, therefore, likely to be more socially mobile, both upwards and downwards, than the white population.

Girls regularly out-perform boys in exams. Even though the way we live our lives has changed dramatically in the last 30 years, we are faced by the stark fact that attitudes, work cultures and expectations are slow to change. Young females may start with high aspirations but, while parental duties are now more likely to be shared, it is usually the career prospects of women that are impaired by difficulties in finding and affording childcare. Men may no longer be the traditional 'breadwinners', and women may be less inclined to do all the domestic chores, but a report by the Equal Opportunities Commission (EOC) in 2007 (*Completing the Revolution*) highlighted a number of key gender equality gaps that still remain. These include the following:

- Currently only about 20% of MPs in the House of Commons are female. This is a significant rise on the 6% of women MPs in 1987 (and is now the highest proportion in history) but the proportion of female voters is over 50%.
- There are very few women company directors. Women are also much less likely to run their own businesses than men.
- Occupational pensions for women are often much lower than those for men because many women take time off to raise children.
- Despite the passing of the Equal Pay Act in 1970 and the Sex Discrimination Act in 1975, it remains the case that the average pay for full-time male workers is 17% higher than that for full-time female workers. For part-timers the difference in pay is 38%. Ethnic differences can exaggerate the situation even further.
- There is continuing widespread discrimination against pregnant women.

In response, the EOC identified five priorities:
- closing the income gap between men and women
- giving better support to families
- modernising public services
- providing equal access to justice and safety at work
- sharing power equally

The EOC was subsumed by the Commission for Equality and Human Rights in 2007, and one of the biggest tasks of the new organisation is to continue the battle against gender discrimination. It is not easy. As local councils seek to ensure that there is equal pay for equal work between men and women, following an EU ruling in 2004 on the 1970 Equal Pay Act, it is estimated that costs will be as much as £3 billion. Male employees are reluctant to accept pay cuts so that money can be transferred to female colleagues. Ultimately, that may mean redundancies and higher taxes.

It is over 20 years since the *Wall Street Journal* first used the phrase 'the **glass ceiling**' and it remains difficult for many women to break through this invisible barrier to reach the top in business and in professions such as law. The UK is some distance from a recent law in Norway that requires Norwegian companies to have at least two women on their board of directors. Not all reformers favour such examples of 'positive discrimination'.

The Disability Discrimination Acts have helped to improve access to public buildings

Further concern has been expressed about the plight of the elderly and the disabled, despite recent legislation designed to give both groups protection against discrimination. As medical science advances, many people are living for longer and significantly more severely disabled children survive.

In both cases more demands are made on social services and on a hidden army of family carers. Resources have been increased, but not at a rate that matches growing numbers and costs. Public responsibility rests uneasily between the NHS and local councils, which are often responsible for meeting the costs of those who have to be placed in private care homes. In England many elderly people have to sell their homes to meet care costs.

For disabled people, the Disability Discrimination Acts have helped to improve access to shops and leisure facilities, although provision is often patchy. Buses have been redesigned to facilitate wheelchair access both onto and inside them.

Ultimately, like 'class', '**inequality**' has become almost a taboo word. According to the Office for National Statistics, after 10 years of Labour government income equality had changed little by 2007. The poorest fifth of the population pay the highest proportion of their income in taxes despite measures such as tax credits, designed particularly to help the working poor with families. Meanwhile, a survey by Barclays Bank revealed that in 2007 the average annual salary of residents in the London borough of Kensington and Chelsea exceeded £100,000.

New Labour has championed equality of opportunity — the ability of people to rise by their talents rather than by an accident of birth or through inherited privilege. There are images of 'level playing fields' and equal life chances — a true meritocracy; but even in a meritocracy, the winners might have little regard for the losers.

Westminster School got nearly 50% of its pupils into Oxford or Cambridge. It is an excellent school with some exceptionally talented pupils — but fees are in the region of £25,000 a year. The reality is that, just as there are rich and poor parts of the country, the 7% of young people educated at private schools usually gain 45% of Oxbridge places. Arguably they do so on merit, and in a free society parents and their children are entitled to make free choices. Equality of opportunity may be considered a desirable and prized social goal. It is also one that is likely to remain both elusive and illusory.

Pupils educated at private schools gain 45% of Oxbridge places

Ask the examiner

Q **Is enough being done to reduce inequality?**

A Parliament has made great efforts since 1970 to pass legislation that will at least help to secure greater equality. This has undoubtedly had some success – how much success is partly a matter of judgement based on a selection from a huge amount of evidence.

For many groups — women, ethnic minorities, the disabled — the situation is better than it was, say, 20 years ago. Whether the progress made is deemed to be sufficient is difficult to prove one way or another, and that is why it is so difficult to reach a conclusion.

It is one thing for Parliament to pass a law requiring something to happen, and another thing for it actually to happen. We have clear and straightforward laws restricting the speed at which we can drive, yet most people are likely to break them on a daily basis. The barriers to change might include:

- problems of enforcing any laws because of a lack of human or financial resources
- habits — which are difficult to break
- the process of socialisation — we are brought up to believe certain things and these beliefs may be slow to change
- deliberate attempts to disobey or get round a law which might be difficult to detect and prove
- cultural factors which influence our beliefs and values
- slow progress in terms of educating people about what might be deemed fair and unfair in society
- genuine disagreement about what constitutes 'progress' and about the extent and speed of change

Viewpoints

It is sometimes said that class divisions and inequality, even elitism, are features of a free society and a market economy. Social engineering, in whatever form, is never likely to succeed.

Arguments for and against social engineering and greater state intervention to reduce inequality

In favour

- Economies organised on the basis of communist ideology, which claims that inequalities can be removed, have often not succeeded because of the massive bureaucracy of the state that is needed to support them.
- The state already interferes too much in people's lives.
- Even in communist countries, elites — often based on party membership and privilege — have quickly emerged.
- People need incentives to fuel their ambition.
- Some people are naturally more talented than others and need scope to develop their talents. It is a matter of nature and genetics rather than nurture and environment.
- People should be rewarded for achieving success.
- A dynamic economy cannot be sustained without talented leaders.
- While it might be possible to eliminate gross inequalities, it is unrealistic to pretend that full equality can ever exist.
- Britain is not a closed society and people with drive, ambition and talent can achieve considerable social mobility.

Against

- While a meritocracy might be a desirable goal, it is unlikely to be achieved while there are such massive differences in the quality of schooling.
- Talent is being wasted if opportunities for poor but able children are so limited.
- Equality is a matter of social justice and it is desirable that the state should intervene to promote this.
- Actions based on ignorance and prejudice should always be challenged; this is the basis for a just society.
- Significant differences in wealth and income are likely to result in more social unrest and crime.
- Opponents distort the arguments. They use emotive words such as 'social engineering'. Supporters of greater equality acknowledge that equality of outcomes cannot be achieved. What they are seeking is greater equality of opportunity.
- Elites are interested in their own status and achievement rather than the wider social good.
- Without state intervention and protection, too many people in society would be abused and exploited by the ignorant and the unscrupulous.

Practice question

The following question is typical of those that might be used in Section B of Unit 4.

It is around 40 years since the Equal Pay Act, in which Parliament first tried to tackle discrimination between men and women. Since then, there have been many new laws against discrimination on the grounds of gender, ethnicity, age, disability and sexual orientation.

Explain why such parliamentary intervention was necessary.

Discuss the claim that little progress has been made in discriminatory behaviour in the United Kingdom in the last 40 years.   *(25 marks)*

Social and economic trends and constraints

Education

- The 1944 Education Act, passed a year before the end of the Second World War, was of great importance because it brought in its wake free secondary education for all.
- On the basis of a test known as the 11 +, most children progressed to what were called 'secondary modern' schools for a practical education, initially without examinations.
- A small minority of children were deemed to be 'academic' and went to grammar schools, where examinations were important.
- A handful of areas had 'technical grammar schools' as a concession to those who might progress in more technical subjects.
- For those working-class children selected for a grammar school, there was a clear route to social mobility and a respectable 'white-collar' job with status and a pension. Very few went on to university.
- Although there was meant to be 'parity of esteem', the 80% who went to secondary moderns were quickly labelled '11 + failures', and by the 1960s the reliability of testing at a relatively early age was increasingly questioned.
- Comprehensive schools, catering for pupils of all abilities, were increasingly common, particularly after they received government approval in the later 1960s.
- At the same time, there was a significant expansion in the number of universities.
- As the number of comprehensives increased, the number of grammar schools fell, although they remain today in a few parts of the country — most notably in Kent, Lincolnshire and Buckinghamshire.
- The great majority of secondary schools are now comprehensive, including a number of faith schools — mostly Church of England and Roman Catholic.

- Both Sixth Form and Further Education colleges have expanded significantly.
- Over the last 10 years, some secondary schools have become 'city academies', often with some support from private business.
- The growth in higher education has been rapid and a much higher proportion of 18-year-olds go on to university, despite the introduction of top-up fees.

Education debates

Comprehensives and selective education

When the Conservatives — traditional supporters of selective education — returned to power in 1979, many were surprised that the rate of grammar-school closures did not slow down under Margaret Thatcher. Under the leadership of David Cameron, the Conservatives — although not threatening to close those still in existence — appeared less committed to grammar schools, as they had ceased to provide a route to greater social mobility for poorer but able children. (Only 2% of those attending grammar schools qualify for free meals compared with the national average of 12%.)

In the UK, 36 of the 150 local education authorities in England still retain at least one grammar school and there is considerable competition for the limited number of places. Many parents resort to private tutoring to give their children a head start.

Most grammar schools have a reputation for academic excellence and some send particularly high numbers to Oxford and Cambridge universities. Wales has no grammar schools, while Northern Ireland retains a relatively large number. There are few private schools in Northern Ireland and more working-class students go on to university.

Viewpoints

Arguments in favour of comprehensive schools

- Selection at 11 is too early, particularly for boys, who tend to mature later than girls.
- It is claimed that the 11+ is unreliable and culturally biased. Doubts have been cast on the relationship between IQ and test scores.
- Supporters argue that a central aim of education should be to promote a greater equality of outcome and more social integration.
- The existence of grammar schools means that other schools in the areas concerned, although often called 'comprehensives', do not get an intake covering the complete ability range because the most able are creamed off by the grammar schools.
- Grammar schools are increasingly socially, as well as academically, selective and it is unfair that educated and better-off families can use their advantages to secure grammar-school places for their children.

- Comprehensive schools often contain a social mix and this is good preparation for life outside school.
- Comprehensive schools are much fairer and allow for children who develop after the 11+ barrier.
- There are some extremely successful comprehensives that out-perform grammar schools.
- The country needs to provide a good education for pupils of all abilities and backgrounds, not just the most able.

Arguments in favour of selective grammar schools

- Because they are selective, grammar schools can offer the best academic education that the state can provide.
- Education is naturally selective and not everyone has the same ability and potential. The most able can progress more quickly if taught together.
- Late developers can transfer to a grammar school at 12+ and 13+.
- Grammar schools can still offer an excellent education to clever children from disadvantaged backgrounds.
- There is still much public support for grammar schools.
- There is evidence that high-ability children achieve better examination results in selective schools.
- A 'one size fits all' approach is not appropriate for secondary education.

The private sector and the public sector in education

Over 90% of secondary-age children attend a non-fee-paying school in the public sector. Apart from a tiny number educated at home, the rest are privately educated in fee-paying schools. Fees at a prestigious school such as Eton, where David Cameron was educated, can be as high as £25,000 per year.

Viewpoints

Arguments in favour of education in the private sector

- It helps to ensure that parents have freedom of choice.
- It offers financial support, bursaries and scholarships for able children from disadvantaged backgrounds.
- It provides smaller classes.
- Some private schools are acknowledged centres of excellence.
- They offer more chance to get to university.
- People who have been to private schools can often get better jobs.

Arguments against education in the private sector

- Only the better-off can have freedom of choice.
- The existence of private schools helps to reinforce social and class divisions.

- Opportunities and spending are unequal. The average cost of educating a secondary-school pupil in the state system is £4,500 but the figure for a private school pupil is over £8,000.
- Independent schools get significant tax breaks because of their charitable status but do not always do a lot for the less privileged to justify this.
- If there were no private schools, many more able pupils and influential parents would be involved in driving forward the state system.

Paying for higher education: grants or loans?

Before the expansion of universities in the late 1960s and beyond, only 5% of the age group went on to university education. Fees were paid for all students and, on the basis of a means test of parental income, most students qualified for a grant from their local authority to cover living costs while living away from home. As the numbers studying at university expanded, the cost of maintaining them rose dramatically and student loans were introduced to meet maintenance costs. These replaced student grants and had to be paid back on a long-term basis.

In 2006, much-debated top-up fees of up to £3,000 per year (a figure subject to review in 2009) were introduced to provide universities with additional sources of revenue to meet the cost of expansion. The government is aiming for 50% of young people to enter higher education by 2010.

Viewpoints

Arguments in favour of student grants
- Many young people accumulate large debts by the time they leave university and, unlike grants, these eventually have to be repaid.
- Grants made it much easier than loans for students from poorer families to go to university.
- Young people have enough difficulties establishing themselves in working life after they leave university, especially as the cost of buying a house has increased so much. The burden of paying back student loans makes this even more difficult.

Arguments in favour of student loans
- It is important for economic growth for the UK to remain competitive, and this means that more young people must be better educated. Because this is very costly, the individuals concerned must be prepared to make a contribution to the cost of their studies.
- Taxpayers cannot be expected to meet all the additional costs of the expansion of higher education.
- Loans teach young people about the cost and value of education.
- They do not have to be repaid until graduates are working and have reached a minimum salary level.
- They can be repaid over a long period.

Ask the examiner

Q Are A-levels too easy?

A It is difficult to compare A-levels now with those of, say, 1970. Forty years ago the range of questions was much narrower, knowledge was more likely to be tested than skills, and fixed percentages of entrants were awarded each grade. Examinations and their marking were then a highly secretive process and only a tiny minority of the age group sat A-levels, which were essentially a test of suitability for university entrance.

Modern A-levels may not require the same depth of knowledge but they do need a wider range of skills. Because jobs are more difficult to get, 16–18-year-olds work hard to pass exams and get the best grades. Examination boards make more information available to teachers, and teachers are more aware of what is necessary for their students to reach the top grades. A-levels are now taken by many more people than in the past and from a much wider range of ability.

A-levels are often seen as the 'gold standard' of exams for 18-year-olds, but sections of the media, despite the lack of conclusive evidence, argue that they have become too easy. A new A* grade has been introduced, and some schools have switched to the International Baccalaureate, which has more breadth. A new system of diplomas is currently being introduced. Even examiners cannot agree whether or not A-levels are easier. They are certainly different, are marked with a much more detailed mark scheme, are taken by far more 18-year-olds, and still require a lot of effort and ability to gain a grade A.

Ask the examiner

Q Do schools need uniforms?

A Many European countries do not require their school students to wear a uniform. In the UK, uniforms were widely associated with private and grammar schools and have been copied by schools trying to emulate them and gain status. They are widely favoured by parents, help to avoid fashion competitions in school dress, do not show up children from poorer homes and can reinforce a sense of identification with the school and a feeling of pride.

Critics feel that they deny freedom to individuals, are often excessively expensive if there are exclusive contracts with suppliers and are frequently the cause of disagreement between teachers and the taught. Often they also conflict with human rights legislation and, occasionally, with pupils' religious beliefs, especially among Muslims.

World population trends, poverty and food production

World population and poverty

With Britain's population growth accelerating by the end of the eighteenth century, the Reverend Thomas Malthus predicted that the rapid growth would outstrip the growth of resources. Consequently there would need to be checks on population growth based on either 'moral restraint' (such as contraception or abstention) or events such as famine, disease or war. The UK population continued to grow rapidly in the nineteenth century, but so did the economy and food supplies; yet the warnings of Malthus can be applied to the situation today in some parts of the world.

It is estimated that the world's population is currently about 6.5 billion, but the United Nations has warned that it could rise to over 9 billion by 2050 — a figure in line with projections from the United States Census Bureau. The UN also predicts that the population of the world's 50 poorest countries will double by 2050. However, predicting future population figures is notoriously difficult because birth rates vary and death rates can vary considerably as a result of war, disease, other catastrophes or advances in medical knowledge. Virtually all the population growth is in less economically developed countries (LEDCs) and it is thought that two in three babies are born in poverty.

In contrast, it is estimated that the population of developed countries is likely to remain near to its current level of 1.2 billion because they have low birth rates and low death rates. Indeed, population within the European Union is likely to decline by several million by 2050, although projections for the UK indicate a possible rise from 61 million to 77 million by then.

The most populous nations, by some margin, are China (with 20% of the world's population) and India (with 17%), although it is estimated that India will overtake China as the world's most populous country, perhaps by 2020. The third most populous country, the USA, has less than 5% of the world's population and the most populous European country, Germany, is fourteenth on the world list with 1.3% of the world's population. Added together, all the countries in the EU would account for less than 8% of the world's population.

Rises in the birth rate in LEDCs may be caused by:
- the need for children as labour
- ignorance of contraceptive techniques, perhaps because of illiteracy
- inability to afford contraceptives
- poor supply of contraceptives
- religious opposition to contraception, for example from the Catholic Church, which forbids artificial contraception
- people compensating for high levels of infant mortality

In terms of the dangers of overpopulation, much will depend on factors such as changes in trade patterns and advances in science that might raise agricultural productivity. Food production may require extensive irrigation schemes, non-sustainable fertilisers and reliance on genetically modified techniques; and may also depend on the extent to which productivity is diverted towards biofuels. As in the times of Malthus, war, drought and pestilence can still have a significant impact on the rate of population growth.

The possible consequences of over-rapid population growth might include:
- shortages of drinking water
- inadequate/irregular food supplies leading to hunger, malnutrition and starvation
- pressure on housing
- threats to the countryside and bird/animal habitats
- the adoption of more intensive farming and animal-rearing methods
- greater consumption of non-renewable resources
- more pollution
- the speeding up of global warming and subsequent impact on weather patterns
- the greater likelihood of conflict and war as resources become more scarce

China, where the population was increasing rapidly, introduced the one child policy in 1979. Couples have to gain official permission to give birth, and keeping to one child means

Advertisment for China's one-child policy

that they qualify for a range of social benefits that are lost if another child is born. While this slowed down the increase in population, abortion increased, babies were abandoned and an imbalance of males and females occurred as parents, limited to one child, often tried to ensure that their one child was male.

International organisations such as the Red Cross and Médecins Sans Frontières battle constantly against endemic poverty, malnourishment and illnesses, and often also against the results of the political instability and violence that swell the numbers of refugees trying to escape from war zones in African countries such as Darfur and Somalia.

The global rush to switch from fuel oil to crops and plants in order to generate energy may increase problems as crops are grown extensively for fuel rather than food. With growing demand from countries such as China and India, and extreme weather leading to more drought and floods, world food prices are rising sharply, with global corn prices doubling between 2006 and 2007. In 2007 the UN listed 34 countries needing food aid, with sub-Saharan Africa, where HIV/AIDS is rife, experiencing rapidly rising rates of undernourishment.

By 2008, the UN was warning that there was no longer sufficient money available to tackle global malnutrition through the UN's World Food Programme (WFP), which feeds 73 million people in 78 countries — a small fraction of the undernourished people in the world. With world food prices soaring by up to 40% in 2008, and high fuel prices to transport it, the WFP's budget of £1.5 billion is inadequate. Food riots have taken place in countries as far apart as Mexico, Yemen, Senegal and Uzbekistan. Much of the blame has been put on the transfer of foodstuffs to produce biofuels.

After three decades of falling world food prices, the world's richest countries which make up **the G8** made promises at the Gleneagles summit in 2005 to relieve world poverty through more generous aid for development, more preferential trade arrangements or the writing off of debt. However, only the UK and Japan seem to have met their obligations, according to a report by DATA (Debt AIDS Trade Africa), the organisation set up by Bono and Bob Geldof. There is, though, no guarantee that aid will reach those most in need, often because of high levels of political corruption, particularly in a number of African countries.

> ### Key term
>
> **the G8:** an international forum involving representatives from Canada, France, Germany, Italy, Japan, Russia, the UK and the USA. Meetings are held periodically to discuss and address global economic and monetary issues and concerns.

In 1996, at the World Food Summit, 176 world leaders pledged that by 2015 the number of undernourished people in the world would be halved. Yet by 2006, more than 850 million were hungry — an increase of 18 million on the 1996 figure. It is estimated that 6 million children die from hunger annually; and it has to be asked if there really is a political will, and commitment to prioritise, to solve the problem of world hunger. In Sierra Leone, where female life expectancy is 42 years, the mortality rate for children under 5 is 282 per 1,000 live births — the highest in the world. In Iceland, with the world's lowest child mortality rates, the comparable figure is three.

At Gleneagles in 2005, the G8 leaders promised to double international aid by $50 billion a year by 2010, including a doubling of aid to Africa. G8 countries also pledged to write off debts to 40 highly indebted countries. It seems most unlikely that the 2010 target will be reached. Debts have been written off for over 50% of the countries targeted.

Other countries will qualify for debts to be written off once economic and political conditions have been met, but as many as 25 additional countries, outside the scheme, may also require debt relief and cancellation. The Food and Agriculture Organisation of the United Nations, the world body coordinating efforts to reduce world hunger, is powerless if the world's wealthiest countries do not cooperate fully.

The UN's goals for 2015 are:

- reducing extreme poverty by halving the number of people who live on less than $1 a day
- universal primary education, by ensuring that children will have full primary schooling
- gender equality, by eliminating gender disparity in primary and secondary education
- reversing the spread of HIV/AIDS
- reducing child mortality by two-thirds
- reducing the maternal mortality rate by 75%
- integrating principles of sustainable development into the policies of individual countries
- halving the proportion of people without sustainable access to basic sanitation

The ageing population in more economically developed countries

It is extremely unlikely that fertility levels will rise significantly in the future because people in more economically developed countries (MEDC's) have widespread access to birth control techniques and are likely to seek to protect their rising living standards by limiting the size of their families. Consequently population ageing is seen as irreversible. Globally the proportion of older people in the population is increasing much more rapidly than growth of the population as a whole, and the population of older people is itself ageing as average life expectancy increases.

As the proportion of people aged over 60 increases, there is a reduction in the normal working population of those aged 16–60. Consequently the burden on the working population to support older people, and finance their welfare benefits, is greater.

The following are some of the issues that arise with an ageing population.

- Pension costs rise. Occupational pension schemes might not be adequate to support people in old age.
- Older people require more health services, increasing NHS costs.
- Older people may be more at risk from loneliness, isolation and depression.
- There is a change in housing needs. Older people require smaller, perhaps specially adapted, dwellings.
- Problems of care increase. Residential care is expensive, and care is often provided by younger members of the family.
- Patterns of consumption change. Not all old people are poor; retirement may take place earlier and some older people will be well provided for financially. The 'grey pound' might be quite a powerful economic force.
- Older people are more likely to vote and this may have an impact on election results.
- Older people are sometimes less willing to change. Society may become less innovative and dynamic, although it could benefit from the experience of older people.

Fair Trade

- The Fair Trade movement has increased in momentum in the last two decades. In the USA, Fair Trade coffee is part of a movement dating back to the 1940s, when US churches sold handicrafts made by European refugees.
- Fair Trade certification began in the Netherlands in 1988, following a dramatic fall in world coffee prices which threatened to bankrupt many producers.

Key term

Fair Trade: a system in which the purchasing company or agent operates directly with farmers, growers and other producers. Together they seek to establish a fair price for the product, trying to ensure that potentially disadvantaged producers receive sufficient remuneration and that acknowledgement is given to following sustainable environmental practices. Fair Trade items sold in the UK can be identified by the Fairtrade logo.

Co-operative Group

- Today, 20 countries have their own labelling schemes and an increasing number of Fair Trade products are seen on supermarket shelves, including coffee, tea, chocolate, bananas, sugar and flowers, as well as a great many Fair Trade handicrafts sold in specialist shops.

- Total UK sales of Fair Trade products exceed £300 million per year and are increasing rapidly. It is estimated that they could be worth in excess of £500 million by 2011.

- Around the world, there are 23 national initiatives and all are members of FLO International which sets and reviews Fair Trade standards and helps producers to take advantage of market opportunities. According to FLO, global consumer spending on Fair Trade products was over £1 billion in 2006.

- Producers are paid a guaranteed payment above world market prices. Producers often form cooperatives and surplus monies can be invested in improving production techniques or building up the local infrastructure, perhaps improving education and health or developing power supplies.

- According to the Fairtrade Foundation, which gives accreditation, and which operates a strict certifying system based on five core principles, Fair Trade is one of the fastest-growing retail sectors, with British consumers spending over £450 million annually.

- This is not least a result of pioneering initiatives undertaken by the Co-op, which operates 2,700 stores across Britain and was the first major British retailer to champion the Fairtrade label when it launched Cafédirect coffee in 1992.

- Some of Britain's top retailers, such as Marks and Spencer, Next and Debenhams, are developing new clothes options based on ethically certified cotton, and over 100 have been awarded the Fairtrade mark.

Unfair production

Part of the consumer revolution in countries like the UK is based on clothes and leisure goods. Supermarkets such as Asda, with its 'George@Asda' range, and Tesco have diversified into cheap clothes, and one of the major retailing successes on the high street in recent years has been that of Primark, which responds quickly to fashion trends, emulating fashion spin-offs at a fraction of the original prices and combining quality, style and value. Two men's shirts can be bought for £5 and a pair of jeans for less than that in a buoyant and rapidly expanding market. However, concerns have been expressed about sustainability and the exploitation of labour in producing countries.

- The charity War on Want has joined forces with the anti-sweatshop pressure group Labour Behind the Label, which is seeking to secure better wages for garment workers in less economically developed countries, where wages can be as low as a few pence an hour.
- Questions are frequently asked about working conditions in factories owned by exporters in countries like India and Bangladesh. Such factories often supply clothes sold on British high streets.
- Wages in garment factories may be little higher than £1 a day, often with compulsory overtime and unsafe working conditions.
- Such allegations are not always easy to prove. Living standards in LEDCs cannot always be compared to those in Western countries and any efforts to improve wages may result in unemployment and adverse effects on the families concerned.
- However, even in the poorest countries, at least £2 per day is likely to be closer to a living wage. Given the unlimited labour supply, it is not difficult to see how employees might be exploited.
- Child labour is another emotive issue. Children's meagre wages are often an important contribution to the family income, and orphans may have no other means of support.
- It is also argued that, deprived of any other source of income, more children might turn to prostitution.
- Unions are weak and employees who complain about pay and conditions are likely to be dismissed.
- Women, who often make up the bulk of the labour force in garment manufacturing, are also likely to be exploited.

The possibilities of labour exploitation in the manufacturing process presents some shoppers in the UK with an ethical dilemma. Many high-street brands might be produced under conditions that workers in MEDCs would not tolerate. Cheap but 'chic' clothing has become widely available in the UK during the last few years. 'Rock bottom' prices are attractive but they can often only be secured at a cost. It is a cost that we might choose to ignore. British companies claim that they have ethical standards on worker welfare. To what extent they are able to enforce these, thousands of miles away, remains a matter for debate.

World trouble spots

In 2008, **Iraq** and **Afghanistan** remained two of the world's most notorious trouble spots. As the allies sought an 'exit strategy' from Iraq, Afghanistan was a more enduring problem, as it had been for over a century. The Taliban fundamentalists who supported al-Qaeda regrouped constantly and the world opium trade continued to flourish from its base in Afghanistan. Increasingly, the mountain regions of Pakistan, which borders Afghanistan, acted as a training ground for terrorists.

In **Pakistan**, where the military remained the overwhelming influence, President Musharraf continued to cling to power in 2008, supported by Western countries that feared a fundamentalist uprising in a volatile area of the world. The assassination of the popular opposition politician, Benazir Bhutto, dealt a further blow to the country's stability.

Turkish troops withdrawing from Iraq, February 2008

Elsewhere in Africa, violence in **Somalia** in 2007 reached levels not seen since 1992. The United Nations deemed Somalia to be the worst humanitarian crisis in Africa as Ethiopian troops battled with the Union of Islamic Courts, reducing Somalia's capital, Mogadishu, to anarchy. Millions fled their homes and it became increasingly difficult to get aid through to the most vulnerable.

Darfur, in the western region of Sudan, was another part of Africa deep in crisis. In Darfur, it is estimated that civil war cost half a million lives in the 4 years to 2007. Four million people in Darfur became dependent on food aid because their homes and fields were destroyed as the government-backed Arab militia, the Janjaweed, operated an unforgiving system of enforcement. While the African Union pressed for peace and the UN hovered on the sidelines, Arab and non-Arab tribal leaders remained divided. At its worst, Darfur is a country where babies are shot on their mother's backs and children are thrown into bonfires.

A 2007 survey by charities such as Oxfam, *Africa's Missing Billions*, says that 50% of African countries have been involved in conflict since 1990. Where there has been conflict there is far more undernourishment, malnutrition and poverty, and life expectation is often lower. Rape and HIV infections are much more common. Long-standing conflict in countries such as Burundi, the Democratic Republic of Congo, Eritrea, Rwanda and Sierra Leone has led to a massive waste of resources.

Intervention

There is a plethora of international organisations and agencies: the African Union, the United Nations, the Commonwealth, G8, the World Bank, the World Trade Organisation, and the International Monetary Fund are among the most prominent.

The principle of non-interference in the affairs of other nation states was first established by the Peace of Westphalia in 1648. In an ideal world, it helps to protect the independence and sovereignty of individual nations. How far this is moral may vary, according to individual circumstances and the extent to which countries should stand by when acts of extreme cruelty or the suppression of human rights are taking place. British intervention in Sierra Leone has led to the emergence of a more stable and democratic country. Similarly, in Kosovo a bloodbath may well have been averted by intervention.

The situation in Afghanistan and Iraq remains unresolved. The Taliban regime was overthrown but has regrouped to hold certain parts of a country where, again, tribal loyalties remain important. In Iraq, Saddam Hussein was a brutal tyrant who had crushed all opposition; but such undesirable characteristics were far from unique among world leaders. The allegation that he was holding weapons of mass destruction in breach of UN resolutions now appears a flimsy pretext for invasion; and the country's possession of significant oil reserves, and the inability of the USA to press home a previous advantage, always generated suspicions about the real motives.

Without a second UN Security Council resolution, the justification for sending British and American troops was never secure, and both countries have become targets for terrorist retribution. It seems that neither country anticipated the consequences of intervention in Iraq and the intensity of the Shia–Sunni rivalry. Yet if other strategies fail, armed liberal interventionism is sometimes the only way of beating what many deem to be tyranny and extreme suffering.

Practice questions

The following two questions are typical of those that might be used in Section B of Unit 4.

(1) The debate about aid or trade to help less economically developed countries continues. Sometimes the need is so urgent that emergency aid is the only option. In the longer term, LEDCs require more technology to improve their infrastructure, greater availability of contraception and better trading terms.

Explain the different circumstances that lead to less economically developed countries needing aid.

Discuss the difficulties in determining which forms of aid are likely to have the most important longer-term effect on the prosperity of less economically developed countries. *(25 marks)*

(2) Conflict, whether it is in Iraq, Afghanistan, the countries of Africa or in any other trouble spot in the world, is disastrous for everyone involved. It is a drain on resources and causes great human misery and suffering.

Examine the reasons for conflict in any named part of the world.

Discuss the claim that intervention in the affairs of another country can only be justified if it is properly sanctioned and carried out by an international body such as the United Nations. *(25 marks)*

Characteristics of science and understanding of scientific methods, principles and their application

Space exploration

Even in the 1950s, the exploration of space seemed to belong to the world of science fiction. Dan Dare of *The Eagle* comic enthralled boys — and it was assumed that only boys would be interested in space exploration — and millions gripped the edges of their seats listening to the popular BBC radio serial, *Journey Into Space*.

Yet at the height of the Cold War, in October 1957, Russia launched the *Sputnik I* satellite into space, followed a month later, unsuccessfully, by the launch of a dog. Not to be outdone, the USA launched *Explorer I* from Cape Canaveral, Florida, at the start of 1958. Later in the year NASA was set up by the Americans, and in the 1960s it pioneered satellite communications, including Telstar, remembered as the title of a successful instrumental hit by the Tornados in the newly burgeoning pop-music industry.

There are many obstacles to overcome in developing successful space travel:
- harnessing sufficient energy to get off the ground
- the vacuum of space
- heat management

> **Key term**
>
> **NASA:** the National Aeronautics and Space Administration, which was established in the USA on 1 October 1958 'to provide for research into the problems of flight within and outside the earth's atmosphere and for other purposes'. It succeeded the National Advisory Committee for Aeronautics as the US government agency with responsibility for developing flight and space-related technology after the Russians had shown the way with Sputnik. NASA's initial annual budget was $100 million; by the new millennium it was responsible for ten research and spaceflight centres.

- orbital mechanics
- space debris
- cosmic and solar radiation
- internal logistics in a weightless environment
- acceptable and balanced food
- re-entry

In 1961 the so-called 'space race' was won by the Russians when cosmonaut Yuri Gagarin became the first human to enter space and return safely, which made him an instant worldwide celebrity. Three weeks later, with the launch of *Freedom 7*, Alan Shepard became the first American to fly into space, and shortly afterwards President John F. Kennedy announced that the USA intended to send astronauts to the moon by the end of the 1960s. In 1963, after the intervention of President Khrushchev, Valentina Tereshkova became a national hero as the first woman in space. In 1965, Edward H. White became the first American to make a spacewalk — only to die 2 years later in the Apollo tragedy.

Almost immediately a space treaty was signed and later refined as the Outer Space Treaty of 1967, followed by later treaties culminating in the Moon Agreement of 1979. It was agreed that the exploration and use of outer space should be carried out for the benefit of all countries and that no national claims could be made. It was also agreed that no weapons of mass destruction should be placed in orbit or on celestial bodies and that individual nations should be liable for any damage caused by their space objects.

Space tragedies

Early efforts were not without both failure and tragedy. In 1965 millions watched on television screens as a space probe crashed into the moon. Double tragedy struck in 1967. At the start of the year, *American Mission AS-204* (later renamed *Apollo 1*) was hit by a flash fire that swept through its command module during a launch pad test, killing three astronauts. Shortly afterwards, Russia lost Vladimir Komarov, who became the first person to die in a space mission when his *Soyuz I* spacecraft crashed on return to Earth.

Three more Russians died in 1971 during the re-entry of their *Soyuz 11* spacecraft, following 24 days in an orbiting space laboratory, after it was depressurised by a faulty valve. However, it was the Americans who had the most fatalities. In 1986 the space shuttle *Challenger* exploded only a minute after take-off when a leak in the joints of one of two solid rocket boosters caused the main liquid fuel tank to explode, killing the seven astronauts on board. Seven more were killed in 2003 when the space shuttle *Columbia* broke apart in flames over Texas shortly before it was due to touch down in Florida.

Men on the moon

There were triumphs as well as tragedies in 1967. The first test flight of the *Saturn V* rocket took place. In the years to come it would carry many spacecraft into space. As the decade ended, even though President Kennedy had been assassinated, the American dream was realised when Neil Armstrong and Edwin 'Buzz' Aldrin became the first men to walk on the moon.

They raised the Stars and Stripes and unveiled a plaque signed by President Richard Nixon. It read: 'Here men from the planet Earth first set foot upon the Moon July 1969AD. We came in peace for all mankind.' Armstrong summed up the massive technological achievement with his words 'That's one small step for a man, one giant leap for mankind.' It was — but at a cost of $25 billion.

Edwin 'Buzz' Aldrin, photographed by Neil Armstrong — the first men on the moon

A hundred years earlier, Jules Verne had written *From the Earth to the Moon* (in which three astronauts were sent to the moon after being fired from a cannon), and in 1898 H. G. Wells wrote *The War of the Worlds,* telling a tale of Martians invading the Earth and causing destruction in London. In 1950, another science fiction writer, Ray Bradbury, described in *The Martian Chronicles* how humans got to Mars, and in Philip K. Dick's 1964 sci-fi novel *Martian Time-Slip*, Mars had been colonised by humans.

More progress was made from the 1970s onwards:

- In 1972, the unmanned *Pioneer 10* became the Earth's first space probe to travel through the asteroid belt to an outer planet. It made close-up observations of Jupiter and was the first man-made object to leave the solar system. Its last communication to Earth was received in 2003.
- In 1973 the USA launched *Skylab*, its first experimental space station.
- In 1975, the Apollo–Soyuz Test Project was the first human spaceflight mission conducted jointly by two nations — the USA and the Soviet Union.
- In 1976 both *Viking 1* and *Viking 2* landed safely on Mars and sent back the first set of images and data from the planet. By 2004, NASA was looking for water on Mars.

In 1981, nearly 10 years after President Richard Nixon announced America's intention to develop the first space shuttle for travel into space, the shuttle *Columbia* was sent into orbit. It landed safely, starting a new era in the US space programme.

- A year later, it carried a four-person crew. There was a setback when the shuttle *Challenger* exploded in 1986, but *Discovery* – in the first shuttle flight since the *Challenger* disaster – carried its five-person crew safely and successfully in 1988. Space shuttles are the world's first re-usable spacecraft. All components are re-used with the exception of the external fuel tank, which burns up in the atmosphere after the launch.
- Two years later, the Hubble Space Telescope (named after US astronomer Edwin Hubble) was launched into orbit to provide high-resolution astronomical observations. The Hubble's orbit above the Earth's atmosphere provided unblurred images and benefited from its very steady and accurate pointing mechanisms. It was a technological triumph but cost $1.5 billion to build and required periodic and expensive service missions. Not for the first time, the very high costs of space exploration became an issue.
- By 1995, with the Cold War almost a distant memory, the shuttle *Discovery* made a non-docking rendezvous with the space station *Mir*, which the Russians had launched in 1986, passing close enough for the crews to wave at each other.
- In 1998, the first two modules of the International Space Station (ISS) were launched and joined together in orbit. Other modules were added, and by 2000 the first crew had arrived.

Viewpoints

Is the expense of space exploration worth the cost and the risk?

Yes

- There has been a fascination with landing a human on the moon for a long time and scientists were keen to test the hypotheses that this was possible and that another form of life might exist there.
- The lure of the unknown is considerable and the human sense of adventure is irresistible.
- There is great scientific and public curiosity about the mysteries of outer space. The imagination of young people who might become scientists is stimulated by the quest for further discovery.
- It is important to explore other planets to see if they could be colonised or if we can learn from the evidence that space probes provide.
- Much scientific progress (e.g. the marvels of the Hubble Space Telescope) has resulted from the quest for space travel.
- Science done aboard the shuttle or International Space Station is difficult to replicate elsewhere.
- Possibilities for space tourism are an exciting new development with great potential.
- The glamour associated with space exploration makes it seem more expensive than it is.
- In terms of priorities and moral justification, 40 times more per year is spent on gambling in the USA than space exploration.

No

- It is too costly and the money could be spent on other, more worthwhile, things on Earth, such as the needs of the underprivileged.
- The benefits of space exploration may be real but they are rarely self-evident.
- The USA is heavily committed to the costly battle against world terrorism and cannot afford the billions of dollars spent on space exploration.
- The USA is the fulcrum of the world economy but its budget deficits are getting larger. Uncertainty affecting the US economy can have global economic repercussions.
- The risks to human life are too great.
- There are dangers because of the amount of 'space junk' that is now circulating, with unpredictable results.
- Space travel is simply an indulgence for the fabulously wealthy.
- Much of the cost of space travel is related to the safety of human space travellers. More unmanned probes could be deployed.

Space tourism

Space tourism is a recent and mostly uncharted venture. Although the Space Tourism Society was founded in Los Angeles in 1996, it was not until 2001 that the American Dennis Tito became the first fee-paying tourist in space. Because it is extremely expensive (Tito is reputed to have paid $20 million) it is the preserve of the super-rich, usually with the Russians providing the transport. (Tito travelled by the *Soyuz* capsule to spend 7 days on the International Space Station.) It allows an elite few to experience what astronauts experience in looking at Earth from space and discovering what it is like to be weightless.

Bearing in mind the tragic malfunction at lift-off of the space shuttle *Challenger* in 1986, and the disintegration of *Columbia* shortly before touchdown in 2003, space tourism is decidedly risky; and some participants may experience space sickness. Weightlessness may be a novel experience but it may also be an unwelcome one. In a microgravity environment there is a short-term impact on gravity receptors that affects balance, a loss of plasma in the bloodstream affecting fluids, and a possibility of muscle atrophy and loss of bone tissue.

By 2007, there had been five space tourists — a South African and four Americans, including Iranian-born Anousheh Ansari who became the first female space tourist in 2006. The most recent traveller, Charles Simonyi in 2007, spent $25 million on his experience of 14 days in space. As one of those responsible for developing Word and Excel software, maybe he was one of the few who could afford it.

The future of space tourism is uncertain. Despite the massive cost, there is a waiting list of those who wish to join the list of space tourists, and what was once the 'space race' between the USA and Russia is now 'the race for space tourism' as companies compete to become leaders in space tourism. Development is likely to be slow, even though optimists talk of space hotels, and the Russians are warning that after 2009 there may no longer be room for space tourists on the Russian capsule serving the International Space Station.

Perhaps unsurprisingly, one person who does claim to see the business potential of space travel is the British entrepreneur responsible for the Virgin brand, Richard Branson. Using the Esrange space centre in the north of Sweden, Branson plans that his new creation, *Virgin Galactic*, will offer travellers who can afford £100,000 the possibility of a 2-hour spaceflight through the aurora borealis — the northern lights — by 2010. Before that, Branson's company is planning to start commercial space flights from a purpose-built spaceport in New Mexico.

Practice question

The following question is typical of those that will be used in Section B of Unit 4.

> Space exploration, whether for exploration or tourism, can never be justified. It is a waste of resources that could be directed to more worthwhile projects, and the only people to benefit are a handful of space scientists, politicians and super-rich tourists.

> **To what extent do you consider that the development of space exploration in the last 50 years has been worthwhile scientific and technological investment?**

> **Discuss the claim that the only people to benefit from the development of space travel have been 'a handful of space scientists, politicians and super-rich tourists'.**

> *(25 marks)*

The question of progress in science and the social sciences

Transport

In 2000, 3 years after returning to power, the Labour government published a 10-year transport plan. As 2010 gets closer, targets to cut congestion, develop tramways and triple cycle trips have been largely abandoned — much as many feared. With so many conflicting interests in transport it has been difficult for politicians to develop clear strategies and policies for transport planning and development.

Public transport is the subject of repeated complaint in the UK. It is regularly deemed to be:

- expensive
- unreliable
- dirty
- vandalised
- cramped
- overcrowded
- infrequent or non-existent in rural areas
- dangerous in terms of the possibility of assault

For most people, it is important — and frequently necessary — to have their own private transport, particularly in the form of a car. Personal mobility and the flexibility it brings are important in modern life for work or recreation, and there are now more and more cars and lorries on the nation's roads. In 25 years the number of vehicles on British roads has increased by 70% to more than 32 million, and it is anticipated that the growth will continue.

Since the completion of Britain's first motorway — the M1 — in 1959, the country's motorway and trunk-road network has increased by almost 5,000 miles. As quickly as roads are improved or extended, they fill up with vehicles; it is feared that Britain's roads are grinding to a halt, and the Confederation of British Industry (CBI) has estimated that traffic congestion costs the UK economy up to £20 billion per year. However, there seems to be a series of intractable problems for politicians over whether to:

- increase taxes on bigger 'gas-guzzling' cars such as 4x4s
- increase 'green' petrol taxes at a time when world oil prices are at an all-time high
- promote alternative power sources, as in electric or hydrogen-powered cars
- encourage more investment in bioethanol fuel
- sanction the construction of more motorways
- support more toll roads
- provide incentives for local authorities to use congestion charges, similar to those in London, in town and city centres
- charge drivers by the mile through satellite-tracking technology linked to recording boxes in cars, (although outline proposals in 2007 resulted in an opposing e-petition on the prime minister's website containing over a million signatures)
- allow rail fares to increase while subsidies to train operators decline, placing more of the responsibility for railway funding on those who use the railways
- make train operators simplify the confusing system of many different types of rail fares
- encourage the building of more airports — the effect of aviation on global warming is becoming a key battleground

In making decisions, the government needs to take into account:
- the economic needs of the British Isles
- increasing difficulties caused by road congestion
- carbon-cutting obligations to the European Union — emissions under Labour have continued to grow despite a commitment to reduce carbon dioxide levels by 20% by 2010

Car ownership continues to increase, and motorists and motoring organisations are quick to defend their personal freedoms from what they consider to be 'government interference'. Yet they are increasingly aware of the consequences of global warming, and millions experience the daily personal misery of congestion and long delays. However, outside London, buses are largely in decline and the railway network is near to full capacity. More intensive use of air travel has particularly undesirable environmental effects. The Department of Transport's 2010 target of increasing public transport by 12% over the previous decade looks to be well out of reach.

The key question of the extent to which public transport should be thought of as a form of public service rather than a profit-making business remains unresolved.

One of Britain's mototways — grinding to a halt

Traditionally, Conservatives have favoured a market-based approach: deregulating buses and privatising the railways and British Airways, to subject transport to the discipline of competition, which they claimed would bring greater efficiency. Labour's approach has not been dissimilar, and the market has favoured the car and personal freedom.

Driving a car is clearly easier and more convenient than relying on public transport. In addition, despite rising fuel costs and petrol in excess of £1 per litre, it may also be cheaper. In some areas, traffic congestion at peak times has risen to a point where roads are saturated, especially in outer London and some of the home counties, and increased numbers travelling by rail in the last decade have done little to ease the pressure on roads. It is estimated that road traffic increased by 12% between 1997 and 2006, with an additional 5.5 million cars on the road.

Campaign for Better Transport: a pressure group

Known as 'Transport 2000' until 2007, the Campaign for Better Transport is both a research and dissemination trust and a campaign group for better transport policies. The group's campaigning activities involve:
- lobbying politicians at local and national level
- undertaking research and supplying information to policy makers
- supporting local groups fighting against transport problems
- working with transport companies
- working with the media to make the case for sustainable transport

The Campaign for Better Transport seeks:

- reduced car use
- more comfortable, affordable and accessible public transport
- improved pedestrian and cycle routes
- reduced traffic
- easier access to jobs, services, friends and family
- recognition that road building does not solve congestion
- easier access to sustainable travel for businesses
- better use of the planning process to reduce the need to travel
- urgent action to reduce transport's contribution to climate change

Railways

- The British railway system was privatised by John Major's Conservative government in 1996.
- There are now a number of different train operators working as private companies for profit, with government subsidies amounting to over £5 billion.
- The railway infrastructure, including most stations, track and signals, is separately owned; the initial owner was Railtrack until it was placed in administration in 2001; the 'not-for-profit' Network Rail then took over. (The separation of train and track ownership has been one of the most criticised aspects of rail privatisation.)
- The Office of Rail Regulation (ORR) protects the public interest wherever possible and its remit has included railway health and safety since 2006.
- In addition, although railways are a particularly safe form of travel, accidents can be both tragic and spectacular. Over 30 people were killed in a crash at Ladbroke Grove near London in 1999 when a signal known for its poor visibility was passed at 'Danger'. There were more fatalities a year later when a London to Leeds express was derailed by a shattered rail at Hatfield at a speed of 115 mph. In 2002 another high-speed train was derailed by defective points at Potters Bar.
- Such accidents led to serious public disquiet about the private sub-contracting system used for track maintenance. The media image of 'fat cats' making large sums of money and being more interested in profit than public safety has endured.
- Despite many criticisms, the numbers travelling by rail have increased significantly since privatisation — mostly due to increased road congestion, higher parking and congestion charges and rising petrol prices — and over 1 billion rail journeys per year are currently made in Britain. (Railway freight transport has also increased substantially.)

- Despite significant investment by private companies in new trains and rolling stock, commuter trains to London, in particular, are becoming simultaneously more expensive and more overcrowded. On too many lines, more passengers have meant fewer seats for them to sit in.

Despite the success of the privatised rail companies in attracting more travellers, railway services in the UK often compare unfavourably with those in comparable European countries such as France, Germany and the Netherlands.

Ultimately, we expect the impossible from rail services. Across the world railway services have proved unprofitable. None of the following options is likely to be taken up:

- Services could be cut dramatically so that only the few that generate so much traffic that they might be profitable remain. The workings of the free market would determine which lines survived and which did not. This was Dr Beeching's approach in the early 1960s. The axing of many 'non commercial' lines proved extremely unpopular and, in the twenty-first century, would be politically unthinkable.

The numbers travelling by rail have increased significantly since privatisation

- The railways could be renationalised but this would involve huge compensation costs. The nationalised British Rail service was widely criticised and suffered from chronic under-investment.
- Public subsidies could be increased in recognition that public transport is a public service as much as a commercial opportunity. The costs would be borne primarily by the taxpayer rather than the railway traveller.

In determining which train operating company should win a line franchise, a company's ability to reduce its need for public subsidies seems to be crucial. As subsidies go down train fares inevitably increase, as operating companies seek to protect their investment and to offer good returns to their shareholders.

In terms of punctuality and reliability, railway performance is improving and much of the rolling stock now used is significantly better, but it all comes at a price, either for the individual traveller or the public purse. Although people do not like higher fares, they are likely to be even less sympathetic to higher taxes.

Buses

- Although it is still commonly assumed that bus services are run by local authorities, this has not been the case since 1986, when public bus services, except in London, were privatised and routes deregulated.
- Although one of the main aims of privatisation was to encourage competition that would keep fares down, bus services in many areas are dominated by large national concerns such as Stagecoach, Arriva and First Group.
- This has led to accusations of 'cherry picking' — concentrating on heavily used routes and swamping them with buses while ignoring other routes.
- So that some people do not have to go without bus services, many councils still subsidise some services, although they do not themselves operate them. This means that some services that would otherwise be unprofitable are able to continue, albeit at minimal levels, in areas where there might otherwise be no public transport facilities, especially in the evenings and at weekends.
- Modern buses are now more accessible than was once the case, complying with disability discrimination legislation and making things easier for older people — with over sixties now eligible for free bus travel — and mothers with pushchairs. Both groups may be frequent users of buses.
- The creation of dedicated urban bus lanes has made bus travel faster, but buses are not a popular form of public transport and Margaret Thatcher's view that a man going to work on a bus after the age of 26 should consider himself a failure might still ring true with many.

- One reason why bus travel is low on the political agenda is that the services are used predominantly by the poorer and less influential sections of society.
- Long-route coach travel is relatively cheap but often slow, because of speed limits, the fact that coach stations are poorly situated in city centres, and journeys are poorly coordinated.

Air transport

- In recent years there has been a boom in low-cost air travel with the emergence of 'budget' airline companies such as easyJet and Ryanair.
- According to the Civil Aviation Authority (CAA), passenger traffic at UK airports has increased at an average rate of 6% since the mid-1970s, although this slowed to 2% in 2006 and 2007.
- Britain now has one of the slowest growing markets in air travel in the more established countries of the European Union. Nevertheless, the British market remains one of the largest in the world, with nearly 230 million passengers travelling through UK airports each year, with the biggest demand coming for holiday flights abroad.
- The CAA has also estimated that the annual number of passengers travelling from UK airports in 2030 could be as high as 465 million.
- Environmental pressure groups believe that green taxes should be imposed on air travel. This would raise money for the Exchequer and perhaps slow down the growth of air travel (Britain's airports are planning to treble the number of flights by 2030). Green taxes might help to slow the rise in greenhouse gas emissions, which is faster than in any other sector.
- Currently, aircraft fuel is untaxed and air travel only lightly taxed. However, increasing the cost of air travel, though environmentally desirable if it acted as a deterrent, would hit potential passengers on lower incomes disproportionately.
- When a government White Paper was published in 2003 it encouraged aircraft expansion; and if all of Britain's 71 airports carry out their development plans (significant expansion is envisaged at Luton, Bristol, Manchester, Newcastle, Stansted, Gatwick and Glasgow together with a third terminal at Heathrow) there will be a massive increase in carbon emissions. Such plans do not sit easily with the conclusions of the Stern Report.
- The aircraft industry sees its salvation in the European Union's Emission Trading Scheme (ETS), through which it expects to be able to purchase permits to continue emissions while reductions are made elsewhere.

Viewpoints

Will the government be successful in encouraging more people to use public rather than private transport?

Yes

- There has already been a massive increase in railway travel since privatisation.
- The roads are now so crowded that public transport may be quicker.
- Bus travel in some areas is beginning to increase. There is free bus travel locally for the over-60s and this scheme was extended to include other areas in 2008.
- Success in public transport in London has shown what can be achieved through coordinated travel planning and management.
- Increases in the costs of fuel, vehicle tax and insurance are making private transport more and more expensive.
- People are becoming more concerned about the environmental effects of private transport. Public transport is much more environmentally friendly.

No

- The facts speak for themselves. There has been a massive increase in private car ownership in recent years.
- Private transport often enhances status but public transport does not.
- Private transport is more direct and offers greater personal freedom for the individual.
- If the hard shoulder can be used for driving on motorways there will be fewer delays at peak times.
- Public transport (particularly railways) is too expensive. As government subsidies to transport operators are reduced, fares will increase.
- The provision is too patchy, especially in rural areas.
- Public transport can be overcrowded and dirty.
- It is not always reliable and suffers from poor timekeeping.

Practice question

The following question is typical of those that might be used in Section B of Unit 4.

As more roads are built, they are quickly filled by an increasing number of cars because people will always prefer personal choice and mobility to the inadequacies of public transport, irrespective of the impact of cars on the environment.

To what extent do you consider that public transport is inadequate?

Discuss the ways in which the impact of the increase in cars and other forms of transport can be modified to protect the environment. *(25 marks)*

Sport

The changing face of football

Football was once thought to be a working-class game, at a time when the working class was readily identifiable, and professional footballers were limited by a maximum wage that would be considered derisory by present standards. Crowds were huge, with nearly everyone standing on terraces open to the elements. Facilities were, at best, primitive.

Three things have changed football: the end of the maximum wage; income for the game from television; and the globalisation of football, with British clubs attracting foreign investment and foreign players.

The end of the maximum wage

Professional football has existed in England for over a century, and the Football League, founded in 1888, was made up of 12 professional clubs. By 1901 a maximum wage of £4 per week had been fixed for professional footballers, and for over 50 years there was a battle between players and clubs over this. Early players' unions were not effective. By 1920 the maximum wage was £9 per week; and in 1947 it was fixed by a wage tribunal at £12. Professional footballers, though they might be retained by their clubs, were often forced to take summer jobs to make ends meet.

Jimmy Hill, later to achieve fame as a football commentator, brought a new professionalism to the footballers' union when he reorganised it as the Professional Footballers' Association (PFA) in 1956. Following threats of a strike, the maximum wage ended in 1961. Almost immediately, the Fulham and England international Johnny Haynes became the first £100-a-week footballer — a sum far in excess of the previous £20 maximum. Soon afterwards, working with the professional footballer George Eastham, Hill helped to transform the players' position over retain and transfer by their clubs.

In 1981 Gordon Taylor became chief executive of the PFA, proving himself to be an astute operator on behalf of the players. Some players currently earn in excess of £100,000 per week and often undertake lucrative advertising deals. Taylor is one of the most highly paid union bosses, reflecting his skills and success.

Viewpoints

Are professional footballers worth such high wages?

In favour

- It is difficult for anyone to determine, using commonly accepted criteria, what any individual job is 'worth'.
- Wages are determined by market forces of supply and demand. World demand to watch live football is seemingly insatiable. Few players are able to supply truly world-class skills. Such scarcity, as with any other commodity, can only force up prices.
- Exceptional footballers are entertainers and celebrities and should be rewarded as such.
- Professional football is a relatively short career, usually lasting no more than 20 years. Footballers need to earn as much as they can over their working life.

Against

- High wages lead to high admission prices, which are increasingly excluding many lower earners and poorer families.
- Few footballers have truly world-class skills. Far too many less skilled players are over-rewarded for their more limited talents.
- Professional footballers can become arrogant and some top English players are caught up in a culture of drinking, gambling and irresponsible social behaviour.
- Highly paid professional footballers often do not do enough for the community.

Money from television and sponsorship

Once live televised football was a rarity confined to the FA Cup Final and the occasional international game. In the 1960s BBC's *Match of the Day* attracted large Saturday night audiences with its recorded highlights, but the major financial breakthrough for clubs came in 1992 when the Premier League was set up. A contract was signed with Rupert Murdoch's satellite television company, BSkyB, allowing it to show live Premier League games exclusively — a position it held until 2007, making a huge financial input into Premier League football.

The major change was the showing of live Premier League games, for which BSkyB (and Setanta from 2007) paid huge sums, by 2008 amounting to an average income for each of the 20 Premier League clubs of £45 million per year. The Premiership is screened in over 200 countries — more than any other league in the world. It is that sort of exposure that makes English Premiership football an extremely lucrative business proposition. However, there are few certainties in football — for players, managers or owners — and much depends on the extent to which an individual club can gain and, crucially, retain a place in European football competitions. Links between sport and sponsorship are strong with individual deals being worth millions of pounds, especially in football with its worldwide appeal and audiences. For sponsors it:

- is an excellent form of advertising reaching massive audiences
- establishes a brand name and corporate image
- furthers customer relations and facilitates hospitality
- helps build employee–community relations

Some of the biggest-spending has been on football where Barclays Bank has a deal to sponsor the English Premier League between 2004 and 2010. The shirts of the teams acknowledged as 'the big four' in the English Premier League in 2008 carry advertising as shown in the table.

Club	Shirt brand	Business sector
Manchester United	AIG	Finance
Arsenal	Fly Emirates	Aviation
Chelsea	Samsung	Electronics
Liverpool	Carlsberg	Drinks

One particularly controversial area, now prohibited, has been sponsorship offered by tobacco companies. In the absence of such sponsorship, the fortunes of snooker have declined but Formula One motor racing has continued to prosper, attracting sponsorship from other areas of business and industry.

Foreign owners and players in the Premiership

- In 1997 Mohamed Al Fayed, an Egyptian who has made a number of attempts to secure British citizenship, bought Fulham Football Club for £30 million. At the time this was thought to be unlikely to catch on.
- What really changed things was the purchase of Chelsea FC in 2003 by the Russian oil billionaire Roman Abramovich, after which Chelsea quickly became one of the 'Big Four'. Abramovich paid £60 million for Chelsea and settled club debts of £80 million.
- In 2005 one of the world's wealthiest and most famous clubs, Manchester United, was bought by the American Glazer family for £790 million.
- In 2007 two other American sports franchise owners, Tom Hicks and George Gillett Junior, purchased Liverpool FC for £240 million and in 2008 it was rumoured that a Dubai-based consortium might be interested in a buyout as relations between the two Americans became strained.

- So far, the only club in the 'Big Four' to avoid a takeover by foreign buyers has been Arsenal, where the American Stan Kroenke paid £65 million for 12% of the club's shares.

- In addition, by 2008 four other Premiership clubs — Manchester City, West Ham, Aston Villa and Portsmouth — had all been bought by foreign interests.

- The English Premier League is now the world's richest football league and there is much to be earned from foreign markets, not least in the USA, where various attempts to establish football have proved unsuccessful, and in Asia.

- In 2007 Manchester City was purchased for £81 million by the popular Thai politician Thaksin Shinawatra, who was ousted by a military junta coup in 2006 and who was accused by his opponents of corruption. Per capita viewing figures for football are higher in Thailand than in any other country in the world.

- Football has become part of the global economy and, as foreign investors buy into British public utilities, pub chains, banks and vehicle manufacturers, it is no surprise that football is another economic investment. However, as admission prices have risen dramatically, and marketing becomes ever more aggressive, critics have claimed that traditional supporters have been driven out of the game.

- Just as investors see an opportunity to make money, many foreign footballers now play in England, attracted in no small way by the very high wages of the Premier League.

- Crowds have increased and many supporters enjoy seeing world stars live.

- However, British players are in a minority in most Premier League sides. At the start of the 2007–08 season, over 300 overseas players from 66 countries were registered to play in the Premier League.

- The richest clubs can afford to buy the best players, and there is a growing gap between them and other clubs in the Premier League that have fewer assets or lack wealthy benefactors. Invariably, the world's best players attract the biggest crowds.

Not surprisingly, the fortunes of the UK's national sides have declined. It is over 40 years since England won the World Cup and in 2007 the team failed even to qualify for the 2008 European Championships. There is great concern about the lack of young UK players coming through the system, although some blame the poor quality of youth-team coaching. With the exception of the long-serving Sir Alex Ferguson at Manchester United, many of the leading Premier League sides are managed by outstanding foreigners. In 2007 the Italian Fabio Capello was appointed as the England team manager in the hope that he could restore the fortunes of the national team.

It is unlikely that any attempt to limit the number of foreign players in the Premier League, perhaps by setting quotas, would succeed because it would be contrary to European law. The same applies to control over transfer fees — with exceptional players commanding transfer fees in excess of £20 million — and wages. Football is no longer a working-class sport and now cuts across class and economic boundaries.

Corruption and cheating in sport

Sport is often seen as a national obsession; for many people, it plays a bigger part in their lives than almost anything else. Some watch, some participate and some do both. Newspapers are full of sporting news, there are dedicated sports channels on television and sport is a regular topic of discussion. Football dominates but there is considerable interest in horse racing, limited-over cricket and the fortunes of England in test matches, athletics, rugby union (particularly in Wales), rugby league in the north of England and tennis — usually in the form of the annual Wimbledon fortnight.

People are often passionate about sport and it generates intense emotions — which sometimes take the form of fervent nationalism, which can lead to both racism and violence. Victory and success are important. Supporters want their side, or players, to win. Success in sport brings individual glory and substantial financial returns. Some, though, look back to a different era of 'playing the game' and playing it in a good spirit, even if this resulted in defeat. Cheating was looked upon with contempt.

Times have changed and so has sporting behaviour, although perhaps not as much as might be imagined. Sport is now a global phenomenon and big business. Scientific and medical advances mean that there are more ways to cheat but also that cheating can be more readily detected. The all-encompassing media guarantee that instances of cheating are widely reported. Fairly or unfairly, many sports have become tainted by the actions of a small minority.

Some sports have been more tainted than others. Horse racing is subject to doping despite stringent security to prevent this. Jockeys may be involved in malpractice in a sport in which betting is particularly significant. In 2007, following a 3-year investigation which cost £6 million, the six-times champion jockey, Kieren Fallon, was one of six men cleared of allegations of race fixing. Soon afterwards, Fallon was suspended from riding for 18 months after failing a drugs test. In 2008, news of the first cloned champion racehorse emerged from Italy after a foal was bred using a skin cell of a world champion in equine endurance races.

Cycling (and the Tour de France in particular) has long been blighted by allegations of drug taking, as has athletics. In both cases, performance-enhancing drugs can have a significant impact on individual performance and in the 2006 Tour de France two favourites were banned for suspected drug taking and the 'winner', Floyd Landis, was disqualified.

In athletics, Dwain Chambers, a former European 100-metres champion banned for 2 years in 2004 for the illegal use of the designer steroid drug tetrahydrogestrinone (THG), launched a comeback which, against the wishes of many, saw him return to the British team. Shortly before that, the American athlete Marion Jones, who won a women's record five track and field medals in the 2000 Olympics, admitted that she had cheated her way to success by using prohibited performance-enhancing drugs.

Dwain Chambers on the podium after winning the 60-metre final in Sheffield in February 2008

Even cricket, that most gentlemanly of sports, saw the Pakistan side forfeit a test match against England amid allegations of cheating; and the Indian team threatened to leave Australia after one of their number was suspended for allegedly making a racist remark to an opposing player of mixed race. These events came after a life ban was imposed on Hansie Cronje, the South African cricket captain, for match-fixing.

The number of sportspeople taking drugs is likely to be far in excess of those detected, partly because there are ways to counter the effect of drug taking and partly because regulatory bodies are not always as diligent in their approach as they might be. Sport is big business and there are many entrenched and powerful vested interests. How far the attitudes of individuals have changed, and whether they are more willing to cheat, is difficult to determine.

The science behind illegal drug taking is complex and sportspeople who test positive often become involved in protracted legal cases in an effort to prove their innocence. Dick Pound, chairman until 2008 of the World Anti-Doping Agency (WADA), raised the issue of gene doping following work in genetic therapy by Dr Lee Sweeney at the University of Pennslyvania. So far, in his experiments to help muscle growth and repair — something that might be a considerable help in the treatment of diseases such as muscular dystrophy — Sweeney had used only rodents.

Pound warned that unscrupulous coaches with links to unregulated laboratories and ambitious athletes might seek to use the legitimate scientific research of Dr Sweeney for the illegal enhancement of performance in the 2008 Beijing Olympics. The potential consequences of any form of doping that alters an athlete's genetic make-up could be catastrophic. It is a measure of the seriousness of the threat of genetic doping that the WADA has been working on counter-measures since 2002.

Ask the examiner

Q **Is there more cheating in sport and, if so, is this a reflection of falling standards of behaviour?**

A Cheating is likely to have taken place in the past but there were fewer incentives to cheat as the rewards for winning were smaller. There were fewer drugs available and fewer ways of testing for the presence of drugs.

Now rewards are large and there are big investors involved in many sports, particularly those that carry advertising revenue from being televised or sponsored. Nobody wants to lose their money and some sportspeople are paid highly for success. The pressures leading to errors of judgement are considerable.

There are now more ways of enhancing performance — but also more ways of detecting this due to scientific advances. There is more public awareness, and even cynicism, and media reporting of examples of cheating is often high profile.

If there is more cheating, is this a reflection of falling standards of behaviour? We are sometimes reminded of a supposed golden age when the game was the thing, fairness was a watchword, and sport was an honourable pastime. It was the age of the gentleman amateur.

This was probably sometimes the case but almost certainly not the norm, especially where there were links between sport and gambling or when working men with sporting talent could earn a little more from their sporting skills but had to do so in the context of a short career.

Standards of behaviour may well, on the whole, be lower than they once were. 'Respect' has taken on a different meaning. Attitudes to authority have changed. Society is less deferential. More people seem to lack what were once considered manners and common courtesies.

Yet we must be wary of making sweeping statements, unfounded assumptions and wild generalisations. Certain forms of behaviour are unacceptable, even abhorrent, to the majority of people, but the media tend to focus on the worst excesses. We hear less about the many people who have high standards of both private and public morality — and who are thoroughly tired of being stereotyped on the basis of the behaviour of a few.

Data handling and the interpretation of other evidence in Section A of the Unit 4 case study

In addition to the essay questions in Section B of Unit 4, there are some case study questions in Section A of this unit. The case study is based on a set of pre-released documents on a theme taken from the Unit 4 specification. The theme might be scientific, or based on the social sciences or, most commonly, based on a combination of scientific and socioeconomic knowledge of a non-specialist nature. The aim will be to focus on a contemporary issue that might have formed the basis for discussion as a part of General Studies teaching.

There will usually be five or six separate extracts and these will be released to centres some weeks before the examination. Centres will be permitted to teach to these sources. There will be four questions in the case study and each question is compulsory. Of the five or six sources, Source A will be based on data, perhaps with brief additional comments. Several different pieces of data will form the basis of Source A. There follow some typical examples of data that might be used in Source A, based on the theme of health and human behaviour.

Other sources will usually be taken from newspaper articles or similar media. Each source will be approximately 800–1,300 words in length. Shortened versions of typical sources appear on the following pages.

Source A

Figure 1 Percentage of men and women who had drunk alcohol on 5 days or more a week prior to interview by age: Great Britain, 2002

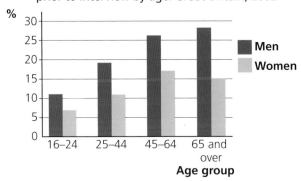

Figure 2 A summary of changes over time in Great Britain: smoking

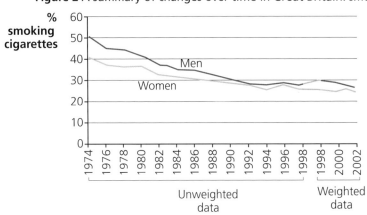

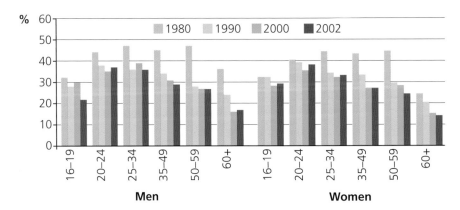

Figure 3 Life expectancy at birth: by sex, UK

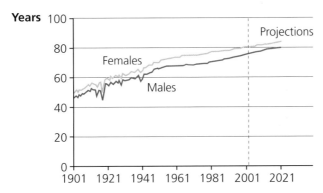

Figure 4 *Clostridium difficile* (*C. difficile*): number of deaths between 2001 and 2006

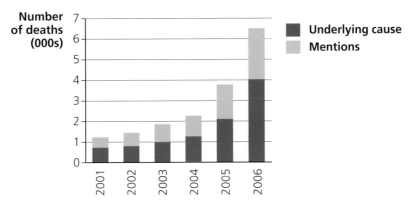

Source for Figures 1–4: Office for National Statistics

Source B

Britain's binge drinking culture: are we a nation of boozers?

Binge drinking among the young is increasing at an alarming rate and it is often the case that crimes and various forms of antisocial behaviour associated with teenagers, or even younger children, are drink-fuelled. The Home Secretary, Jacqui Smith, promised a clampdown on underage drinking, making available extra cash for policing during school holidays.

Alcohol seems to be easily accessible for young people. Sometimes it is purchased for them by those who are over 18. Supermarkets have been branded as irresponsible for cheap drink promotions; there are suggestions that some alcoholic drinks are sold at less than cost price, making them cheaper than bottled water.

The attractions of alcohol are obvious and there is enormous peer pressure on teenagers, irrespective of background and social class. Teenagers, often outwardly bold but inwardly insecure, use alcohol as a way of losing inhibitions. They see it as bold and daring, and getting 'hammered' or 'wasted' has become part of the initiation into adult life.

Despite the efforts of those involved in alcohol education, teenagers either don't see the dangers of excessive drinking or prefer to ignore the advice of those who might be considered 'uncool'. Friday and Saturday nights in any major Accident and Emergency department can be chaotic. Staff are abused and often assaulted by drunken teenagers, and security staff — who represent an added cost to the NHS budget — have to be used in greater numbers.

Uninhibited behaviour can result in higher rates of teenage pregnancies and sexually trans-mitted diseases. Longer-term problems are less obvious, especially to young people who see themselves as immortal. Doctors report that more and more young people are being treated for serious liver disease — something once associated with middle-aged and older drinkers.

According to the Office for National Statistics, children as young as 12 are drinking regularly with the aim of 'getting drunk'. This trend is contributing to the rise in teenage crime and antisocial behaviour and, according to the Home Secretary, we are reaching the point where more under-13s have drunk alcohol than have not.

Part of the problem is that teenagers see little need for restraint. Both they and an increasing number of parents are not prepared to take responsibility in what is becoming a 'me first' society.

And the problem of binge drinking is not confined to teenagers.

Source C

GPs do less work but get 60% rise in pay

It's not so many years since we were all worried about the shortage of general practitioners. The British Medical Association was issuing dire warnings about the lack of GPs, particularly in inner-city areas. Soon, we were told, a great many doctors would be reaching retirement age. The situation would be similar to that of finding a dentist. More doctors would be tempted into private practice, and when a new doctor came to town there would be queues round the block as desperate patients sought to register.

How much truth there was in all this, nobody knows. But the warnings worked. By 2003 new contracts had been agreed, and by 2004 they were in operation, with more community care being undertaken in surgeries. Doctors became part of the target culture so beloved by the Labour government. If their surgeries gave so many flu injections, provided regular monitoring of chronic heart disease patients, identified more people with diabetes... (and so it went on), the doctors would qualify for extra payments.

The deal succeeded, probably beyond the wildest dreams of the doctors. By 2008 many of them were sitting pretty. According to the National Audit Office, the earnings of GPs had soared by nearly 60% between 2004 and 2006. Yet they appeared to be doing 5% less work. They no longer had to provide out-of-hours services themselves, and surgeries were not open later in the evening, or at weekends, when a lot of working people might need them.

Can you blame the doctors or the BMA? Is it a question of money-grabbing first and ethics second by some distance? I think not. Doctors are self-employed and they have a number of costs to meet, including staff salaries and the running costs of their surgeries. By 2006, the average annual salary for a partner in general practice was £113,000.

It's a lot of money, but mostly we only hear the bad news. Training for doctors is long, arduous and expensive. The responsibility is big and there are plenty of people with chronic illnesses who are likely now to be getting more effective monitoring and treatment. The situation with NHS dentists is a national disgrace, but since the new contracts the number of GPs has risen by 15%. GPs have done what we all do. They have responded to financial incentives. They have met their quality targets.

If the finger needs pointing, point it in the direction of the government. The salary increases were not evenly spread and partners did far better than salaried GPs. Productivity may not appear to be higher. Yes, I'd like the chance to attend an evening or weekend surgery. Yes, I wish it weren't as difficult to make an appointment. The politicians and their negotiators got what they wanted. More target hitting. Unfortunately they didn't get all the targets right.

Let's get this thing into perspective. I don't have private insurance so I depend on the NHS. I have friends in America in chronic ill health who struggle to make ends meet because of the opposition there to what the Americans call 'socialised medicine'. The time you least want to be worried about money and medical bills is when you're ill. GPs earning over £100,000 a year? So what? We've got footballers getting that in a week. We are quick to be told when a doctor makes a once-in-a-lifetime mistake. Ethics? Just ask the football commentators what's meant by a 'professional foul'!

Source D

Change your lifestyle or you'll stay unhealthy

It is often said that lifestyle is a matter of personal choice, although the introduction in 2007 of a law that banned smoking in pubs and other public places was a blow to pressure groups like FOREST that promote the rights and freedoms of smokers. Now people wishing to exercise those rights have to go outside to do so, sometimes lurking like naughty schoolchildren seeking to satisfy their addiction to nicotine behind the bicycle sheds.

The demand that smokers take greater personal responsibility is increasing. One Lincolnshire smoker seeking treatment for the narrowing of the arteries in his leg was told that he must give up smoking for 6 months before he could be treated. Another Primary Care Trust in the East Midlands advised smokers that quitting for a month prior to surgery would improve recovery times, although it stressed that the final decision to operate would be that of the clinician.

It is a complex issue. Individuals choose to smoke but many become addicted to nicotine. In recent years there has been significant investment in preventive measures designed to help people to stop smoking. The dangers of smoking and its links with lung and heart disease are well known. The cost to the National Health Service of treating smokers is considerable. It is known that smokers take longer to recover than non-smokers, and hospitals ban smoking on their property and in their grounds.

Besides the threats to personal liberty, smokers also argue that it is unethical for them to be refused treatment, especially if their condition might worsen. As cigarettes are heavily taxed, smokers contribute significantly to the funds of the Chancellor of the Exchequer. Where, they might ask, will 'selective surgery' end?

Resources are always finite. The number of specialists is not unlimited. Already there are accusations of a 'postcode lottery' in the health service, which means that patients may or may not be entitled to certain drugs that could extend their lives, on the basis of which health trust is responsible for their treatment.

Besides smokers, heavy drinkers and the obese might find certain forms of treatment difficult to get unless they agree to changes in their lifestyle. It is estimated that about 10% of hospitals refuse some forms of surgery to heavy smokers and obese patients as hospitals battle to combat debt.

Source E

Will obesity become the developed world's biggest health problem?

The facts are clear. The human body stores fat if the calories in the food consumed by an individual exceed the energy burnt up — and increasingly we lead more sedentary lives. Rates of adult obesity in the UK have quadrupled in the last 25 years. Over 20% of adults are officially classified as obese and over 60% are either obese or overweight. Being obese can reduce life expectancy significantly and makes people far more susceptible to:
- diabetes
- gall bladder disease
- heart disease
- high blood pressure
- infertility
- strokes
- depression

It was once the case that obesity was primarily a problem associated with middle-aged adults, but the number of children who are obese has tripled in the last 10 years. In fact, the data are likely to underestimate the scale of the problem as they are based on the voluntary weighing of primary school children. Over 30% of English children in Year 6 were deemed to be overweight or obese in 2007. (A healthy weight is usually based on a body mass index of between 18.5 and 25. A BMI of 25 to 30 is considered to be overweight and a figure above 30 is deemed obese. BMI is calculated by dividing the weight of an individual in kilograms by the square of their height in metres.)

Children and young adults need to take stock of their lifestyles. Sport is more likely to be promoted in schools these days but, too often, playing fields have been sold off. Sport is often unpopular, especially among girls, and schools have often struggled to squeeze the recommended time for sport and physical education into an already overcrowded curriculum.

Parents claim that they are subject to 'pester power' and, despite Jamie Oliver's campaign for healthier school dinners and restrictions on school vending machines, too many young people prefer to snack on sugary drinks and foods that contain an excess of saturated fat and salt. Fast-food outlets such as McDonald's now promote healthy eating options but the temptations of the Big Mac remain considerable.

It is also the case that parents are increasingly reluctant to let younger children 'play out' because of concerns about their safety and welfare. Many children are happy to confine themselves to their bedrooms where they can play the latest Xbox games or network in chat rooms.

Increasingly, adults are resorting to surgery to tackle obesity. The last 5 years have seen a sharp rise in referral rates for obesity surgery, which was once reserved only for the most serious, life-threatening cases.

Yet surgery is not an attractive option. Surgery to restrict the intake of calories can usually only be done in two ways: restriction (which involves reducing the size of the stomach through the use of devices such as a gastric band) and malabsorption (bypassing the small intestine so that fewer calories from food are absorbed by the body).

What we seem to lack is will-power. Once again, in our 'blame-led' culture, the issue is one of rights and responsibilities. Dieting may still provide the answer and bookshops are stacked high with books on the subject. Yet dieting requires both discipline and deprivation. So does taking regular exercise. The easy way out is to assume that the NHS can come to our rescue or that an operation performed privately is money well spent. Quick fixes seem to match our cash-rich and time-poor lifestyle.

Perhaps there need to be more controls on advertising, especially of unhealthy foods that might appear attractive to children, because too many people rely too much on junk food. Maybe we should use the car less, especially on journeys to and from school. Young people often respond to incentives, so perhaps more could be used to promote exercise.

One answer could be the rediscovery of will-power; however, recent research suggests that genetic factors may be more important than was once thought, so we may no longer be able to assume that personal sacrifice will necessarily lead to any discernible weight loss. As is so frequently the case when science meets society, the problems are complex and the answers, such as they are, are far from simple.

Questions on pre-released case study material shown above

(1) In what ways does the data shown in Source A have implications for
the National Health Service? *(11 marks)*

(2) Using Source B and your own knowledge, discuss the measures that
could be taken to reduce binge drinking. *(12 marks)*

(3) Using Source C and your own knowledge, consider the extent to which
you think the recent large salary increases for GPs are justified. *(11 marks)*

(4) Using Sources D and E, consider whether treatment for illnesses related
to smoking or obesity should be conditional on individuals changing
their lifestyle. *(11 marks)*

SCIENCE AND SOCIETY
Chapter 31

Social, ethical and environmental implications of scientific discoveries and technological developments

Health, hygiene and disease: the National Health Service

One of the most remarkable achievements in British social policy was the establishment of the National Health Service in 1948 as part of the Labour government's plans to expand the welfare state. Prior to that, those who could pay for the services of a doctor, dentist, or optician did so. Although lower-paid workers could get access to a doctor, their spouses and children could not. Healthcare was a luxury and those who could not pay relied on whatever charitable services might be available or resorted to devices like taking out their own teeth, buying glasses (without an eye test) from a selection at shops like Woolworths or relying on often dubious homespun remedies to fight illness.

Until 1948 thousands died from infectious diseases such as diphtheria, pneumonia, polio and tuberculosis, and infant mortality was high, with 1 in 20 children dying before their first birthday. Many of the elderly and mentally ill ended up in facilities provided by local authorities, many of which were similar to the dreaded workhouses. Voluntary hospitals were often close to financial collapse.

Suddenly the lives of millions of people were transformed. The National Health Service was to be paid for out of general taxation and was to be free to all at the point of demand — the first time that any country in the world had attempted such an ambitious scheme. It was a remarkable plan, but one that was soon overwhelmed. The health of the nation was poor, not least in areas like dental treatment and properly prescribed spectacles. When the NHS was being planned, it was anticipated that its annual running cost would be £110 million. By 1950–51 it was £384 million and the Labour Party was divided by the need to introduce prescription charges to help meet rapidly rising costs.

Things have changed considerably during the 60 years of the NHS:

- It remains a service that is greatly valued and used by the great majority of the population despite the proliferation of schemes offering private alternatives. For many years, investment levels in the NHS did not keep up either with the expectation of patients or the rapid increases in medical knowledge and health technology, which would inevitably raise costs.
- In comparison with many other European countries, UK investment levels in health were relatively low and there were widespread concerns about shortages of both doctors and nurses.
- Spending on health has increased significantly since Labour returned to power in 1997, and between 2002–03 and 2007–08 the average annual increase in NHS funding, in real terms, was 7.4%, taking total net NHS expenditure from £56 billion to £90 billion — yet criticisms remain, often relating to wasted spending, excessive bureaucracy or unhygienic practices.
- Many reforms in structure, administration and management have taken place — some more successful than others.

Some of the media criticism is probably justified but, as with the environment (where some newspapers appear to give more publicity to sceptics than their numbers might warrant), we do not always get a balanced view of the achievements of the NHS.

Criticisms of the NHS

Shortage of dentists

- Dental care has often been seen as the poor relation of the NHS.
- In 1999 Tony Blair promised that everyone who wished would have access to an NHS dentist, but we remain a long way from that.
- Politicians and dentists have often been locked in contractual disputes and the outcome has been that some dentists have left the NHS for private practice.
- For the last 20 years, the trend has been for most dentists to offer both private and NHS treatment, with the proportion of private work increasing.
- Since 1951, most NHS adult patients have paid a financial contribution towards their dental treatment.
- Charges for private dentistry vary widely.

- Some areas now have few, or no, NHS dentists, and those who do open quickly become full, leaving local people dependent on paying for private care.
- Budgets for NHS dentists have now been passed to Primary Care Trusts responsible for planning health provision in their areas.
- A report by the Office of Fair Trading in 2003 revealed that few checks on the quality of private dentistry existed and concluded that the free market did not work well for many dental patients.

Doctors' pay and access to surgeries

One of the most powerful pressure groups in the UK is the British Medical Association. It was the BMA that was able to negotiate a significant rise in pay and improvement in conditions for general practitioners in 2004, when the targets for patient monitoring and care proved easier to reach than government negotiators anticipated.

In 2005–06 the pay of GPs averaged £110,000 a year, making them among the highest paid family doctors in the world, compared with £81,556 in 2003–04. At the same time, nearly all GPs have opted out of out-of-hours services, and surgeries are frequently not open in the evenings or weekends. Many patients complain that they have difficulty in getting through to surgeries on the phone and making appointments when they do so.

Postcode lottery

Because funding and responsibility are devolved from central government to local health trusts, there are variations in policy and practice. This leads to variations in the treatments available in different parts of the country. It means that some health trusts are prepared to pay for particular drugs while others are not; this often affects people with certain forms of cancer or seeking fertility treatment.

Teenage pregnancies

Teenage pregnancies remain high, and the rates in Britain are the highest in western Europe. Although there is criticism of sex education and the provision of birth control for teenage girls, research suggests that key factors are social deprivation and family breakdown.

Care of the elderly

- Like many European countries, the UK has an ageing population.
- Due to better healthcare and higher living standards, a high proportion of people are living longer; but many depend on an army of friends and relatives for care.

- In recent years the number of older people in Britain has been increasing at a faster rate than any other age group.
- In 1971, the average age of a Briton was 34. Now it has risen to 39.
- More old people now end up in residential care, which is the responsibility of the social services departments of local councils; but many end up in hospital, either in the short term or on a longer-term basis in geriatric wards. Criticisms have been made by relatives in a number of areas that the standard of care of the elderly in some hospitals falls below acceptable levels.

Targets, management and rationalisation

Nobody doubts that spending on the NHS has increased significantly in real terms in the last 10 years. However, critics have argued that the money has not necessarily been spent wisely and that Labour ministers have been too preoccupied with increasing layers of hospital management, setting endless targets and trying to close local Accident and Emergency and maternity hospitals so that provision can be concentrated in larger, more specialised hospitals. These are often less accessible for many patients and have led to local protests.

UK variations

Devolved government has meant that there are differences in provision in the four countries that make up the United Kingdom. Waiting lists are lower in England; funding for the personal care of the elderly is more generous in Scotland; Northern Ireland integrates health and social care; and prescriptions are free for everyone in Wales.

Hospital infections

Few aspects of healthcare have received more publicity than hospital-acquired infections and poor levels of hospital cleanliness. It is believed that every year 100,000 people who enter hospital catch an infection. Two infections have received particular attention:

- **Methicillin-resistant *Staphylococcus Aureus* (MRSA)** is the best known, although it accounts for less than 50% of all hospital-acquired infections. Although MRSA rates vary from hospital to hospital, cases have increased by 600% in the past 10 years and some strains of MRSA are resistant to almost all known antibiotics. It is estimated that MRSA claims more than 1,500 lives annually. Efforts to combat it and other hospital-acquired infections, and to improve hospital cleanliness and hygiene, cost the NHS over £1 billion a year, and every health trust has infection-control teams. In the last couple of years, cases of MRSA have begun to fall.

● ***Clostridium difficile (C. difficile)*** is another serious hospital-acquired infection which can cause severe illness and death in patients who have undergone surgery. It has become a particularly virulent strain and is the major infectious cause of hospital-acquired diarrhoea, with older people particularly at risk. (There were 56,000 cases in 2006 affecting the over 65s — an increase of 8% on the number of reported cases in 2005.) Many consider it more of a danger than MRSA especially in hospitals with a high bed occupancy rate as they seek to meet government treatment targets. Ironically, with MRSA patients requiring more powerful antibiotics, patients become more vulnerable to *C.difficile* infections because the antibiotics knock out more beneficial bacteria in the gut. It is constantly mutating and very difficult to tackle successfully because it creates spores which are difficult to destroy, and claims more than 3,500 lives annually, outnumbering the yearly figures for road deaths.

Pseudomonas often contaminates water and is defeating cleaning agents used by hospitals to kill bacteria. Like *C. difficile*, it is proving resistant to antibiotics. There are not yet any official statistics on deaths from *Pseudomonas*. It is less common than the two major sources of hospital-acquired infections but it is proving to be untreatable in a number of cases.

According to official figures, the number of deaths linked to MRSA increased by 39% in 2005, with the equivalent *C. difficile* figures rising by 69%, although part of the reason for the higher figures may be greater awareness of the infections and more stringent reporting rules. Both patients and visitors are constantly bringing MRSA and *C. difficile* bugs into hospital wards; and despite great efforts to get doctors and nurses to wash their hands between patients, this does not always happen, even though hospitals increasingly have a bottle of alcohol gel beside each bedside. The bugs thrive among people whose immune system is weak, and the ageing population means that many elderly people, who are particularly susceptible, are treated in hospital.

Inspectors from the Healthcare Commission now make unannounced visits to the 120 English health trusts, which face being served with an 'improvement notice' if they fail to make sufficient progress in tackling MRSA and *C. difficile*. Hospitals will be checked against the government's hygiene code, which sets out 11 compulsory duties to combat hospital-acquired infections.

David Cameron has threatened that the Conservative Party would deduct funding from health trusts for each case of hospital-acquired infection. Ministers remain confident that they will reach their target of halving MRSA infections by 2008. *C. difficile* is likely to prove more difficult to counter, even though infection rates are beginning to slow down, as high bed occupancy continues.

The government has plans to screen all new patients for MRSA when they enter hospital for a pre-planned operation. Those who test positive for the bug will be isolated from the rest of the hospital. The programme is based on experience in the Netherlands. In 2004 there were 9.6 MRSA cases per 100,000 patient days — a figure that was slightly lower than France and slightly higher than Germany. In the Netherlands, the comparable figure was 0.4 and in both Sweden and Norway it was even lower than that.

Viewpoints

Successes of the NHS

- We tend to read about the few patients with a bad experience of the NHS instead of the many with a good one.
- Despite significant improvements already made in areas like cutting waiting lists and reducing heart attacks, the better and more market-oriented the NHS gets, the more people want it to improve even further and to offer more choice.
- After 5 years of unprecedented spending and investment in the NHS, it has moved up the table of European health spending, reaching 9% of gross domestic product. This matches the EU-15 average (i.e. in the 15 countries that comprised the EU prior to its expansion in 2004).
- Life expectancy has increased dramatically for both men and women. Both live for an average of at least 10 years longer than they did when the NHS was first established.
- Both nurses and doctors have benefited from higher salaries, and more have been recruited, often from abroad.
- In dentistry, recruitment has been eased by employing dentists from EU countries.
- Since Labour came to power in 1997 there are about 50,000 more nurses and 14,000 more doctors, although some of these are part-timers. There were 35,000 GPs in 1992 and 43,000 in 2005.
- NHS Direct has been introduced so that people can obtain information and advice from medically qualified staff round the clock, reducing demands on frontline services.
- Over 60 new major hospitals have been built, allowing the NHS to treat more inpatients and outpatients.
- Patients now have more choice over which hospital they go to and are often offered a list of NHS and private hospitals as the NHS works more closely with private health providers. This has limited benefits because patients have to be well advised and GPs do not always have the time or knowledge to provide such advice.

- Transplant surgery has advanced considerably, and there are moves for British doctors to follow the French example of face transplants.
- Without the NHS, high-quality treatments would be confined to more wealthy people.
- Cardiac care is one of the government's main priorities and one of its great successes. More attention is now paid to prevention, and statins that attack cholesterol are used more widely.
- Cardiac departments are better equipped and clot-buster drugs, vital in the early stages of a heart attack, are more accessible. In the last 10 years, deaths from heart disease have fallen by 36%.
- Cancer is another main priority and another major success area. GPs who suspect that one of their patients may have cancer are required to refer the patient to a hospital consultant within 2 weeks, and nearly 100% now receive an appointment within that time.
- A cure for cancer remains elusive but survival rates have improved considerably, especially for breast cancer and leukaemia. In the last decade, cancer deaths have been cut by 16%.
- Although the time people have to wait before receiving a hospital appointment varies, the reduction in hospital waiting lists is another key area of success. In the last 20 years, average waiting times for an appointment have fallen from 10 to 3 months. In England, the target is a maximum wait of 18 weeks for an operation by 2008.

Failures of the NHS

- There is far too much bureaucracy in the NHS.
- There are too many managers — a theme often featured in the television programmes *Holby City* and *Casualty*.
- There are significant regional differences in life expectancy. On average, those living in Dorset and the more affluent London boroughs of Kensington and Chelsea are likely to live up to 10 years longer than people in certain parts of Manchester and Glasgow.
- Doctors and nurses have often been recruited from poorer countries that can ill afford to lose highly qualified medical staff.
- There remain significant shortages in areas like therapy and midwifery.
- Many people are unable to register with an NHS dentist and cannot afford private treatment.
- A number of hospitals have been built using private finance initiatives (PFIs that result in long-term debts for health trusts.
- Patient choice is often an illusion. Few professionals have the time or expertise to advise patients.
- There are about 2,000 transplants a year but there is an enduring shortage of organ donors. About 8,000 people are on a transplant waiting list.
- Politicians are widely criticised for what is claimed to be their obsession with targets.
- There are accusations of a 'postcode lottery', i.e. access to treatment and the availability of potentially life-saving drugs may depend on where a patient lives.

A particularly interesting government appointment has been that of Ara Darzi (Lord Darzi), an Iraqi-born surgeon who combines surgical work with acting as a health minister — an unusual example of a doctor–politician. One of his briefs was to conduct a 'once in a generation' review of the NHS in England. He is likely to be correct in assuming that (in 2008) one of the main problems in the NHS is no longer lack of money or expertise but connecting different parts of the service; one of the needs that Lord Darzi envisages is the appointment of 'navigators' to help patients to work through the complex systems that underpin the different health provision and treatments available.

One eventuality might be an extension of 'market choice principles', to incorporate the right of a British patient to seek treatment anywhere in the EU, particularly where there was quicker access to the required care than would be the case in the UK. The cost of treatment in another country would be reimbursed by the NHS. Seemingly attractive, it might be an administrative nightmare and issues might arise over follow-up treatment. Such a plan, if it does go ahead, is unlikely to come into operation until 2010 at the earliest.

Practice question

The following question is typical of those that might be used in Section B of Unit 4.

The problem with advances in medical science over the last 50 years is that we can no longer afford to sustain them. Treatment often becomes a postcode lottery and we can no longer care adequately for the growing number of elderly people.

Examine some of the main advances in medical science since the setting up of the National Health Service in 1948.

Discuss the extent to which the National Health Service will be able to cope with rising public expectations and the growing proportion of elderly people in the population.

(25 marks)

The relationship between technology, science and society

Development in genetics and biotechnology

Selective breeding was known in biblical times and played a significant part in the British agricultural revolution of the later eighteenth century, bringing improved strains of animals. It is often a time-consuming process, not always predictable, and cannot be used to combine the traits of two wholly different species.

Ever since the monk Gregor Mendel conducted experiments on plant hybrids, scientists have been trying to gain more understanding of genetic codes, even if the word 'genetics', as relating to heredity, was not introduced until the early 1900s.

Central to our make-up as individuals is DNA (deoxyribonucleic acid — identified as the carrier of genetic information in the 1940s), which makes up the nucleus of the cell. It acts as a code and is often referred to as a 'blueprint'. DNA is divided into functional units — the **genes** that carry all the instructions for making up our body and determining what we look like. It is DNA that establishes the individuality of an organism; the information stored in the DNA determines each biochemical process.

Segments of DNA associated with specific features or functions of an organism are called genes, and a gene is a region of DNA that controls a hereditary characteristic. Genes are working sub-units of DNA and each one contains a particular set of instructions — a form of coding for a particular protein. Genes are sometimes described as the body's instruction manual.

DNA is responsible for an organism's life, growth and unique features. It was only after the scientists James Watson and Francis Crick (with important, but less acknowledged, contributions from Rosalind Franklin and Maurice Wilkins) published news of their discovery of the double helix structure of DNA in 1953, that we had a clearer understanding of genetics in terms of the molecules involved and the full significance of DNA in the process of heredity.

Key term

genes: strings of chemicals that help to create the proteins that make up someone's body. Genes are found in long, coiled chains known as chromosomes and are located in the nuclei of the body's cells. As a result of sexual reproduction, a child gets half its genes from the mother's eggs and half from the father's sperm.

One highly contentious area of science is genetic engineering, generally considered to be a modern branch of **biotechnology**. Genetic engineering is a technique involving modifying — perhaps by removing or adding to — a DNA molecule to change the information it contains. Genetic engineering involves the alteration or movement of the genetic material of living cells.

1977 marked the beginning of a new phase of biotechnology. In this year the first human protein was cloned and manufactured using the techniques of genetic engineering, and soon afterwards genetically engineered insulin was produced to help the treatment of diabetics. The first genetically modified fruit or vegetables were tomatoes; they reached the American public in 1994 after 10 years of development but were not a commercial success. UK critics, mindful of the fictional figure Dr Frankenstein, were quick to describe such genetically modified products as 'Frankenfood', and scare stories were not uncommon. GM tomatoes were never marketed in the UK.

'Genetic fingerprinting', using a polymerase chain reaction, emerged in the 1980s. This meant that sufficient DNA could be extracted from a small drop of a person's blood, a hair or a tiny semen sample to identify the individual concerned. This has been a considerable aid in the field of criminal investigation.

The Human Genome Project

- 1990 saw the beginning of what many consider to be the greatest achievement of biotechnology — the Human Genome Project (HGP), which involved the sequencing of over 3 billion nucleotides of DNA in the human nucleus.
- Some saw this ambitious international project, which originally had a 15-year time span and was capable of soaking up much of the money available for other areas of scientific research, as the biotechnological equivalent of landing a person on the moon or splitting the atom.

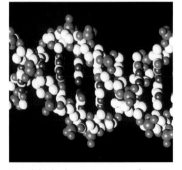

Double-helix structure of DNA

- It was an international project, with the USA playing a prominent role, although Britain made a considerable contribution through work undertaken by the Wellcome Trust Sanger Institute, which invested £150 million in the project.

- Thanks to developments in robotics and computer technology, a working draft of the HGP appeared in 2000. Work was completed in 2003.
- Knowing virtually the complete sequence of DNA nucleotides will afford scientists the opportunity to explore everything in our lives that is genetically determined, and identifying genes can now be done much more quickly than was previously the case.
- The real challenge for scientists and doctors worldwide is to move from the identification of a malfunctioning gene to the knowledge of how to correct it and a clearer understanding of how proteins interact to keep people healthy.
- Many biomedical advances, particularly in the treatment of diabetes and cancers, will enter the trial stage and then go on for patient use as a result of the astounding accuracy of the HGP.
- In 2007 scientists made a significant advance following further large-scale analysis linked to the HGP. By studying the DNA from 17,000 people, researchers have been able to identify a number of new genetic links related to Crohn's disease (a debilitating bowel condition), diabetes, bipolar disorder (formerly known as manic depression), coronary heart disease (the most frequent cause of death in Britain), hypertension (high blood pressure) and rheumatoid arthritis.
- These are diseases affecting millions of people, and the research findings raise real possibilities of improved treatment and even cures in time to come.

Organisms that have new genes inserted into them can be described as 'transgenic' — genetically modified — organisms (GMOs) and, as genetic engineering has gradually become common practice, two of its main aims are:

- the modification of plants and cereals to increase their yield and make them more resistant to disease
- the correction of abnormalities present in human genes in an effort to counter serious and possibly life-threatening conditions

Food modification

- Genetically modified plants or animals are those that have experienced an artificially induced alteration in their DNA.
- This process is sometimes referred to as 'biotechnology', 'gene technology', 'recombinant DNA technology' or, most commonly by non-scientists, 'genetic engineering'.
- The process allows selected individual genes to be transferred between organisms and also between non-related species.

- The main impetus for the production of GM food, beside raising crop yields, has come from the drive to improve crop protection through the introduction of resistance against plant diseases caused by insects or viruses or through increased tolerance towards herbicides.

- Much of the early work on GM food, starting with tomatoes and soybeans, was undertaken in the USA. This is a vast and largely unregulated market, whereas in the UK and the rest of the European Union GM food is closely regulated by legislation.

- On the whole, American consumers have raised few objections against GM food, and vast tracts of land are now assigned to the production of crops such as GM maize and soybeans.

- Reaction in the UK is mixed and even sceptical, although it is difficult to find unbiased coverage that makes a detached analysis of the potential benefits and disadvantages of GM foods.

- Supporters offer a favourable gloss while opponents often see profit-driven conspiracies based on corporate, rather than consumer, advantage.

Because genetic modification is relatively new, it is unlikely that a scientifically accurate assessment of the effects of GM products can be made because they can be viewed only in the short term. Critics have pointed to potential health hazards such as allergic reactions, the potential dangers of gene transfer from GM foods to cells of the body or to bacteria in the gastro-intestinal tract, and outcrossing (the movement of genes from GM plants into conventional crops or related species in the wild). Similar concerns exist about potential environmental damage, including the loss of biodiversity and the increasing use of chemicals in agriculture.

It is estimated that over 250 million acres of transgenic crops have been planted in over 20 countries across the world, with corn, cotton and soya beans being among the most common. Millions of farmers are involved. The USA, where confidence in GM foods seems high, accounts for over 50% of global transgenic crops, some way ahead of the next biggest producers, Argentina and Brazil. As researchers gain more access to genomic resources, and technologies develop further, more GM crops are likely to appear in less economically developed countries.

Such developments are already controversial and disputes often focus on: human and environmental safety; labelling and consumer education; food security; and the contribution of GM foods to a reduction in world poverty. Some critics are uneasy about the increasing dominance of a few major concerns such as Monsanto.

Viewpoints

Advantages of genetically modified food

■ Crop and animal yields can be increased, often quite dramatically.

■ It is possible to accelerate the growth cycle, reducing maturation time.

■ Resistance to disease and pests is improved.

■ Crops may be less dependent on climatic conditions.

■ Profits are higher for producers.

■ There is wider availability, perhaps at cheaper prices, for consumers.

■ Genetic modification may be of particular help to less economically developed countries, especially in the development of drought-resistant crops.

■ The growth of biotech companies helps to increase employment.

■ GM food has increased consumer appeal through taste, colour etc.

Disadvantages of genetically modified food

■ It is not necessary: the world problem is less a matter of shortage and more a question of distribution and low income.

■ GM means increased dependence of developing countries on industrialised nations.

■ New developments may focus mostly on the interests of more economically developed countries.

■ Higher doses of pesticides may work into the surrounding food chain.

■ The stability of altered DNA is unknown. (Critics point to the unanticipated and unwelcome results of other developments, such as the use of DDT and the impact of chlorofluorocarbons that floated into the upper atmosphere and destroyed ozone.)

■ The influence and control of biotech companies in agriculture is increased.

■ Biosecurity in laboratories, perhaps involving the use of bacteria, is a growing concern.

■ Genetic modifications cannot be contained by fences — there may be an unintended transfer of transgenes through cross-pollination. (A gene designed to resist herbicides might transfer to a weed and evolve into a 'super-weed' that could not then be controlled.)

■ There are potential health dangers, such as allergic reactions from newly introduced allergens, increased resistance to antibiotics, or exposure to newly produced toxins.

■ Natural elements and features may be lost.

Ethical considerations

■ How can what may be short-term gains be balanced against longer-term risks?

■ To what extent can developments, once started, be stopped?

■ To what extent should one generation commit a future generation?

■ Should nature be interfered with by mixing genes among species?

Q Who should you believe when trying to make a judgement about how far to support developments in GM food?

A This is difficult because many of those involved have vested interests and there is sensationalism and scare-mongering in the popular press which might or might not be justified. Clear scientific evidence and well-supported, rational arguments are difficult to come by. Monsanto is a company that is heavily involved in genetic engineering and will clearly make statements in favour. Greenpeace, as a well-known pressure group, is opposed and suggests more sustainable alternatives. GM trials have to take place in secret because of the danger of interference through direct action campaigns by opponents.

Inevitably there are those who resist almost any new technology on the grounds that it interferes with nature, and stories and images of 'Frankenfoods' add little to the debate. Conversely, supporters of new technology and scientific techniques see almost no limits to what might be possible. For example, scientists at the Rockefeller Foundation have developed Golden Rice, which, through its genetically engineered fortification with Vitamin A, may help to reduce blindness resulting from a deficiency of that vitamin in parts of Africa and Asia.

With the presence of vested interests, bias, emotive terminology, political spin, point-scoring and positions that may not be open to change irrespective of contrary evidence, it may be a question of seeking to balance advantages and disadvantages, on a global basis, over both the long and the short term. As with any new technology, it is unlikely that all the risks inherent in genetic engineering have been identified.

Human genetic engineering

Many people are affected by diseases resulting from inherited defective genes. Genetic screening, either of the foetus during pregnancy, or in later life, can help to detect defective genes that might result in mental impairment or physical deformity. Different techniques have been used in an effort to change the genetic structure that results in such diseases. Huntington's disease and cystic fibrosis are caused by a defective gene, and the hope is that a cure can eventually be found for such diseases either by modifying an existing gene or inserting a corrected one.

Somatic-cell therapy

- Somatic cells are all the cells within the body except the germ (or sex) cells.
- Consequently, this is a form of genetic engineering that manipulates defective genes in specific organs and tissues of a person without affecting their eggs or sperm.

- Because it is specific, its alterations are not passed on to future generations. It is still considered to be experimental and the aim is to insert a healthy gene somewhere in the chromosomes.
- In future, a healthy gene in the respiratory tract might help to treat a disease such a cystic fibrosis.

Germ-line therapy

- This is a form of genetic engineering that targets the genes in eggs, sperm or very early embryos.
- New DNA is introduced so that it can recombine with DNA in the reproductive cells. This means that the genetic profile of a child whose parents carry a genetically based disease can be changed.
- The alterations affect every cell in the body and are passed on to future generations.
- Still in its early stages, germ-line therapy has been tested on animals.
- Because of the potential for genetic enhancement — a non-therapeutic use of genetic alteration — and the unpredictability of potentially irreversible changes, it is unlikely that germ-line therapy will be used, legally, on humans.

Cloning

- Cloning is the experimental process of producing genetically identical copies from a single body cell of the parent.
- Cloning occurs naturally in identical twins, and bacteria and yeast survive because of natural cloning.
- Single-cell organisms reproduce simply by splitting in two, and gardeners have used cloning techniques for centuries by taking cuttings of the stems or roots of plants and replanting them.
- The word 'cloning' was first used in the 1960s. Before that, artificial cloning was referred to as 'nuclear transfer'.
- Whether we refer to 'DNA cloning', 'gene cloning', 'molecular cloning' or even 'recombinant DNA technology', the process is one of transferring a DNA fragment from one organism to a self-replicating genetic element such as a bacterial plasmid.

Reproductive cloning

- Usually when the media refer to 'cloning', they are referring to reproductive cloning.
- Reproductive cloning is a process used to generate an animal with the same DNA as another current or previously existing animal, using a process called 'somatic cell nuclear transfer'.

- Reproductive cloning can also be used to repopulate endangered species, but it is both expensive and inefficient in terms of creating viable offspring.
- There are also concerns about the immune functions and higher infection rates of cloned animals, which may not live long enough to generate good data.
- With so many unknowns concerning the reproductive cloning of animals, human reproductive cloning is banned in the UK and many other countries.

Therapeutic cloning

- Therapeutic cloning is used to study human development and treat disease.
- The cloning procedure produces a clonal embryo, which is used to generate **stem cells**.
- These can be used to generate virtually any type of specialised cell in the human body.
- Stem cells are taken from the egg after it has divided for 5 days (a blastocyst) — a process that destroys the embryo and thus gives rise to ethical concerns.
- Ultimately, medical researchers hope to use stem cells as replacement cells in the treatment of diseases such as heart disease and cancer, and it may eventually be possible to use therapeutic cloning to generate tissues and organs for human transplants, significantly reducing the need for human donors.

> **Key term**
>
> **stem cells:** primordial cells capable of developing into a variety of types of cell. They can be found in the adult body or in very early embryos and can be cultured in Petri dishes. Stem cells can grow into any of the 300 different types of cell in the human body. They have the potential to generate therapeutic tissues or spare organs.

Dolly the sheep, the first DNA-cloned mammal

Many experiments attempted to clone mammals, but success only came with Dolly the sheep in 1996. Scientists at the Roslin Institute in Edinburgh implanted the nucleus of a cell from the mammary gland of a sheep into the embryo of another sheep's unfertilised egg that had had the nucleus removed. Once the egg began to divide following the use of an electrical pulse, the resulting embryo was implanted into the uterus of another sheep.

Dolly, the resultant lamb, was a clone of the sheep that supplied the mammary gland (and therefore identical to it). Dolly eventually mated and produced an offspring, but she developed arthritis and lung problems. Dolly lived for 7 years — about half of her expected lifespan. By 1999 cattle had also been cloned, and there have been successful clones of goats, mice, pigs, cats and rabbits using nuclear transfer technology. The cloning of animals, despite its low success rate, has much potential in terms of medical and pharmaceutical research.

Human cloning, talked of after the Dolly experiment, remains confined to the realms of science fiction, despite claims that reproductive cloning could, in the future, be developed to replace terminally ill children with genetically identical copies or even to enable an adult to live on in a new body.

Regulation and ethical concerns

Religious groups in particular have expressed concerns about how stem cells are created. Some are the by-product of attempts by infertile couples to have children through **in vitro fertilisation (IVF)**: unused embryos are harvested that would otherwise be discarded. Others are created deliberately for research. Scientifically, it has been proved that blastocysts do not have a nervous system and can thus have no feelings, but some religious groups are uneasy about such artificial creations and cite the possible existence of a 'soul'. They oppose embryonic stem cell research because the start of each cell line involves the destruction of a blastocyst. In 2005 the claims of a South Korean researcher, Hwang Woo-Suk, to have produced stem cell lines by cloning were disproved.

> **Key term**
>
> **in vitro fertilisation (IVF):** a method of medical intervention used to help women who have found it difficult to conceive, perhaps because of damaged Fallopian tubes. It is a laboratory procedure in which sperm are placed with an unfertilised egg in a Petri dish to achieve fertilisation. The embryo is then transferred into the uterus or frozen for future use. The first IVF baby was born in England in 1978.

The UK's Human Fertilisation and Embryology Authority was established in 1991 as part of the 1990 Human Fertilisation and Embryology Act. Its main tasks are to license and monitor clinics that carry out IVF, donor insemination and human embryo research. It also regulates the storage of gametes (eggs and sperm) and embryos. It granted its first licence for the therapeutic cloning of human cells in 2004. The 1-year licence was issued to the Newcastle Centre for Life, allowing it to create human embryonic stem cells for research purposes.

In 2003 a £9 million stem cell bank was established by the Medical Research Council, where it is planned to hold every kind of stem cell created in Britain, with many from other countries. It is envisaged that the bank will be able to supply cells to scientific and medical researchers throughout the world. Embryonic stem cells are able to grow into any body tissue and may hold the key to the future successful treatment of illnesses such as Parkinson's, motor neurone disease and cystic fibrosis. However, because they are collected from early-stage embryos — which would otherwise be of no use to an IVF clinic — critics regard this as intrusive and unethical. The bank will allow scientists to work on cells without having to undertake the very difficult process of creating them.

Equally controversial are plans to create embryos that are part human and part animal. (Scientists are seeking to do this because of difficulties in obtaining human stem cells for experimentation.) Politicians are reluctant to give their support because they fear a backlash from the tabloids (already referring to 'chimp-manzees' and 'pig-girls'), religious groups and voters. Scientists would take a human cell and place it in a hollowed-out animal egg to produce an embryo that would be 99.9% human. After a few days, embryonic stem cells would be extracted and grown into nerves and other tissues, giving scientists insight into how disease develops.

Under existing laws, embryos must be destroyed no later than 14 days after creation and cannot be implanted. The Human Fertilisation and Embryology Authority is undecided about whether or not licences for this form of research on part-human embryos should be made available. However, researchers say it may soon be possible to take normal adult cells and reprogramme them to act as embryonic stem cells, although, on the basis of current scientific knowledge, the process would be difficult and costly.

New legislation designed to update the 1990 regulatory framework for fertility treatment has proved difficult to draft:

- the specific issue of so-called animal/human embryo research is highly controversial
- there is a clash between medicine and ethics that has set scientists against bishops
- it has caused division in the cabinet, especially among Roman Catholic members
- MPs are torn between voting according to their conscience rather than with the party whip
- newspaper reporting has influenced public opinion

Clashes between church and state, especially those that involve medical ethics are rarely easily resolved. Newspaper headlines are sensationalised and rational analysis and debate — the very thing General Studies seeks to encourage — is likely to be conspicuous by its absence. Perhaps this is a fitting, if unwelcome, conclusion.

Practice question

The following question is typical of those that might be used in Section B of Unit 4.

Whether in food production or the cloning of living things, genetic engineering is undesirable and leads to moral dilemmas that cannot be resolved and that threaten the values that are important to a stable society.

Examine the arguments for and against the further development of genetically modified food.

Consider the extent to which embryonic research represents acceptable scientific advance.   *(25 marks)*

Index

Note: page numbers in **bold** type refer to key terms.